Politics 1B:
Introduction to
Comparative Politics

We work with leading authors to develop the strongest educational materials bringing cutting-edge thinking and best learning practice to a global market.

Under a range of well-known imprints, including Financial Times/Prentice Hall, Addison Wesley and Longman, we craft high quality print and electronic publications which help readers to understand and apply their content, whether studying or at work.

Pearson Custom Publishing enables our customers to access a wide and expanding range of market-leading content from world-renowned authors and develop their own tailor-made book. You choose the content that meets your needs and Pearson Custom Publishing produces a high-quality printed book.

To find out more about custom publishing, visit www.pearsoncustom.co.uk

A Pearson Custom Publication

Politics 1B: Introduction to Comparative Politics

Compiled from:

European Politics Today Third Edition
by Gabriel A. Almond, G. Bingham Powell, Jr.,
Russell J. Dalton, and Kaare Strøm

Comparative Politics Today: A World View
Ninth Edition
by Gabriel A. Almond, Russell J. Dalton,
G. Bingham Powell, Jr. and Kaare Strøm

Comparative Politics: An Introduction
by Peter Calvert

PEARSON

Custom
Publishing

Pearson Education Limited
Edinburgh Gate
Harlow
Essex CM20 2JE

And associated companies throughout the world

Visit us on the World Wide Web at:
www.pearsoned.co.uk

First published 2008

Taken from:

European Politics Today Third Edition
by Gabriel A. Almond, Russell J. Dalton,G. Bingham Powell, Jr. and Kaare Strøm
ISBN 978 0 321 23652 4
Copyright © 2006 Gabriel A. Almond, Russell J. Dalton,G. Bingham Powell, Jr. and
Kaare Strøm

Comparative Politics Today: A World View Ninth Edition
by Gabriel A. Almond, G. Bingham Powell, Jr., Russell J. Dalton and Kaare Strøm
ISBN 978 0 205 52931 5
Copyright © 2008 Gabriel A. Almond, G. Bingham Powell, Jr., Russell J. Dalton and
Kaare Strøm

Comparative Politics: An Introduction
by Peter Calvert
ISBN 978 0 582 43823 1
Copyright © Peter Calvert 2002

ISBN 978 1 84776 061 6

Printed and bound in Great Britain by Henry Ling Limited at the Dorset Press,
Dorchester, DT1 1HD

Contents

Section 1
Comparative Politics

ISSUES IN COMPARATIVE POLITICS

WHAT IS POLITICS?

Some people love politics. They relish the excitement of political events, such as a presidential election, as they would an exciting athletic contest (the World Series of baseball or the World Cup of soccer, perhaps). Others are fascinated with politics because they care about the issues and their consequences for people in their own communities and around the world. Still others hate politics, either because it sets groups and individuals against each other, or because it involves abuse of power, deceit, manipulation, and violence. Finally, some people are indifferent to politics because it has little to do with the things that matter most to them. All of these reactions involve kernels of truth about politics. Indeed, most of us react to politics with a mixture of these sentiments. Politics has many faces and can be a force for good as well as evil. The core of politics, however, is about human beings making important decisions for themselves and for others.

This book is about the comparative study of politics. In order to make political comparisons, we need to understand what politics is as well as what it means to study politics comparatively. Comparative politics thus involves two separate elements:

- It is a subject of study—comparing the nature of politics and the political process across different political systems.
- It is a method of study—involving how and why we make such comparisons.

We address the first point in this chapter, Chapter 2 discusses the second.

Politics deals with human decisions, and political science is the study of such decisions. Yet, not all decisions are political, and many of the social sciences study decisions that are of little interest to political scientists. For example, consider when you go with a friend to an event, such as a concert or a soccer match. You can spend your money on the tickets (to get the best seats possible) or on food and drink, or you can save your money for the future. Economists study the sorts of spending decisions people make, and perhaps how they reach them. Psychologists, on the other hand, might study why you went to the event with this friend and not another, or who suggested going in the first place.

Political scientists seldom examine such personal experiences, unless they have political consequences. Instead, we examine the political process and its impact on the citizens. Political decisions constantly touch our lives in many ways, our careers, and our families. Our jobs are structured by government regulations, our homes are built to conform to government housing codes, our public schools are funded and managed by the government, and even when we go to a concert or sporting event, we travel on roads maintained by the government and monitored by the police. We might not think of politics as omnipresent in our lives, but it affects us in many important ways. Therefore, it is important to study how political decisions are made and what their consequences are.

Political decisions are *public* and *authoritative*. There is no such thing as political solitaire, playing politics by yourself. Political decisions take place within some community that we call a *political system*, which we describe below. Yet, not all social decisions are public. Most of what happens within families, among friends, or in social groups belongs to the *private sphere*. Actions within this sphere do not bind anyone outside that group. In most societies, your choice of concert partners and food are private decisions.

The *public sphere* deals with collective decisions that extend beyond the individual, typically involving government action. In totalitarian societies, like Hitler's Third Reich and some communist nations, the public sphere is very large and the private sphere is very limited. The state tries to dominate the life of its people, even intruding into family life. On the other hand, in some less developed nations the private domain may almost crowd out the public one. People in many African nations, for instance, may be unaware of what happens in the capital city and untouched by the decisions made there. Western democracies have a more balanced mix of private and public spheres. However, the boundaries between the two spheres get redrawn all the time. A couple of decades ago, the sex lives of U.S. presidents or members of the British royal family were considered private matters, not to be discussed in public. These norms are changing in Britain and the United States, but the traditional standards remain in other countries. Similarly, at one time in British history certain religious beliefs were considered treasonous. Today, religious beliefs are considered private matters in most modern democracies, but not in many other parts of the world. Even though politics may be influenced by what happens in the private domain, it deals directly with only those decisions that are public.

Politics is also *authoritative*. Authority means that formal power rests in individuals or groups whose decisions are expected to be carried out and respected. Thus, political decisions are binding for members of that political system. Governments may use force to ensure compliance, although authority is not always backed up by force. For instance, a religious authority, such as the Pope, has few coercive powers. He can persuade, but rarely compel, the Catholic Church's followers. In contrast, tax authorities, such as the U.S. Internal Revenue Service, can both exhort and compel people to follow their rules.

Thus, politics refers to activities associated with the control of public decisions among a given people and in a given territory, where this control may be backed up by authoritative means. Politics involves the crafting of these authoritative decisions—who gets to make them and for what purposes.

We live in one of the most exciting times to study politics. The end of the Cold War created a new international order, although its shape is still uncertain. The democratic transitions in Eastern Europe and many developing nations have transformed the world, although it is unclear whether these new democracies will endure and what forms they might take. In Western nations, new challenges and choices have arisen that divide their citizens. Some of these problems—such as confronting global warming and achieving international peace—are transnational. Part of their solutions, we hope, lies in the political choices that people make about their collective future. Our goal in this book is to give you a sense of how governments and politics function to address these challenges.

GOVERNMENTS AND THE STATE OF NATURE

Governments are organizations of individuals who have the power to make binding decisions on behalf of a particular community. Governments thus have authoritative and coercive powers. Governments do many things. They can wage war or encourage peace; cultivate or restrict international trade; open their borders to the exchange of ideas and art or close them; tax their populations heavily or lightly and through different means; allocate resources for education, health, and welfare or leave such matters to others. People who are affected by such decisions may well agree with them and indeed welcome them, but there is also often heated disagreement about the proper role of government decisions.

Debates over the nature and appropriate role of government are far from new. They reflect a classic polemic in political philosophy. For centuries, philosophers have debated whether governments are a force for good or evil. In the seventeenth and eighteenth centuries—the time of the English, French, and American revolutions—much of this debate was couched in arguments concerning the **state of nature.**

Philosophers thought about the state of nature as the condition of humankind if no government existed. In some cases, they thought that such a situation existed before the first governments were formed. These philosophers used their ideas about the state of nature to identify an ideal social contract (agreement) on which to build a political system. Even today, many philosophers find it useful to make such a mental experiment to consider the consequences of having governments.

These debates have shaped our images of government, even to the present. The contrast between Thomas Hobbes' and Jean-Jacques Rousseau's ideas about the state of nature is most striking. Hobbes was the ultimate pessimist. He thought of the state of nature as mercilessly inhospitable, a situation of eternal conflict of all against all, and a source of barbarism and continuous fear. He pessimistically argued that "[i]n such condition, there is no place for Industry; because the fruit thereof is uncertain: and consequently no Culture of the Earth; no Navigation, nor use of the commodities that may be imported by Sea; no commodious Building,... no Arts; no Letters; no Society; and which is worst of all, continuall feare, and danger of violent death; And the life of man, solitary, poor, nasty, brutish, and short."[1]

Rousseau, in contrast, was more optimistic. For him, the state of nature represented humanity before its fall from grace, without all the corruptions that governments have introduced. "Man is born free," Rousseau observed in *The Social Contract*, "and yet everywhere he is in chains." Rousseau saw governments as the source of power and inequality, and these conditions in turn as the causes of human alienation and corruption. "The extreme inequality in our way of life," he argued, "excess of idleness in some, excess of labor in others;... late nights, excesses of all kinds, immoderate ecstasies of all the passions; fatigues and exhaustion of mind, numberless sorrows and afflictions... that most of our ills are our own work; that we would have avoided almost all of them by preserving the simple, uniform, and solitary way of life prescribed to us by nature."[2]

John Locke's ideas have been particularly important for the development of Western democracies. He took a position between those of Hobbes and Rousseau. Compared with Hobbes, Locke thought of human beings as more businesslike and less war prone. Yet, like Hobbes he proposed a social contract to replace the state of nature with a system of government. While Hobbes thought the main task for government is to quell disorder and protect against

violence and war, Locke saw the state's main role as protecting property and commerce and promoting economic growth. He believed government would do this by establishing and enforcing property rights and rules of economic exchange. Whereas Hobbes thought government needed to be a Leviathan—a benevolent dictator to whom the citizens would yield all their power—Locke favored a limited government.[3]

Although these debates began centuries ago, they still underlie current discussions on the appropriate role of government. To some, government is the solution to many human needs and problems—a theme that former U.S. President Bill Clinton often advocated. To others, the government is often part of the problem—a theme that former U.S. President Ronald Reagan articulately argued. To some, government exists to create the social order that protects its citizens; to others, the government's rules limit our freedoms. This tension is part of the political discourse in many contemporary nations, including the United States. We explore these contrasting views and different examples of government structures in this book.

WHY GOVERNMENTS?

A recent libertarian science fiction book begins with the scenario of a group of travelers landing at an airport after a long overseas flight. As they disembark from the plane, they notice there are no police checking passports, no customs officers scanning baggage, and no officials applying immigration rules.[4] They had landed in a society without government, and the puzzle was what having no government would mean for the citizenry. The answer is a lot (see Box 1.1). As philosophers have pointed out, there are many reasons why people create governments and prefer to live under such a social order. We shall discuss some of these, beginning with activities that help generate a stable community in the first place and then those that help this community prosper.

Community- and Nation-Building

One of the first purposes of governments is to create and maintain a community in which people can feel safe and comfortable. While humans may be social beings, it is not always easy to build a community in which large numbers of people can communicate, feel

---

U.S. Government's Top Ten List

BOX 1.1

Paul Light surveyed 450 historians and political scientists to assess the U.S. government's greatest achievements in the past half century. Their top ten list is as follows:

- Help rebuild Europe after World War II
- Expand the right to vote for minorities
- Promote equal access to public accommodations
- Reduce disease
- Reduce workplace discrimination
- Ensure safe food and drinking water
- Strengthen the nation's highway system
- Increase older Americans' access to health care
- Reduce the federal deficit
- Promote financial security in retirement

Source: Paul Light, *Government's Greatest Achievements of the Past Half-Century* (Washington, DC: Brookings Institution, 2000) (www.brookings.edu/comm/reformwatch/rw02.pdf).

---

at home, and interact constructively. Governments can help generate such communities in many different ways, for example, by teaching a common language, instilling common norms and values, creating common myths and symbols, and supporting a national identity. However, sometimes such actions create controversy because they threaten the values of minority groups.

Nation-building activities help instill common world views, values, and expectations. Using a concept discussed more in Chapter 3, governments can help create a national **political culture.** The political culture defines the public's expectations toward the political process and its role within the process. The more the political culture is shared, the easier it is to live in peaceful coexistence and engage in activities for mutual gain, such as commerce.

Security and Order

Government activities partially reflect Hobbes' belief that only strong governments can make society safe for their inhabitants. Providing security and law and order is among the most essential tasks that governments perform. Externally, security means protecting against attacks from other political systems. Armies, navies, and air forces typically perform this function. Internally, security means protecting against theft, aggression, and violence from members of one's own society. In most societies providing this protection is the function of the police.

Providing security and order is a critical role of modern governments. While governments worldwide have privatized many of the services they once performed—for example those involving post offices,

railroads, and telecommunications, few, if any, governments have privatized their police or defense forces. This shows how security is one of the most essential roles of government. The international terrorist attacks in New York City and Washington, D.C. on September 11, 2001, and subsequent attacks in London, Madrid and other cities underscore the importance of security.

Protecting Rights

John Locke considered property rights to be particularly critical to the development of prosperous communities. Without effective protection of property rights, people will not invest their goods or energies in productive processes. Also, unless property rights exist and contracts can be negotiated and enforced, people will not trust their neighbors enough to engage in trade and commerce. Anything beyond a subsistence economy requires effective property rights and contracts. Therefore, Locke believed that the primary role of government is to establish and protect such rights. Similarly, contemporary authors argue that social order is a prerequisite for development and democratization.[5]

Effective property rights allocate ownership and provide security against trespass and violations. Such rights must also make the buying and selling of property relatively inexpensive and painless. Finally, people must have faith that their property rights can be defended. Thus, many analysts argue that one of the most restrictive limitations on development in the Third World is the government's inability (or unwillingness) to guarantee such rights. Peasant families who have lived for generations on a plot of land cannot claim ownership, which erodes their incentive and opportunity to invest in the future.

Although Locke was most concerned with economic property rights, governments also protect many other social and political rights. Among them are freedoms of speech and association and protection against various forms of discrimination and harassment. Indeed, the protection of these rights and liberties is one of the prime goals of government—with other factors such as nation-building, security and property rights providing a means toward this goal. Governments also play a key role in protecting the rights of religious, racial and other social groups. Human development stresses the expansion of these rights and liberties, and governments play a key role in this process.

Promoting Economic Efficiency and Growth

Economists have long debated the government's potential role in promoting economic development. Neoclassical economics shows that markets are efficient when property rights are defined and protected, when competition is rigorous, and when information is freely available. When these conditions do not hold, markets may fail and the performance of the economy may suffer.[6] At least in some circumstances, governments can lessen the results of market failure.

Governments may be especially important in providing **public goods,** such as clean air, a national defense, or disease prevention. Public goods have two things in common. One is that if one person enjoys them, they cannot be withheld from anyone else. The second is that one person's enjoyment or consumption of the goods does not detract from anyone else's. Consider clean air. For most practical purposes, it is impossible to provide one person with clean air without also giving it to his or her neighbors. Moreover, my enjoyment of clean air does not mean that my neighbors have any less of it. Analysts therefore argue that people in a market economy will not pay enough for public goods. They claim that only government can provide such public goods. Otherwise, people will not voluntarily pay for public goods because they can benefit from the goods that others provide, or they will not act until they are assured others will also contribute.

Governments can also benefit society by controlling the **externalities** that occur when an activity produces costs that are not borne by the producer or the user. For instance, many forms of environmental pollution occur when those who produce or consume goods do not pay all of the environmental costs. Polluting factories, waste dumps, prisons, and major highways can impose large costs on those who live near them. NIMBY ("not in my backyard") groups are an example of citizens complaining about these costs. Governments can help protect people from such unfair externalities or ensure that burdens are fairly shared.

Governments also can promote fair competition in economic markets. For example, governments can assure that all businesses follow minimum standards of worker protection and product liability. In other cases, the government may control potentially monopolistic parts of the economy to ensure that suppliers do not take advantage of their market power. This happened in the nineteenth century with railroad monopolies, and now in the twenty-first century with technology monopolies, such as Microsoft, or telecommunications companies. In these cases the government acts as the policeman to ensure that the economically powerful do not exploit their power. Sometimes, the government itself may become the monopolist. There are some markets in which very large start-up costs or prohibitive costs of coordination mean that there should be only one producer. The government may then set itself up as that monopolist, or it may decide to tightly control a private monopolist. Telecommunications have commonly been a government monopoly, as have mail services and strategic defense industries.

Social Justice

Governments can also play a role in dividing the fruits of economic growth in equitable ways. Many people argue that governments are needed to promote social justice by redistributing wealth and other resources among citizens. In many countries the distribution of income or property is highly uneven. Moreover, in many societies income and wealth inequalities worsen over time. Brazil, for example, has one of the most severe income inequalities in the world, an inequality that grew in every decade from the 1930s to the 1990s.

Under such circumstances, social justice may require a "new deal," especially if inequalities deprive many individuals of education, adequate health care, or other basic needs. Government can intervene to redistribute resources from the better-off to the poor. Some theorists argue that such transfers should attempt to equalize the conditions of all citizens. Others prefer governments to redistribute enough to equalize opportunities, and then let individuals be responsible for their own fortunes.

Many private individuals, organizations, and foundations attempt to help the poor, but they generally lack the capacity to effect large-scale redistribution. Governments do, at least under some circumstances. Many tax and welfare policies effectively redistribute income, although the degree of redistribution is often hotly disputed. Yet most individuals agree that governments should provide their citizens with the opportunities to reach certain minimum standards of living and a social safety net.

Protecting the Weak

We commonly rely on the government to protect individuals and groups that are not able to speak for themselves. Groups such as the poor or the homeless or future generations cannot effectively protect their own interests. Governments, however, can protect the interests of the unborn and prevent them from getting saddled with economic debts or environmental degradation. In recent decades, governments have become much more involved in protecting groups that are politically weak or disenfranchised, such as children, the old, and the infirm or disabled, as well as nonhumans—from whales and birds to trees and other parts of our natural environment.

WHEN DOES GOVERNMENT BECOME THE PROBLEM?

There are many reasons that governments may become involved in human affairs, but such intervention is not always welcomed. When and how government intervention is necessary and desirable are among the most disputed issues in modern politics. During the twentieth century, the role of governments expanded enormously in most nations. At the same time, criticisms of many government policies have persisted and sometimes intensified. Such skepticism is directed at virtually all government activities, especially the economic role of government.

Destruction of Community

Whereas some see governments as a way to build community, others argue that governments destroy natural communities. Government, they hold, implies power and inequality among human beings. And power corrupts. In Lord Acton's famous words, "Power corrupts, and absolute power corrupts absolutely."

While those who have power are corrupted, those without it are degraded and alienated. According to Rousseau, only human beings unfettered by government can form bonds that allow them to develop their full human potential. By imposing an order based on coercion, hierarchy, and the threat of force, governments destroy natural communities. The stronger government becomes, the more it creates inequalities of power that have negative consequences. Such arguments stimulated Western criticism of communism as limiting the potential and freedom of its citizens.

Others argue that strong governments create a "client society," in which people learn to be subservient to authorities and to rely on governments to meet their needs. In such societies, governments patronize and pacify their citizens, as seen in many developing nations today.

Violations of Basic Rights

Just as governments can help establish many essential rights, they can also use their powers to violate these rights in the most serious manner. The twentieth century witnessed enormous progress in the extension of political, economic, and social rights in societies worldwide. At the same time, however, some governments violated basic **human rights** on an unprecedented scale. The millions of lives lost to political persecution is the most serious example of this. Such horrors happened not only in Nazi extermination camps and during Stalin's Great Terror in the Soviet Union, but also on a huge scale in China, Cambodia, and Rwanda, and on a smaller scale in Iraq, Argentina, the Sudan, and Afghanistan.

These extreme abuses of government power illustrate a dilemma that troubled James Madison and other Founders of the American Revolution: the tension between creating a government strong enough to govern effectively but not so strong that it could destroy the rights of its citizens. They understood the irony that to protect individuals from each other, societies can create a government that has even more power to coerce the individual.

Economic Inefficiency

Governments can help economies flourish, but they also can distort and restrict a state's economic potential. President Robert Mugabe, for instance, has destroyed the economy of a once developing Zimbabwe, and similar examples exist in many struggling economies. Economic problems might arise even if government officials do not actively abuse their power. Government regulation of the economy may distort the terms of trade and lower people's incentives to produce. Further inefficiencies may arise when governments actually own or manage important economic enterprises. This is particularly likely if the government holds a monopoly on an important good, since monopolies generally cause goods to be undersupplied and overpriced. Moreover, government industries may be especially prone to inefficiency and complacency because management and workers often have better job protection than those in the private sector. Therefore, they may worry less about the economic performance of the firm. Such experiences stimulate calls to restrict the economic role of governments in both developing and advanced industrial economies.

Government for Private Gain

Society also may suffer if government officials make decisions to benefit themselves personally, or select policies to get themselves reelected regardless of whether those policies would be the best for the society. These actions are like a game in which one person's gain is another person's loss. A politician or political group may use the government to unfairly reap benefits at the public's expense—what is called "rent seeking." *Rents* are benefits created through government intervention in the economy—for example, tax revenue or profits created because the government has restricted competition. Rent seeking refers to efforts by individuals, groups, firms, or organizations to reap such benefits. The idea is really quite simple. For instance, a local mayor plans an economic development project that will benefit his friends who own land in the area or who will supply contracts for the project. Rent seeking can impose large net costs on society because policies are chosen for the private benefits that they produce rather than for their social efficiency and because groups may expend large amounts of resources to control the spoils of government. Rent seeking may turn into outright corruption when influence is traded for money or other advantage (see Box 1.2).

Political exploitation is a particularly serious problem in poor societies. Holding political office is often an effective way to enrich oneself when other political actors are too weak to constrain the abuse of government officials. Besides, many developing societies do not have strong norms against using government for private gain. On the contrary, people often expect those in government to use their power to benefit themselves, their families, and their neighbors. Even in many advanced democratic societies public officeholders are expected to appoint their supporters

---

The Case of Mobutu Sese Seko

BOX 1.2

What happens if politicians use their power in their own self-interest or to benefit individuals or groups that support them? President Mobutu Sese Seko (1930–1997) of Zaire offers a tragic example of the costs that rent-seeking politicians can impose on their societies. After seizing power in a 1965 coup, Mobutu ruled the large African state of Congo (which he renamed Zaire) for more than thirty years. During his long rule, President Mobutu used government funds, including aid from Western states such as the United States, to amass a huge personal fortune, which he invested abroad. In addition to large sums of money, he is reported to have owned about thirty luxury residences abroad, including a number of palatial estates on the French Riviera. Meanwhile, living standards in Zaire, a poor country despite significant natural resources, plummeted, and the country was racked with epidemic disease and civil war. Mobutu died of natural causes shortly after his ouster.

to ambassadorships and other public posts, constrained in part by civil service rules designed to reward merit over patronage. The temptations of officeholding are great. Despite formal rules, press scrutiny, and citizen concerns, few governments anywhere finish their terms of office untainted by some corruption scandal.

Vested Interests and Inertia

Government-created private gains are difficult to change or abolish once they have been established. Some people enjoy the benefits of government jobs, contracts, or other favors that they otherwise might not have had. The larger the government and the more attractive the benefits it provides, the more likely it is that such vested interests will resist change (unless change means even larger benefits). Therefore, any government will foster a group of people with a vested interest in maintaining or enlarging the government itself. Such groups may become a powerful force in favor of the status quo.

Vested interests make it difficult to change government policies or make them more efficient. Once established, agencies and policies can live on far beyond their usefulness. For example, when the Spanish Armada threatened to invade England in 1588, the government posted a military observation post at Land's End in southwest England. This observation post remained in place for four centuries! In the United States, the Rural Electrification Administration was created in 1935 to bring electricity to rural America; it persisted for almost sixty years until it was finally merged into the Rural Utilities Service in 1994.

Vested interests are particularly likely in political systems that contain a lot of safeguards against rapid political change. While the checks and balances in political systems as the United States are designed to safeguard individual rights, they may also protect the privileges of vested interests. Yet, even political systems that contain far fewer such checks may exhibit an excess of political inertia. Britain is an excellent example. Until recently, the House of Lords represented the social groups that dominated British society before the Industrial Revolution more than 200 years ago (noblemen, bishops, and judges). Only in the last few years has Britain begun reforming the House of Lords to eliminate features that reflect Britain's feudal and preindustrial past.

This debate and struggle over the proper role of government are an ongoing part of politics. In the past twenty-five years or so, there has been a clear trend away from extensive government regulation of many economic sectors. Since the 1970s especially, many societies have moved to privatize many economic sectors and to deregulate others. Government regulation has become less extensive in some areas, but it has grown in others—for example, through enacting laws to protect the environment or the rights of children. The overall size of governments in advanced industrial countries has not changed very much. In the former communist countries and in some developing countries, however, the government's size has shrunk quite dramatically. Yet, countries vary widely in the size of their governments, and they are likely to continue to do so.

POLITICAL SYSTEMS AND STATES

We began by discussing governments, but governments are only one part of a larger political system. Since the term **political system** is a main organizing concept of this book, it deserves a full explanation. A system necessarily has two properties: (1) it has a set of interdependent parts, and (2) it has boundaries between its environment.

Political systems are a particular type of social system that is involved in the making of authoritative public decisions. Central elements of a political system are the institutions of government—such as parliaments, bureaucracies, and courts—that formulate and implement the collective goals of a society or of groups within it.

Political systems also include important parts of the society in which governments operate. For example, political organizations, such as political parties or interest groups, are part of the political system. Such organizations do not have coercive authority, except insofar as they control the government. Likewise, the mass media only indirectly affect elections, legislation, and law enforcement. A whole host of institutions—beginning with the family and including communities, churches, schools, corporations, foundations, and think tanks—influence political attitudes and public policy. The term *political system* refers to the whole collection of related, interacting institutions and agencies.

The political systems that we compare in this book are all independent states. They represent some of the important countries in the contemporary world. At the same time, they reflect the diversity of political systems that exist today. A **state** is a particular type of political system. It has **sovereignty**—an independent legal authority over a population in a particular territory, based on the recognized right to self-determination. Sovereignty rests with those who have the ultimate right to make political decisions.

External sovereignty means the right to make binding agreements (treaties) with other states. For instance, France's external sovereignty means that it can enter into treaties with other states. The city of Bordeaux, however, does not have this right (nor do other subnational units of government in France). Internal sovereignty means the right to determine matters having to do with one's own citizens. For example, the French government has internal sovereignty so that it can impose taxes on French citizens.

Yet, states mold and are molded by a domestic environment and an international environment. The system receives inputs from these environments and shapes them through its outputs. The boundaries of political systems are defined in terms of persons, territory, and property. Most people have citizenship rights in only one country. Similarly, territory is divided between states. A given piece of land is supposed to belong to only one country. Of course, disputes over citizenship, territory, and property are by no means uncommon and are among the most frequent causes of international conflict.

Every state faces some constraints on its external and internal sovereignty. For example, with the increasing integration of France into the **European Union (EU),** the French government has given up parts of its sovereignty to the EU, and this loss of sovereignty is a major topic of political debate. In the United States, we confuse things a bit by calling the fifty constituent units "states," even though they enjoy much less sovereignty than France. The states of the United States share the power and authority of the "state" with the federal government in Washington, D.C.

We often think of the world as a patchwork of states with sizable and contiguous territories and a common identity shared by their citizens. A nation is a group of people, often living in a common territory, who have such a common identity. We call the cases in which national identification and sovereign political authority largely coincide **nation-states.** We have come to think of nation-states as the natural way to

organize political systems, and often as an ideal. The national right to self-determination—the idea that every nation has a right to form its own state if it wants to do so—was enshrined in the Treaty of Versailles signed at the end of World War I.

Nation-states are often a desirable way to organize a political system. However, the national right to self-determination—is a relatively modern invention. Until the end of the Middle Ages, Europe consisted of many very small political systems and a few very large ones, whose territorial possessions were not always very stable or contiguous. Nor did states always consist of people with the same national identity. Gradually, a set of European nation-states evolved, and the 1648 Treaty of Westphalia established that principle for the political organization of Europe. The nation-state thus emerged as the dominant political system during the eighteenth and nineteenth centuries in Europe.

Since then, Europe has transformed itself into distinct nation-states. This did not happen accidentally—indeed, the governments of the emerging nation-states had a lot to do with it. They sought to instill a common national identity among the peoples they controlled. They did so, often heavy-handedly, by promoting a common language, a common educational system, and often a common religion. While this process of *nation-building* was often harsh, it produced a Europe in which the inhabitants of most states have a strong sense of community.

Many societies in the developing world today face similar challenges. Especially in Africa, the former colonial powers (particularly Britain and France) left the newly independent states with very weak national identities. In many parts of Africa, large-scale national communities simply did not exist at the time of colonization. Even where they did exist, they were rarely reflected in the boundaries that the colonial powers drew between their possessions. After independence, many new states have therefore faced huge nation-building tasks.

There are additional challenges to contemporary nation-states. After World War II, power in Western states began to shift downward from the state to local governments, and upward to supranational organizations, such as the EU. Most of the industrialized countries of Western Europe have gradually created a common market economy. Originally consisting of six countries—France, Germany, Italy, Belgium, the Netherlands, and Luxembourg—the EU has expanded to twenty-seven members with the addition of two members in 2006.

The **United Nations (UN),** formed at the end of World War II in 1945, has also acquired new responsibilities since the collapse of the Soviet Union in the 1990s. As of early 2006, UN forces were peacekeepers in fifteen countries. These operations—involving more than 100,000 peacekeepers—separate combatants in domestic and international conflicts, settle disputes, and form effective governing institutions. The UN has increased authority over world security, constraining, supporting, and sometimes replacing the unilateral actions of individual states. While the sovereignty of states may be diminishing, they are still the most important political systems. That, of course, is the main reason that they are the subject of our study.

THE DIVERSITY OF STATES

Just about the entire surface of the world today is covered by independent states. There were 192 UN "member-states" in 2006.[7] A few countries are not members of the UN (Taiwan, Switzerland, and the Vatican), and some independence movements would create even more states. When the United States declared its independence in 1776, most independent states were European (see Figure 1.1). Much of the rest of the world existed as colonies to one of the European empires. In the nineteenth and early twentieth centuries, the number of states increased, principally in Latin America, where the Spanish and Portuguese empires broke up into twenty independent states. In Europe, newly independent countries emerged in the Balkans, Scandinavia, and the Low Countries.

Between the two world wars, national proliferation extended to North Africa and the Middle East; and Europe continued to fragment as the Russian and Austro-Hungarian empires broke up. Since World War II, the development of new states has taken off. By 2006, 125 new countries have joined the sixty-eight states that existed in 1945. The largest group of new states is in Sub-Saharan Africa. More than twenty new countries formed in the 1990s—mostly the successor states of the Soviet Union, Yugoslavia, and Czechoslovakia.

All these countries—new as well as old—share certain characteristics. They have legal authority over their territories and people; most have armies, air forces, and

The United Nations is the most inclusive organization of states. As of 2006, the United Nations had 192 member states, represented by the flags flying outside its headquarters in New York City.

Joseph Sohm–ChromoSohm, Inc./Corbis

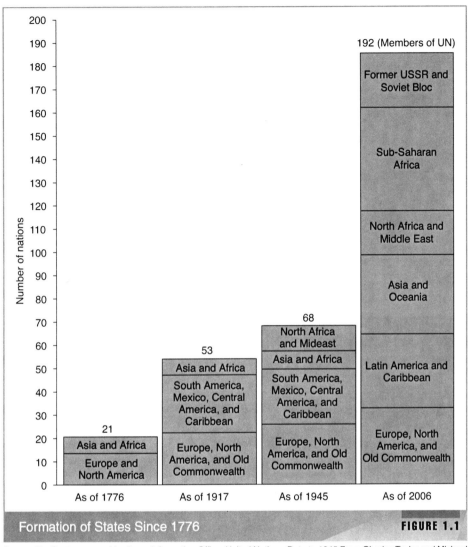

Formation of States Since 1776

FIGURE 1.1

Source: For Contemporary Members, Information Office, United Nations. Data to 1945 From Charles Taylor and Michael Hudson, *World Handbook of Political and Social Indicators* (New Haven, CT: Yale University Press, 1972), 26 ff.

in some cases navies; they collect taxes and spend money; they regulate their economies, maintain public order, and pursue their general welfare. Countries send and receive ambassadors; most belong to several international organizations. They also vary, often profoundly, in physical size, histories, institutions, cultures, religions, economies, and social structures—factors that shape their politics.

Big and Small States

Nations come in all sizes. The smallest legally independent political entity in both geographic extent and population is Vatican City, the headquarters of the Catholic Church, with less than half a square kilometer of turf and less than a thousand residents.

The contrasts between geographic size and population size can be graphically seen in the following two maps. Map 1.1 is the familiar global map in which countries are displayed according to their size. Russia, with its landmass extending over eleven contiguous time zones, is the world's largest state with more than 17 million square kilometers. The United States falls about midpoint in this range, with just more than 9 million square kilometers. Many of the established democracies in Europe are relatively small (Britain has 242,000 square kilometers and Germany 349,000).

Map 1.2 is more provocative because is displays nations by their population size. Instantly we see China and India balloon in size because of their large populations. China alone accounts for almost a quarter of the world's population (with 1.3 billion people), and India is not far behind (with 1.1 billion). The European democracies we compare—Britain, France, and Germany—look smaller in these comparisons because their populations range from about 60 million to 80 million. Even more dramatically, Australia shrinks from a continent in the first map to a small dot in the population map because of its small population size (20 million). The United States in this global perspective seems relatively small in population terms

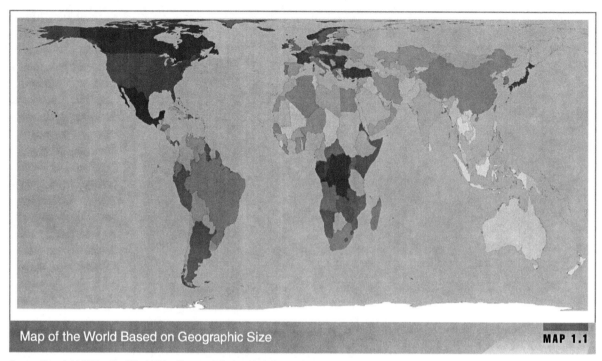

Map of the World Based on Geographic Size   **MAP 1.1**

Source: Copyright © *The Real World Atlas,* Thames & Hudson, Ltd., London, 2008.

(298 million), even though it has roughly the same area as China and is geographically larger than India. And even though Russia has almost twice as much land as any other country, it has a modest population size (142 million) that is barely half as large as the United States and Russia is shrinking.

The political implications of these striking contrasts in population size and geographic area are not always obvious. Big countries are not always the most important and do not always prevail over the small ones: Cuba has challenged the United States for almost forty years; Israel stands off the Arab world; and tiny Vatican City has great power and influence. Nor do area and population size determine a country's political system. Both little Luxembourg and large India are democracies. Authoritarian regimes are found in small, medium, and large countries. These enormous contrasts in size show only that the states now making up the world differ greatly in their physical and human resources.

A state's geographic location can also have important strategic implications. In the sixteenth through nineteenth centuries, European states typically required a large land army to protect themselves from the threats of their neighbors. These nations had difficulties developing free political institutions, since they needed a strong government to extract resources on a large scale and keep the population under control. Britain was protected by the English Channel and could defend itself through its navy, a smaller army, lower taxation, and less centralization of power—which aided political liberalization. Most peoples of Asia, Africa, and Latin America were colonized by the more powerful Western nations. Those that had the richest natural resources and the most benign climates tended to attract the largest numbers of settlers.

Whether they are old or new, large or small, most of the world's states face a number of common challenges. The first is building community. Most states do not have a homogeneous population, and instilling a sense of shared identity can be a serious challenge. Second, the ability to foster economic and social development is a challenge that is shared even by the wealthiest states. Finally, most states face significant challenges in advancing democracy and civil liberties. These challenges should be familiar from our discussion of the purposes and dangers of governments. In the remainder of this chapter, we discuss these challenges successively.

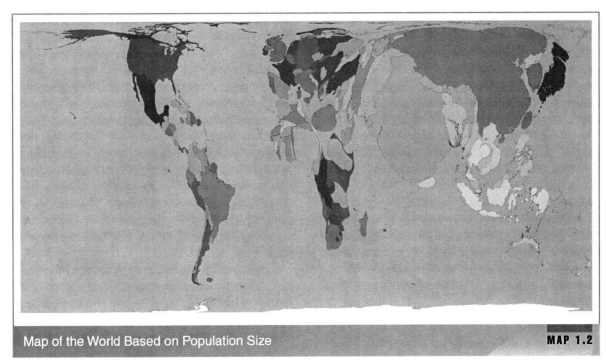

Map of the World Based on Population Size   **MAP 1.2**

Source: Copyright © *The Real World Atlas,* Thames & Hudson, Ltd., London, 2008.

BUILDING COMMUNITY

One of the most important challenges facing political systems worldwide is to build a common identity and a sense of community among the citizens. The absence of a common identity can have severe political consequences. Conflicts over national, ethnic, or religious identities are among the most explosive causes of political turmoil, as we have witnessed in Northern Ireland, the former Yugoslavia, Rwanda, and elsewhere. But while building community is a pervasive challenge, some countries are in a much better situation than others. Japan, for example, has an ethnically homogeneous population, a common language, and a long national political history. A large majority of the Japanese share in the religions of Buddhism and Shintoism, and the country is separated by miles of ocean from its most important neighbors. Nigeria, in contrast, is an accidental and artificial creation of British colonial rule and has no common precolonial history. The population is sharply divided between Muslims and Christians; the Christians are divided equally into Catholics and Protestants. There are some 250 different ethnic groups, speaking a variety of local languages, in addition to English. Obviously, the challenges of building community are much greater in Nigeria than they are in Japan. Although few countries face problems as complicated as those of the Nigerians, the community-building challenge is one of the most serious issues facing many states today.

States and Nations

The word *nation* is sometimes used to mean almost the same as the word *state*, as in the name the United Nations. Strictly speaking, however, we wish to use the term **nation** to refer to a group of people with a common identity. When we speak of a "nation," we thus refer to the self-identification of a people. That common identity may be built upon a common language, history, race, or culture, or simply upon the fact that this group has occupied the same territory. Nations may or may not have their own state or independent government. In some cases—such as Japan, France, or Sweden—there is a close correspondence between the memberships of the state and the nation. Most people who identify themselves as Japanese do in fact live in the state of Japan, and most people who live in Japan identify themselves as Japanese.

In many instances, the correspondence between the nation and the state is not so neat. Nor is it obvious that it should be. In some cases, states are *multinational*—consisting of a multitude of different nations. The Soviet Union, Yugoslavia, and Czechoslovakia were multinational states that broke apart. In other cases, some nations are much larger than the corresponding states, such as Germany for most of its history, or China. Some nations have split into two or more states for political reasons, such as Korea today and Germany between 1949 and 1990. Some groups with claims to be nations have no state at all, such as the Kurds, the Basques, and the Tamils. When states and nations do not coincide, it can cause explosive political conflict, as discussed later. At the same time, the presence of several nations within the same state can also be a source of diversity and cultural enrichment.

Nationality and Ethnicity

There is a fine line between nations and *ethnic groups,* which may have common physical traits, languages, cultures, or history. Like nationality, **ethnicity** need not have any objective basis in genetics, culture, or history. The German sociologist Max Weber defined ethnic groups as "those human groups that entertain a subjective belief in their common descent because of similarities of physical type or of customs or both, or because of memories of colonization and migration.... [I]t does not matter whether or not an objective blood relationship exists."[8] Similarly, groups that are physically quite similar, but differ by language, religion, customs, marriage patterns, and historical memories (for example, the Serbs, Croats, and Muslim Bosnians) may believe they are descended from different ancestors and hence are physically different as well. Over centuries, originally homogeneous populations may intermix with other populations, even though the culture may continue. This is true, for example, of the Jewish population of Israel, which has come together after more than two millennia of global dispersion.

Ethnic differences can be a source of political conflict.[9] Since the end of the Cold War, many states of the former Soviet bloc have come apart at their ethnic and religious seams. In the former Yugoslavia, secession by a number of provinces triggered several wars. The most brutal of these was in Bosnia-Herzegovina, where a Muslim regime faced rebellion and murderous "ethnic cleansing" by the large Serbian minority. Intervention by the UN, the North Atlantic Treaty Organization (NATO), and the United States contained Serbian aggression and led to an uneasy settlement, but considerable tension remains. Similar tensions and violent aggression occurred in Kosovo as well.

With the Chinese government encouraging economic growth and foreign investment, the Shanghai skyline is now a mix of highrises and construction cranes.

Wolf Kern/VISUM/The Image Works

In many developing countries, boundaries established by former colonial powers cut across ethnic lines. In 1947 the British withdrew from India and divided the subcontinent into a northern Muslim area—Pakistan—and a southern Hindu area—India. The most immediate consequence was a terrible civil conflict and "ethno-religious" cleansing. There still are almost 100 million Muslims in India. Similarly, thirty years ago the Ibo "tribe" of Nigeria fought an unsuccessful separatist war with the rest of Nigeria, resulting in the deaths of millions of people. The Tutsi and Hutu peoples of the small African state of Rwanda engaged in a civil war of extermination in the 1990s, with hundreds of thousands of people slaughtered, and millions fleeing the country in fear of their lives.

The migration of labor, forced or voluntary, across state boundaries is another source of ethnic differentiation. The American descendants of Africans forcefully enslaved between the seventeenth and the nineteenth centuries are witnesses of the largest coercive labor migration in world history. In contrast, voluntary migration takes the form of Indians, Bangladeshi, Egyptians, and Palestinians seeking better lives in the oil sheikhdoms around the Persian Gulf; Mexican and Caribbean migrant workers moving to the United States; and Turkish and North African migrants relocating to Europe. Some migration is politically motivated, triggered by civil war and repression. Two scholars refer to the contemporary world as living through an "Age of Migration,"[10] comparable in scale to that of the late nineteenth and early twentieth centuries.

Table 1.1 provides examples of politically significant "ethnicity," broadly defined, in our selected twelve countries. Five sets of traits are included, beginning with physical differences, then language, norms against intermarriage, religion, and negative historical memories. The table illustrates the importance of each distinction to ethnic identity. The most important bases of distinction lie in intermarriage, religion, and historical memories. Language differences are of great importance in four cases and of some importance in six; and finally, and perhaps surprisingly, physical differences are of great importance in only two cases. Recent migration has made such previously homogeneous states as France, Japan, and Germany more multiethnic. Other countries, such as the United States and Canada, have long been multiethnic and have become even more so. Indeed, globalization and migration seem destined to increase the diversity of many societies worldwide.

Examples of Ethnicity: Its Bases and Their Salience*					TABLE 1.1
	Physical Differences	Language	Norms Against Intermarriage	Religion	Negative Historical Memories
Brazil: Blacks	XX	O	XX	X	X
Britain: South Asians	X	O	X	XX	X
China: Tibetans	X	XX	XX	XX	XX
France: Algerians	X	X	XX	XX	XX
Germany: Turks	X	XX	XX	XX	O
India: Muslims	O	X	XX	XX	XX
Iran: Kurds	X	XX	XX	XX	XX
Japan: Buraku-min	O	O	XX	O	XX
Mexico: Mayan	X	X	XX	X	XX
Nigeria: Ibo	O	X	XX	XX	XX
Russia: Chechens	X	XX	XX	XX	XX
United States:					
African-Americans	XX	X	XX	O	XX
Hispanics:	X	X	X	O	X

*Salience is estimated at the following levels: O = none or almost none; X = some; XX = much importance in affecting differences.

Language

Language can be a source of social division that may overlap with ethnicity. There are approximately 5,000 different languages in use in the world today, and a much smaller number of language families. Most of these languages are spoken by relatively small tribal groups in North and South America, Asia, Africa, or Oceania. Only 200 languages have a million or more speakers, and only eight may be classified as world languages.

English is the most truly international language. There are approximately 380 million people who speak English at home, and 1.8 billion who live in countries where it is one of the official languages. Other international languages include Spanish (more than 300 million home speakers), Arabic (200 million), Russian (165 million), Portuguese (165 million), French (100 million), and German (100 million). The language with the largest number of speakers, though in several varieties, is Chinese (1.2 billion). The major languages with the greatest international spread are those of the former colonial powers—Great Britain, France, Spain, and Portugal.[11]

Linguistic divisions can create particularly thorny political problems. Political systems can choose to ignore racial, ethnic, or religious differences among their citizens, but they cannot avoid committing themselves to one or several languages. Linguistic conflicts typically show up in controversies over educational policies, or over language use in the government. Occasionally, language regulation is more intrusive, as in Quebec, where English-only street signs are prohibited and large corporations are required to conduct their business in French.

Religious Differences and Fundamentalism

States also vary in their religious characteristics. In some—such as Israel, the Irish Republic, and Pakistan—religion is a basis of national identity for a majority of the population. Iran is a theocratic regime, in which religious authorities govern and religious law is part of the country's legal code. In other societies, such as Poland under communism, religion can be a rallying point for political movements. In many Latin American countries, the clergy have embraced a liberation theology that fosters advocacy of the poor and criticism of government brutality.

Table 1.2 indicates that Christianity is the largest and most widely spread religion, which is divided into three major groups—Roman Catholics, Protestants (of many denominations), and Orthodox (e.g., Greek and Russian). The Catholics are dominant in Europe and Latin America; there is a more equal distribution of Catholics and Protestants elsewhere. While the traditional Protestant denominations have declined in North America in the last decades, three forms of Protestanism—Fundamentalist, Pentecostal, and Evangelical—have increased.

The Muslims are the second largest religious group and the most rapidly growing religion. Muslims are primarily concentrated in Asia and Africa, as well as substantial numbers in Europe and North America, and are becoming revitalized in the Asian successor

Adherents of All Religions by Six Continents (mid-2004, in millions)								**TABLE 1.2**
Religion	Africa	Asia	Europe	Latin America	North America	Oceania	Total	Percentage
Christians	401.7	341.3	553.6	510.1	273.9	26.1	2,106.2	33.0
Muslims	350.4	892.4	33.2	1.7	5.1	.4	1,283.4	20.1
Nonreligious and Atheists	6.4	724.2	130.6	18.6	33.1	4.2	917.7	14.4
Hindus	2.6	844.5	1.4	.8	1.4	.4	851.2	13.3
Buddhists	.1	369.3	1.6	.7	3.0	.4	375.4	5.9
Jews	.2	5.3	1.9	1.2	6.1	.1	14.9	.2
Other	107.7	693.5	3.2	17.6	6.3	1.0	828.8	13.1
Total	869.1	3,870.5	725.5	550.7	328.9	32.6	6,377.6	100%

Source: Adherents as defined in *Encyclopedia Britannic 2006*.

states of the Soviet Union. Muslims have been particularly successful in missionary activities in Sub-Saharan Africa.

Religion can be a source of intense antagonism, since beliefs may take the form of deep personal convictions that are difficult to compromise. Religious groups often battle over such issues as the rules of marriage and divorce, childrearing, sexual morality, abortion, euthanasia, the emancipation of women, and the regulation of religious observances. Religious communities often take a special interest in educational policies in order to transmit their ideas of nature and humankind, right and wrong. On such issues, religious groups may clash with one another as well as with more secular groups. Although religious groups can coexist peacefully, and are often the source of exemplary acts of compassion and reconciliation, they may also commit acts of violence, cruelty, and terrorism.[12]

Even societies in which most people supposedly belong to the same community of faith may be split by conflicts between "fundamentalists" and those who are more moderate in their beliefs. **Religious fundamentalism** has recently emerged in some form in all major faiths in reaction to social modernization. Fundamentalists have frequently been technologically adaptive, even while militantly rejecting some elements of modernity (see Box 1.3).

Judaism, Christianity, and Islam are all "religions of the book," although not exactly the same book. The Jews believe only in the Old Testament; the Christians add on the New Testament; and the Muslims add the Koran to these two. While each religion disagrees over the interpretation of these texts, Jewish, Christian, and Muslim, fundamentalists all believe in the truth of their respective sacred books and attack some of their own clergy for lukewarm defense of these sacred texts. There are also Hindu and Buddhist fundamentalists. The rise of fundamentalism has affected the entire world.

The extremist wings of fundamentalist movements employ violence in many forms: from threats and property destruction to assassination and destructive suicide, as young people turn themselves into bombs. The terrorism of these acts lies in their enormity. They stagger the imagination and are intended to weaken the will. From this point of view, the September 11, 2001, attacks on the World Trade Center and the Pentagon were acts of mega-terrorism, involving not only suicide pilot-hijackers but also aircraft filled with volatile fuel and innocent passengers converted into immense projectiles. (See Box 19.1 in Chapter 19.) These attacks were followed by terrorist assaults in Bali, Madrid, London, Riyadh, and other cities. Dealing with international terrorism by religious fundamentalists is now a challenge that faces many nations worldwide.

FOSTERING ECONOMIC DEVELOPMENT

Two major forces are transforming political systems and nations, and the lives of their citizens; they provide major sources of comparison across the nations in this book. The first is the process of economic development, and the second is political democratization.

The Origins of "Fundamentalism"

BOX 1.3

Fundamentalism got its name in the decades before World War I when some Protestant clergymen in the United States banded together to defend the "fundamentals" of religious belief against the secularizing influences of a modernizing society. This was a reaction to new biblical scholarship at the time that questioned the divine inspiration and authorship of the Bible, and to the expansion of science and Darwinist theories of evolution. These church leaders were also distressed by the apparent erosion of morality and tradition in the United States. In 1920, a journalist and Baptist layman named Curtis Lee Laws appropriated the term "fundamentalist" as a designation for those who were ready "to do battle royal for the Fundamentals." The fundamentalists affirmed the inerrancy (the absolute truth) of the Bible and formed enclaves to protect themselves from error and sin. Religious fundamentalism has recently emerged in some form in all major faiths in reaction to social modernization.

A political system cannot generally satisfy its citizens unless it can foster social and economic development. Thus, as significant as nation-building may be, the level of economic and social development and the rate of economic growth are exceptionally important. Economic development implies that citizens can enjoy new resources and opportunities. Many people are primarily concerned that government can improve their living conditions through economic growth, providing jobs and raising income standards. However, development can also create social strains and damage nature. For better or worse, the social changes that result from economic development transform the politics of developing countries. The success of governments—both democratic and autocratic—is often measured in these terms.

For many affluent advanced industrial societies, contemporary living standards provide for basic social needs (and much more) for most of the public. Indeed, the current political challenges in these nations often focus on problems resulting from the economic successes of the past, such as protecting environmental quality or managing the consequences of growth. New challenges to social welfare policies are emerging from the medical and social security costs of aging populations. For most of the world, however, substantial basic economic needs still exist, and governments focus on improving the socioeconomic conditions of the nation.

Over the past two decades, globalization, democratization, and marketization have begun to transform living conditions in many nations. The United Nations Development Program (UNDP) combines measures of economic well-being, life expectancy, and educational achievement into what it calls the Human Development Index (HDI).[13] The HDI shows dramatic improvements in life conditions in many regions of the world over the past three decades (Figure 1.2). East Asia and South Asia have made substantial improvements since 1975. For instance, in 1975 South Korea and Taiwan had

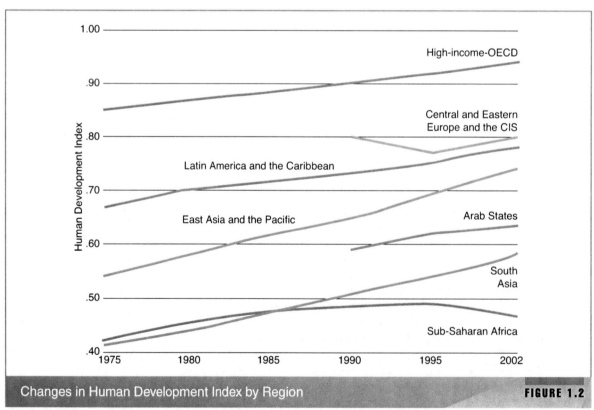

Changes in Human Development Index by Region   **FIGURE 1.2**

Source: United Nations Development Program, *Human Development Report 2004*. (New York: United Nations, 2004) 134.

a standard of living close to many poor African nations, and they are now affluent societies. Even more striking is the change in the two largest nations in the world. China improved from a HDI of .52 in 1975 (the same as Botswana or Swaziland) to .75 in 2003 (similar to the Philippines or Ecuador); India improved from an HDI of .41 to .60. These statistics represent improved living conditions for billions of people. At the same time, other regions of the world are not sharing in these advances. Living conditions have changed only marginally in Sub-Saharan Africa over this period—the poorest of the poor nations have not improved. In addition, many of the postcommunist nations of Central and Eastern Europe have suffered economically following the transition from communism to capitalism and democracy. The HDI for Russia, for instance, has stagnated since 1990.

The process of economic development typically follows a similar course. One element is a transformation of the structure of the labor force. The five advanced industrial countries in our comparisons all have agricultural employment as less than 10 percent of the labor force. The three poorest countries—China, India, and Nigeria—have more than two-thirds of their labor forces employed in agriculture. The middle-income countries—Mexico and Brazil—have about a third to a

fifth of their labor forces in agriculture. In addition, economic development is typically linked to urbanization, as peasants leave their farms and move to the cities. In nations undergoing rapid economic development, such as China, urban migration creates new opportunities for the workers but also new economic and social policy challenges for the governments.

The UNDP's Human Development Index provides a means to compare the differences in current life conditions across the twelve comparison nations in this chapter (Table 1.3). Perhaps the most striking feature of this table is the wide gap in living standards that still exist across nations worldwide. For instance, the **gross national product (GNP)** per capita, which is a measure of national economic development, is nearly thirty times higher in the Western advanced industrial democracies than in Nigeria.[14] Similarly, there are notable gaps in life expectancy and educational opportunities between the affluent Northern societies and the developing nations in Africa and Asia. In highly industrialized countries, education is virtually universal and practically everyone over age 15 can read and write. In India and Nigeria, less than two-thirds of the adult population has this minimal level of education. Moreover, the countries with the fewest literate citizens also have the fewest radios and television sets—even

TABLE 1.3

Human Development Indicators

Nation	Life Expectancy	Percent Enrolled in School	GNP/capita (ppp)	2003 HDI	1975 HDI	2003 World Rank
United States	77.4	93	37,562	.944	.867	10
Japan	82.0	84	27,967	.943	.857	11
United Kingdom	78.4	—	27.147	.939	.845	15
France	79.5	92	27,677	.938	.853	16
Germany	78.7	89	27,756	.930	—	20
Mexico	75.1	75	9,168	.814	.689	53
Russia	65.3	90	9,230	.795	—	62
Brazil	70.5	91	7,790	.792	.645	63
China	71.6	69	5,003	.755	.525	85
Iran	70.4	69	6,995	.736	.566	99
India	63.3	60	2,892	.602	.412	127
Nigeria	43.4	64	1,050	.453	.318	158

Source: United Nations Development Program, *World Development Report 2005* (New York: United Nations, 2005) (www.undp.org).

though these devices do not require literacy. Economic development is also associated with better nutrition and medical care. In the economically advanced countries, fewer children die in infancy, and the average citizen has a life expectancy at birth of over seventy-five years. Improvements in living conditions have substantially increased life expectancy in many low-income nations, such as Mexico and China. However, the average life expectancy of an Indian is sixty-three years; and the Nigerian little more than forty years. Material productivity, education, exposure to communications media, and longer and healthier lives are closely interconnected.

In order to become more productive, a country needs the resources to develop a skilled and healthy labor force and to build the infrastructure that material welfare requires. Preindustrial nations face most urgently the issues of economic development: how to improve the immediate welfare of their citizens yet also build and invest for the future. Typically, these are newer nations that also face the challenges of building community and effective political institutions. Political leaders and celebrities, such as Bono and Angelina Jolie, have mobilized public awareness that these differences in living conditions are a global concern—for those living in the developing world, the affluent nations and their citizens, and international organizations such as the United Nations and the World Bank.

Problems of Economic Development

The HDI or GNP per capita measure the overall wealth, income, and opportunity in a nation, but these factors are not evenly distributed within nations. The unequal distribution of resources and opportunities is among the most serious causes of political conflict. A large GNP may conceal significant differences in the distribution of resources and opportunities. A high rate of national growth may benefit only particular regions or social groups, leaving large parts of the population unrewarded or even less well off than before. The "inner cities" of the United States, the older parts of such Indian cities as Delhi and Calcutta, the peripheral ramshackle settlements around the cities of Latin America, many rural areas in China, and the arid northeast of Brazil all suffer from poverty and hopelessness. At the same time, other parts of the countries experience growth and improved welfare. Moreover, there is some evidence that rapid economic development tends to increase such inequalities.

A country's politics may be sharply affected by internal divisions of income, wealth, and other resources. Table 1.4 displays income distributions for our twelve comparison countries. Generally speaking, economic development improves the equality of income, at least past a certain stage of economic growth. Wealthy nations like Japan, Germany, and

Poverty in Third World cities is illustrated by this scene of a back street in Calcutta, in India, where the poor make their beds in the street. Similar scenes, though on a lesser scale, are to be encountered in modern American cities where homeless people sleep on the sidewalks and in doorways.

Jehangir Gazdar/Woodfin Camp & Associates

Income Distribution for Selected Nations				TABLE 1.4
Country	Year	Wealthiest 10%	Poorest 40%	Wealthy/Poor Gap
Germany	2000	22.1	22.2	−0.1
Russia	2002	23.8	20.9	2.9
Japan	1993	21.7	24.8	3.1
France	1995	25.1	19.8	5.3
India	1999	28.5	21.2	7.3
Britain	1999	28.5	17.5	11.0
United States	2000	29.9	16.2	13.7
Iran	1998	33.7	19.5	14.2
China	2001	33.1	13.7	19.4
Nigeria	1996	35.4	12.6	22.8
Mexico	2000	43.1	10.3	32.8
Brazil	2001	46.9	8.3	38.6

Source: World Bank, *World Development Indicators 2005*, table 2-7 (www.worldbank.org); distribution of income or consumption.

France have relatively more egalitarian income distributions than middle- or low-income countries. Still, the wealthiest 10 percent in Japan receive about the same total income as the poorest 40 percent receive. This is a large gap in life conditions between rich and poor, but the gap is even wider in less affluent nations. In Mexico, a middle-income country, the ratio is closer to 10 to 1; and in Brazil it is more than 20 to 1. The table also suggests that a nation's political characteristics make a difference. India has consciously worked to narrow inequality, which places it higher in the table, while inequality in the United States is as great as several poor nations, such as China.

Although industrialization and high productivity may eventually encourage a more equal distribution of income, the first stages of industrialization may actually increase **income inequality.** As economies modernize they create a dual economy—a rural sector and an urban industrial and commercial sector, both with inequalities of their own. These inequalities increase as education and communication spread more rapidly in the modern sector, which may contribute to the political instability of developing countries. Moreover, there is no guarantee that inequality will diminish in later stages of development. In Brazil, for instance, income inequality has increased for decades, even as the economy has developed. In the United States, income inequality increased substantially from the 1970s to the mid-1990s because of changes in economic structure, the increase in single-parent families,

and a lowering of income taxes. In Russia and other postcommunist societies, the development of new capitalist markets was accompanied by new income inequalities. Inequality is an issue that many nations face.

Several studies have proposed various policy solutions to mitigate the hardships economic inequality causes in developing societies.[15] Taiwan and South Korea are models showing how early land reforms equalized opportunity at the outset of the developmental process. Investment in primary and secondary education, in agricultural inputs and rural infrastructure (principally roads and water), and in labor-intensive industries produced remarkable results for several decades. A comparative advantage in cheap and skilled labor enabled Taiwan and South Korea to compete effectively in international markets. Thus, some growth policies mitigate inequalities, but it can be very difficult to put them into practice, especially where substantial inequalities already exist.

Another correlate of development is population growth. The book *The Population Explosion* drew attention to the social burden that may follow from the population growth that typically accompanies economic development.[16] As health care improves, living standards increase, and life expectancies lengthen, population sizes grow. This is a positive development because it represents improved living conditions for these people, but rapid population growth also can pose policy challenges for many developing nations.

	In 1990		Projected to 2015	
Economic Development Level	**Number**	**Percentage**	**Number**	**Percentage**
Low-income economies	1,777	33.9	2,794	39.4
Middle-income economies	2,588	49.3	3,299	46.5
High-income economies	887	16.8	1,007	14.1
Total	5,252	100	7,100	100

TABLE 1.5 Population by Economic Development Level in 1990 and Projected to 2015 (in millions)

Source: World Bank, *World Development Report Indicators 2005*, table 2-1 (www.worldbank.org) population dynamics.

Table 1.5 puts this issue in sharp relief. The table divides the world population into three strata: low-income economies, middle-income economies, and high-income economies. In 1990 the low-income countries had a population total of almost 2 billion, or about a third of the total world population. In contrast, the high-income nations had about a sixth of the world's population.

Some projections estimate that world population in 2015 will increase to 7 billion and that the poorer countries will see a more rapid rate of growth. In 2005, Hania Zlotnik of the UN population division estimated that "out of every 100 persons added to the [world's] population in the coming decade, 97 will live in developing countries."[17] Rapid economic growth in the developing world can create significant burdens for these nations.

These prospects have produced a development literature that mixes both light and heat. Economist Amartya Sen warns of a "danger that in the confrontation between apocalyptic pessimism on one hand, and a dismissive smugness, on the other, a genuine understanding of the nature of the population problem may be lost."[18] He points out that the first impact of "modernization" on population is to increase it rapidly, as new sanitation measures and modern pharmaceuticals reduce the death rate. As an economy develops, however, changing conditions tend to reduce fertility. With improved education (particularly of women), health, and welfare, the advantages of lower fertility become clear, and population growth declines.

Fertility decreased in Europe and North America as they underwent industrialization. Today, in many European nations the native populations are decreasing because fertility rates are below levels necessary to sustain a constant population size. This pattern appears to be occurring in the developing world. Thus annual

population growth in the world has declined from 2.2 percent to 1.7 percent in the last two decades. The rate of population growth in India, for example, rose to 2.2 percent in the 1970s and has since declined. Latin America peaked at a higher rate and then came down sharply. The major problem area is Sub-Saharan Africa, with an average growth rate of more than 2.7 percent each year during the 1990s.[19] The fertility rate in Africa has recently dropped dramatically because of the tragically rising death rate from the AIDS epidemic.

While population growth rates appear to be slowing, governments are addressing this issue in different ways. China adopted a coercive policy of limiting families to a single child, which in urban areas produced dramatic results at great costs. India followed a collaborative approach involving governmental intervention and market and education to affect family choices.[20] Kerala in southern India is a dramatic example of what can be accomplished by the collaborative approach, where expanding education (particularly among women) and otherwise improving living conditions has reduced fertility more than in China.

Economic growth can have other social costs. For instance, advanced industrial societies are dealing with the environmental costs of their industrial development. Despoiled forests, depleted soils and fisheries, polluted air and water, nuclear waste, endangered species, and a threatened ozone layer now burden their legislative dockets. With increasing industrialization and urbanization in the developing world, many of these environmental problems could worsen. Thus, economic development can impose serious environmental costs as well as benefits. At the same time, some environmental problems are even more acute in less developed countries, where rapid increases in population and urbanization create shortages of clean air, clean water, and adequate sanitation.[21] Thus,

The world's increasing energy use is causing serious environmental challenges. The burning of fossil fuels—such as coal, oil, and gas—polllutes our air, water, and atmosphere, whereas nuclear power plants, such as this one in Northern Bohemia, pose the risk of nuclear radiation.

Sean Sprague/Panos Pictures

economic development generally improves living conditions of the public, but in the process it produces new policy problems that governments must address.

FOSTERING DEMOCRACY, HUMAN RIGHTS, AND CIVIL LIBERTIES

The second major force transforming contemporary political systems is the process of democratization, which includes the enhancement of human rights and the expansion of freedom. Democracy is the form of government to which most contemporary countries, more or less sincerely and successfully, aspire. A **democracy,** briefly defined, is a political system in which citizens enjoy a number of basic civil and political rights, and in which their most important political leaders are elected in free and fair elections and are accountable under a rule of law. Democracy literally means "government by the people."

In small political systems, such as local communities, it may be possible for "the people" to share directly in debating, deciding, and implementing public policy. In large political systems, such as contemporary states, democracy must be achieved largely through indirect participation in policymaking. Elections, competitive political parties, free mass media, and representative-

assemblies make some degree of democracy, some degree of "government by the people," possible. This indirect, or representative, democracy is not complete or ideal. But the more citizens are involved and the more influential their choices, the more democratic the system.

The most important general distinction in classifying political systems is between democratic systems and authoritarian systems. *Authoritarian* states lack one or several of the defining features of democracy. In democracies, competitive elections give citizens the chance to shape the policymaking process through their selection of key policymakers. In authoritarian systems the policymakers are chosen by military councils, hereditary families, dominant political parties, and the like. Citizens are either ignored or pressed into symbolic assent to the government's choices.

Authoritarian states can take several forms. (See Chapter 6.) In **oligarchies,** literally "rule by the few," important political rights are withheld from the majority of the population. South Africa until the abolition of apartheid in the early 1990s is a good example. Other authoritarian states, such as Egypt, are controlled by an individual dictator and his party or military supporters. **Totalitarian systems**—such as Nazi Germany, or the Soviet Union under Stalin, or North Korea today—are systems in which the government constricts the rights and privacy of its citizens in a particularly severe and intrusive manner.

As societies become more complex, richer, and more technologically advanced, the probability of citizen involvement and democratization increases. In the first half of the twentieth century most Western states were transformed from authoritarian regimes or oligarchies to democracies. After World War II, a second democratic wave—which lasted from 1943 until the early 1960s—saw both newly independent states (such as India and Nigeria) and defeated authoritarian powers (such as Germany and Japan) set up the formal institutions of democracy.[22]

Another round of democratic transitions began in 1974, involving Southern Europe, East Asia, Latin America, and a number of African states. The most dramatic changes came in Central and Eastern Europe, where in a few short years the Soviet empire collapsed, the nations of Eastern Europe rapidly converted to democracy, and many of these nations have now joined the European Union. The people power revolution in the Philippines, the end of the apartheid regime in South Africa, and the public protests for democratization in Indonesia were equally dramatic. Samuel P. Huntington speaks of this latest move toward democracy as a "Third Wave" of worldwide **democratization**.[23]

As a result of these three democratization waves, democracy has become a common goal of the global community (see Figure 1.3). As late as 1978, only a third of the world's independent countries had competitive party and electoral systems. Communist and other single-party governments and other authoritarian regimes dominated the landscape. By 2004, almost two-thirds of states had a system of electoral democracy, and human rights and liberties were similarly spreading to more of the world's population.[24] This democratization trend is continuing in the new millennium, with prospects for further progress in many nations.

This democratization process results from a combination of factors. Economic development transforms societies in ways that typically encourage democratization by creating autonomous political groups that demand political influence, by expanding the political skills of the citizenry, and by creating economic complexity that encourages systems of self-governance. Social modernization transforms the political values and political culture of the public, which increases demands for a more participatory system (see Chapter 3). New democracies are also much more likely to endure when founded in economically developed societies.[25]

Democracy is not an all-or-nothing proposition, however. No democracy is perfect, and we can speak of shades or gradations of democracy. Democracy typically does not come about overnight. It often takes time to establish democratic institutions and to have citizens recognize them and comply with the rules of the democratic process.

It can be especially difficult to consolidate democracy in less economically developed societies. Not all of the newly democratizing countries are succeeding beyond the first few years. In some, democratic processes fail to produce stable institutions and effective public policies and give way to some form of authoritarianism. In Nigeria, a democratic-leaning regime installed in 1979 was overthrown by a military coup in 1983, and a partial movement toward redemocratization was again aborted by the military in 1993 before being reestablished in 1999. Nigeria is by no

Growth in Free Governments over Time   **FIGURE 1.3**

Legend: Not free | Partly free | Free

Source: Freedom House, *Freedom in the World 2006* (www.freedomhouse.org).

Women and Political Development

BOX 1.4

If a poor nation could do one thing to stimulate its development, what should it do? Opening the fiftieth session of the United Nations Commission on the Status of Women in 2006, UN Deputy-Secretary General Louise Fréchette said the international community finally comprehends that empowering women and girls around the globe is the most effective tool for a country's development. She stated that studies have repeatedly shown that by giving women equal education and work opportunities and access to a society's decision-making processes, a country can boost its economic productivity, reduce infant and maternal mortality rates and improve the general population's nutrition and health. These results are achieved because women's education and participation in the labor force increase family output, increase the likelihood that children will be better educated and benefit from health care, improve nutrition in the family, and better the quality of life for women and their families.

Source: UN News Center, February 27, 2006.

means unique. Transition can move in either direction, toward or away from democracy. The recent wave of democratization is supported by the more favorable environments of more modernized societies and because there are now more democracies in the world to support new democracies. However, democracy is difficult to sustain when severe economic or political problems face a nation, or where the public remains uncertain about democracy.

Even when states democratize, there is no guarantee that they will grant human rights and civil liberties to all their people. In some countries, majority rule turns into a "tyranny of the majority" against ethnic or religious minorities. Therefore, democracies have to balance between respecting the will of the majority and protecting the rights of the minority. Even when political rulers sincerely try to promote human rights and civil liberties (which is by no means always the case), they do not always agree on the nature of those rights.

A good example of the spread of rights and liberties—and cultural differences in the definition of rights—involves gender issues. Governments in Western industrial societies favor gender policies that guarantee equality for women in society, the workplace, and politics. The United Nations and other international organizations have become advocates of women's rights. But gender norms often vary across cultural zones. The UN's statistics indicate that many developing nations hesitate to grant equal rights to women, restricting their education and involvement in the economy and politics.[26] Restrictions on women's rights are even starker in many Arab states. Ironically, other research indicates that improving the status of women is one of the most productive ways to develop a nation politically and economically (see Box 1.4). In short, expanding human rights is an ongoing process in the world today, and there is much room for further progress.

LOOKING FORWARD

The last several decades have been a period of tremendous social, economic, and political change in the world. Economic development, improved living standards, the spread of human rights, and democratization improved the life chances and life conditions of billions of individuals. In most of the world, the average child born today can look forward to a longer, better, and freer life than his or her parents—especially if she is a girl.

At the same time, continuing social, economic, and political problems remain. Progress in one area can create new opportunities, but also new problems in another. Economic development, for example, can sometimes stimulate ethnic strife and destabilize political institutions. Economic development can also disrupt social life. And the process of development has been uneven across and within nations. Many basic human needs still remain in too short supply.[27]

Even in the affluent democracies, as one set of policy issues is addressed, new issues come to the fore. Western democracies struggle to address issues of environmental quality, changing lifestyles, and the challenges of globalization and multiculturalism. A more affluent and information-driven citizenry can also limit the effectiveness of political parties, interest groups, parliaments, and political executives. Success in meeting these old and new challenges can improve the living conditions for the world's populations, decrease international conflict, and come closer to meeting the ideals of humankind.

Governments and politics have played a large role in promoting the successes and failures of the past. Just as we can point to governments whose actions improved life for their citizens, there are other governments that took regressive actions. Governments and their activities are central to our political futures. Our goal in this book is to examine the ways in which citizens, policymakers, and governments address the policy challenges that face them today.

REVIEW QUESTIONS

- What is politics?
- What are the contrasting images of the "state of nature" of humankind?
- What are the potential positive and negative outcomes of government activity?
- What are the main challenges that countries face in building a political community?
- What are the causes and consequences of economic development?
- What are the causes and consequences of democratization?

KEY TERMS

democracy
democratization
ethnicity
European Union (EU)
externalities
governments

gross national product (GNP)
human rights
income inequality
nation
nation-states

oligarchies
political culture
political system
public goods
religious fundamentalism
sovereignty

state
state of nature
totalitarian systems
United Nations (UN)

SUGGESTED READINGS

Chenery, Hollis et al. *Redistribution With Growth.* New York: Oxford University Press, 1981.

Cornelius, Wayne et al., eds. *Controlling Immigration: A Global Perspective.* Stanford, CA: Stanford University Press, 1995.

Dalton, Russell, and Doh Chull Shin, eds. *Citizens, Democracy, and Markets Around the Pacific Rim.* Oxford: Oxford University Press, 2006.

Diamond, Larry, ed. *Developing Democracy: Towards Consolidation.* Baltimore: Johns Hopkins University Press, 1999.

Ehrlich, Paul, and Anne Ehrlich. *The Population Explosion.* New York: Simon & Schuster, 1990.

Horowitz, Donald. *Ethnic Groups in Conflict.* Berkeley: University of California Press, 1985.

Huntington, Samuel. *The Third Wave: Democratization in the Late Twentieth Century.* Norman: University of Oklahoma Press, 1991.

———. *The Clash of Civilizations and the Remaking of World Order.* New York: Simon & Schuster, 1996.

Lijphart, Arend. *Patterns of Democracy.* New Haven, CT: Yale University Press, 1999.

Linz, Juan, and Alfred Stepan, eds. *Problems of Democratic Transitions and Consolidation.* Baltimore: Johns Hopkins University Press, 1996.

Marty, Martin, and Scott Appleby. *Fundamentalism Observed.* Chicago: University of Chicago Press, 1991.

Putnam, Robert. *Making Democracy Work: Civic Traditions in Modern Italy.* Princeton, NJ: Princeton University Press, 1993.

Przeworski, Adam et al. *Democracy and Development: Political Institutions and Well-being in the World 1950–1990.* New York: Cambridge University Press, 2000.

Sachs, Jeffrey. *The End of Poverty: Economic Possibilities for Our Time.* New York: Penguin, 2005.

United Nations. *World Development Report.* New York: Oxford University Press, annual editions.

Weiner, Myron. *The Global Migration Crisis: Challenge to States and to Human Rights.* New York: HarperCollins, 1995.

Zakaria, Fareed. *The Future of Freedom: Illiberal Democracy at Home and Abroad.* New York: Norton, 2003.

ENDNOTES

1. Thomas Hobbes, *Leviathan,* ed. C. B. Macpherson (New York: Penguin, 1968), 186.

2. J. J. Rousseau, *Second Discourse on Inequality, The First and Second Discourses* (New York: St. Martin's Press, 1964), pp. 109–10.

3. Two other philosophical groups are especially outspoken critics of government: libertarians and anarchists. Adherents of **libertarianism** are individualists who see society as composed of individual human beings with fundamental rights that must be protected. The main problem with government, libertarians argue, is that the more tasks it takes on, the more prone it is to violate such basic rights. Adherents of **anarchism** claim that governments produce undesirable effects; they see societies not as collections of individuals but as communities of people who in their natural condition are equal. Governments and power corrupt such communities and lead to oppression and alienation.

4. Martin Greenberg and Mark Tier, *Visions of Liberty* (New York: Baen Publishers, 2004).

5. See, for example, Fareed Zakaria, *The Future of Freedom: Illiberal Democracy at Home and Abroad* (New York: Norton, 2003).

6. See, for example, Douglas North, *Institutions, Institutional Change, and Economic Performance* (Cambridge: Cambridge University Press, 1990), Mancur Olson, "The New Institutional Economics: The Collective Choice Approach to Economic Development," in C. Clague, ed., *Institutions and Economic Development.* (Baltimore: Johns Hopkins University Press, 1997; S. Knack and P. Keefer, "Institutions and Economic Performance," *Economics and Politics* 7 (1995) 207–29.

7. The Vatican and Switzerland are not members of the UN but maintain permanent observer missions at the UN headquarters. Taiwan was expelled from the UN in 1971 to accommodate mainland China (the People's Republic).

8. Max Weber, *Economy and Society,* ed. Guenther Roth and Claus Wittich (Berkeley: University of California Press, 1978), 389.

9. Even before the end of the Cold War, ethnic autonomy movements in parts of old countries—such as the United Kingdom (the Scots and Welsh) and Canada (the Quebecois)—sought to break free or achieve greater autonomy.

10. Stephen Castles and Mark J. Miller, *The Age of Migration: International Population Movements in the Modern World* (New York: Guilford, 1994).

11. Erik V. Gunnemark, *Countries, Peoples, and Their Languages: The Geolinguistic Handbook* (Gothenburg: Lanstryckeriet, 1991).

12. A book dealing with this theme is R. Scott Appleby, *The Ambivalence of the Sacred* (Lanham, MD: Rowman & Littlefield, 2000).

13. United Nations Development Program, *Human Development Report 2005* (New York: United Nations). See also www.undp.org. for additional data and interactive presentations.

14. The per capita *gross national product (GNP)* is the total economic output per person. Rather than the traditional measures computed according to the exchange rates of the national currencies, the *purchasing power parity (PPP)* index takes into account differences in price levels from one country to another. Most analyses assume that the GNP/ppp statistics are more comparable measures of living conditions. The income gap increases, however, if one uses the traditional exchange rate measure of GNP.

15. For example, see Hollis Chenery et al., *Redistribution With Growth* (New York: Oxford University Press, 1981).

16. Paul Ehrlich and Anne Ehrlich, *The Population Explosion* (New York: Simon & Schuster, 1990).

17. Hania Zlotnik, "Statement to the Thirty-Eighth Session of the Commission on Population and Development," April 4, 2005 (www.un.org/esa/population/cpd/Statement_HZ_open. pdf).

18. Amartya Sen, "Population: Delusion and Reality," *New York Review of Books,* 22 Sept., 1994, pp. 62ff.

19. World Bank, *World Development Report, 1998–1999* (New York: Oxford University Press, 1999).

20. Sen, "Population: Delusion and Reality."

21. Regina Axelrod, David Downie, and Norman Vig, eds., *The Global Environment: Institutions, Law, and Policy* (Washington, DC: CQ Press, 2004); Yale Center for Environmental Law and Policy and Center for International Earth Science Information Network, *2005 Environmental Sustainability Index: Benchmarking National Environmental Stewardship* (New Haven, CT: Yale University, 2005) (http://www.yale.edu/esi/).

22. While many countries became formally democratic in these years, most of them quickly lapsed into authoritarianism. Many of these would-be democracies failed in their first decade; another "reverse wave" in the 1960s and early 1970s swept away some older democracies (Chile, Greece, and Uruguay, for example) as well.

23. Samuel Huntington, *The Third Wave* (Norman: University of Oklahoma Press, 1991).

24. Freedom House, *Freedom in the World 2004* (Washington, DC: Freedom House, 2005) (www. freedomhouse. org).

25. Seymour Martin Lipset, "Some Social Requisites of Democracy," *American Political Science Review* 53 (September 1959), 69–105 Larry Diamond, "Economic Development and Democracy Reconsidered," in G. Marks and L. Diamond, eds., *Reexamining Democracy* (Newbury Park, CA: Sage, 1992); Tatu Vanhanen, *Prospects of Democracy* (New York: Routledge, 1997); Adam Przeworski et al., *Democracy and Development: Political Institutions and Well-being in the World 1950–1990* (New York: Cambridge University Press, 2000).

26. See United Nations Development Program, *Human Development Report 2005* (New York: United Nations) (http://hdr.undp.org/reports/global/2005/), tables 25-30, and associated discussion.

27. Many of these issues are addressed by the United Nations' Millennium Development Goals. Visit the UN website (http://www. un. org/ millenniumgoals/) or see United Nations, *Millennium Development Goals Report 2005* (New York: United Nations) (http:/ /unstats. un. org/ unsd/ mi/ pdf/ MDGBook. pdf).

COMPARING POLITICAL SYSTEMS

WHY WE COMPARE

The great French interpreter of American democracy, Alexis de Tocqueville, while traveling in America in the 1830s, wrote to a friend explaining how his own ideas about French institutions and culture entered into his writing of *Democracy in America*. Tocqueville wrote: "Although I very rarely spoke of France in my book, I did not write one page of it without having her, so to speak, before my eyes."[1]

On a more general note about the comparative method, he offered this comment: "Without comparisons to make, the mind does not know how to proceed."[2] Tocqueville was telling us that comparison is fundamental to all human thought. We add that it is the methodological core of the humanistic and scientific methods. It is the only way we can fully understand our own political system. Comparing our experience with that of other countries deepens our understanding of our own institutions. Examining politics in other societies permits us to see a wider range of political alternatives. It illuminates the virtues and shortcomings of our own political life. By taking us beyond our familiar arrangements and assumptions, comparative analysis helps expand our awareness of the possibilities of politics.

Comparison is also at the methodological core of the scientific study of politics. Comparative analysis helps us develop explanations and test theories of the ways in which political processes work and in which political change occurs. The goals of the comparative methods used by political scientists are similar to those used in more exact sciences. But political scientists cannot normally design experiments, a major path to knowledge in many of the natural sciences. We cannot control and manipulate political arrangements and observe the consequences. We are especially limited when dealing with large-scale events that drastically affect many people. For example, researchers cannot and would not want to start a social revolution to see its effects.

We can, however, use the comparative method to describe and explain the different combinations of political events and institutions found in different societies. More than two thousand years ago, Aristotle in his *Politics* contrasted the economies and social structures of Greek city-states in an effort to determine how the social and economic environments affected political institutions and policies (see Box 2.1). More contemporary political scientists also try to explain differences between the processes and performance of political systems. They compare two-party democracies with multiparty democracies, parliamentary with presidential regimes, democracies in poor countries with those in rich countries, elections in new party systems with those in established democracies. These and many other comparisons have greatly enriched our understanding of politics.

HOW WE COMPARE

We study politics in several different ways: we describe it; we seek to explain it; sometimes we try to predict it. These are all parts of the scientific process. Each of them may use the comparative method.

Aristotle's Library	BOX 2.1

There is historical evidence that Aristotle had accumulated a library of more than 150 studies of the political systems of the Mediterranean world of 400–300 B.C. Many of these had probably been researched and written by his disciples.

While only the Athenian constitution survives of this library of Aristotelian polities, it is evident from the references to such studies that do survive that Aristotle was concerned with sampling the variety of political systems then in existence, including the "barbarian" (Third World?) countries, such as Libya, Etruria, and Rome: "[T]he references in ancient authorities give us the names of some 70 or more of the states described in the compilation of 'polities.' They range from Sinope, on the Black Sea, to Cyrene in North Africa; they extend from Marseilles in the Western Mediterranean to Crete, Rhodes, and Cyprus in the East. Aristotle thus included colonial constitutions as well as those of metropolitan states. His descriptions embraced states on the Aegean, Ionian, and Tyrrhenian Seas, and the three continents of Europe, Asia, and Africa."

Source: Ernest Barker, ed., *The Politics of Aristotle* (London: Oxford University Press, 1977), 386.

The first stage in the study of politics is description. If we cannot describe a political process or event, we cannot really hope to understand or explain it. Much less can we predict what might happen next or in similar situations. In order to describe politics, we need a set of concepts that are clearly defined and well understood. We speak of this as a conceptual framework. The easier this set of concepts is to understand, and the more generally it can be applied, the more helpful it is to the study of politics. Conceptual frameworks are not generally right or wrong, but they may be more or less useful to the task at hand.

POLITICAL SYSTEMS: ENVIRONMENT AND INTERDEPENDENCE

Comparative Politics Today suggests that we compare political systems with a structural-functional systems framework. To do so, we need to discuss three general concepts that we use throughout this book: (1) system, (2) structure, and (3) function. **System,** as we defined it in Chapter 1, suggests an object having interdependent parts, acting within a setting or an **environment.** The **political system** is a set of institutions and agencies concerned with formulating and implementing the collective goals of a society or of groups within it. **Governments** are the **policymaking** parts of political systems. The decisions of governments are normally backed up by legitimate coercion, and obedience may be compelled. (We discuss legitimacy at greater length in Chapter 3.)

Figure 2.1 tells us that a political system exists in both an international environment and a domestic environment. It is molded by these environments and it tries to mold them. The system receives **inputs** from these environments. Its policymakers attempt to shape them through its outputs. In the figure, which is quite schematic and simple, we use the United States as the central actor. We include other countries as our environmental examples—Russia, China, Britain, Germany, Japan, Mexico, and Iran.

Exchanges among countries may vary in many ways. For example, they may be "dense" or "sparse"; U.S.–Canadian relations exemplify the dense end of the continuum, while U.S.–Nepalese relations would be at the sparse end.

Relationships among political systems may be of many different kinds. The United States has substantial trade relations with some countries and relatively little trade with others. Some countries have an excess of imports over exports, whereas others have an excess of exports over imports. Military exchanges and support with such countries as the NATO nations, Japan, South Korea, Israel, and Saudi Arabia have been of significant importance to the United States.

The interdependence of countries—the volume and value of imports and exports, transfers of capital, international communication, the extent of foreign

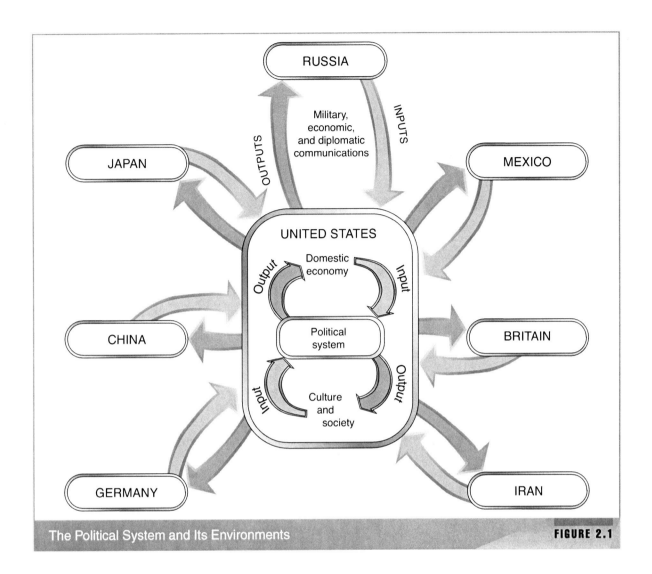

The Political System and Its Environments

FIGURE 2.1

travel and immigration—has increased enormously in the last decades. This increase is often called **globalization.** We might represent this process as a thickening of the input and output arrows between the United States and other countries in Figure 2.1. Fluctuations in this flow of international transactions and traffic attributable to depression, inflation, protective tariffs, international terrorism, war, and the like may wreak havoc with the economies of the countries affected.

The interaction of a political system with its domestic environment—the economic and social systems and the political culture of its citizens—is also depicted in Figure 2.1. We can illustrate this interaction in the U.S. case by the rise of the "high-tech information-based economy."

The composition of the U.S. labor force, and consequently its citizenry, has changed dramatically in the last century. Agriculture has declined to under 2 percent of the gainfully employed. Employment in heavy extractive and manufacturing industries has decreased substantially. Newer, high-technology occupations, the professions, and the service occupations have increased sharply as proportions of the labor force. The last half-century has also witnessed significant improvements in the educational level of the U.S. population. Many more young people complete high school and go on to college. Moreover, people move more easily from one region to another. These and other changes in the U.S. social structure have altered the challenges facing the U.S. system and the resources available to meet these challenges.

These changes in the economy and the citizenry are associated with changes in American **political culture.** (Political culture—the attitudes, beliefs, and values of the people in a country—is discussed at more length in Chapter 3.) People want different things from politics. For example, an educated and culturally sophisticated society is more concerned with quality of life, the beauty and healthfulness of the environment, and similar issues.

At the same time, the globalization of the economy leads to demands from firms and workers in some industries for protection of their jobs. Natural disasters, such as the hurricane that devastated New Orleans in 2005, spur calls for the national government to lead reconstruction. Local issues are seen as the responsibility of the entire country. People live longer. An aging population demands that governments do more to help with medical benefits. In input-output terms, socioeconomic changes transform the political demands of the electorate and the kinds of policies that it supports.

Thus a new pattern of society results in different policy outputs, different kinds and levels of taxation, changes in regulatory patterns, and changes in welfare expenditures. The advantage of the system-environment approach is that it directs our attention to the **interdependence** of what happens between and within countries. It provides us with a vocabulary to describe, compare, and explain these interacting events.

If we are to make sound judgments in politics, we need to be able to place political systems in their domestic and international environments. We need to recognize how these environments both set limits on and provide opportunities for political choices. This approach keeps us from reaching quick and biased political judgments. If a country is poor in natural resources and lacks the capabilities necessary to exploit what it has, we cannot fault it for having a low industrial output or poor educational and social services. Each country chapter in the second half of this book begins by discussing the current policy challenges facing the country and its social and economic environment.

POLITICAL SYSTEMS: STRUCTURES AND FUNCTIONS

Governments do many things—from establishing and operating school systems, to maintaining public order, to fighting wars. In order to carry on these disparate

activities, governments have specialized agencies, or **structures,** such as parliaments, bureaucracies, administrative agencies, and courts. These structures perform **functions,** which in turn enable the government to formulate, implement, and enforce its policies. The policies reflect the goals; the agencies provide the means to achieve them.

Figure 2.2 locates six types of political structures—political parties, interest groups, legislatures, executives, bureaucracies, and courts—within the political system. These are formal organizations engaged in political activities. They exist in most contemporary political systems. This list is not exhaustive. Some structures, such as ruling military councils or governing royal families, are found in only a few countries. Some, such as Iran's Council of Guardians, are unique to their political system.

We might think that if we understand how such structures work in one political system, we can apply this insight to any other system. Unfortunately, that is not always the case. The sixfold classification will not carry us very far in comparing political systems with each other. The problem is that similar structures may have very different functions across political systems. For example, Britain and China have all six types of political structures. However, these institutions are organized differently in the two countries. More importantly, they function in dramatically different ways. They do different things in the political processes of their countries.

The political executive in Britain consists of the prime minister, the ministers assigned to the Cabinet, and the larger ministry, which consists of all the heads of departments and agencies. All these officials are usually selected from Parliament. There is a similar structure in China, called the State Council, headed by a premier and consisting of the various ministers and ministerial commissions. But while the British prime minister and Cabinet have substantial policymaking power, the State Council in China is closely supervised by the general secretary of the Communist Party, the Politburo, and the Central Committee of the party.

Both Britain and China have legislative bodies—the House of Commons in Britain and the National People's Congress in China. Their members make speeches to each other and vote on prospective public policies. But while the House of Commons is a key institution in the policymaking process, the Chinese Congress meets for only brief periods, ratifying decisions made mainly by the Communist Party authorities.

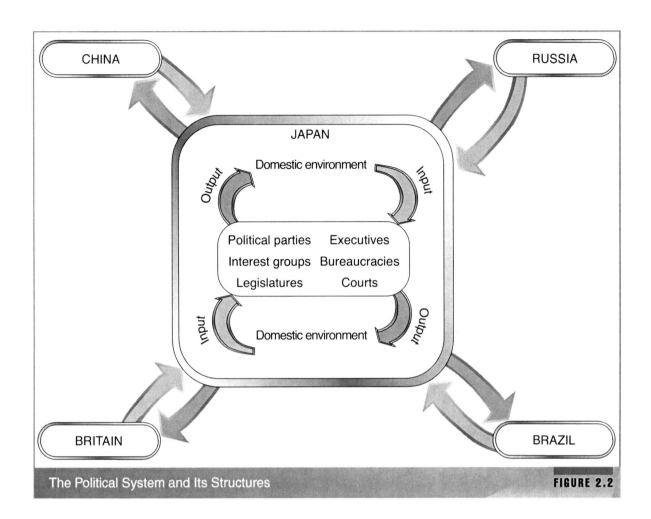

The Political System and Its Structures   **FIGURE 2.2**

Usually the Chinese delegates do not even consider alternative policies.

There are even larger differences between political parties in the two countries. Britain has a competitive party system. The majority in the House of Commons and the Cabinet are constantly confronted by an opposition party or parties, competing for public support. They look forward to the next election when they may unseat the incumbent majority, as happened in 1997, when the Labour Party replaced the Conservatives in government. In China the Communist Party controls the whole political process. There are no other political parties. The principal decisions are taken in the Politburo and to some extent in the Central Committee of the Communist Party. The governmental agencies implement the policies, which are initiated or approved by the top Communist Party leaders.

Thus, an institution-by-institution comparison of British and Chinese politics that did not spell out their

interdependence and the functions that they perform would not bring us far toward understanding the important differences in the politics of these two countries. Each country study in this book includes a figure that shows how some of the major structures select and control each other. Another figure illustrates how they fit into the policymaking process.

Figure 2.3 shows the functions of the political process that we can use to compare all political systems. The center of Figure 2.3 under the heading **"process functions"** lists the distinctive activities necessary for policy to be made and implemented in any kind of political system.

- **Interest articulation** involves individuals and groups expressing their needs and demands.
- **Interest aggregation** combines different demands into policy proposals backed by significant political resources.

This meeting of the National Assembly of the People's Republic of China in the Great Hall of the People in Beijing illustrates the importance of structural functionalism. While this is called the "National People's Congress" and the delegates are raising their hands in a vote, the vote is purely formal, since there is no real choice between alternatives.

Mark Avery/AP Images

- **Policymaking** decides which policy proposals are to become authoritative rules.
- **Policy implementation** carries out and enforces public policies; **policy adjudication** settles disputes about their application.

(We discuss each concept in greater detail in Chapters 4, 5, and 6.) We call these process functions because they play a direct and necessary role in the process of making policy.

Before policy can be decided, some individuals and groups in the government or the society must decide what they want and hope to get from politics. The political process begins as these interests are expressed or articulated. The many arrows on the left of the figure show these initial expressions.

To be effective, however, these demands must be combined (aggregated) into policy alternatives—such as higher or lower taxes or more or fewer social security benefits—for which substantial political support can be mobilized. Thus the arrows on the left are consolidated as the process moves from interest articulation to interest aggregation.

Governments then consider alternative policies. Whoever controls the government backs one of them and authoritative policymaking takes place. The policy must be enforced and implemented, and if it is challenged, there must be some process of adjudication.

Each policy may affect several different aspects of a society, as reflected in the three arrows for the implementation phase.

These process functions are performed by such political structures as parties, legislatures, political executives, bureaucracies, and courts. The **structural-functional approach** stresses two points. One is that *in different countries, the same structure may perform different functions*. A second is that while a particular institution, such as a legislature, may have a special relationship to a particular function, such as policymaking, *institutions often do not have a monopoly on any one function*. Presidents and governors may share in the policymaking function (veto powers), as do the higher courts (judicial review of statutes for their constitutionality).

The three functions listed at the top of the figure—socialization, recruitment, and communication—are not directly involved in making and implementing public policy but are of fundamental importance to the political system. We refer to these three functions as **system functions.** They determine whether or not the system will be maintained or changed. For example, will policymaking continue to be dominated by a military council or be replaced by competitive parties and a legislature? Will a sense of national community persist, or will it be eroded by new experiences?

The arrows leading from these three functions to all parts of the political process suggest their crucial

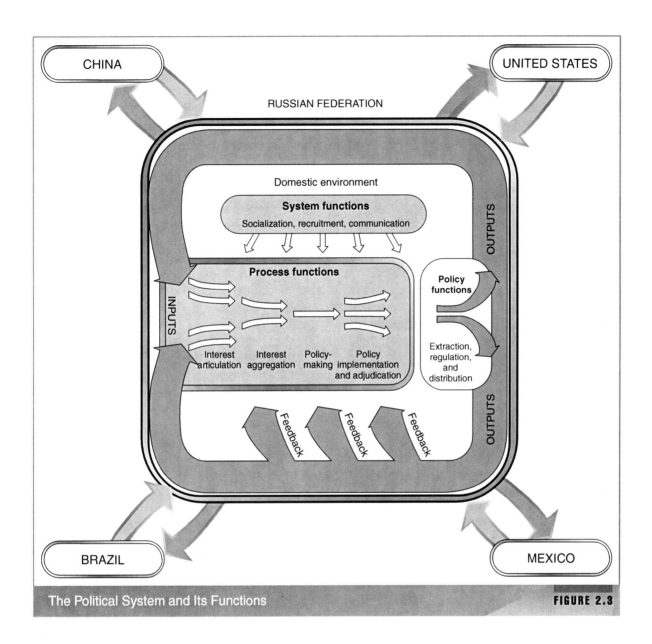

The Political System and Its Functions

FIGURE 2.3

role in underpinning and permeating the political process.

- **Political socialization** involves families, schools, communications media, churches, and all the various political structures that develop, reinforce, and transform the political culture, the attitudes of political significance in the society. (See Chapter 3.)
- **Political recruitment** refers to the selection of people for political activity and government offices. In a democracy, competitive elections play a major role in political recruitment. In authoritarian systems, recruitment may be dominated by a single party, as in China, or unelected religious leaders, as in Iran.
- **Political communication** refers to the flow of information through the society and through the various structures that make up the political system. Gaining control over information is a key goal of most authoritarian rulers, as shown in the elaborate efforts of Chinese leaders to control content on the Internet.

Understanding the performance of the system functions is essential to understanding how political systems respond to the great contemporary challenges of building community, fostering economic development, and securing democracy that we discussed in Chapter 1.

On the right side of Figure 2.3 we see the consequences of the policy process. The **outputs** are the implementations of the political process. These are the substantive impacts on the society, the economy, and the culture. They include various forms of **extraction** of resources in the form of taxes and the like, **regulation** of behavior, and **distribution** of benefits and services to various groups in the population. The **outcomes** of all these political activities reflect the way the policies interact with the domestic and international environments. Sometimes these outcomes are the desired results of public policies. But sometimes the complexities of policy and society result in unintended consequences. Among these may be new demands for legislation or for administrative action, or increases or decreases in the amount of support given to the political system and incumbent officeholders. We shall return to the policy level, after providing an example of a structural-functional comparison.

The functional concepts shown in Figure 2.3 describe the activities carried on in any society regardless of how its political system is organized or what kinds of policies it produces. Using these functional categories, we can determine how institutions in different countries combine in making and implementing different kinds of public policy. Each country study in this book discusses the ways the different political functions are performed.

AN ILLUSTRATIVE COMPARISON: REGIME CHANGE IN RUSSIA

Figures 2.4 and 2.5[3] offer a simplified graphic comparison of structures and functions in Russia before and after the breakdown of communist rule in the Soviet Union. They illustrate the use of the comparative method to assess the way a political regime changed significantly in a short period of time. The point here is to illustrate how we can use the tools of political analysis, rather than provide the details of the Russian case (which are discussed in depth in Chapter 12).

The figures depict the changes in the functioning of the major structures of the political system brought about by the collapse of communism. These include two revolutionary changes. One is the end of the single-party political system dominated by the Communist Party of the Soviet Union, which held together the vast, multinational Soviet state. The other is the dissolution of the Soviet Union itself into its fifteen member republics. As a result of these two remarkable events, Russia, the republic that was the core republic of the old union, became an independent noncommunist state.

In June 1991, Boris Yeltsin, a bitter rival to the Soviet president, Mikhail Gorbachev, was elected president of Russia. Six months later, the Soviet Union collapsed and Gorbachev gave up his office. In December 1993, Russian voters were called on to ratify a new constitution, which provided for a powerful executive presidency and at the same time elected a new parliament dominated by a diverse range of political parties.

In the new Russia, democratic tendencies competed with pressures for authoritarian rule. Overall, the new system was a mixture of pluralism with vestiges of the old, bureaucratically run, state socialist order. New political parties were represented in Parliament and tried to develop national political bases of support for the next elections. A reborn Communist Party—called the Communist Party of the Russian Federation—regularly denounced Yeltsin and called for the restoration of a strong state and more social protection. Parliament had become a meaningful site for policy debate and decisionmaking. The mass media were no longer tightly controlled by the Communist Party. New organized interest groups, such as business associations and labor unions, were actively involved in policymaking. The bureaucracy remained a powerful central player in the political process, however, with substantial continued control over the economy.

These and subsequent changes are reflected in the differences between the two figures. In 1985 (the year that the reform leader Mikhail Gorbachev came to power), the Soviet Union was a communist regime. Its Communist Party ruled the country. The top leader of the country was the general secretary of the Communist Party. Although the country had the formal trappings of democracy, power actually flowed downward from the decisionmakers at the top to government and society.

Figure 2.4 therefore shows how the basic functions of the political system were performed in 1985. The Communist Party was the dominant political institution of the country, overseeing schools and media, the arts and public organizations, the economy and

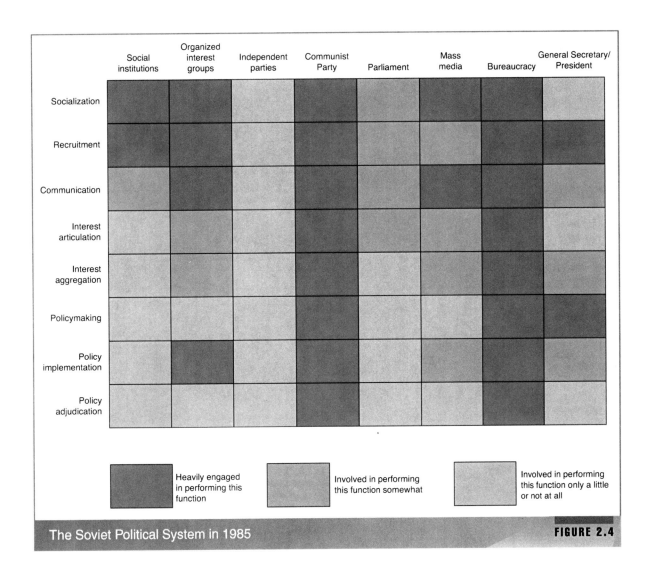

	Social institutions	Organized interest groups	Independent parties	Communist Party	Parliament	Mass media	Bureaucracy	General Secretary/ President
Socialization								
Recruitment								
Communication								
Interest articulation								
Interest aggregation								
Policymaking								
Policy implementation								
Policy adjudication								

Heavily engaged in performing this function

Involved in performing this function somewhat

Involved in performing this function only a little or not at all

The Soviet Political System in 1985   **FIGURE 2.4**

the courts. For this reason, all the cells of the chart in the column marked "Communist Party" are shaded dark, as are the cells under the column marked "Bureaucracy." Although social institutions—such as the family, workplace, arts, and hobby groups—exercised some influence over such system-level functions as socialization, recruitment, and communication, it was the Communist Party and state bureaucracy that dominated process-level functions. Under their tutelage, the mass media in 1985 were a key agent of communist political socialization and communication. Parliament was a compliant instrument for ratifying decisions made by the party and bureaucracy. No other parties could exist beside the Communist Party. The only organized interest groups were those authorized by

the party. The party's general secretary was the most powerful official in the country, since there was no state presidency.

By 2000 the political system had undergone fundamental changes, as shown in Figure 2.5. Many more structures played a role in the political process, as is immediately evident by the larger number of cells that are heavily shaded. In particular, Parliament, independent political parties, and regional governments all acquired important new powers in policymaking. The freedom enjoyed by ordinary citizens to articulate their interests and to organize to advance them had expanded enormously. The Communist Party, no longer an official or monopolistic party, had declined substantially in power and

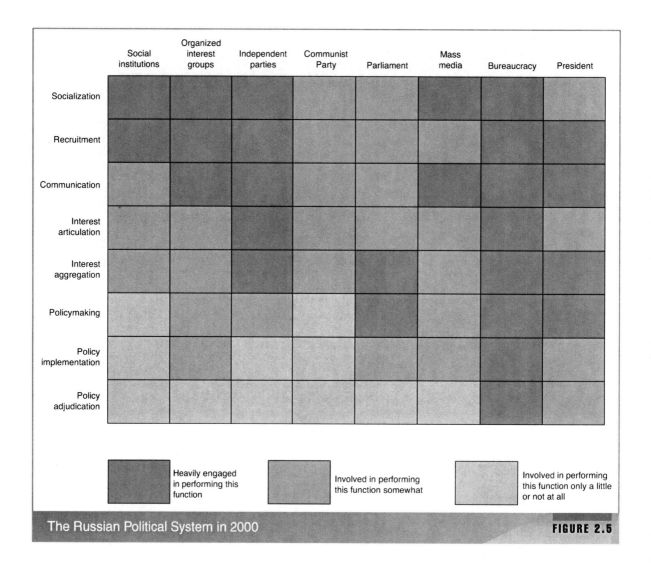

The Russian Political System in 2000

FIGURE 2.5

was playing by the rules of the parliamentary game. The lighter shading for the Communist Party in Figure 2.5 shows its diminished influence. The state bureaucracy remained an important element in the political system, although adapting itself to the new trend of movement toward a market economy by adopting quasi-commercial forms.

The presidency, now occupied by Vladimir Putin, has been a dominating policymaking institution in the new Russia, as shown in Figure 2.5. The Parliament, although fairly representative of the diversity of opinion in the country, was frustrated in its policymaking and oversight roles by the inertia of the vast state bureaucracy, by its inability to compel compliance with its laws, by its weak links with the electorate, and

by the president's power to make policy by decree. Nevertheless, it played a much greater role than before in aggregating interests and making policy, as shown when comparing Figures 2.4 and 2.5.

A further updating of Figure 2.5 would show the eclipse of independent parties and Parliament by President Putin after 2000. This movement in a more authoritarian direction, although not back to communism, would be shown by fewer dark shaded columns in the middle of the figure. These further developments are discussed in detail in Chapter 12.

The brief comparisons presented here illustrate the use of the structural-functional approach. This approach enables us to examine how the same functions are performed in different countries, or in the same country at two different points in time. Similarly, we may examine changes in the functions performed by the same structures over time or across different political systems. In a country undergoing as rapid and dramatic a transition as Russia in the 1990s, this framework helps us to analyze changes in the distribution of power among the major institutions making up the political system.

Neither the analysis of structures nor that of functions is complete without the other. A structural analysis tells us the number of political parties, or the organization of the legislature. It describes how the executive branch, the courts, the bureaucracy, the mass media, interest groups, and other structures of a political system are set up and by what rules or standards they operate. A functional analysis tells us how these institutions and organizations interact to produce and implement policies. This kind of analysis is especially essential when we are comparing very different kinds of political systems.

The country chapters of this book do not present formal structural-functional sketches like Figures 2.4 and 2.5. But at the core of each chapter is a set of discussions of these functions and the structures that perform them. We can see these in the section headings of the country studies and in the analytic guide at the beginning of this book. These tools make it possible to compare the workings of the very different political systems in this book.

THE POLICY LEVEL: PERFORMANCE, OUTCOME, AND EVALUATION

The important question is what these differences in structure and function do for the interests, needs, and aspirations of people. We call this the **policy level** of the political system.

Looking again at Figure 2.3, we see reflections of the relationships between the international environment, the domestic society, and the political system. At the left of Figure 2.3 are arrows signifying inputs of demands and supports from the society and the international system. Inputs also come from the independent initiatives of political leaders and bureaucrats. The structures performing the political process functions convert these inputs into the policies of the government. These policies extract resources, distribute benefits, and regulate behavior. They are designed

to achieve broad goals, such as welfare, justice, and freedom—or control and domination—as well as special benefits for groups and individuals. At the right are arrows signifying outputs and outcomes, the end products of the political process, the things a government does for and to its people.

We call the outputs of a political system—its extractions, distributions, regulations, and symbolic acts—its policy performance. We have to distinguish among these efforts, the things a government does, and the actual outcome of these efforts. Governments may spend equal amounts on education and health, or defense, but with different consequences. Government efficiency or corruption plays a role in the effectiveness of politics. But so do the underlying cultural, economic, and technological levels.

Americans spend more per capita on education than any other people in the world. But their children perform less well in some subjects, such as mathematics, than do children in some other countries that spend substantially less. The United States spent enormous sums and many lives on the war in Vietnam in the 1960s and 1970s, as did the Soviet Union on its war in Afghanistan in the 1980s. Yet, both countries were held at bay by small countries resolved to resist at all costs. Because of these costly failures, they were weakened internally. The outcome of public policy is never wholly in the hands of the people and their leaders. Conditions in the internal environment, conditions and events in the larger external world, and simple chance may frustrate the most thoughtfully crafted programs and plans. Each country study in this book concludes with a discussion of the country's performance, describing both policies and their outcomes.

Finally, we must step even further back to consider the whole situation of political system, process, and policy, and the environment in order to evaluate what political systems are doing. Evaluation is complex because people value different things and put different emphasis on what they value. We will refer to the different things people may value as political "goods." In Chapter 7, we discuss goods associated with the system level, such as the stability or adaptability of political institutions. We also discuss goods associated with the process level, such as citizen participation in politics. Finally, we consider goods associated with the policy level, such as welfare, security, and liberty. To evaluate what a political system is doing, we assess performance and outcomes in each of

The wall dividing California from Mexico illustrates the input-output model of comparative politics. The two men are trying to escape from the poverty of the Mexican economy. The wall is part of the output of the American political system, intended to frustrate illegal immigrants. The two figures illustrate the point that outputs do not necessarily produce the intended outcomes.

Les Stone/Sygma

these areas. We must also be aware of how outcomes affect individuals and subgroups in the society, of specific changes that may often be overlooked in presenting averages.

A particularly important problem of evaluation concerns building for the future as well as living today. The people of poor countries wish to survive and alleviate the suffering of today but also to improve their children's lot for tomorrow. The people of all countries, but especially rich ones, must deal with the costs to their children of polluted and depleted natural resources as the result of the thoughtless environmental policies of the past.

HOW WE EXPLAIN

Once we are able to describe politics with the help of the conceptual framework that we choose, the next task is to explain it. What we mean by explaining political phenomena is seeking to identify relationships among them. For example, we might be interested in the relationship between democracy and international peace (see Box 2.2). Are democratic states more peaceful than others? If so, are they peaceful because they are democratic, are they democratic because they are peaceful, or are they perhaps both peaceful and democratic because they are more prosperous than other states?

These questions show that we often want explanations to go beyond associating one thing with another. Ideally, we want to put many political relationships in causal terms, so that we can say that one political feature is the cause of another, and the latter is the effect of the former.

Theories are statements about causal relationships between general classes of events—for example, about what causes democracy, war, or welfare policies. Scientific theories are always tentative; they are always subject to modification or falsification as our knowledge improves. And theories need to be testable. A good theory is one that holds up after continued trials and experiments. Yet, it can be further confirmed or modified as we test the theory again and again. A well-tested theory allows us to explain confidently what happens in specific cases or groups of cases: these two countries have a peaceful relationship because they are democracies (see Box 2.2).

Researchers in political science distinguish between studies based on large numbers (large "n") and small numbers (small "n"). In large "n" studies, it is often possible and helpful to use statistical analysis. Such studies are usually referred to as *statistical studies;* small "n" studies are usually called *case studies.* Large "n" studies have a sufficient number and variety of cases to enable the researcher to examine the relation among the variables. Variables are the features on which our cases differ—for

BOX 2.2

Statistical Methods

A popular contemporary research program known as *democratic peace research* illustrates the pros and cons of statistical and case study research. It has been of primary interest to international relations scholars, who took the diplomatic history of the Cold War period and asked whether democratic countries are more peaceful in their foreign policy than authoritarian and nondemocratic ones. Many scholars in the democratic peace research group took the statistical route. They counted each year of interaction between two states as one case. With roughly half a century of diplomatic history involving a state system of 100 countries or more, they had a very large number of cases, even after eliminating the many irrelevant cases of countries that never, or rarely, had any relations with one another. Political scientists Andrew Bennett and Alexander George drew these conclusions after surveying the statistical research:

> Statistical methods achieved important advances on the issue of whether a nonspurious interdemocratic

peace exists. A fairly strong though not unanimous consensus emerged that: (1) democracies are not less war-prone in general; (2) they have very rarely if ever fought one another; (3) this pattern of an interdemocratic peace applies to both war and conflicts short of war; (4) states in transition to democracy are more war prone than established democracies; and (5) these correlations were not spuriously brought about by the most obvious alternative explanations.

Yet, although much was learned from the statistical studies, they were not as successful at answering "why" questions. Case studies make clinical depth possible, revealing causal interconnections in individual cases. Careful repetition of these causal tracings from case to case strengthens confidence in these relationships. Thus Bennett and George concluded that the best research strategy uses statistical and case study methods together, with each method having its own strengths.

Source: Andrew Bennett and Alexander George, "An Alliance of Statistical and Case Study Methods: Research on the Interdemocratic Peace," APSA-CP: *Newsletter of the APSA Organized Section in Comparative Politics* 9 (1998) no. 1: 6.

example, "form of government: democracy or dictatorship." Statistical analysis enables us to consider possible alternative causes at the same time, accepting some and rejecting others. Small "*n*" studies permit investigators to go deeply into a case, identify the particularities of it, get the clinical details, and examine each link in the causal process. Most researchers recognize that these methods are complementary (see Box 2.2).

Large "*n*" statistical studies allow us to be more certain and precise in our explanations. On the other hand, we need the depth that case studies provide. They encourage us to formulate insightful hypotheses for statistical testing in the first place. They allow us to trace the nature of the cause-and-effect relations (sometimes called "causal mechanisms") better than large "*n*" studies. In this manner, political scientists may come to know not only whether democracies are more peaceful than dictatorships, but more precisely why democratic leaders behave in the way that they do.

We can also generate and test hypotheses about the causes and consequences of political change by comparing countries at different historical periods. Tocqueville's study of the French Revolution contributed to a general theory of revolution by comparing pre- and postrevolutionary France.[4] Theda Skocpol based her theories of the causes of revolution on a comparison of the "old regimes" of France, Russia, and China with their revolutionary and postrevolutionary regimes.[5]

An example may suggest how you might go about theorizing in comparative politics, going beyond "just mastering the facts." It is well known that rich countries are more likely to be democracies than are poor countries; democracy and economic development are strongly associated. But there are many possible reasons for this association. Some have suggested that this relationship comes about because democracy encourages education and economic development. Others have argued that as countries develop economically, their new middle classes or better organized working class are more likely to demand democratization. Yet others have seen that both democracy and economic development are commonly found in some regions of the world, such as Western Europe, while both tend to be scarce in the Middle East and Africa. This fact suggests that certain cultures may encourage or discourage both of them.

We want to understand the causal nature of this association, for reasons of both science and policy. Fostering economic development and securing democracy are two of the significant political challenges that we discussed in Chapter 1. It is vitally important that we understand how they relate to each other.

A work of Adam Przeworski and his associates examined the full experience of democracies, non-democracies, and transitions between them in all parts of the world between 1950 and 1990.[6] Their statistical analysis led them to conclude that the explanation for the association did not lie in regional effects or superior economic growth in democracy. Moreover, countries at any level of development seemed able to introduce democracy, although economically developed countries are somewhat more likely to do so. They argue that key to the relationship lies rather in the consistently greater fragility of democracies in societies at lower levels of economic development. Democracy can easily be introduced in poor societies with less educated populations. But in these social conditions it is often replaced by some kind of dictatorship. In rich countries, on the other hand, democracy tends to survive once it has been introduced. These democratic failures in poor countries produce a strong association between development and democracy. We still need to understand just why democracy is more precarious in less developed societies. But we are making progress in understanding the causal element in the relationship. We are better able to explain the relationship between development and democracy, as well as the failures of democratization in specific countries.

Comparative analysis is a powerful and versatile tool. It enhances our ability to describe and understand political processes and political change in any country by offering concepts and reference points from a broader perspective. The comparative approach also stimulates us to form general theories of political relationships. It encourages and enables us to test our political theories by confronting them with the experience of many institutions and settings.

REVIEW QUESTIONS

- How do the main elements in the environment of a political system affect the way it performs?

- Why can't we compare political systems by just describing the different structures we find in them?

- What are the functions performed in all political systems as policies are made?

- What is the difference between outputs and outcomes of policy?

- How do we use theories to explain political events?

KEY TERMS

distribution	interdependence	policy level	process functions
environment	interest aggregation	policymaking	regulation
extraction	interest articulation	political culture	structural-functional
functions	outcomes	political communication	approach
globalization	outputs	political recruitment	structures
governments	policy adjudication	political socialization	system
inputs	policy implementation	political system	system functions

SUGGESTED READINGS

Collier, David. "The Comparative Method," in Ada W. Finifter, ed., *Political Science: The State of the Discipline II.* Washington, DC: American Political Science Association, 1993.

Dogan, Mattei, and Dominique Pelassy. *How to Compare Nations: Strategies in Comparative Politics.* Chatham, NJ: Chatham House, 1990.

Goodin, Robert E., and Hans-Dieter Klingemann. Chapters 2 and 3, and Part 4 of *A New Handbook of Political Science.* New York: Oxford University Press, 1996.

King, Gary, Robert O. Keohane, and Sidney Verba. *Scientific Inference in Qualitative Research.* New York: Cambridge University Press, 1993.

Lichbach, Mark, and Alan Zuckerman. *Comparing Nations: Rationality, Culture, and Structure.* New York: Cambridge University Press, 1997.

Przeworski, Adam, and Henry Teune. *The Logic of Comparative Social Inquiry.* New York: Wiley, 1970.

ENDNOTES

1. Alexis de Tocqueville to Louis de Kergolay, 18 October 1847, in *Alexis de Tocqueville: Selected Letters on Politics and Society,* ed. Roger Boesche (Berkeley: University of California Press, 1985), 191.

2. Alexis de Tocqueville to Ernest de Chabrol, 7 October 1831, ibid, 59.

3. Figures 2.4 and 2.5 and the text of this section were contributed by Thomas Remington.

4. Alexis de Tocqueville, *The Old Regime and the French Revolution,* trans. Stuart Gilbert (New York: Doubleday, 1955).

5. Theda Skocpol, *States and Social Revolutions* (New York: Cambridge University Press, 1979).

6. Adam Przeworski et al., *Democracy and Development* (Cambridge: Cambridge University Press, 2000).

POLITICAL CULTURE AND POLITICAL SOCIALIZATION

Do you remember the first time you traveled to a foreign country? You probably were surprised by how many of the normal things in your life were different there. The food was different, people wore different clothes, houses were constructed and furnished differently, and the pattern of social relations differed (for instance, whether they talked to strangers or stood in queues). You were observing how social norms shape what people eat, how they dress, how they live, and maybe even on which side of the road they drive.

Similarly, each nation has its own political norms that influence how people think about and react to politics. Americans' strong feelings of patriotism, the Japanese deference to political elites, and the French proclivity for protest all illustrate how cultural norms shape politics. The way political institutions function at least partially reflects the public's attitudes, norms, and expectations. Thus, the English use their constitutional arrangements to sustain their liberty, while the same institutions were once used as a means of repression in South Africa and Northern Ireland. When a new regime forms, a supportive public can help develop the new system, while the absence of public support may weaken the new system. To understand the political tendencies in a nation, we must begin with public attitudes toward politics and their role within the political system—what we call a nation's political culture.

Chapter 1 stated that one main goal of any government, and a special challenge for a new government, is to create and maintain a political community. In part, this involves developing common structures and systems (such as a single economy), common political institutions, and common political processes. At the level of the public, this involves developing common world views, values, and expectations among the public that together comprise the nation's political culture. So studying political culture partially explains how a political community is created and sustained.

In this chapter we map the important parts of political culture. We then discuss political socialization: how individuals form their political attitudes and thus, collectively, how citizens form their political culture. We conclude by describing the major trends in political culture in world politics today.

MAPPING THE THREE LEVELS OF POLITICAL CULTURE

A nation's **political culture** includes its citizens' orientations at three levels: the political system, the political and policymaking process, and policy outputs and outcomes (Table 3.1). The *system* level involves how people view the values and organizations that comprise the political system. Do citizens identify with the nation and accept the general system of government? The *process* level includes expectations of how politics should function, and individuals' relationship to the political process. The *policy* level deals with the public's policy expectations for the government. What should be the policy goals of government and how are they to be achieved?

The Aspects of Political Culture TABLE 3.1	
Aspects of Political Culture	**Examples**
System	Pride in nation
	National identity
	Legitimacy of government
Process	Role of citizens
	Perceptions of political rights
Policy	Role of government
	Government policy priorities

The System Level

Orientations toward the political system are important because they tap basic commitments to the polity and the nation. It is difficult for any political system to endure if it lacks the support of its citizens.

Feelings of national pride are considered an affective, emotional tie to a political system. National pride seems strongest in nations with a long history that has emphasized feelings of patriotism—the United States is a prime example (see Figure 3.1). Such a common sense of identity and national history often binds a people together in times of political strain. The figure indicates that high levels of pride exist in nations with very different political and economic systems, such as the United States and Poland. In contrast, national pride is low in Japan and Germany, two nations that have avoided nationalist sentiments in reaction to the World War II regimes and their excesses. In other cases, ethnicity, language, or history divide the public, which may strain national identities and ultimately lead to conflict and division.

Feelings of popular **legitimacy** are another foundation for a successful political system. When people believe that they ought to obey the laws, legitimacy is high. If they see no reason to obey or if they comply only from fear, legitimacy is low. Because it is much easier for government to function when citizens believe in the legitimacy of the system, virtually all governments, even the most brutal and coercive, try to encourage people to believe that they should obey the laws. A political system and a government with high legitimacy are typically more effective in carrying out policies and are more likely to overcome hardships and reversals.

Citizens may grant legitimacy to a government for different reasons. In a traditional society, legitimacy may depend on the ruler's inheriting the throne or on the ruler's commitment to religious customs. In a modern democracy, the legitimacy of the authorities depends on their selection by voters in competitive elections and on the government following constitutional procedures. In other political cultures, the leaders may base their claim to legitimacy on their special wisdom or ideology, which they claim will transform people's lives for the better, even though the government does not respond to specific public demands or follow prescribed procedures.[1] Theocratic regimes, such as Iran, base their legitimacy on adherence to religious principles. Thus, legitimacy also presumes an agreement on the broad form of government that defines the political system and thus the standards of legitimacy: monarchical rule, a tribal system, a communist order, or a democratic system.

Whether legitimacy is based on tradition, ideology, elections, or religion, feelings of legitimacy reflect a basic understanding between citizens and political authorities. Citizens obey the laws and in return the government meets the obligations set by the terms of its legitimacy. As long as the government meets its obligations, the public is supposed to be supportive and act appropriately. If legitimacy is violated—the line of succession is broken, the constitution is subverted, or the ruling ideology is ignored—the government may expect resistance and perhaps rebellion.

In systems with low legitimacy, people often resort to violence or extra-governmental actions to solve political disagreements. Legitimacy is lacking where the public disputes the boundaries of the political system (as in Northern Ireland or Kashmir), rejects the current arrangements for recruiting leaders and making policies (as when Indonesians took to the streets in 1998 demanding a new democratic regime), or loses confidence that the leaders are fulfilling their part of the political bargain (as when the Thai opposition forced the prime minister from office in 2006).

The Soviet Union disintegrated in the early 1990s because all three legitimacy problems appeared. After the communist ideology failed as a legitimizing force, there was no basis for a national political community in the absence of common language or ethnicity. Similarly, the loss of confidence in the Communist Party as a political organization led many people to

100	Egypt
	United States/Poland
	Mexico/Canada/Iran
	Peru/Finland
	India/Argentina
90	Nigeria
	France
	Britain/Hungary/Turkey
	Sweden/Italy
	Israel
	China
80	Latvia/Czech Republic
	Netherlands
	Germany (East)
70	Russia
	Estonia
	Germany (West)
60	Japan/Lithuania

Feelings of National Pride (in percent) **FIGURE 3.1**

Source: Selected nations from the 2000–2002 *World Values Survey* and the 1999 *European Values Survey*. Figure entries are the percent "proud" and "very proud"; missing data are excluded from the calculation of percentages.

call for institutional reform. Finally, shortages of food and consumer goods caused people to lose faith in the government's short-term economic and political policies. Soviet President Mikhail Gorbachev failed in his efforts to deal with all three problems at the same time.

The Process Level

The second level of the political culture involves what the public expects of the political process. Whether you are English or Nigerian, what do you think about the institutions of your political system and what is expected of you as a citizen?

Broadly speaking, three different patterns describe the citizen's role in the political process:[2]

- **Participants** are, or have the potential to be, involved in the political process. They are informed about politics and make demands on the polity, granting their support to political leaders based on performance.
- **Subjects** passively obey government officials and the law, but they do not vote or actively involve themselves in politics.
- **Parochials** are hardly aware of government and politics. They may be illiterates, rural people living in remote areas, or simply people who ignore politics and its impact on their lives.

As shown in Figure 3.2, in a hypothetical modern industrial democracy a majority are participants, a third are simply subjects, and a small group are parochials. This distribution provides enough political activists to ensure competition among political parties and sizable voter turnout, as well as critical audiences for debate on public issues by parties, candidates, and pressure groups. At the same time, not all citizens feel the need to be active in or concerned about the political system.

The second column in Figure 3.2 shows the pattern we expect in an industrialized authoritarian society, such as the former communist nations of Eastern Europe. A small minority of citizens are involved in a one-party system, which penetrates and oversees the society, as well as decides government policies. Most other citizens are mobilized as subjects by political institutions: political parties, the bureaucracy, and government-controlled mass media. People are encouraged and even forced to cast a symbolic vote of support in elections and to pay taxes, obey regulations, and follow the dictates of government. Because of the effectiveness of modern social organization and the efforts of the authoritarian power structure, few people are unaware of the government and its influence on their lives. If such a society suddenly attempts to democratize its politics, many people must learn to become democrats and participants.

The third column shows an authoritarian society that is partly traditional and partly modern, such as in Iran or China. In spite of an authoritarian political system, some participants—students and intellectuals, for example—oppose the system and try to change it

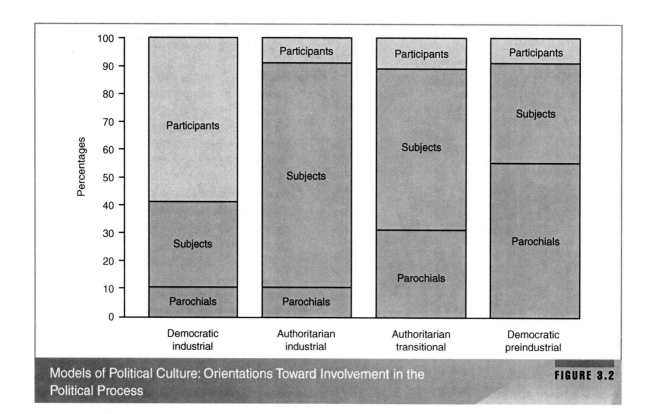

Models of Political Culture: Orientations Toward Involvement in the Political Process

FIGURE 3.2

by persuasion or acts of protest. Favored groups, like business people and landowners, discuss public issues and engage in lobbying. Most people in such systems are passive subjects, aware of government and complying with the law but not otherwise involved in public affairs. The parochials—poor and illiterate urban dwellers, peasants, or farm laborers—have limited contact with the political system.

The fourth column shows the democratic preindustrial system, perhaps India or Nigeria, which has a predominantly rural, illiterate population. In such a country, the few political participants are chiefly educated professionals, business people, and landowners. A much larger number of employees, workers, and farmers are directly affected by government taxation and other official policies. The largest group of people are illiterate peasants, whose knowledge of and involvement with national politics are minimal. Such a society faces a significant challenge to create a more aware public that can participate meaningfully and shape government policies through democratic means.

Attitudes toward the citizen's role are also shaped by the political form of the regime. In the early 1900s, many different political systems existed worldwide.

Fascism was on the rise in Europe, communism was establishing itself in the Soviet Union, colonial administrations governed large parts of the world, and monarchical or authoritarian governments ruled other nations. All of these systems encouraged a restrictive role for the citizens. Western Europe and North America were the democracies in this sea of conflicting currents.

Today, many of these nondemocratic forms of governance are no longer widely accepted. Communism still has strongholds in China and Cuba, but it has lost its image as a progressive force for global change. Some nations still accept autocratic or religiously based systems of government. However, the global wave of democratization since the early 1990s has raised democratic principles to a position of prominence (see Figure 1.3 in Chapter 1). Democratic norms emphasize the importance of a participatory system, majority rule and minority rights, and the values of political tolerance. Most of the people in the world today seem to favor democratic principles even if they differ in how those principles should be applied.[3]

The distribution of these citizen types and political norms is affected by the process of social and

vid Smith report how one
ed to a question about how his
y made him feel. "Sometimes like 9
ns a yard wide. Here in the factory
ny machine can twist any way I want a

piece of steel that all the men in my home village together could not begin to bend at all." Such
experiences—and the parallel changes in educational
levels and access to information—can create a more
modern political culture.

and David Smith, *Becoming Modern* (Cambridge, Harvard University Press, 1974), 158.

ization that we introduced in
ation, urbanization, and improved
orm the social base of a nation.
through work, education, and
ividual's personal experiences
it norms in other societies. It
ipation, a sense of individual
nproved living standards and
, and government legitimacy
mance. It also frequently dis-
life, traditional bases of legi-
arrangements that depend on
ochials or subjects. In addition,
iences of science can alter eco-
stems, which then reshapes the
modernization trend has power-
trates societies (or parts of soci-
and David Smith's classic study of
phasized how factory experience
eness of the possibilities of organi-
control over nature that empowers
Box 3.1).

ization process is spread unevenly
The advanced industrial societies have
rtion of citizens who are participants
engaged in politics. The recent eco-
East Asia is similarly transforming the
and political behavior in these nations.[4]
dernization has proceeded more slowly
y in Africa and Arab nations. Some polit-
these nations even reject the principles of
n as incongruent with their national val-
r, there is persuasive evidence that where
onomic modernization occurs, it trans-
litical culture to emphasize self-expression,
y values, and autonomy.[5]

n great
cal rela-
lingness

res

cte
it
c

The Policy Level

What is the appropriate role of government? If you ask
political theorists, you get a wide range of answers—
from the minimal state to the all-encompassing polity
(see Chapter 1). And if you travel to other nations, you
quickly realize that there is wide variation in how people answer this question.

The policy activities of a country are influenced
by public images of what constitutes the good society
and the government's role in achieving these goals.
Should government manage the economy, or should
private property rights and market forces guide
economic activity? Should the state intervene in
addressing social and moral issues, or should it follow
a minimalist strategy? The ongoing debates over "big
government" versus "small government" in democratic states, and between socialist and market-based
economies reflect these different images of the scope
of government.

We can illustrate differences in policy expectations with an opinion survey question that asks
whether the government is responsible to provide for
everyone (see Figure 3.3). The range in opinions is
considerable, about three-quarters of respondents in
Nigeria and Sweden believe this is a government
responsibility compared with only a quarter of the
French or West Germans. In general, people in developing nations and in the formerly communist nations
of Eastern Europe are more supportive of a large government role—reflecting both their social condition
and their past political ideologies. In some Western
nations, such as Sweden and Finland, traditions
include a large role for the government. In general,
however, support for government action generally
decreases as national affluence increases.[6]

Cubans wave flags at a pro-government rally organized by the Castro government.

AP Images

Policy expectations also involve specific issue demands.[7] Indeed, each country study in this book begins with a discussion of the policy challenges facing the nation and the public's issue concerns. This sets the agenda of politics that responsive governments should address.

Some policy goals, such as economic well-being, are valued by nearly everyone. Concern about other policy goals may vary widely across nations because of the nation's circumstances and because of cultural traditions. People in developing countries are more likely to focus on the government's provision of basic services to ensure public welfare. Advanced industrial societies have the resources to provide for basic needs. In these nations, people are often more concerned with quality-of-life goals, such as preservation of nature and even government support for the arts.[8] One basic measure of a government's performance is its ability to meet the policy expectations of its citizens.

Another set of expectations involves the functioning of government. Some cultures put more weight on the policy outputs of government, such as providing welfare and security. Other cultures also emphasize how the process functions, which involves values such as the rule of law and procedural justice. Among

Germans, for example, the rule of law is gi[ven] importance; in many developing nations poli[tical rela]tions are personally based, and there is less w[illingness] to rely on legalistic frameworks.

Consensual or Conflictual Political Cul[ture]

Although political culture is a common cha[racteristic] of a nation, values and beliefs can also vary [.] Political cultures may be consensual or conf[lictual on] issues of public policy and, more fundame[ntal,] views of legitimate governmental and politica[l arrange]ments. In some societies, citizens generally ag[ree on the] norms of political decisionmaking and the[policy] expectations. In other societies—because of d[ifferences] in histories, conditions, or identities—the ci[tizens are] sharply divided, often on both the legitima[cy of the] regime and solutions to major problems.[9]

When a country is deeply divided in its po[litical val]ues and these differences persist over time, [distinct] **political subcultures** may develop. The citizen[s in these] subcultures may have sharply different points [of view on] some critical political matters, such as the bou[ndaries of] the nation, the nature of the regime, or the cor[e ideol]ogy. They may affiliate with different politic[al parties] of peoples into new areas—made possible by easier transportation and encouraged by wars, political conflicts, and the desire for economic betterment—can seem to threaten the way of life of the host society. The exposure to values from other cultures also may intensify one's own self-image, which may increase cultural tensions. Although such exposure may eventually lead to greater tolerance, that outcome is not guaranteed.

WHY CULTURE MATTERS

Political culture does not explain everything about politics. Even people with similar values and skills might behave differently from each other when they face different situations. Nor is political culture unchangeable. However, cultural norms typically change slowly and reflect stable values. Thus, political culture is important first because it encapsulates the history, traditions, and values of a society. To understand how most people in a nation think and act politically, we can begin by understanding their political culture. Political culture can create the common political community that is one goal of government.

In addition, the distribution of cultural patterns is typically related to the type of political process that citizens expect and support. This is the principle of *congruence theory*. For instance, support for a democratic system is typically higher in societies that have a more participatory political culture. Authoritarian states are more likely to endure when the public is characterized by subjects and parochials—where individuals lack the skills or motivations to participate and the state discourages their participation. These cultural norms represent the "rules of the game" for the political system, and the system works better when citizens accept these rules. Where political structures and political cultures are mutually reinforcing, a more stable political system is likely to emerge.

We can illustrate the logic of congruence theory in terms of the relationship between political culture and the democratic development of a nation (Figure 3.4). The horizontal axis of the figure displays the public's adherence to self-expressive values, reflecting the participatory norms we discussed earlier. The vertical axis represents the democratic development of the nation based on a variety of expert evaluations. You can see that as participatory values increase, so too does the democratic development of the nation. The nations

The Government Should Ensure Everyone Is Provided For (percent agreeing)

FIGURE 3.3

Source: Selected nations from the 2000–2002 *World Values Survey* and 1999 *European Values Survey*; missing data are excluded from the calculation of percentages.

and interest groups, read different newspapers, and even have separate social clubs and sporting groups. Thus, they are exposed to different information about politics. For instance, such subcultural differences characterize the publics in India, Nigeria, and Russia today.

In some instances, historical or social factors generate different cultural trajectories. For instance, *ethnic*, *religious*, or *linguistic* identities in many parts of the world shape citizen values.[10] Moreover, as such groups increase their political skills and self-confidence, they may express their identities and demand equal treatment. In fact, the processes of globalization might actually heighten these cultural contrasts.[11] The migration

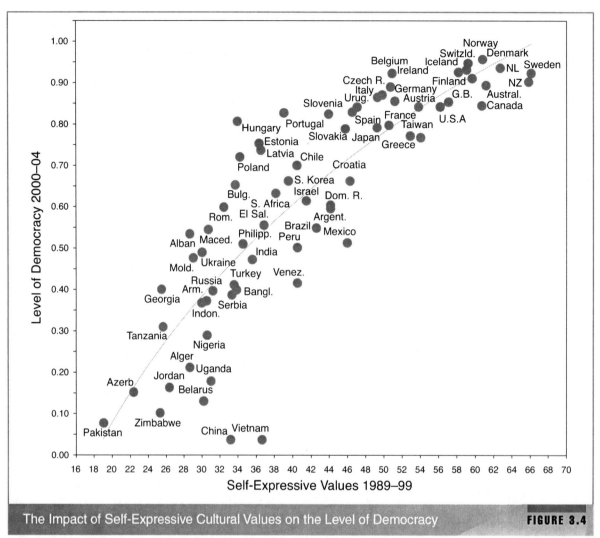

The Impact of Self-Expressive Cultural Values on the Level of Democracy   **FIGURE 3.4**

Source: The self-expressive values measure is from the *World Values Survey*; higher scores represent more citizen emphasis on self-expression. The level of democracy measure is a composite of the ranking of democracy by the Freedom House and other national rankings. Higher scores indicates a higher level of democratic development. For additional discussion of these measures see Ronald Inglehart and Christian Welzel, *Modernization, Cultural Change and Democracy: The Human Development Sequence* (New York: Cambridge University Press, 2005).

in this book that are included in these analyses show a clear differentiation between the established Western democracies, relatively new democracies (such as Russia and other East European nations), and nondemocracies (such as China and several Middle East nations). Structure and culture do overlap in these nations.[12]

Do democracies create a participatory democratic public or does such a political culture lead to a democratic political system? It works both ways. For example, immediately after World War II, Germans were less supportive of democracy, but political institutions and political experiences transformed their culture over the next generation.[13] At the same time, democracy

endured in Britain during the strains of the Great Depression and World War II, at least in part because the British public supported the democratic process. The important conclusion is that there is normally a relationship between political culture and political structures.

Beyond shaping the structure of the political system, a nation's political culture also influences the style of politics and the content of policymaking. We have stressed how the policy elements of a political culture can influence the content of policy. In addition, research suggests that cultural factors, such as social trust and engagement, influence the efficiency and effectiveness of government.[14]

Finally, while the political culture may help build a national community, it may also provide a basis of division. For instance, where political subcultures coincide with ethnic, linguistic, or religious differences—as in Northern Ireland, Bosnia, and Lebanon—the divisions can be enduring and threatening. The fragmentation of the Soviet empire, the breakup of Yugoslavia, and the impulses toward autonomy and secession among ethnically distinct regions (such as in Scotland or separatist movements in Africa) all reflect the lasting power of language, culture, and historical memory to create and sustain the sense of ethnic and national identity among parts of contemporary states. In broader international terms, Samuel Huntington has divided the world into different civilizations defined by their religious and cultural traditions.[15] He then predicted that these cultural differences will be a major source of international conflict in this century. While culture may have the power to divide, it is counterbalanced by its potential to build a common political community.

POLITICAL SOCIALIZATION

Political cultures are sustained or changed as people acquire their attitudes and values. *Political socialization* refers to the way in which political values are formed and the political culture is transmitted from one generation to the next. Most children acquire their basic political values and behavior patterns by

adolescence.[16] Some of these attitudes will evolve and change throughout their lives, while other attitudes may remain part of their political self throughout life.

At any specific time, a person's political beliefs are a combination of various feelings and attitudes. At the deepest level, there are general identifications, such as nationalism, ethnic or class self-images, religious and ideological commitments, and a fundamental sense of rights and duties in the society. At the middle level, people develop attitudes toward politics and governmental institutions. Finally, there are more immediate views of current events, policies, issues, and personalities. All these attitudes can change, but those in the first level usually were acquired earliest, have been most frequently reinforced, and tend to be the most durable.

Three points about political socialization deserve mention. First, the socialization process can occur in different ways. Direct socialization involves an actor explicitly communicating information, values, or feelings toward politics. Examples of direct socialization include civics courses in the schools, public education programs of the government, and the political information campaigns of interest groups. Communist political systems also heavily use direct indoctrination programs (see Box 3.2). Indirect political socialization occurs when political views are inadvertently molded by our experiences. For example, children normally learn important political values by observing the behavior of their parents, teachers, and friends. Or, people may learn by observing the political and social

---

Socializing Values

BOX 3.2

Communist East Germany had a special ceremony for eighth graders to mark their passage to adulthood. The heart of the ceremony was the endorsement of the following four pledges:

- As young citizens of our German Democratic Republic, are you prepared to work and fight loyally for the great and honorable goals of socialism, and to honor the revolutionary inheritance of the people?
- As sons and daughters of the worker-and-peasant state, are you prepared to pursue higher education, to cultivate your mind, to become a master of

your trade, to learn permanently, and to use your knowledge to pursue our great humanist ideals?
- As honorable members of the socialist community, are you ready to cooperate as comrades, to respect and support each other, and to always merge the pursuit of your personal happiness with the happiness of all the people?
- As true patriots, are you ready to deepen the friendship with the Soviet Union, to strengthen our brotherhood with socialist countries, to struggle in the spirit of proletarian internationalism, to protect peace and to defend socialism against every imperialist aggression?

context that surrounds them, watching what governments do and how other citizens react.

Second, socialization is a lifelong process. Early family influences can create an individual's initial values, but subsequent life experiences—becoming involved in new social groups, moving from one part of the country to another, shifting up or down the social ladder, becoming a parent, finding or losing a job—may change one's political perspectives. More dramatic experiences—such as relocating to a new country or suffering through an economic depression or a war—can alter even basic political attitudes. Such events seem to have their greatest impact on young people, but people at any age are affected to some degree.

Third, patterns of socialization can unify or divide. Governments design public education systems, for instance, to create a single national political culture. Some events, such as international conflict or the death of a popular public figure, can affect nearly the entire nation similarly. In contrast, subcultures in a society can have their own distinctive patterns of socialization. Social groups that provide their members with their own newspapers, their own neighborhood groups, and perhaps their own schools can create distinctive subcultural attitudes. Divisive patterns of socialization can lead to a political gap among members of a nation.

AGENTS OF POLITICAL SOCIALIZATION

Individuals in all societies are affected by **agents of political socialization:** individuals, organizations, and institutions that influence political attitudes. Some, like civics courses in schools, are direct and deliberate sources of political learning. Others, like playgroups and work groups, affect political socialization indirectly.

The Family

The direct and indirect influences of the family—the first socialization source that an individual encounters—are normally powerful and lasting. The family has distinctive influences on attitudes toward authority. Participation in family decisionmaking can increase a child's sense of political competence, providing skills for political interaction and encouraging active participation in the political system as an adult. Similarly, unquestioning obedience to parental decisions may lead

a child toward a role as a political subject. The family also shapes future political attitudes by defining a social position for the child: establishing ethnic, linguistic, class, and religious ties; affirming cultural values; and influencing job aspirations.

The nature of the family is changing in many societies. Family sizes are generally decreasing, which changes the pattern of family life. In addition, there has been a marked rise of single-parent families, especially in the advanced industrial democracies. The impact of these structural changes on family socialization patterns is still unclear.

In addition, gender roles are changing in many industrial nations, although they persist in many less-developed nations.[17] The rise of the women's movement and self-help groups has encouraged women to become politically active and change social cues about how women should relate to politics. The lessening of gender differences in self-images, in parental roles, and in relations to the economy and the political system is significantly affecting patterns of political recruitment, political participation, and public policy. A more open family, equality of parenting, and the early exposure of children to childcare and preschool group experiences have modified the impact of the family in the socialization process. Especially in the developing world, the changing role of women may have profound influences in modernizing the society.[18]

Schools

Schools educate children about politics and their role in the process, provide them with information on political institutions and relationships. Schools can also help shape attitudes about the political system, the rules of the political game, the appropriate role of the citizen, and expectations about the government. Schools typically reinforce attachments to the political system and reinforce common symbols, such as the flag and pledge of allegiance, that encourage emotional attachments to the system. When a new nation comes into being, or a revolutionary regime comes to power in an old nation, it usually turns immediately to the schools as a means to supplant "outdated" values and symbols with new ones more congruent with the new ideology.

In some nations, educational systems do not provide unifying political socialization but send starkly different messages to different groups. For instance, some Muslim nations segregate girls and boys within the school system. Even if educational experiences are intended to be equal, segregation creates different experiences and expectations. Moreover, the content of education often differs between boys and girls. Perhaps the worst example occurred under the Taliban in Afghanistan, where for several years young girls were prohibited from attending school. Such treatment of young girls severely limits their life changes, and ensures they will have restricted roles in society and the economy—which was the intent of the Taliban system. The new Afghanistan government reversed this policy, and now young girls are being included in the education system, and their future life prospects are improving as a result.

Education also affects the political skills and resources of the public. Educated people are more aware of the impact of government on their lives and pay more attention to politics.[19] The better educated have mental skills that improve their ability to manage the world of politics. They also have more information about political processes and participate in a wider range of political activities.

Religious Institutions

The religions of the world are carriers of cultural and moral values, which often have political implications. The great religious leaders have seen themselves as teachers, and their followers have usually attempted to shape the socialization of children through schooling, preaching, and religious services. In most nations, there are formal ties between the dominant religion and the government. In these instances, religious values and public policy often overlap. Catholic nations, for instance, are less likely to have liberal abortion policies, just as Islamic governments enforce strict moral codes.

Religious institutions of many kinds offer valuable moral and ethical guidance that individuals often need to make choices in complex societies. Religious affiliations are often important sources of partisan preferences and can guide people in making other political choices. Thus, even though church attendance is decreasing in many nations, the political relevance of religion continues.

Where churches teach values that may be at odds with the controlling political system, the struggle over socialization can be intense. These tensions can take a

wide variety of forms: the clash between secular and religious roles in the French educational system, the efforts of American fundamentalists to introduce prayer in the schools, or the conflict between Islamic fundamentalists and secular governments in Algeria and Egypt. In such cases, religious groups may oppose the policies of the state, or even the state itself.

The emergence of religious fundamentalism in recent decades has influenced the society and politics of countries as diverse as the United States, India, Israel, Lebanon, Iran, Pakistan, Algeria, and Nigeria. Such **fundamentalism** is often a defensive reaction against the spread of scientific views of nature and human behavior, and the libertarian values and attitudes that accompany these views.[20] The influence of fundamentalism has been most visible in the Middle East and in Muslim countries, but it is important in Christian countries as well. Both Protestant and Catholic versions of fundamentalism exist in the United States, Europe, and Latin America. Versions of fundamentalism also exist, combined with ethnic and nationalist tendencies, in the Confucian, Buddhist, and Hindu countries of Asia. Broadly speaking, fundamentalism seeks to raise conservative social, moral, and religious issues to the top of the contemporary policy agenda.

Peer Groups

Peer groups also shape political attitudes. They include childhood playgroups, friendship cliques, school and college fraternities, small work groups, and other groups in which members share relatively equal status and close ties. They can be as varied as a group of Russian mothers who meet regularly at the park, to a street gang in Brazil, to a group of Wall Street executives who are members of a health club.

A peer group socializes its members by motivating or pressuring them to conform to the attitudes or behavior accepted by the group. Individuals often adopt the views of their peers because they like or respect them or because they want to be like them. Similarly, an individual may become interested in politics or attend a political demonstration because close friends do so. One example of peer networks is the international youth culture symbolized by rock music, T-shirts, and blue jeans (and more liberal political values). Some observers claim that it played a major role in the failure of communist officials to mold Soviet and

Eastern European youth to the "socialist personality" that was the Marxist-Leninist ideal. Likewise, the "skinheads" groups that have sprouted up among lower class youth in many Western countries have adopted political views that are based on peer interactions.

Social Class

Most societies have significant social divisions based on class or occupation. Individuals live in different social worlds defined by their class position. For instance, industrialization in Britain created a working class that was concentrated in particular neighborhoods. This working class developed its own forms of speech, dress, recreation, and entertainment, as well as its own social organizations (such as social clubs, trade unions, and political parties). Similarly, the life experience of the rural peasantry in many less developed nations is radically different from urban dwellers. Often, these social divisions are politically relevant: identifying yourself as a member of the working class or the peasantry leads to distinct political views about what issues are important and which political groups best represent your interest.

Interest Groups

Interest groups, economic groups, and similar organizations also shape political attitudes. In most industrial countries, the rise of trade unions transformed the political culture and politics, created new political parties, and ushered in new social benefit programs. Today, unions are active participants in the political process and try to persuade their members on political matters. Other professional associations—such as groups of peasants and farmers, manufacturers, wholesalers and retailers, medical societies, and lawyers—also regularly influence political attitudes in modern and modernizing societies. These groups ensure the loyalty of their members by defending their economic and professional interests. They can also provide valuable political cues to nonmembers, who might identify with a group's interests or political ideology. For instance, when a group that you like (or dislike) publicly supports a policy, it gives you information on the likely content of the policy.

The groups that define a civil society are also potential agents of socialization. These groups might include ethnic organizations, fraternal associations, civic associations (such as parent-teacher associations), and policy groups (such as taxpayers' associations, women's groups, and environmental groups). Such groups provide valuable political cues to their members and try to reinforce distinct social and political orientations. They also provide settings to learn about how making political choices in small groups can be extended to politics. For instance, Vietnam has an active network of social groups that socialize individuals into the norms of the communist regime; while civil society groups in the United States are treated as

The international press cover an emergency summit of the Organization of the Islamic Conference (OIC) called to discuss the Iraqi crisis in March 2003.

AP Images

democracy-building organizations.[21] In addition, these groups—using the media and other sources—send out large quantities of information on political, social, and economic issues to the public and elites.

Political Parties

Political parties normally play an important role in political socialization. In democratic systems, political parties attempt to mold issue preferences, arouse the apathetic, and find new issues to mobilize support. Party representatives provide the public with a steady flow of information on the political issues of the day. Party organizations regularly contact voters by mail or phone, and in many nations party activists visit voters at home. In addition, every few years there is an election in which parties present their accomplishments and discuss the nation's political future. Elections can serve as national civics lessons, and the political parties are the teachers.

In competitive democratic party systems, partisan socialization can be also a divisive force. In their efforts to gain support, party leaders may appeal to class, language, religion, and ethnic divisions and make citizens more aware of these differences. The Labour and Conservative parties in Britain, for example, use traditional symbols of class to attract supporters. Similarly, the Congress Party in India tries to develop a national program and appeal, but other parties emphasize the ethnic and religious divisions. Leaders of preindustrial nations often oppose competitive parties because they fear such divisiveness. Although this is sometimes a sincere concern, it is also self-serving to government leaders, and is increasingly difficult to justify against contemporary demands for multiparty systems.

Authoritarian governments often use a single party to inculcate common attitudes of national unity, support for the government, and ideological agreement. The combination of a single party and controlled mass media is potent: the media present a single point of view, and the party activities reinforce that perspective by directly involving the citizen. In a closed environment, single-party governments can be potent agents of socialization.

Mass Media

The mass media—newspapers, radio, television, magazines—are important in socializing attitudes and values in nations around the globe. The mass media are typically the prime source of information on the politics of the day. There is virtually no place so remote that people lack the means to be informed about events elsewhere: in affluent nations the public is wired to the Internet, satellite dishes sprout from houses in Iran, inexpensive transistor radios are omnipresent even in Third World villages far removed from urban centers.

There is one thing most people in the world share in common: we sit before our televisions to learn about the world.[22] Television can have a powerful cognitive and emotional impact on large public audiences by enlisting the senses of both sight and sound. Watching events on television—such as the broadcasts of government affairs or the war in Iraq—gives a reality to the news. Seeing the world directly can shape political attitudes. Today, the Internet provides another powerful source of news for those with access to it.

Access to information thus becomes an important political commodity in the contemporary world. Western democracies put a premium on freedom of the media, even if they frequently complain about what the media reports. In many European nations, the government still manages television and radio stations because it views the media as a public service. Autocratic governments typically seek to control the media and what they can report, as well as the public's access to information (see Box 3.3). Similarly, the communist regimes of Eastern Europe had tried to limit access to news reports from the West because they feared it would undermine their regimes, and the movements for democracy in the region were partially created by the image of the way of life in the West. In the contemporary world of Internet and satellite broadcasting, it is becoming increasingly difficult for governments to control the spread of information.

Direct Contact with the Government

In modern societies, the wide scope of governmental activities brings citizens into frequent contact with various bureaucratic agencies. One survey of Americans found that about a third had had contact with a government official (federal, state, or local) in the preceding year.[23] Citizens contacted a wide range of government offices, from federal officials, to state and local governments, to school boards and the police. In addition, the government touches our lives in a myriad of other ways, from running the public schools to providing retirement

BOX 3.3

The Great Firewall of China

The People's Republic of China currently has the largest number of Internet users of any nation in the world, except the United States, and this fact has government officials worried. Chinese "netizens" find themselves surfing in the shadow of the world's most sophisticated censorship machine. There is now an estimated 30,000-strong Internet police force, which—with the aid of Western-provided technology—is dedicated to monitoring websites and e-mails. On a technical level, the five gateways that connect China to the global Internet filter traffic coming into and going out of the country. Keyword blocking technology—much of it provided by U.S. companies such as Microsoft and Google—prevents access to offending sites. Even the country's 110,000 Internet cafes are now highly regulated and state-licensed, and all are equipped with standard surveillance systems.

Source: Richard Taylor, "The Great Firewall of China," *BBC News*, January 6, 2006.

checks to providing social services. The degree of government intervention in daily life, and hence the necessity for contacts with government, varies greatly across nations as a function of their political system and the role of government in the society.

These personal experiences are powerful agents of socialization, strengthening or undercutting the images presented by other agents. Does the government send retirement checks on time? Do city officials respond to citizen complaints? Are the schools teaching children? Do unemployment offices help people find jobs? Are the highways well maintained? These are very direct sources of information on how well the government functions. No matter how positive the view of the political system that people have learned as children, citizens who face a different reality in everyday life are likely to change their early-learned views. Indeed, the contradictions between ideology and reality proved to be one of the weaknesses of the communist systems in Eastern Europe.

In summary, the country chapters in this book all examine the patterns of political socialization for several reasons. The sources of political socialization often determine the content of what is learned about politics. If people learn about new events from their friends at church, they may hear different information than people who rely on their workplace or the television for information. The role of these different socialization agents and the content of their political messages also vary systematically across nations. In addition, the ability of a nation to recreate its political culture in succeeding generations is an important factor in perpetuating the political system. Finally, cultures change when new elements are added to the process of political learning.

Thus, socialization provides the feedback mechanism that enables a political culture to endure or change.

TRENDS SHAPING CONTEMPORARY POLITICAL CULTURES

A political culture exists uniquely in its own time and place. Citizens' attitudes and beliefs are shaped by personal experiences and by the agents of political socialization. Yet, in any historical period there may be trends that change the culture in many nations. The major social trends of our time reflect both general societal developments and specific historic events.

For the past two decades, a major new development is the trend toward democracy in Eastern Europe, East Asia, and other parts of the developing world. This **democratization** trend reflects long-term responses to modernity as well as immediate reactions to current events. Modernization gradually eroded the legitimacy of nondemocratic ideologies, while the development of citizens' skills and political resources made their claim to equal participation in policymaking (at least indirectly) more plausible. Thus, many studies of political culture in Eastern Europe and the former Soviet Union uncovered surprising support for democratic norms and processes among the citizenry as the new democratic system formed.[24]

Ironically, as democracy has begun taking root in Eastern Europe, citizens in many Western democracies are increasingly skeptical about politicians and political institutions. In 1964, three-quarters of Americans said they trusted the government; today only a third of the public say as much—and the malaise is spreading to

Western Europe and Japan.[25] At the same time, public support for democratic norms and values has strengthened over time in most Western democracies. Thus, these publics are critical of politicians and political parties when they fall short of these democratic ideals. Although this cynicism is a strain on democratic politicians, it presses democracy to continue to improve and adapt, which is ultimately democracy's greatest strength.

Another recent major trend affecting political cultures is a shift toward **marketization**—that is, an increased public acceptance of free markets and private profit incentives, rather than a government-managed economy. One example of this movement appeared in the United States and many Western European nations beginning in the 1980s, where economies had experienced serious problems of inefficiency and economic stagnation. Margaret Thatcher in Britain and Ronald Reagan in the United States rode to power on waves of public support for reducing the scale of government. Public opinion surveys show that people in these nations felt that government had grown too large (see again Figure 3.3).

Just as Western Europeans began to question the government's role in the economy, the political changes in Eastern Europe and the Soviet Union transformed the discussion. The command economies of Eastern Europe were almost exclusively controlled by state corporations and government agencies. The government set both wages and prices and directed the economy. The collapse of these systems raised new questions about public support for marketization. Public opinion surveys generally find that Eastern Europeans support a capitalist market system and the public policies that would support such an economic system.[26]

Globalization is another trend affecting political cultures of many nations. Increasing international trade and international interactions tend to diffuse the values of the overall international system. Thus, as developing nations become more engaged in the global economy and global international system, the development of certain norms—such as human rights, gender equality, and democratic values—increases.[27] People in developing nations also learn about the broader opportunities existing in other nations, which can spur cultural change as well as economic change. Thus, although globalization has been a deeply divisive political issue for the past decade in many nations, the Pew Global Values Survey found broad support for globalization among citizens worldwide—especially in developing nations where it is seen as improving living standards and life chances.[28]

Clearly, political culture is not a static phenomenon, so our understanding of political culture must be dynamic. It must encompass how the agents of political socialization communicate and interpret historic events and traditional values. It must juxtapose these factors with the exposure of citizens and leaders to new experiences and new ideas. But it is important to understand the political culture of a nation, because these cultural factors influence how citizens act, how the political process functions, and what policy goals the government pursues.

REVIEW QUESTIONS

- What are the three key elements of a political culture?
- Why does political culture matter?
- Why is the process of political socialization important?
- What are the main agents of political socialization?
- What are the major trends in cultural change in the contemporary world?

KEY TERMS

agents of political socialization
democratization
fundamentalism

legitimacy
marketization
modernization

parochials
participants
political culture

political socialization
political subcultures
subjects

SUGGESTED READINGS

Almond, Gabriel A., and Sidney Verba. *The Civic Culture.* Princeton, NJ: Princeton University Press, 1963.

——, eds. *The Civic Culture Revisited.* Boston: Little Brown, 1980.

Barnes, Samuel, and Janos Simon, eds. *The Postcommunist Citizen.* Budapest: Erasmus Foundation, 1998.

Bratton, Michael, Robert Mattes, and E. Gyimah-Boadi. *Public Opinion, Democracy, and Market Reform in Africa.* Cambridge: Cambridge University Press, 2004.

Cleary, Matthew, and Susan C. Stokes. *Democracy and the Culture of Skepticism: Political Trust in Argentina and Mexico.* New York: Russell Sage, 2006.

Dalton, Russell. *Democratic Challenges, Democratic Choices: The Erosion of Political Support in Advanced Industrial Democracies.* Oxford: Oxford University Press, 2004.

Harrison, Lawrence, and Samuel P. Huntington, eds. *Culture Matters: How Values Shape Human Progress.* New York: Basic Books, 2000.

Horowitz, Donald. *Ethnic Groups in Conflict.* Berkeley: University of California Press, 1985.

Huntington, Samuel. *The Clash of Civilizations and the Remaking of World Order.* New York: Simon & Schuster, 1996.

Inglehart, Ronald, and Pippa Norris. *Sacred and Secular: Religion and Politics Worldwide.* Cambridge: Cambridge University Press, 2004.

Inglehart, Ronald, and Christian Welzel. *Modernization, Cultural Change, and Democracy: The Human Development Sequence.* New York: Cambridge University Press, 2005.

Inkeles, Alex, and David H. Smith. *Becoming Modern.* Cambridge: Harvard University Press, 1974.

Jennings, M. Kent. "Political Socialization," in Russell Dalton and Hans-Dieter Klingemann, eds. *Oxford Handbook of Political Behavior.* Oxford: Oxford University Press, 2007.

Jennings, M. Kent, and Richard Niemi. *Generations and Politics: A Panel Study of Young Adults and Their Parents.* Princeton, NJ: Princeton University Press, 1981.

Klingemann, Hans Dieter, Dieter Fuchs, and Jan Zielonka, eds. *Democracy and Political Culture in Eastern Europe.* London: Routledge, 2006.

Norris, Pippa, ed. *Critical Citizens: Global Support for Democratic Government.* Oxford: Oxford University Press, 1999.

Norris, Pippa, and Ronald Inglehart. *Rising Tide: Gender Equality and Cultural Change Around the World.* New York: Cambridge University Press, 2003.

Pharr, Susan, and Robert Putnam. *Disaffected Democracies: What's Troubling the Trilateral Democracies?* Princeton, NJ: Princeton University Press, 2000.

Putnam, Robert. *The Beliefs of Politicians.* New Haven, CT: Yale University Press, 1973.

——. *Making Democracy Work: Civic Traditions in Modern Italy.* Princeton, NJ: Princeton University Press, 1993.

Pye, Lucian W., and Sidney Verba, eds. *Political Culture and Political Development.* Princeton, NJ: Princeton University Press, 1965.

Rochon, Thomas. *Culture Moves: Ideas, Activism, and Changing Values.* Princeton, NJ: Princeton University Press, 1998.

Rose, Richard, Christian Haerpfer, and William Mishler. *Testing the Churchill Hypothesis: Democracy and Its Alternatives in Post-communist Societies.* Cambridge, UK: Polity/Baltimore: Johns Hopkins University Press, 2000.

ENDNOTES

1. This concept of legitimacy and its bases in different societies draws on the work of Max Weber. See, for example, Max Weber, *Basic Concepts in Sociology,* trans. H. P. Secher (New York: Citadel Press, 1964), chs. 5–7.

2. These terms were developed in Gabriel A. Almond and Sidney Verba, *The Civic Culture: Political Attitudes and Democracy in Five Nations* (Princeton, NJ: Princeton University Press, 1963).

3. Ronald Inglehart and Christian Welzel, *Modernization, Cultural Change, and Democracy: The Human Development Sequence* (New York: Cambridge University Press, 2005); Pippa Norris, ed., *Critical Citizens: Global Support for Democratic Government* (Oxford: Oxford University Press, 1999).

4. Russell Dalton and Doh Chull Shin, eds., *Citizens, Democracy, and Markets Around the Pacific Rim* (Oxford: Oxford University Press, 2006).

5. Inglehart and Welzel, *Modernization, Cultural Change, and Democracy.*

6. Ronald Inglehart, *Modernization and Postmodernization* (Princeton, NJ: Princeton University Press, 1997), chs. 6–7.

7. Ole Borre and Elinor Scarbrough, eds., *The Scope of Government* (Oxford: Oxford University Press, 1995).

8. Ronald Inglehart, *Culture Shift in Advanced Industrial Societies* (Princeton, NJ: Princeton University Press, 1990).

9. Even within established Western democracies, there are internal differences in the appropriate role of government, the role of the citizen, and the perceived goals of government. See Max Kaase and Ken Newton, *Beliefs in Government* (Oxford: Oxford University Press, 1995).

10. W. Kymlicka and N. Wayne, eds., *Citizenship in Divided Societies* (Oxford: Oxford University Press, 2000); Donald Horowitz, *Ethnic Groups in Conflict* (Berkeley: University of California Press, 1985).

11. Amy Chua, *World on Fire: How Exporting Free Market Democracy Breeds Ethnic Hatred and Global Instability* (New York: Doubleday, 2003).

12. See also Inglehart and Welzel, *Modernization, Cultural Change, and Democracy*.

13. Kendall Baker, Russell Dalton, and Kai Hildebrandt, *Germany Transformed* (Cambridge: Harvard University Press, 1981).

14. Robert Putnam, *Making Democracy Work: Civic Traditions in Modern Italy* (Princeton, NJ: Princeton University Press, 1993); Robert Putnam, *Bowling Alone* (New York: Simon & Schuster, 2000).

15. Samuel P. Huntington, *The Clash of Civilizations and the Remaking of World Order* (New York: Simon & Schuster, 1996); see also Fareed Zakaria, *The Future of Freedom* (New York: Norton, 2003).

16. See Almond and Verba, *Civic Culture*, ch. 12; M. Kent Jennings, Klaus R. Allerbeck, and Leopold Rosenmayr, "Generations and Families," in Samuel H. Barnes, Max Kaase, et al., *Political Action* (Beverly Hills, CA: Sage, 1979), chs. 15–16.

17. Pippa Norris and Ronald Inglehart, *Rising Tide: Gender Equality and Cultural Change Around the World* (New York: Cambridge University Press, 2003).

18. Martha Nussbaum and Jonathan Glover, eds., *Women, Culture, and Development* (New York: Oxford University Press, 1995).

19. For example, see Sidney Verba, Norman H. Nie, and Jae-on Kim, *Participation and Political Equality* (New York: Cambridge University Press, 1978); Barnes, Kaase, et al., *Political Action*, ch. 4.

20. See Martin Marty and Scott Appleby, *Fundamentalism Observed* (Chicago: University of Chicago Press, 1991).

21. Robert Putnam, ed., *Democracies in Flux* (Oxford: Oxford University Press, 2002).

22. The Pew Global Attitudes Project found that over two-thirds of the public in most nations cited television as their main source of political information. Only in poor African nations did this statistic fall below 50 percent, and in these nations the radio provided an alternative. Pew Global Attitudes Project, *What the World Thinks in 2002* (Washington, DC: Pew Global Attitudes Project, 2002) (http://pewglobal.org/).

23. Sidney Verba et al., *The American Participation Study 1990* (Ann Arbor: Interuniversity Consortium for Political and Social Research, University of Michigan).

24. Arthur Miller, William Reisinger, and Vicki Hesli, eds., *Public Opinion and Regime Change* (Boulder, CO: Westview Press, 1993); William Mishler and Richard Rose, "Trajectories of Fear and Hope: Support for Democracy in Post-communist Europe," *Comparative Political Studies* 28 (1995): 553–81. Compare to Robert Rohrschneider, "Institutional Learning Versus Value Diffusion," *Journal of Politics* 58 (1996): 442–66.

25. Norris, *Critical Citizens*; Russell Dalton, *Democratic Challenges, Democratic Choices*.

26. See William Zimmerman, *The Russian People and Foreign Policy: Russian Elite and Mass Perspectives* (Princeton: Princeton University Press, 2002), ch. 2; Raymond Duch, "Tolerating Economic Reform," *American Political Science Review* 87 (1993): 590–608. Russian support for marketization noticeably lags behind that of most Eastern Europeans.

27. Wayne Sandholtz and Mark Gray, "International Integration and National Corruption," *International Organization* 57 (Autumn 2003): 761–800; Mark Gray, Miki Kittilson, and Wayne Sandholtz, "Women and Globalization: A Study of 180 Countries, 1975–2000," *International Organization* 60 (Spring 2006): 293–333.

28. Pew Global Attitudes Project, *Views of a Changing World, June 2003* (Washington, DC: Pew Global Attitudes Project, 2003): 71–81 (http://pewglobal.org/reports/display.php?ReportID=185).

Democracy and Its Rivals

CHAPTER TWO

Learning Objectives

By the end of this chapter, the reader will be able:

- to understand the basic features of liberal democracy;

- to identify alternative forms of government and to show how these forms have been categorised and how they relate to one another;

- to clarify the differences between, for example, authoritarianism and totalitarianism;

- to develop understanding of the emergence, development and modern practice of confederation, federalism and federal government.

Liberal Democracy

The overwhelming majority of modern states claim to be 'democracies'. We call this form of democracy **liberal democracy**. On the one hand, liberal democracy is *representative*, distinguished from the older classical notion of 'direct' democracy in that, under it, citizens do not govern themselves directly but choose representatives to govern. On the other, it is *limited* – the government is restricted in what it can do. Liberal democracies are states in which government is limited in its powers by a written constitution, a system of law and/or an independent judiciary, and is responsive to the popular will as expressed through free and fair elections. Under such a government certain basic freedoms (often termed *civil rights*) will be guaranteed to the individual (Holden 1993). In the political sense, *liberalisation* means extending the range of rights and freedoms available to the citizen, and it is important to distinguish between this usage and the so-called liberalisation of an economy by removing constraints on investment and trade. *Democratisation* refers to both the process by which other forms of government evolve (or are transformed) into democracies and the process by which existing democracies become more democratic, as for example by improvements in electoral representation or the defence of civil rights.

However, democracy is an 'essentially-contested' concept, that is to say, a concept on which *by definition* agreement is not possible. Democracy is about a contest for power and the outcome of that struggle colours people's perception of it. Hence it is not possible to determine *with certainty* which states are liberal democracies and which are not. There are broadly three working possibilities.

An *inclusive* definition allows the label to all governments which call themselves democratic and can claim to have been chosen by the people. Lincoln spoke of 'government of the people, by the people, for the people' (*Gettysburg Address*, 1863) but the United States of 1863 would not be accepted as a liberal democracy today. Schmitter and Karl hold that democracy does not consist in a single specific set of institutions. 'There are many types of democracy, and their diverse practices produce a similarly varied set of effects' (Schmitter and Karl 1993, p. 40).

A *procedural* definition focuses on the way in which this process of choice is achieved. 'The democratic method is that institutional arrangement for arriving at political decisions in which individuals acquire the power to decide by means of a competitive struggle for the people's vote' (Schumpeter 1943, p. 269). It is easy enough to tell whether or not an election has been held, but it is another matter to tell whether it has been 'free and fair' (see Chapter 7). A criticism of this approach is that it can lead to low standards being applied and the acceptance of 'low intensity democracy' (Gills, Rocamora and Wilson 1993) as an adequate substitute for the real thing.

An *exclusive* definition concentrates on determining whether or not features exist that are incompatible with free popular choice: there must be no military intervention, no armed repression of the opposition or of minorities, no secret police, no limits on candidature at elections and no ballot rigging. In addition some claim that there must be a vibrant civil society/civic culture. The point is that consent in itself does not make a government democratic (Partridge 1971; Ginsburg 1982) – citizens may see no alternative to passive consent to oligarchy or dictatorship.

Schmitter and Karl warn us not to expect too much. Democracies are not necessarily more efficient economically than other forms of government, they argue. They are not necessarily more efficient administratively, either, and they are not likely 'to appear more orderly, consensual, stable, or governable than the autocracies they replace'. Lastly, 'democracies will have more open societies and polities than the autocracies they replace, but not necessarily more open economies'. What they will have, however, is a much better chance of delivering, in the end, a stable, peaceful and prosperous society (Schmitter and Karl 1993, pp. 49–51). And Diamond points out that three tensions or paradoxes are inherent in the very nature of democracy: conflict v. consensus, representativeness v. governability, consent v. effectiveness (Diamond 1993).

Those of us who live in the English-speaking world take democracy so much for granted that we easily forget just what a modern phenomenon it is. Liberal democracy originated in a much older concept of representation: the idea that it will be easier to get people to pay taxes if their representatives are asked to agree to do so first.

Representative government was achieved before it became general practice to allow all citizens to vote, displacing the older idea that only the well-to-do had a stake in society. Hence there is general agreement that the appearance of democracy is associated with a certain minimum level of economic development. Here, however, agreement ends.

Again there are broadly speaking three alternative views of the relationship between economic development and the change to democracy. Those who take the *modernisation approach* believe that at a certain stage of economic development democracy becomes possible, and that, in the words of Seymour Martin Lipset, 'the more well-to-do a nation, the greater the chances that it will sustain democracy' (Lipset 1960, pp. 49–50). The reasoning is clear: since the seventeenth century it has been recognised that sufficient economic resources to bring a certain sense of security are needed for people to take part in politics, and the better educated they are the more likely they are to be able to participate successfully. The emergence of an educated middle class has therefore been seen as a precondition for the emergence of liberal democracy.

Those who take a *structural approach* see the nature of structures of class and power as central. The accumulation of wealth gives rise to a middle class. But at a certain point in time it is the class as a whole that challenges the old elites for a share in political power, if necessary by force. Or, as Barrington Moore put it, 'no bourgeoisie, no democracy' (Moore 1969, p. 37). This would imply that liberal democracy was in practice an instrument of class rule and that its institutions function to maintain the rule of middle-class elites and to disempower ordinary citizens. A growing disenchantment with democracy seems evident in the steadily declining turnout in US elections (already very low by European standards) since the 1960s.

The *transition approach* sees the agreement to democratise less starkly, as a matter of elite choice, bargaining and negotiation, the impetus for which comes from the historical conflict over scarce resources. 'A people who are not in conflict about some rather fundamental matters would have little need to devise democracy's elaborate rules for conflict resolution' (Rustow 1970, p. 362). Again the question is: why do these conflicts arise, and how far do the mechanisms that purport to resolve them actually work to do so?

Liberal democracy is well established in Western Europe, North America, Japan and other leading countries. However, economic development is not a prerequisite for people to want democracy, as is demonstrated by the persistent reappearance of the liberal tradition in Latin America over the past century and a half, and some striking examples from South Asia, the Middle East and the Caribbean. Liberal democracy has proved adaptable and responsive to the pressures of survival in a competitive world, and with the collapse of the rival Soviet model, it currently has no effective competitor. However, this does not mean that all liberal democracies are the same.

Since the nineteenth century, it has been a widespread assumption, particularly in English-speaking countries, that stable democratic systems required a high level of social consensus. Where this was achieved, political stability was enhanced and society unified. Where it was not, there was a tendency for political order to break down and democracy to collapse. For some time it has been accepted that the key determinant of political stability is the number and nature of *social cleavages* in society (Lipset and Rokkan 1967; Rae and Taylor 1970; Lane and Ersson 1991). There are many factors dividing groups in all societies. If the dividing lines between these groups do *not* coincide with each other, competitive democratic politics can and does take place without endangering the whole structure. The problem comes when they do coincide with one another and a major split opens up, as in Belgium between the Flemings and the Walloons.

However, there are several states which are among the most democratic in Europe in which, on the contrary, a high level of agreement is obtained in divided societies. Hence special interest attaches to what is now termed **consociational democracy**, a term originally formulated by Arend Lijphart, as a result of comparative studies by political scientists from Austria, Belgium, the Netherlands and Switzerland (Lijphart 1969, 1974, 1977; Lembruch 1967; Steiner 1972, 1974).

Consociational democracy, Lijphart argued, exists in societies which are clearly and apparently permanently divided vertically into a number of communities, whether ethnic, religious or linguistic. These communities, after Dutch practice, are often referred to as 'pillars' and their division as 'pillarisation' (*verzuiling*). It is characterised by an elaborate process of *negotiation* between the elites of the different 'pillars' leading to *accommodation* and *compromise*. Four basic principles are used to diffuse and to resolve conflict:

1. **executive power-sharing**: the executive is not vested exclusively in one group; all pro-system groups are represented in the government;
2. **autonomy**: each group has a right to regulate its own affairs in certain respects;
3. **proportionality**: jobs are shared in proportion to representation in Parliament or Congress;
4. **minority veto**: the minority have a right to veto any proposal which they regard as violating their basic interests.

In fact, as Table 2.1 shows, Lijphart's argument is that it is the behaviour of the elite that makes this system possible. What is of particular interest is whether the strategy of seeking agreement is really successful, or whether its apparent success in the Netherlands was simply the necessary product of coalition government in a highly fragmented party system. It is true that it has not served to maintain a unitary state in the highly

Table 2.1 Lijphart's typology of democratic systems

	Political culture – homogeneous	Political culture – fragmented
Elite behaviour – coalescent	Depoliticised democracy	Consociational democracy
Elite behaviour – competitive	Centripetal democracy	Centrifugal democracy

Source: after Lijphart 1969

unpromising circumstances of Belgium, where ethnic, linguistic and religious cleavages between Flemings and Walloons coincide with a clear-cut geographical split. It is also true that with depillarisation in the Netherlands it seems to have come to an end (van Mierlo 1986). But it seems to have worked well both there (see Gladdish 1991) and in Austria (Gerlich 1987) over a substantial period and there is evidence that where the same strategy has been adopted in other states – Germany in Europe, Canada in the Americas, Malaysia in South-East Asia – it has achieved a much higher degree of political stability than might otherwise have been expected. Conversely its abandonment in Colombia, Cyprus, Lebanon and Nigeria has led to political instability, unrest and even civil war.

This reminds us that all states, even liberal democracies, exist in an evolutionary context and may well have diverged considerably from the ideal types they profess to represent (cf. Macpherson 1977). Moreover on many occasions in recent years rulers have argued that for reasons of national security, or otherwise, they have found it 'necessary' to suspend or dispense with any or all of the notions of individual rights, limitation of government power or the right to a fair trial.

Identifying alternative forms

From the beginning of the study of politics, observers have tried to order their ideas by the use of various systems of classification. Modern systems utilise the basic concept of participation, in conjunction with other criteria. However, political systems are in constant evolution. Static typologies are therefore of little use compared with developmental models.

Classification as a means of organising information is essential, and the first system of classification propounded for states was that used by Aristotle himself, who divided them between those ruled by the one, by the few, and by the many (Aristotle 1968, p. 113). This distinction, even though it was not developed for use on modern complex states at all, is still useful, but only in a limited sense. It appeals to the most important of popular feelings about politics, the sense of how far – if at all – the system appears to respond to one's own individual wishes. In an age when democracy is almost universally espoused as the ambition of each and every political system, it still operates as the chief criterion for determining just how far any given state or political system can be truly regarded as democratic.

But the mere number of the rulers (read decision-makers) in a modern system is not an adequate guide to the way in which the system as a whole actually operates, even assuming that the exact number could be determined. Concepts such as the few and the many are irritatingly imprecise. One of the few definite things that can be said, for example, about the 'Fourteen Families' traditionally said to control El Salvador is that intermarriage and breeding combine to make the actual number quite meaningless. For another thing, the capacity of the ultimate decision-makers is determined by their effectiveness. This depends both on the amount and accuracy of the information that reaches them, and on their capacity to implement their decisions once taken. Even 'Ramfis' Trujillo of the Dominican Republic, who in 1962 personally shot his political prisoners with a machine-gun, had in other, more complex respects to depend on others to act on his orders and so found himself forced to flee the country regardless (Diedrich 1978, p. 248).

Once a ruler depends on others, autocracy is qualified, and so, in practice, the rule of the one becomes the rule of the few. Not only must the others continue to render their services, but they may and do act in the name of the one person who bears the responsibility for all decisions of government. To understand other countries, therefore, one has to identify a set of criteria by which they can be sorted into recognisable categories.

Participation

The key concept for this purpose is the concept of **participation**. Almost all states nowadays consider that they are either democratic or aspiring to democracy. That is to say, their rulers believe that under their form of government, as far as human fallibility allows, the ultimate decisions are either taken by the people at large, or will be, as soon as they can be taught how to do it. Unhappily, there are two basic strands of thought as to what is meant by democracy. The fact that these differences involve differences of technique rather than belief makes them of as much interest to the student of comparative politics as to political philosophers, and indeed they reflect the observations by those who first formulated them of the political systems of their own day.

Both views are concerned with the process of choice by which the people select their representatives and that by which people or representatives reach decisions on specific issues. The older view, represented in ancient times by Roman practice, and in modern theory by the writings of Rousseau, see both as aspects of what Rousseau termed 'the general will' (*volonté générale* – Rousseau 1958, pp. 20, 22–30). The general will of the people is not just the will of the majority, nor even of all individual people, it is a coherent expression of the feeling of the society as a whole. It is therefore possible to say that the general will cannot be understood and interpreted by a series of individual choices, but that anyone who can perceive what the general will is can point it out and advocate its support to his or her fellows. This was the view of Robespierre and the Jacobins during the French Revolution, and it is one congenial to individuals or groups under the 'mixed' constitutions of most modern societies.

The more modern view, represented by Locke and Mill among theorists, is that all government is a process of compromise, and that the general will – if it exists – cannot be arrived at except by approximation. This approximation can be arrived at by accepting the decision of the majority in all processes of choice involving large numbers, but in the self-restraint also of that majority in tolerating the views of the minority (Locke 1956, pp. 49–50, 95–8; Mill 1958, pp. 102–3). Thus a series of shifting coalitions becomes possible on individual issues. Recent American writers, beginning with Dahl (1964a, b) and Kornhauser (1959), have increasingly emphasised the importance of keeping the process of choice essentially one of bargaining in a 'free market' of ideas.

Competitive v. non-competitive systems

Like the Jacobins, Russian and Chinese Communists believed that there could be no antagonistic conflict within their states, but have gone further in claiming that their party, as vanguard of the proletariat, was therefore the sole body able to interpret the general will correctly. A similar argument has been used by various self-appointed rulers to justify their actions as being guided by a superior form of legitimacy. Writers on these aspects of government have therefore propounded a number of schemes of ideological classification which take these facts into account. Some have chosen to focus on the location of power in the system, others on the degree to which theory is reflected in a valid attempt to replace counting heads by a system for reaching a consensus of views.

Thus Talmon distinguishes between 'representative' and 'totalitarian' democracy in his study of the conflict of the emergent ideas in the French revolutionary period (Talmon 1961), while Almond and Coleman distinguish in Asia and Africa between 'Western' systems based on the acceptance of majority decision, and 'non-Western' systems in which attempts are made to include criteria of value on the process of decision, and to promote the solidarity of turbulent states by making decisions only when they command universal assent (Almond and Coleman 1960, p. 17). Both terminologies, however, are highly unsatisfactory, and '**competitive**' and '**non-competitive**' are better.

Whatever the terminology employed, the fact is that structures of similar names perform different functions in each type of system. Thus political parties, which for some 'competitive' systems are largely concerned with articulating and aggregating interests, are for the 'non-competitive' systems primarily a means of mobilising support. 'Non-competitive' systems, abhorring overt conflict, do not allow for interest groups openly to operate as pressure groups, abolish or co-opt competing parties and predetermine the result of elections by various devices designed to monopolise political power for those favoured by the regime, often with the ideological justification that, because of their special knowledge, such matters should be the preserve of a small group or elite. But these facts are not the product of the differences in terminology; the terminology has been selected to reflect just those differences.

Participation may be either *qualitative* or *quantitative*. A football match involves twenty-two players, a polo match eight. That is a quantitative difference. But a football match may also involve the participation of a handful of spectators, if amateur, or of thousands, if professional, but the differences may have little impact on the performance of the players compared with the quantitative difference in the teams themselves if a member of one is sent off the field. And participation can be further restricted or enhanced, other than by simple, clean-cut numerical criteria. Thus the fact that a goalkeeper's function is to remain within a defined area of the field is counter-balanced by allowing him increased freedom to handle the ball, while the fact that other players have greater freedom on the field is limited by the fact that the goal is only of a certain size, and so on.

In politics the most important differences between modern states are the number of *levels* on which, and *channels* through which, participation can take place.

There are many possibilities of participation in European states short of taking part in government itself, the actual decision-making process. These include: first of all, interest in politics; secondly, voting; thirdly, political organisation – taking part in some kind of mechanism designed to influence the political process, party membership, possible candidature for the assembly, and actual choice to be a member of the government itself. These are all *levels* of participation involving greater involvement in the system and a greater say in what goes on.

But at each level, except at the top, there are a number of alternative *channels* through which participation can be effective, and include elections or referenda, interest groups, political parties and local government organs. The same is true even in such apparently unpromising instances as, for example, China under the Cultural Revolution, but there the channels included such unfamiliar devices as the wall poster, the Red Guards, and the revolutionary committees (Robinson 1969). And when one system is compared with another, what varies is not simply participation, but what is considered to be political. In other words, political participation varies with the definition of what is properly the concern of politics and what the proper way of being political is.

It is for this reason that one has to make a functional separation between one aspect of government and another, rather than a purely institutional one, because what is defined as being one thing in one country may be defined as being something quite different in another. To take the obvious case, in almost all modern countries people 'participate' in elections. But what this *means* in terms of the individual varies from country to country, depending on what the actual likely outcome of the vote is – that is, the degree to which it is connected to the rest of the political process.

Authoritarianism

It was in the age of the Cold War (1946–90) that a new term, **totalitarianism**, came into use in the West to describe a syndrome of features believed to be characteristic of both fascism in Hitler's Germany and communism in the Soviet Union, China and Eastern Europe. These states, it was thought, differed from all previous states as having both the will and the ability to exercise unlimited control over their populations (Friedrich and Brzezinski 1975) and will be discussed further in the next section. By contrast an older word, '**authoritarian**', gained a new popularity as a convenient term to designate more traditional dictatorships. The beliefs which underpinned those systems designated as 'authoritarian' systems included: belief in the transcendental importance of the principle of authority; an emphasis on the exclusive use of political power, unfettered by juridical restraint or civil liberties; and a tendency to excuse the excesses either of arbitrary decision-making or of despotic methods of political and social control.

Consequently, various writers have since 1960 sought to identify a number of criteria by which to distinguish between the two broad types of political system, democratic and authoritarian, which they see as opposites.

Thus Dahl, who began with the Aristotelian criterion as his point of departure (Dahl 1964a, p. 26), first distinguished between two broad types of political system which he termed *polyarchies* and *hierarchies*, according to criteria such as the existence of a separation of powers, the independence or otherwise of the judiciary and civil service, the existence or otherwise of competitive parties, and formally organised pressure groups with open access to the decision-makers (Dahl 1964b, pp. 84–7). Subsequently he went on to divide the categories using two criteria, *competitiveness* and *inclusiveness*, the extent to which the system encourages popular participation. The result is four categories: closed hegemonies, low on both criteria; inclusive hegemonies, high on participation but low on competition (Cuba, for example); competitive oligarchies, low on participation but high on competition; and polyarchies, with high levels both of participation and competition (Table 2.2). This generates three categories of authoritarian systems and is still widely used.

In a key study Linz defined the new authoritarian states as 'political systems with limited, not responsible, political pluralism; without elaborate and guiding ideology (but with distinctive mentalities); without intensive nor extensive political mobilization (except at some point in their development); and in which a leader (or occasionally a small group) exercises power within formally ill-defined limits but actually quite predictable ones' (Linz 1970, p. 255).

On the basis of Linz's definition it is possible to distinguish as he does between new and old authoritarian regimes. The longer established an authoritarian regime is, the less it needs to rely on the overt use of force and the more it tends to develop new forms of legitimacy. However, for Linz authoritarian government is always a transitional state,

Table 2.2 Dahl's typology of political systems

	Competitiveness low	Competitiveness high
Inclusiveness low	Closed hegemonies (hierarchies) Saudi Arabia	Competitive oligarchies Nigeria
Inclusiveness high	Inclusive hegemonies Cuba	Polyarchies France

Source: after Dahl 1964b

either towards democracy or towards totalitarianism. In his recent work with Al Stepan (Linz and Stepan 1996, pp. 42–51) they defend the concept of totalitarianism as still having meaning, while proposing a new category of 'post-totalitarianism' to designate many of the countries of the former Soviet bloc. At least one of these, Romania, is however categorised as 'sultanistic' – a term originally proposed by Max Weber to identify the most extreme form of patrimonial state.

Alternatively, Sahlin (1977) suggests, it is also useful to distinguish between protective authoritarianism and promotional authoritarianism. Protective authoritarianism is the argument of those who intervene by force simply to protect the status quo and the position of those who benefit from it. Following a traditional military coup, which has only the limited aim of displacing the existing government, a period of emergency rule normally follows in which the armed forces emphasise the power available to them, their limited ambitions in making use of it, and their intention to return the country to civilian rule as soon as possible. Some regimes of this type, for example that of Franco's Spain, do survive for a long period and, Sahlin notes, become 'old' authoritarian regimes in Linz's terms, gaining a degree of legitimacy through force of habit, and, generally, needing to depend less on the overt use of force. However, their principal aims remain the same: the de-politicisation of issues and the demobilisation of the masses.

Promotional authoritarianism, by contrast, is characterised by a desire to promote change, by supplanting the existing government and establishing one which will stay in power for a period of years to pursue certain stated aims. Chief among these aims is economic development, the desire for which is in itself rooted in a nationalistic belief in the value of a strong state. But this requires a certain degree of mobilisation of the masses in the interests of productivity. For such neo-authoritarian regimes this can most safely be achieved by appealing to nationalism. However, even this does not resolve, but only postpone, a fundamental conflict between the desire for economic mobilisation and the fear of political mobilisation. There are two possible ways in which this can be done; in each case, significantly, they involve maintaining and not jettisoning the forms of democracy.

Some authoritarian regimes are prepared to mobilise the popular sector for both political and economic purposes, and to live with the consequences. Regimes of this rare type can be classed as authoritarian populist regimes. The classic case of such a regime is to be found in Argentina under General Juan Domingo Perón (president 1946–55, 1973–74). Its success can be gauged by the fact that ever since the coup that displaced the regime in 1955, no government has long survived that did not come to terms with the Peronists. Despite his authoritarian ideology and emphasis on the role of the leader (known as 'verticalism'), Perón was constitutionally elected and re-elected, and it took several attempts for the armed forces to overthrow him (Calvert and Calvert 1989).

Other regimes have been able to achieve such a degree of economic success that their citizens are prepared to wait for democracy. It is probably not just coincidence that the so-called 'tiger' economies of East and South-East Asia – Singapore, Taiwan, South Korea, Malaysia and Thailand – are in states where for a variety of reasons and in varying degrees the governing style, and often the substance, is authoritarian. However, as we shall see later (Chapter 5), there are other explanations for their apparent success.

Oligarchy or totalitarianism?

Other writers have sought to utilise the concept of totalitarianism. The word 'totalitarian' was originally coined by Mussolini to designate a state in which the power of the state worked without hindrance and the individual citizen had no rights at all. Friedrich (1972) distinguishes totalitarian states from others, by six criteria:

1. an official ideology, to which everyone is supposed to adhere;
2. a single mass party usually led by one man, organised hierarchically;
3. monopoly of the effective use of all weapons by party and bureaucracy;
4. monopoly of the means of effective mass communication;
5. a system of terroristic police control;
6. central control and direction of the economy (Schapiro 1972, p. 18).

In the late 1960s the concept of totalitarianism came under strong attack, both from writers in Eastern Europe and from specialists on Eastern Europe. The former pointed out that the six criteria were chosen to link together three principal historical instances: Mussolini's Italy (1922–44), Hitler's Germany (1933–45) and the Soviet Union under Stalin (1928–53). They rejected this linking as propagandist, principally (though not entirely) because they saw the purpose of the Soviet Union as being entirely opposed to that of the other two instances. The 'leadership principle' was not, they argued, a basic principle of communism, but an aberration. The latter, on the other hand, had failed to find evidence that the overwhelming control claimed for the state by the proponents of the model did in fact exist in the Soviet Union at that time. They were able to identify a limited number of competing power-centres and interest groups within Soviet society (Skilling and Griffiths 1971; Hough 1976; Kelley 1976) and some even argued that a degree of **pluralism** existed (the view that the will of the individual is best served by the multiplication of competing groups – Solomon 1983). Hence they could dismiss the totalitarian model of Soviet decision-making as the product of a single authoritarian will (essentially a 'rational actor' model) in favour of a scheme which saw decisions as being the product of competing individuals and interests within government (a 'bureaucratic politics' interpretation; see Allison 1971, p. 5; Gustafson 1980; Dawisha 1980; and Chapter 8, this volume). Other Eastern European states, notably Poland and Hungary, had diverged from the model substantially on the criteria of centralised control of the economy, and acceptance of the ruling ideology (Ball and Millard 1986).

A more serious problem is presented by the difficulty of distinguishing between 'true' democracy and what Finer (1970) called '**façade democracy**': that is to say, a system that is nominally democratic, but in fact oligarchical. Where does the dominance of an elite end and **oligarchy** begin?

This problem is well illustrated by Shils's early model which formalised concepts widely used at the time in speech and in the press (Parsons and Shils 1962). He distinguished, on the one hand, the rule of the few, which he called oligarchy, from the rule of the many, democracy. He then proceeded to subdivide these types by two different criteria: what he took to be the actual effective degree to which the concept is applied, and for what purpose the government concerned advocated it.

He thus derived two types of democracy: *political democracy*, that is to say liberal democracy, such as exists in Western Europe and the United States, characterised by free elections, competitive parties, pressure groups, and so on; and *tutelary democracy*, such as was characteristic of Pakistan under Ayub Khan (1958–68), where the government holds many rights in abeyance on the pretext that the people need to be educated before being ready for political democracy. This category might include many military governments that, as in Bolivia, Ecuador, Peru and Brazil in the 1970s, promise free elections once they have ended illiteracy, taught everyone who to vote for, and given them an official party to support – but there must surely be serious doubts whether democracy is the right word for it.

And it is in fact very difficult to distinguish tutelary democracy from the first of Shils's three categories of oligarchy, which he calls *modernising oligarchy*. This is where the rulers justify their restraint on public self-assertion on the grounds that to do so will promote economic development. Naturally modernising oligarchy can be made to look attractive, particularly if judiciously contrasted with its old-fashioned counterpart, *traditional oligarchy*, where nothing is ever done because the rulers like things the way they are. Lastly, however, Shils offers a third category, that of *totalitarian oligarchy*. This is rule from the centre directed by an ideology which justifies it on the grounds that it is in the true interests of the masses and backed by a coercive apparatus which demands positive and not merely negative acceptance.

Although these three types correspond to popular ideas of differences between states – and especially to types which were fashionable in the 1950s when the scheme was outlined – the way in which the differences are drawn is not really up to the strain of actual classification. Was Brazil under General Medici (1969–74) a modernising oligarchy, as it professed to be, or a totalitarian oligarchy, as Amnesty International tended to regard it? Not only is there, it seems, no very hard-and-fast line to be drawn between democracy and oligarchy, but the divisions between the subtypes are just as uncertain. And the scheme makes no mention of perhaps the most fruitful subtype proposed: *totalitarian democracy* (Talmon 1961). The so-called people's democracies of Eastern Europe after the Second World War ruled in the name of the people, and claimed to be much more democratic than the liberal democracies, precisely because they set out to give the people what they believed they needed, not what they actually wanted. Talmon was not of course the first thinker to warn of the dangers of the dictatorship of the majority.

For unfortunately in the meantime the word 'totalitarian' continued to be widely used, and indeed still is, otherwise it would not be necessary to have this discussion here. By loosening the definition somewhat, Crick extended to eleven the number of criteria by which he distinguishes between *autocratic, totalitarian* and *republican* regimes (Crick 1973, pp. 44–81). This raised two new problems. First, extending the number of criteria makes for a very unwieldy typology, and the aim of classifying should be to make things clearer. Secondly, it does not enable us to distinguish authoritarian regimes; in fact by preferring the word 'totalitarian', it confuses the boundary between the two. And it is authoritarian regimes that we need to clarify, since even those who have employed the totalitarian model have never been able to argue that outside its specific time-frame it was worth distinguishing.

The notion of totalitarianism enjoyed a brief renaissance in the 1980s, when it was incorporated in the notorious distinction of Jeane Kirkpatrick between 'totalitarian' governments and 'moderately repressive authoritarian' governments (MRAGs). She argued that their control mechanisms were such that 'totalitarian' states could not evolve into liberal democratic states. The United States should therefore, she argued, be prepared if necessary to support 'moderately repressive authoritarian' states, such as Pinochet's Chile, rather than run the risk of allowing a state to succumb to totalitarianism (Kirkpatrick 1982). The collapse of Soviet power in Eastern Europe in 1989 and the disintegration of the Soviet Union two years later has exposed the specious assumption on which this argument was based.

Static Typologies

The problem is, however, one common to all *static typologies* of political systems (see Table 2.3). The best approach would be to return to first principles and determine a number of *clearly defined criteria* by which states can be categorised and the different labels employed by politicians and others related to one another. Blondel (1969, p. 40) has pointed out that three axes of classification could enable us to link all such criteria: a radical–conservative dimension, a democratic–monarchical dimension, and a liberal–authoritarian dimension (see Figure 2.1). The importance of this approach is that it makes us think clearly, not just why some 'cells' of a given typology are full, but why others are empty, and it will be helpful to bear in mind in what follows. For this book is based on an approach which is rather different, but is, nevertheless, based on the same imperative, to relate the universe of states to underlying processes. The problem is twofold. On the one hand, the number of possible axes of classification is potentially infinite. On the other, all classifications, however detailed, will be actively misleading in so far as they distinguish categories only at one moment of historical time. For within the universe of states order can be found only if it is understood that all static typologies

Table 2.3 Static typologies of political systems

Aristotle	Shils (1962)	Dahl (1964b)	Finer (1970)	Crick (1973)
Monarchy Tyranny			Dynastic state	Totalitarian
Aristocracy Oligarchy	Modernising oligarchy Traditional oligarchy Totalitarian oligarchy	Hierarchy	Military regime Façade democracy Quasi democracy Totalitarian regime	Autocratic
Polity Democracy	Political democracy Tutelary democracy	Polyarchy	Liberal democracy	Republican

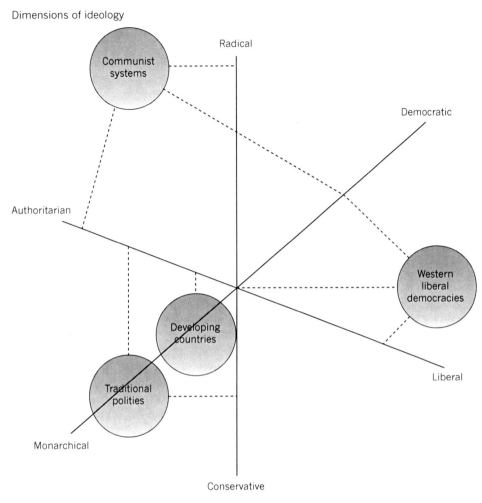

Dimensions of ideology

Source: after Blondel 1969, p. 39

Figure 2.1 Blondel's three dimensions of classification

are only 'snapshots' of an evolving pattern, and that the confusion stems from the conflict of two principles:

1. Each political system has some freedom to evolve according to its own internal political dynamics.
2. All political systems have been shaped by the influence of two successive periods of political evolution which have occurred in the last 200 years, each of which has altered (in ways that are not wholly compatible) prevailing ideas about the relationship of the individual to the state.

Constitutions

Since 1787, it has been customary to draw up a written document called a Constitution which provides the ground rules for the operation of the political system. Here such a document will be given a capital C, to distinguish it from the term constitution which is still sometimes used to refer to these ground rules whether written or unwritten. However, today virtually all modern states have Constitutions (the UK is the only major exception, and in this case it is more correct to say that the constitution is uncodified rather than unwritten).

Four basic features are to be found in virtually all Constitutions:

1. A **preamble**, stating on whose authority the Constitution has been written – this in itself has no legal force.
2. The **text**, which establishes political institutions, assigns powers to them and gives ground rules for the system to work.
3. A **Bill of Rights**, stating certain fundamental rights which all individuals have and listing what governments may not constitutionally do to breach them. (However, the French Constitution of 1958 initially did not have constitutional guarantees, which were subsequently incorporated from its predecessor by the Conseil Constitutionel.)
4. An **amending procedure**, which enables the Constitution to be changed to fit new circumstances.

Lawyers have in the past distinguished between rigid and flexible constitutions according to the ease with which they can be amended. In practice, however, there is a wide range of variation. The United States Constitution has only been successfully amended 26 times since 1787; the Mexican Constitution has been amended more than 330 times since 1917. The important thing is that amendment should be possible – the first Constitution of a united Italy, the Piedmontese *Statuto* of 1859, could not be amended, with the unfortunate consequence that Italian politicians of the Liberal era increasingly tended to disregard it, paving the way for Mussolini.

Governments of states gaining independence after 1945 soon became impatient with the constitutional restraints imposed on them. It was not long, therefore, before many of these Constitutions were scrapped or extensively rewritten to introduce an executive presidency, formalise a one-party state and curb the power of the judiciary. Experience has shown, however, that changing a Constitution to try to entrench partisan provisions is a risky business. The temptation is strong for the next government to write a new Constitution, thus inaugurating an era of *faction constitutionalism* such as plagued Latin America during the nineteenth century – Venezuela, the most striking example, has now (2001) had 23 Constitutions. There is also a strong temptation to incorporate *programmatic provisions* which deal not just with what the form of government should be but also with what it should do. These are to be found in both the Italian Constitution of 1947 and the German Basic Law of 1949 but the classic example is the Mexican Constitution of 1917, which contains the basis for the later land reform programme (Article 27) and Labour Code (Article 123) and even a provision empowering the president to expel any foreigner from the country whose presence he finds inconvenient (Article 33).

Two other features of Constitutions have a continuing relevance. These are the **separation of powers** and *checks and balances*. Because both are well-known features of the US Constitution, it is particularly interesting to see how they may turn up in a very different form elsewhere.

The differentiation between the **executive** and the **legislative** 'powers' was first formulated by Locke, but it was Montesquieu who in his visit to Britain in 1739 popularised the notion by describing it as a basic principle of British liberties (Montesquieu 1966). The framers of the American Constitution in making it the basis of their document

Case Study   Court Rules on Land Control

The US supreme court yesterday curtailed the power of the federal government to regulate local land and water use, in a decision closely watched by business groups and environmentalists. The court split 5–4 along lines which have become familiar in its battle over the balance of power between the federal government and the states.

The court found the federal government, under the landmark Clean Water Act, did not have the power to prevent a group of Chicago localities from building a landfill on seasonal ponds used by migrating birds. But it stopped well short of a broader challenge to the authority of Congress to regulate the environment under the constitution.

Congress did not intend the legislation to cover such small bodies of water, Chief Justice William Rehnquist wrote for the majority. 'Permitting the (government) to claim federal jurisdiction over ponds and mudflats would also result in a significant impingement of the states' traditional and primary power over land and water use,' he wrote.

Writing for the four traditional dissenters on federalism matters, Justice John Paul Stevens criticised the decision: 'Today the court takes an unfortunate step that needlessly weakens our principal safeguard against toxic water,' he wrote.

The US Chamber of Commerce, which argued in support of the Chicago localities, welcomed the decision as striking down an instance of 'regulatory overreach' by the federal government. The ruling will free property developers from one kind of federal intervention, and will potentially give farmers, mining companies and other businesses more say over how they use their land.

Source: *Financial Times*, 10 January 2001

---

also arranged that there were some formal links between executive and legislature (the president has to report annually to Congress and could veto legislation, the Congress has to approve taxation and could in the last resort impeach the president). They were wise to do so, since without these checks and balances the system could not have worked at all. It is because in practice the powers are not rigidly divided that Almond and Coleman preferred rather to identify the functions of rule-application and rule-making.

Federalism

Locke also spoke of a third 'power', but this one has scarcely ever been specifically incorporated into the Constitution of any modern state, though it is implicit in the structure of all states. This was the **federative power** – the power to conduct relations with other states (Locke 1964, p. 383). An exception was the former Soviet Union, where the 1936 Constitution was amended after the United Nations was created to give individual Union republics the right to conduct direct relations with other states. This enabled Moscow, through branch 'foreign offices' in Bielorussia (now Belarus) and the Ukraine, to have three votes in the UN instead of one, for there is no recorded instance of either state voting independently of the Union as a whole as long as it lasted. The federative power never aroused much interest in other theorists, who were very reluctant to apply it to the actual study of states. It appeared that the federative power, such as it was, was exercised either by the executive, or, worse, by the army. However, the question of the distribution of powers did arise, and was of particular importance when a number of states joined together to form a larger union. The simplest form is what we may term a *league* of states, each retaining the full power to act but joining together to create institutions for specific purposes. This was the position of the American colonies under the Association (1774) or of the European Economic Community (EEC) when first established in 1957.

A closer union, in which a range of powers are given to a central government, but most powers remain with the constituent states, is a *confederation*, such as Switzerland before 1848 or the United States under the Articles of Confederation (1777). In practice, however, many people regard Switzerland today as a **federal system** or *federation*, along with Australia, Canada, India, Malaysia, etc.

The situation is enormously complicated by the fact that for some purposes the term 'federal' has come to mean exactly the opposite in Britain and the United States from what it does in Continental Europe. In France 'federation' means *decentralised* government; in the 'Anglo-Saxon' terminology it means *centralised*. The problem arises from the fact that in *The Federalist Papers* (1987) Alexander Hamilton chose to use the term 'federal' to refer to the new central government he was advocating for the United States.

The problem that the framers of the American Constitution sought to solve was how to maintain representative democracy over a vast area divided into at least thirteen different states surrounded by potentially hostile powers. They came up with the concept of the division of powers which is characteristic of the Constitutions of all true federal states. In a federal system, powers are divided between a central ('federal') government and a number of regional ('state') governments, each of which has the full authority to act within its own boundaries in all matters assigned to it (Wheare 1963; Duchacek 1970). There are therefore four categories of powers assigned under the US Constitution: *enumerated*, clearly stated to be assigned to the federal government (the power to coin money); *concurrent*, available both to the states and the federal government (the power to tax); *reserved*, allowed to the states but denied to the federal government (administration of criminal justice); and *denied*, permitted neither to the federal government nor to state governments (imprisonment without trial). In the US system the presumption is that any unspecified powers belong 'to the States respectively, or to the People', a phrase whose guileless simplicity has caused a surprisingly large amount of trouble.

The history of independent states in the nineteenth century was one of constant struggles to define their identity. In these struggles the major factor was the struggle between centre and the periphery of the newly emergent states, as the centre sought to extend its control over the periphery and the peripheral provinces sought autonomy or even independence. This struggle continues today. Though Belgium is in some respects an exception, it is still probably true that all true federal governments have been created by the unification of separate states and none has ever been created by the *devolution* of powers from a central government. The Russian Soviet Federated Socialist Republic (RSFSR) formed in 1918 was not a true federal state; 'Russia's "federalism" was essentially administrative and formal, with its constituent parts lacking constitutionally protected autonomous powers' (Lapidus 1995, p. 85). Unlike the Soviet Union, in which it was merged in 1922, it was not created by a formal federation treaty, and since 1991 the new Russian Federation has not allowed any of its components to go their separate ways.

Yugoslavia's federal structure was initially imposed at the end of the Second World War by Marshal Josip Tito. It was subject at all levels to control by the Communist Party operating under the principle of 'democratic centralism'. It was then transformed by

Case Study: Fischer Predicts EU Will Become Federation

The European Union is set to develop into a federation of nation states, according to Joschka Fischer, Germany's foreign minister. 'I would dare to prophesy that things will go this way. Certainly, not without crises or problems, but the pressure is in that direction,' the Green party member predicted. Mr Fischer said such a federation seemed the only effective way to handle a European Union with up to 27 member states once its expected enlargement got under way from 2004.

He said in an interview with the Financial Times: 'We have three possibilities – intergovernmentalism; federalism; or a federation of nation states. In the light of experience, it would seem advisable to seek the third option as our next step even if the second has my full sympathy.'

He cited November's speech by Tony Blair in Warsaw – in which the prime minister put forward a model in which national legislatures would provide delegates to a future second chamber of the European parliament – as a decisive contribution to the debate on Europe's future.

'Irrespective of my agreeing with all of it, for a British prime minister, he made the most important speech since Churchill's landmark speech on Europe' in Zurich in 1946, said Mr Fischer, referring to Sir Winston's call for a united states of Europe.

Mr Fischer's comments come a year after his landmark speech at Berlin's Humboldt university setting out a vision for the future of Europe.

He said on Wednesday: 'I'm a convinced believer in the federal state. But visiting Westminster, I understood for the first time Britain's resistance above all to a transfer of the sovereignty of the House of Commons.

'As I see Britain as an essential part of Europe and the EU, my question was: how should an integrated Europe be constituted, so that even England could cross this bridge? Or France, where nation cannot be divided from state?'

Mr Fischer's thinking has developed in the light of reaction to his speech, especially with regard to the role of the Council of Ministers in the balance of power with the Parliament and the Commission.

A year ago, he put forward alternatives for an executive – developing the Council into a fully-fledged European government or expanding the Commission, including direct election of a president. Today, he is convinced the former is the only answer.

'The Council must become the executive, with the Commission, and give up its legislative responsibilities to the European parliament. Otherwise we will slide back into intergovernmentalism and have the problem that, in a union of 25 or 27 members, stagnation or negotiating difficulties will dominate.'

Source: *Financial Times* (FT.com), 16 May 2001

the 1974 Constitution designed by Edvard Kardelj into a unique 'system of delegation' which at one and the same time turned not only the six constituent republics (Slovenia, Croatia, Serbia, Montenegro, Bosnia and Hercegovina, and Macedonia) but also two autonomous areas within Serbia (Kosovo and Vojvodina) into eight proto-states with their own presidencies and parliaments, enhanced the rivalries between them and atomised the federal government by replacing it with a collective presidency and a parliament almost destitute of powers. Once Communist Party control had also been lost, this unusual arrangement simply disintegrated (Dyker and Vejvoda 1996, pp. 16–17). It too, however, was not a true federal system.

Constitutional courts

The Americans also adopted the concept of a discrete **judicial power** originally hailed by Montesquieu as characteristic of Britain (Montesquieu 1966). It is fair to say that when Montesquieu visited Britain in 1739, by contemporary standards the British judiciary was indeed unusually independent. The 1787 Constitution of the United States, therefore, speaks of three powers: the legislative, executive and judicial. The judicial power has been transplanted into modern terminology by Almond under the functional name of rule-adjudication, and this reminds us that in two respects the United States is an exception. In most states, the judiciary is part of the executive branch of government, even where the belief exists that there is an abstract entity called law existing independently of the power of government. And under the US system of '**dual federalism**' (McKay 1997, pp. 69–70) federal and state governments have dual sovereignty and there are separate and overlapping judicial systems of federal and state courts. Each of the fifty states has a separate constitution, its own courts and its own system of local government.

Changes in the Federal Constitution require the approval of two-thirds of both houses of Congress as well as three-fourths of the states. Since 1796, however, it has been taken as read that the federal Supreme Court and Circuit Courts have the power to declare state law unconstitutional as repugnant to the Constitution of the United States as a whole, and, following the precedent set by *Marbury* v. *Madison* (1803), the Supreme Court subsequently successfully asserted that it could also declare federal law invalid. In other federal systems, such as those of Australia and Canada, the doctrine of parliamentary sovereignty (see below) leaves much less room for judicial interpretation. Understandably under the American system many of the key decisions have been concerned with the distribution of economic powers, which were matters which were not clearly spelt out in the Constitution (see Peterson 1995).

There are three distinctive features of the role of the United States Supreme Court as interpreter of the Constitution:

1. The Court is an ordinary court with original jurisdiction in a few specified matters and appellate jurisdiction (acts as a court of appeal) in all other matters. It is not a special administrative court whose sole task is to interpret the Constitution.
2. It does not give advisory judgments or opinions on hypothetical cases. Hence if no appropriate case comes before it, it is unable to rule on the constitutionality of laws. Hence they remain constitutional.
3. For most of its existence the Court has operated under the doctrine of 'judicial self-restraint'. Only in the most unusual cases has the Court questioned the constitutionality of a law and it has frequently shown great skill in avoiding having to do so.

The German system of **collaborative federalism** is radically different from the American. The sixteen *Länder* do not have separate constitutions. Under the 1949 Basic Law a special Constitutional Court interprets the Basic Law and rules on the validity of legislation. Constitutional changes require the agreement of the Bundesrat, the upper house of the federal legislature. The powers of the federal and *Land* governments are not distinct but shared: it is the responsibility of the sixteen *Länder* to enforce federal law under the principle of *subsidiarity*. Hence the federal government passes 'framework laws' which are developed and enforced by the *Land* governments. As in the United States, federal and *Land* governments have concurrent powers in a number of areas, e.g. transport, and the

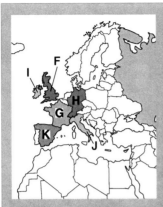

The European Union

THE UNITED KINGDOM

Official name: The United Kingdom of Great Britain and Northern Ireland
Aka: UK; Great Britain; Britain; England (incorrectly)
Type of government: Constitutional parliamentary monarchy with some regional devolution of power
Capital: London
Area: 244,100 sq km
Population (2000): 59,000,000
GNP per capita (2000): $21,400 (PPP $20,640)

Evolution of government: In England medieval assembly began to meet c. 1260; merged with Parliaments of Scotland (1707) and Ireland (1801). Emergence of representative government after Civil War and 'Glorious Revolution' of 1688 (Chapter 11); evolved into liberal democracy after extension of the franchise 1832, 1867, 1884 but votes for women conceded only after struggle 1918. Leading colonial power despite loss of American colonies in 1783 (see USA); after independence for India (q.v.) in 1947 systematic decolonisation followed. Welfare state introduced after 1945 under influence of Labour Party backed by unusually strong trade union movement. Globalisation's impact evident in uncritical acceptance of US influence and belief in 'special relationship'. City of London however remains a major centre of finance capital and Thatcher government (1979–90) pioneered deregulation, privatisation and economic 'liberalisation' (Chapter 5).

Main features of government: Constitution uncodified (Chapter 1). Single-ballot single-member electoral system (Chapter 7) gives party system in which two dominant parties have shared power (Chapter 6) for more than two centuries. Unarmed civilian police introduced 1829 (Chapter 10). Civil service introduced 1850s widely admired and copied but for ideological reasons (Chapter 4) undermined and made less accountable by transfer of power to agencies in 1980s. Strongly centralised decision-making system created in two World Wars modified by devolution of powers to Scotland and Wales in 1997 (Chapter 8). Parliament an arena. No separate system of administrative courts.

federal government uses equalisation grants to iron out regional differences. But unlike the United States, Germany does not have separate laws and judicial systems for each *Land*. There is a unified judicial system, in which the higher courts and judges are federal and the lower courts and judges are *Land*-based, and the civil service is organised on similar lines.

France too has a special body charged with interpreting the Constitution, the Constitutional Council (Conseil Constitutionel). Under the 1958 Constitution either the president, the prime minister, the president of the National Assembly or the president of the Senate may request an opinion from the Council on the constitutionality of an

FRANCE

Official name: The French Republic
Type of government: Unitary semi-presidential republic
Capital: Paris
Area: 544,000 sq km
Population (2000): 59,000,000
GNP per capita (2000): $24,940 (PPP $22,320)

Evolution of government: Medieval assembly disunited and ceased to meet in early seventeenth century. Financial crisis of government led to summoning in 1789 and beginning of French Revolution, type example of a 'great social revolution' (Chapter 11). Imperial rule under Napoleon I (1804–14) marked by militarism (Chapter 10) which paved the way for imperial expansion in later nineteenth century. Parliamentary republic emerged as compromise in 1875 but discredited in 1930s by scandal and defeated by Germany in 1940 when a dictatorship was established (1940–44). The Republic was restored in 1944 but following a crisis of decolonisation in Algeria and the revolt of the army in 1958 (Chapter 10) General de Gaulle was recalled to power and Fifth Republic established. Major centre of opposition to globalisation in the form of US ('Anglo-Saxon') influence; similarly resisted economic liberalisation throughout the 1990s.

Main features of government: Constitutional Council has only limited powers to check constitutionality of laws (Chapter 2). Semi-presidentialism: president has reserved sphere in defence and foreign affairs; prime minister and Cabinet responsible for day-to-day administration (Chapter 2). Unitary government in which continuity of policy maintained before 1958 through powerful and well-trained civil service (Chapter 8) which transcends ideology (Chapter 4). Traditional multi-party system effectively modified 1958 by introduction of single-member second-ballot system (Chapter 7) for National Assembly, which lost most of its power to challenge governments. A separate system of administrative courts handles grievances.

item of legislation. They must do so within a fixed period of time after its approval. If they do not do so, or there is no decision, the law is constitutional, whether it appears to be or not, and there is no further appeal. In this way in 1962 General de Gaulle was able to call a referendum on extending the powers of the president, without first getting the approval of parliament.

Spain's Constitutional Court was established by the 1978 Constitution. Like the German one, it is *concentrated*, dealing exclusively with the interpretation of the Constitution, and *abstract*, in that, unlike the Supreme Court of the United States, it does give advisory judgments. Initially it could be asked for a decision before the event (*a priori*), but in 1985 this possibility was abolished except for the special case of international treaties, since it resulted in delays which were assiduously exploited by the opposition to hold up legislation. A large number of authorities, including lower courts, have the power to refer cases to the Court but some 90 per cent of its work comes from individuals

GERMANY

Official name: The German Federal Republic
Type of government: Federal parliamentary republic
Capital: Berlin
Area: 357,000 sq km
Population (2000): 82,200,000
GNP per capita (2000): $25,850 (PPP $20,810)

Evolution of government: The multitude of German states in existence before 1789 were partially consolidated by Napoleon and linked in a customs union after 1815. The 39 remaining states were eventually incorporated in 1871 in a German Empire led by Prussia. The Weimar Republic created in 1918 was displaced in 1933 by a Fascist dictatorship led by Adolf Hitler, which is often taken to be a type example of totalitarianism (Chapter 2). Hitler led Germany to a disastrous defeat at the hands of the United Nations in 1945. Under the influence of the Cold War two German states emerged, the German Federal Republic in the West and the German Democratic Republic in the East. They were re-unified by general consent with the agreement of the Soviet Union after the fall of the Berlin Wall in 1989 (Chapter 11).

Main features of government: The Basic Law of 1949 continues as the constitution of the re-united Germany. It was designed to limit the powers of central government. System of 'collaborative federalism' (Chapter 2) in which central government makes framework laws implemented by state (*Land*) governments under principle of 'subsidiarity'. Chancellor (prime minister) chosen by popular vote independently of parliamentary majority and can only be overthrown by 'constructive vote of no-confidence' (Chapter 2); president has largely ceremonial role. 'Mixed' proportional electoral system for lower house, the Bundestag (Chapter 7), introduced under Basic Law 1949. Elements of consociationalism and neocorporatist features (Chapter 6) in economic policy-making have limited social conflict.

who have exhausted all other remedies. The twelve judges are chosen by the Congress (four), the Senate (four), the Cabinet (two) and the judiciary (two).

The problem with giving judges the power to decide on the constitutionality of legislation is that it is hard to justify in terms of democratic theory, particularly where (as in the US case) they are appointed and not elected. The problem is compounded when the judgment is one which the majority of voters do not support. In 1985 the Spanish Court, on the casting vote of its president, gave a conditional approval to a 1983 law permitting abortion in the first twelve weeks of pregancy. Following German experience, the law was very limited in its effect and carefully drafted with a view to resisting the challenge which came when the opposition Alianza Popular (AP) referred it to the Court. Hence though it did uphold the constitutionality of the measure, the Court laid down conditions which were to be followed, thus venturing into areas which the minority argued were properly the province of the legislature (Barreiro 1999).

Official name: Ireland ('Eire', though often used in the UK, is simply the Irish for Ireland and 'Republic of Ireland' is incorrect)
Type of government: Unitary parliamentary republic
Capital: Dublin
Area: 70,280 sq km
Population (2000): 3,750,000
GNP per capita (2000): $18,340 (PPP $18,340)

Evolution of government: As part of the UK after 1801 developed movement for Home Rule in later nineteenth century. Failure to grant this led to abortive revolt in 1916 (the 'Easter Rising'); transformed into fully developed movement for secession following its suppression. In 1918 representatives elected seceded from Westminster Parliament and established their own (Dáil Eireann). In 1922 the Anglo-Irish Treaty granted 'Dominion status' (full internal self-government) to 26 of the 32 counties, the remainder remaining part of the UK. In the Civil War that followed the republicans were defeated but came to power with an electoral mandate in 1932 and their 1937 Constitution limited residual British influence. In 1949 Ireland was declared a Republic.

Main features of government: Directly elected presidency with largely ceremonial powers. Parliamentary government; executive power with Cabinet appointed by prime minister (Taoiseach) elected by Dáil. Despite highly proportional electoral system (STV – Chapter 7) has evolved system dominated by two main parties.

ITALY

Official name: The Italian Republic
Type of government: Unitary parliamentary republic with limited regional devolution
Capital: Rome
Area: 310,000 sq km
Population (2000): 57,500,000
GNP per capita (2000): $20,250 (PPP $20,200)

Evolution of government: Italy was unified between 1860 and 1870 under the House of Savoy as a constitutional monarchy. The Piedmontese Constitution could not be amended and was increasingly disregarded. After the First World War discontent with government paved the way for the rise of Benito Mussolini who became prime minister in 1922. Mussolini used his party militia to establish an authoritarian (and would-be totalitarian) regime (Chapter 3) which lasted until 1942. Discredited by its association with the dictatorship, the monarchy was deposed in a referendum and Republic established (1946).

Main features of government: From 1946 on a long period of dominance by the Christian Democrats (DC) supported by Cold War polarisation and funds from the USA (Chapter 6). Extreme multipartism sustained by Imperiali largest-remainder system of proportional representation, replaced in 1990s by a less-proportional mixed system (Chapter 7). One-party dominance led to prevalence of clientelism and corruption (Chapter 9).

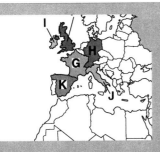

SPAIN

Official name: Kingdom of Spain
Type of government: Constitutional parliamentary
monarchy with substantial regional devolution
Capital: Madrid
Area: 505,000 sq km
Population (2000): 40,200,000
GNP per capita (2000): $14,080 (PPP $16,060)

Evolution of government: Absolute monarchy until invasion by Napoleon in 1807; influence of French Revolution brought Liberal revolt against restored government in 1820 and institution of representative government. Carlist civil wars of early nineteenth century however were accompanied by rise of militarism (Chapter 10), and influence of anarchism in late nineteenth century brought ideological polarisation (Chapter 4). In 1931 the king left the country and a Republic was proclaimed but in 1936 the armed forces revolted and after a bitter Civil War (1936–39) General Francisco Franco established a dictatorship. On his death in 1975 the monarchy was restored and personalist dictatorship gave way to liberal parliamentary democracy.

Main features of government: Parliamentary government. Elections to lower house (Cortés) by list system on provincial basis (Chapter 7). Considerable degree of autonomy since 1978 for 17 self-governing regions, notably two problem areas of the former Republic: Catalonia (Catalunya) and the Basque provinces (Euzkadi).

Developmental Typologies

Once the bases of classification have been clarified it should be easier to see how political systems change over time. *Developmental typologies* are those that take the time dimension into consideration (see Table 2.4).

The oldest of these typologies was that of Aristotle, as modified by the historian Polybius, who saw governments as following an endless chain of evolution: from monarchy, to aristocracy, to democracy, and then by way of tyranny, back to monarchy.

Marx's typology is one of economic systems, but each has a corresponding political order. He argues that human society will ultimately go through four stages. It began with an era of 'primitive accumulation', in which people start to garner resources from the world around them. With the rise of powerful families, powerful hereditary rulers use force to compel the peasantry to work for them and so concentrate land and wealth in their own hands. This 'feudal' society is organised in a pyramid of power based on landownership. With the rise of commerce and industry, economic power passes into the hands of those who own capital, the bourgeoisie. In the great bourgeois revolutions, the English and the French, they seized political power from the decaying aristocracies and created a new and much more powerful form of state based on their ability to expropriate and then to control the surplus labour of the industrial workers. Finally, in the last

Table 2.4 Developmental typologies of political systems

Aristotle/Polybius (c. 146 BC)	Marx and Engels (1962 [1848])	Almond and Powell (1966)
Monarchy Aristocracy Democracy Tyranny Monarchy etc.	Primitive accumulation Feudal Bourgeois Socialist	Patriarchal/patrimonial Feudal Premobilised modern Mobilised modern Democratic
	Primitive accumulation Oriental mode of production ???	Patriarchal/patrimonial Historical bureaucratic Premobilised modern Mobilised modern Authoritarian

stage, the industrial workers will then in turn rise in revolt, overthrow the rule of the bourgeoisie, establish the dictatorship of the proletariat, and build a socialist society.

Almond and Powell (1966, 1996) proposed a developmental model of politics, and their structural-functional analysis continues to be employed to structure their view of comparative politics (Almond *et al.* 2000). Their developmental model rests in the first instance on the concept not of power but of authority, and follows the distinction made by Weber between patriarchal, patrimonial and feudal authority (Weber 1965, p. 346).

For feminists, **patriarchy** is a form of rule characterised by male dominance and the subordination of women. The purpose of the state is to maintain this subordination, without which men cannot control marriage and with it the assurance that their property will be transmitted to male heirs. As Engels noted in the nineteenth century, it was not a universal characteristic of primitive societies, some of which were matriarchal and some of which lacked established hierarchies. For Weber, however, patriarchal authority means simply authority vested solely in the representative of the lineage and patrimonial authority depends on the possession of goods, or lands having value. Feudal authority involves a bargain between the holders of each of these concepts for a series of reciprocal obligations of service and protection. In other words the representative of the lineage that holds centralised authority holds power only by agreement with other people who have a right to authority within their own limited areas.

Out of the patrimonial states there has been developed, in turn, what has been called the *historical bureaucratic state*. This is Eisenstadt's (1963, p. 4) term for a state in which the system of government has become so routinised that, within limits, it operates regardless of the competence of the nominal ruler. Every so often, human biology being what it is, either the inheritance fails or there is a 'time of troubles' when there are many contenders for the throne. But the bureaucratic structure by that time is such that decisions continue to be made, the system continues to work, the field boundaries are still delimited, the harvest is still gathered, a tenth is dished out to the priests, and a pittance is dished out to the poor (if they are lucky). And it is out of this historical bureaucratic system that modern states have derived.

Almond and Powell provide a special category for the *secularised city states*. These are very small states such as Liechtenstein, San Marino or Monaco, but probably not

Andorra or Luxembourg, because they are too large, or the more recently independent island states such as St Vincent or St Kitts in the Caribbean, or Kiribati, Nauru or Tuvalu in the Pacific. Secularisation refers simply to the fact that the religious element has, in modern times, been taken out of their government, which presumably excludes the Vatican City State, but it is very hard to see why.

It will be noticed that Almond and Powell do not, as is done here, stress the duality of the origins of government. They accept the fact of government, and with it, implicitly, the assumption that it is beneficial to society. But there are always two elements in conflict in government: government and the people, the claim to power and its acceptance, or reward and punishment. Government is interaction, not action. From this point onwards, moreover, they view development as a process of *political mobilisation*: that is, the bringing of more and more people into the political life of the community. Certainly the mobilisation of individuals does mean at the same time taking account of their interests. To bring them into the political system, they have to be getting something out of it if they are going to be required to continue to put something in to it. It is, of course, possible to find, even today, systems in which large sectors of the population are not incorporated in the structure, and so a category is provided for pre-mobilised modern systems.

Finally, they conclude with two categories of mobilised systems, in which mass participation is both required and encouraged, and so is qualitatively different. One is the democratic state in which the desire of the people to produce inputs is fully accepted and channelled, even when it is a question of demands rather than supports. The other is the authoritarian system, where the support is wanted but demands are not.

To summarise, therefore, Almond and Powell see the evolution of modern states as following a historical path from the patriarchal-patrimonial level, through the feudal states and the historical bureaucratic states, to the pre-mobilised modern states – modern, that is, in that they still exist in today's world, but are not mobilised in the sense that the mobilised modern state requires or permits. And in these mobilised modern states, the common factor is that people participate widely in politics, some because they want to do so, some because they are made to do so, and some for both reasons.

Executive and legislature

For the present writer the possibilities are somewhat more complex (see Table 2.5). The categorisation has two distinctive features. First of all, the dualism which Almond and Powell discern as coming into evolution of states at the division between the authoritarian and democratic states of today is here seen as running throughout the whole

Table 2.5 Varieties of government

Primitive	Agrarian	Imperial	Assembly	Apparat
Tribe	Kingdom	Empire	Presidential	Party
	Theocracy	Tyranny	Caesarism	Praetorian
Band	Horde	Feudal	Federal	
	City	Anarchy	Parliament	

course of human history. Indeed, this conflict, natural because politics is institution-alised conflict, provides the basic dynamic for all experimentation with political forms. People in Western Europe or the United States may have forgotten or become habitu-ated to the essentially violent and self-imposed way in which their governments first emerged. But the facts are still fundamental to their understanding of how they work today. All governments exercise just as much power as they believe they can get away with. It is in the extension or, conversely, in the limitation of these powers that all modern governments have been shaped. Governments who try to mobilise their peoples in order to get them to work harder and pay their taxes soon find that the people will demand a greater say in government in return.

Secondly, precisely because this dynamic is continuous and fundamental, it is con-sistent with the observation that the process of political change ebbs and flows. It does not follow a cycle of change from one form of government to another, returning to the beginning, as Plato and later Polybius suggested (Calvert 1970a, pp. 40, 43–4). Nor, as the Victorians (including Marx) would have it, is there an irresistible progress in the sense that political systems evolve along a single line towards a predictable future state. Of course, human beings learn by experience, but even with books to aid them, mem-ories grow cold and old men die. Hence the revolutions in Eastern Europe in 1989 should have come as a surprise to no one, least of all to those who were most surprised by them.

All modern states derive their basic political structures from a period of violent dis-ruption and reconstitution. Such a period of disruption may either take the form of an independence struggle, international war or revolution. The phenomenon of revolution is covered in detail in Chapter 11. Here the term is used in the usual sense to refer to political and social changes accompanied by violence, such as people associate particu-larly with England, the United States, France and Russia (Brinton 1952), and in modern times with countries as diverse as Mexico, Turkey, China, Egypt (Leiden and Schmitt 1968), Cuba, Iran and Nicaragua. In all of these instances an important feature of these changes has been the attempt to claim power by people claiming to act directly on behalf of the masses, and in the majority of cases this claim has momentarily led to direct rule by a convention (Verney 1961; see also Brogan and Verney 1963), a special type of **assembly** claiming complete control over every aspect of political and social life.

Convention theory

Most liberal democracies today are of one of two types: the parliamentary or the pres-idential system. But a developmental perspective reminds us that both are historical variants of what Verney called the 'convention theory' state (Verney 1961, pp. 3, 57). By **convention theory** Verney means a rare and short-lived, but historically very significant form of government, in which all conversion functions are exercised by a represent-ative assembly (a 'convention', after the French Revolutionary Convention). This form of government has existed historically after certain major social revolutions, e.g. England 1649–51, United States 1777–89, France 1793–95, Russia 1917–18 ('all power to the Soviets'). However, it has not done so for long and in practice has invariably been modified. At the time of the French Revolution, all power was vested in the National Convention (assembly), and all other centres of authority were for a time destroyed, neutralised, or subordinated. The chairman of the Convention was its servant, not its master. The execution of its policies was entrusted to committees created for that purpose. Thoughout its existence, including the period of the Terror (1793–94), the notorious Committee for Public Safety was re-elected monthly. In the parallel instance in England under the Commonwealth (1649–53), Parliament did not delegate even the ceremonial function of receiving ambassadors. Each was brought before the entire House to be formally introduced, and to bow and be bowed to. Remnants of these and similar practices were still embedded in the Constitutions of communist states, notably those of the USSR (1936), China (1949) and Cuba (1975). In practice, even in those instances, the system was substantially modified in certain well-defined ways.

A second characteristic of convention theory government is a unifying political culture which seeks to make equal that which is not already equal. The consequence, therefore, is a conflict between centre and periphery, and more particularly a conflict between two principles – the principle of *representation*, which favours having a big assembly so that representatives are as close to their constituency as possible, and the principle of *efficiency*, which favours small groups for taking day-to-day decisions. In practical terms this means that under the pressure of business the assembly sits for longer and longer hours, and in the end many of the representatives are tempted to hand the burden of work over to someone else. And popular pressure for them to do so may by then be very great, particularly where, as in the French case, the political system is threatened by attack and a speedy response is called for.

If an assembly is to survive for a long time as an effective and working instrument, it must not only develop a system of committees, it must delegate effective power to them. Such a development is most strikingly illustrated by the United States Congress. However, in the United States the creation of a separate executive has created a **presidential system**. Where, on the other hand, one of the committees has come to assume the executive power while remaining within the assembly, as in Britain, the result is a **parliamentary system**. Both represent compromises by which a government, limited in its powers of decision, is in return guaranteed the right to extract a sufficient quantity of power resources from the society it governs. There are important differences, however, in the terms of the two compromises (see Table 2.6).

Parliamentary systems

In Britain, almost uniquely, the parliamentary system was not embodied in a single written Constitution. Hence what became the prototype statement of the rules of the parliamentary system for most of the rest of the world was the Belgian Constitution of 1831, which was specifically modelled on British practice. Present-day examples of working parliamentary systems include not only Britain and Belgium, but also Australia, Canada, India, Israel, Malaysia, the Netherlands, Sri Lanka, Germany and Japan. There is an independent origin for the parliamentary systems of the Nordic countries in Sweden in the eighteenth century (Verney 1961, p. 18; cf. Hawgood 1939, pp. 145–6); and much earlier than that for the Althing of Iceland and the House of Keys in the Isle of Man. However, despite promising beginnings parliamentarism failed to develop in Poland (as, today, in the European Community) because of the veto each of its individual members could exercise.

In a parliamentary system the functions of rule-application, nominally derived from a *head of state*, are in practice vested in a committee of the assembly, consisting of ministers appointed by the head of state, but responsible to the assembly for their political actions. In countries such as Britain or the Netherlands, where the head of state is a

Table 2.6 Convention theory, parliamentary and presidential systems

Attribute	Convention	Parliamentary	Presidential
Head of state	Chairman	Monarch or president	President
Head of government	Chairman	Prime minister	President
Executive	Committee elected by assembly	Appointed by prime minister from assembly	Secretaries of president
Executive members of assembly?	Yes	Yes	No
Executive can dissolve assembly?	Yes	Yes	No
Fixed term for executive?	No	No	Yes
Assembly checks executive?	Yes	Sometimes	No
Focus of power	Assembly	Parliament	None
Assembly controls own business?	Yes	No	Yes

Source: after Verney 1961

hereditary monarch, his or her functions are ceremonial only. In a state with an elected head, such as Iceland, Ireland or Italy, the president (as s/he is rather confusingly called), may have rather more power, though once elected s/he is expected to stand above the political struggle. And in most states, exceptions being Japan and Sweden, the head of state has to sign documents giving effect to laws, and retains in this, and the choice of a first or prime minister, reserve powers which may be activated by some unexpected crisis.

The prime minister, as *head of government*, chooses the executive committee, or ministry (Weller 1985). This must normally consist of elected members of the assembly. This is not the case in the Netherlands, Luxembourg and Norway and the way in which they are chosen varies a great deal. In Israel the prime minister is separately elected by popular vote; in Germany each party must present its chancellor-candidate at elections; in Britain the sovereign by custom has to call first on the leader of the largest party to form a government; in Italy, with frequently changing coalitions the norm, presidents have played an active role in forming governments, one of the few major prerogatives they enjoy. However, in all cases the government can only survive as long as it can command a majority in the assembly, though in Germany it can only be overthrown by a 'constructive vote of no-confidence' naming someone who is prepared to take on the job of chancellor. This device has only been used successfully once (Larres and Panayi 1996, pp. 74–5).

It is the assembly which normally elects the head of state, where this office is not vested in a hereditary monarch. Five countries that are exceptions are Austria, Finland, France, Iceland and Ireland. There the presidents are directly elected by the people, and in the case of Finland (as in semi-presidentialist France) the president has an important

Table 2.7 Leagues, confederal and federal states

LEAGUE/ASSOCIATION	
European Union 1993	United Arab Emirates 1971

CONFEDERAL STATE	
Switzerland 1291/1849	

FEDERAL STATES	
Parliamentary	Presidential
Canada 1867	United States 1787
Australia 1900	Mexico 1824
Austria 1919	Argentina 1853
India 1947	Brazil 1889
Germany (1871) 1949	Yugoslavia 1945
Malaysia 1957	Micronesia 1990
Nigeria 1963	
Russian Federation 1991	

independent sphere of authority in foreign affairs. However, even there, all power has in practice to be exercised through parliament, the collective entity formed by the head of state, the ministry and the assembly.

The fact that all power decisions pass through parliament has been confused in the past with the idea that power rests in it, or even, more misleadingly still, in the assembly itself. But like any other organisation, a parliament's effective power is limited, sometimes dramatically so, by the constraints of time and space. Hence the powers of the ministry, which is only indirectly responsible to the electorate, may well not be effectively checked by the assembly either.

Presidential systems

The other favoured compromise is the presidential system. This differs fundamentally. The prototype is the 1787 Constitution of the United States. But not only has this been amended substantially over time (Neustadt 1964), as a model it has only been taken up throughout the world since 1946 and in a form which differs substantially from the original intentions of the framers of the American Constitution.

It was perhaps natural that in the first three decades of the nineteenth century, presidential systems should have been adopted by most of the newly independent states of the Americas, with the exception of part of Haiti and of Brazil, which remained a parliamentary monarchy until 1889 (Needler 1963). Only one other presidential state dates from this period: Liberia, a colony for freed American slaves, independent in 1847. After that there was a long gap, until the rising power of the United States created Hawaii (1892; annexed by the United States 1898) and Cuba (1901).

It was only after 1946 when the Philippines, under American tutelage from 1898 onwards, became independent, that the presidential system came to sweep across the rest of the Third World, beginning with the Middle East and North Africa, and spreading throughout Africa south of the Sahara in the wake of the dissolution of the British, French and Portuguese colonial empires after 1960. So powerful was the urge to imitate it that even established parliamentary systems such as those of Pakistan and Sri Lanka were modified in the direction of presidentialism. But few of the systems that have resulted are true presidential systems in the constitutional sense.

In the prototype presidential system the assembly remains separate and distinct from the executive. Rule-making remains the function of the assembly; rule-application is entrusted to one person, the president, elected directly for a limited term, who appoints officials to assist him, which though they are also commonly called a cabinet, are not a committee of the assembly, and are not politically responsible to it. And in the United States the potential conflict of function between president and legislature is met by a variety of devices, but most distinctively by the creation of an independent system of rule-adjudication with power to rule on the constitutionality of specific actions of either of the other two branches of government.

Since there is no focus of power, this system is dynamically unstable, and its invariable tendency has been for the president to destroy the compromise by assuming, often with the aid of force, control over all functions of government. To be a true presidential state, therefore, three conditions have all to be observed.

1. The president must be *elected by the people* according to agreed rules generally regarded as fair. The president must not be a hereditary ruler, be self-appointed, come to power by a military coup, or be nominated by the chiefs of a military regime.

2. He or she must be *elected for a definite term*. There is some difference between being elected for a series of definite terms and being in power indefinitely, but in practice one tends to lead to the other. Consequently constitutional provisions limiting presidential terms are normal, though they are often abused, if necessary by the systematic rewriting of constitutional provisions, as with the Somozas in Nicaragua (Diedrich 1982). Assumption of the presidential office for life invites the corollary that the shorter the life, the shorter the term. In practice, of the eight presidents of Haiti who have been elected for 'life', only Dr François Duvalier actually died in office; his predecessors and his successor were deposed. 'Papa Doc' did realise this might happen and one of the ways in which he ingeniously circumvented the restrictions on re-election was to hold municipal elections in 1961. At the top of each ballot paper was the president's name, and after the votes were counted Haitians were told that they had unwittingly given him an overwhelming vote of confidence (Rotberg 1971, p. 232).

3. The president *must not be able to dissolve the assembly* (or suspend its powers) during its fixed term of office. In practice this is often done, as in Uruguay in 1973, by the leaders of military or military-backed regimes, making use, in most if not all cases, of emergency powers, which will be considered further later (Weinstein 1975, pp. 132–3).

In Switzerland there is a collective presidency in the Council of State, the members of which take it in turns to chair meetings for one year. This example was copied in Uruguay on two occasions, more recently between 1952 and 1967, in a deliberate attempt to weaken presidential power. In principle the sharing of executive as well as legislative functions between parties should be a good thing; however, the case of Bosnia in 1992 showed that the system is particularly vulnerable when rivalries between the parties render decision-making impossible (Silber and Little 1995, pp. 232–3, 239).

Semi-presidentialism

If, in a presidential state, secretaries (see p. 63) become ministers by being given the power to sit and vote in the assembly, they become to an extent responsible to it, and the result is a mixed system which is neither presidential nor truly parliamentary. However, a more recent, and in other respects anomalous example is France. **Semi-presidentialism** is characterised by a dual executive, consisting of an elected president with defined political role and a prime minister and cabinet responsible to the assembly.

Experiments along such lines are not new – among presidential states Chile (1891), Peru (1860) and Cuba (1940) have at different times adopted elements of parliamentarism such as a prime minister and the interpellation of ministers while keeping the executive presidency. Peru, before 1968 and after 1980, is an example which has had a long history (Bourricaud 1970, p. 270).

However, the Constitution of the Fifth Republic in France (1958) did the reverse. It was designed to stabilise the faction parliamentarism of the Fourth Republic by establishing an executive presidency which General de Gaulle would want to occupy (Cerny 1980, p. 32). The Constitution of 1958 was deliberately designed to weaken the powers of the National Assembly as far as possible, while giving the president a substantial area of prerogative power in defence and foreign affairs. In both, the tendency is to make the president one of two foci of power, whereas in the true presidential system there is no focus of power. The president is able to make full use of his or her ability to command attention from the media to set the agenda for government, though in his later years, weakened by terminal illness, President Mitterrand tended rather to react to events (Cole 1997b, pp. 46–7). Moreover the president is able to deal with high-profile matters of international politics while the prime minister retains responsibility for the everyday matters of government – as de Gaulle said, 'the price of milk'. However, the distribution of political power is seldom constant for long. The prime minister not only continues to exercise important powers in concurrence with the president, there are also many functions that the prime minister alone holds (Ardant 1991; Elgie 1993).

The main weakness of the system is the possibility of conflict between the president and the parliamentary majority, especially where (as in France) they are separately elected. In the French case this has already resulted in three periods of 'cohabitation' when the president's party has been opposed by a majority in the Assembly: President François Mitterrand with Jacques Chirac (1986–88) and Edouard Balladur (1993–95), and President Jacques Chirac with premier Lionel Jospin (1997–). These periods have proved to be much less contentious in practice than in theory, since in 1986 President Mitterrand seems to have accepted the convention 'that the leader of the majority party or coalition had the right to be called upon to form a government' (Cole 1997a, p. 41). However, though Mitterrand did withdraw to some extent to a superior position as arbiter above the political battle, it is also true that he continued to intervene from time to time, not only in his reserved domains of defence and foreign affairs, but elsewhere, and not always predictably. One of his most surprising decisions was to dismiss his old rival Michel Rocard in May 1991 and appoint Edith Cresson as France's first woman prime minister. Though she shared the abrasive style of Margaret Thatcher, she lacked her popular mandate and was dismissed in April 1992 (Cole 1997a, p. 49).

Other criticisms of the system have also been made. One is that the direct election of the president instituted in 1962 has made the presidency too responsive to public opinion. Another is that it has made the system too 'leveraged' – a relatively slight move by the president has a considerable effect on the rest of the system so there is a tendency for every matter to be referred right to the top (Wahl and Quermonne 1995). The reduction of the excessively long presidential term from seven to five years should do something to alleviate the latter problem, though at the cost of accentuating the former.

Since the fall of communism in Eastern Europe both Poland (1989) and Russia (1993) have adopted semi-parliamentary systems, though the latter gives the president a much wider range of powers than does the French. In his later years, afflicted by illness, Boris Yeltsin exercised only spasmodic control over government and replaced prime ministers from time to time to create the illusion of activity. To general surprise, the last of these, Vladimir Putin, after heading the Russian punitive campaign against Chechen separatists, was elevated to the presidency when Yeltsin resigned on New Year's Eve 1999. But when the president and premier are unable to agree on a common pro-gramme and the premier has too much independent power to be dismissed, the result can be the complete paralysis of government, as in Slovakia when in 1995–96 the two were not even on speaking terms with one another.

Poland emerged from communist rule in 1989 with the 1952 Constitution still in place (though much amended) and in principle 'unified authority' in the Sejm. The shift in 1990 to direct election of the president gave the new democratically elected leader of Solidarity a separate source of authority to make use of the powers to propose and veto laws and a restricted power to dissolve parliament. The so-called 'Little Constitution' of 1992 (which supplemented rather than replaced the 1952 Constitution) extended the president's powers and established a dual executive. The president was given specific powers in foreign affairs and defence by being designated the 'guardian of the Polish Constitution, the protector of Poland's national sovereignty and security and the integrity of its territory; and the safeguard of its international political and military alliances' (Art. 32[2] cited by Millard 1999, p. 40). Some of those who had previously supported President Walesa's call for a strong presidency, however, became disillusioned by his constant struggles with the fragmented majority in the Sejm. Hence the tendency of the 1997 Constitution was on the contrary to weaken the presidency and strengthen the premiership, while retaining the dual executive and establishing the formal separa-tion of the legislative and executive powers. The presidency lost its primacy in defence and foreign affairs, and the presidential veto was restricted, but President Kwasniewski regained the sole right to appoint the chief of staff and senior commanders of the armed forces and the presidents of the Constitutional Tribunal and the Supreme Court (Millard 1999, p. 46).

The struggle for power

The struggle for power takes place throughout a political system and at a number of levels. The continued working of a liberal democracy depends on some kind of balance being maintained, between executive and legislature, between the chief executive and his/her colleagues, and between the government and the people.

As we have seen in Chapter 1, the key is the balance between executive and legislature. In presidential systems the balance is perhaps easier to maintain when, as happens at regular intervals, the president is elected at the same time as the assembly. Even then, different political parties may, as in the United States between 1981 and 2001 or in Brazil since 1990, be chosen to represent the people in each of the branches of government. In Chile after 1963 the timing of the respective terms was such that political conflict between the branches was actually made worse (Gil 1965, p. 208). Though the Christian Democratic majority in Congress in 1970 properly accepted the verdict of the popular vote and ratified the election of the Marxist President Salvador Allende, he in turn was unable to achieve a popular majority for his proposals for radical reform.

Though there must, if government is to function at all, be a close relationship between the two areas of competence, executive and legislature, summed up in the American phrase 'checks and balances', they must be reciprocal and there must be limits on the president's ability to influence the assembly. This is not as easy as it seems. The executive president is both head of state and head of government, owns no superior, and can – and does – convert the duties of his or her ceremonial role into political power. Speaking on behalf of the government as a whole (particularly in foreign policy or in times of national crisis or disaster), making use of the resources of the media, and in particular being seen visibly associated with concrete evidence of achievement in the form of new roads, airports, dams or military installations, all can be used to generate or to strengthen existing support. And, as Montesquieu observed: 'It is an invariable experience that every man who has power is led to abuse it; he goes on until he finds limits' (Montesquieu 1966, p. 151).

The executive president, unlike the head of government in a parliamentary system, is not limited in the power to recruit and to appoint heads of departments by the need to draw them from the ranks of the assembly. Once appointed, the heads of department are the president's subordinates – his secretaries, literally. They seldom have any independent power-base. If the president's power to choose them is limited to an extent by the need to obtain congressional approval, the power to dismiss them is not, and there is a limit to how long any assembly, however powerful, can go on blocking presidential nominees.

In parliamentary systems, on the other hand, the balance between executive and legislature involves the balance between the chief executive and his/her colleagues. Research into ministerial careers suggests that there is less to choose between the parliamentary and presidential systems than this would suggest. Both are characterised by a very rapid turnover of ministers, some two-thirds of whom hold office for less than a year (Blondel 1985). By reshuffling her Cabinet annually, Mrs Thatcher, prime minister of the United Kingdom 1979–90, was able to achieve an exceptional degree of ascendancy over her colleagues. However, since she had to choose among her colleagues, who each had separate and distinct electoral bases, there came a time when this process brought retribution.

Conversely it has time and again been demonstrated, notably in two World Wars, that in time of crisis the parliamentary system can manage an effective response to the challenge. Nor is there any truth in the suggestion that the parliamentary system is somehow unfitted to manage a programme of economic growth over a long period. In fact, Japan, for forty years the world's most successful state in the economic sense, has managed its economic growth since 1945 through a parliamentary system, and the German system is both parliamentary and federal.

In the Weberian sense, the parliamentary and presidential systems, as described here, therefore, are 'ideal types'. Even in its homeland, the United States, in the age of the 'Imperial Presidency' and in particular under President Richard M. Nixon, there were noticeable deviations from the strict constitutional assumptions of the presidential system. The parliamentary system does not depend on such a rigid set of criteria, and, as the case of the United Kingdom shows, it can evolve within a relatively short period of time. But there must be limits to this process. The president of a republic in a parliamentary system such as France can be given more power. A monarch can be rendered virtually powerless, as occurred in Sweden in 1975 (*Annual Register* 1975, p. 151). Yet such is the complexity of modern political systems that no one could deduce from these facts alone either that the French president or the Swedish Riksdag has become all-powerful. The visible constitutional structures are only a partial guide to the real structure of power and decision-making.

Summary

Liberal democracies are states in which government is limited in its powers by a written constitution, a system of law and/or an independent judiciary, and is responsive to the popular will as expressed through elections.

There are two main forms of government in liberal democracies: parliamentary systems and presidential systems. Both derive from a theoretical model in which power is concentrated in a representative assembly and in the former communist states (and some others) all three forms have been modified by being brought under the control of a ruling party organisation. A substantial number of modern states continue to be under authoritarian rule, either of a traditional ruler or of a military dictator. However, the concept of totalitarianism, though still widely used by politicians and press, has little value.

Some 40 per cent of the world's population live under some form of federal government, a form of liberal democracy characterised by the division of powers between a central government and a number of 'state' governments. These systems emerged from the confederation of a number of smaller units and afford citizens an enhanced ability to participate in politics at more than one level.

Key Concepts

authoritarian, government or state characterised by very limited participation and strong emphasis on the right of the rulers to give orders

collaborative federalism, system in which the powers of federal and state governments are not divided horizontally (as in the USA), but are shared, decisions typically being made at the lowest practicable level according to the principle of subsidiarity

competitive systems, political systems in which a degree of free competition of ideas is permitted, e.g. by competitive elections

consociational democracy, for Lijphart, a political system characterised by strong and long-lasting political cleavages and an elaborate process of negotiation between the elites of the different 'pillars' leading to accommodation and compromise

convention theory, for Verney, a rare form of government in which all conversion functions are exercised by a representative assembly

dual federalism, a federal system characterised by dual sovereignty, in which federal and state governments have separate and distinct constitutions, courts, legislatures and powers

executive power, those persons or bodies whether elected or appointed who are able to make and to enforce binding decisions within the existing structure of rules (laws)

façade democracy, for Finer, a system that is nominally democratic, but in fact oligarchical

federal system, one characterised by the division of powers between a single 'federal' government and a number of 'state' governments

federative power, the power to conduct relations with other states

judicial power, those persons or bodies who have been chosen to decide whether in specific cases rules (laws) have been breached or to resolve disputes about the application of those rules

legislative power, those persons or bodies who are able to make rules (laws) which are authoritative, i.e. can in principle be enforced

liberal democracy, states in which government is limited in its powers by a written constitution, a system of law and/or an independent judiciary, and is responsive to the popular will as expressed through elections

mixed constitution, for Aristotle, a political system that combines elements of monarchy, aristocracy and democracy

non-competitive systems, systems where free electoral choice either is not allowed or does not exist in practice

parliamentary system, a governmental system characterised by the unification of powers, the executive power being vested in a committee of the legislative assembly and so responsible to the assembly

participation, the extent to which citizens take part in politics

patriarchy, for feminists, a form of rule characterised by male dominance and the subordination of women

pluralism, for Dahl, a political system characterised by the free interaction of many competing interest groups in the making of policy; by extension, the belief that this is a desirable state of affairs

presidential system, a governmental system characterised by the separation of powers, the executive power being vested in a president and the legislative power in a separate assembly

oligarchy, for Aristotle, government by the few; systems in which a closed group has a virtual monopoly of political power; generic term of abuse applied to traditional landed elites in Latin America

semi-presidentialism, system in which power is shared between a directly elected president with a reserved sphere of power in defence and foreign affairs and a prime minister and cabinet accountable to the assembly

separation of powers, the belief, popularised by Montesquieu, that the executive, legislature and judiciary should be separate and able to act independently in their own sphere of responsibility

'totalitarian', a term coined by Mussolini to designate a state in which the power of the state worked without hindrance and the individual citizen had no rights at all (see **authoritarian**)

Sample Questions

Candidates should be familiar with a representative selection of typologies of states which have been proposed since the major expansion of comparative politics got under way in the 1960s, and be prepared *critically to analyse* the strengths and weaknesses of each. Given their special relevance to liberal democratic systems, typologies of political parties are common in the literature and a favourite subject for examination questions (e.g. 'How useful is a typology of states to our understanding of comparative politics?'). Other questions could focus on specific issues relating to liberal democracy, participation or applications of the concepts of authoritarianism or totalitarianism:

- What do we mean by the term 'liberal democracy'? Is Britain still a democratic country?

- How useful is the concept of 'totalitarianism' in understanding the nature of traditional communist political systems in the 1970s and 1980s?

- 'The essence of Marxist-Leninist political systems is mass participation combined with the "leading role" of the communist elite.' Discuss.

Further Reading

On the principles of liberal democracy see Holden (1993) and for its philosophical basis Plant (1991a). Lijphart (1969) is the classic formulation of the notion of 'consociational' democracy. Lane and Ersson (1991) discuss social cleavages in the Western European context. Dahl (1964b) is the best starting point for the pluralist model. An excellent overview of competing theories is Dunleavy and O'Leary (1987). Various typologies of states discussed are presented in detail in *inter alia* Parsons and Shils (1962), Almond and Powell (1966), Finer (1970), and Blondel (1973).

For 'totalitarianism' see Schapiro (1972), and for a critique of its application to Eastern Europe before 1989 see Ball and Millard (1986). For 'authoritarianism' and other important political concepts see Foley (1993).

For comparative treatments of federalism Wheare (1963) is dated but sound; see also Duchacek (1970).

Chapter 1

The European Context

For centuries Europeans have dreamed of a prosperous continent leading the world in the pursuit of peace. One of the most fateful expressions of this feeling came from Mikhail Gorbachev, the last General Secretary of the Soviet Union, in his book *Perestroika (Opening)* from 1987. Addressing a then divided and unbelieving world, Gorbachev foresaw an end to the "Cold War" that had divided Europe into two nuclear armed camps for the better part of half a century. "Europe from the Atlantic to the Urals is a cultural-historical entity united by the common heritage of the Renaissance and Enlightenment. . . . Europe's historic chance and its future lie in peaceful cooperation between the states of that continent."[1] Just a few years later the Cold War did end, not in the way that Gorbachev preferred, but creating nonetheless a unique opportunity for European peace and integration.

One reason that Gorbachev's image of a cooperative and peaceful Europe seemed so unrealistic was that it contrasted sharply with the continent's past. Over the past century, Europe experienced not only the tensions and conflicts of the Cold War, but also the horrors of two world wars and the barbarisms, holocausts, and mass oppression of the totalitarian governments of the twentieth century. And previous centuries witnessed unremitting smaller wars and often brutal imperial conquests.

Yet, historic Europe has been an ambivalent force—destructive and creative at the same time. On the creative side, the dominant forms of political and economic organization in the world today—the effective service-producing state, representative democracy, the industrial market economy, and the ideas of universal human rights and freedoms—had their origins in Europe. They were created in a tempestuous period during which Europe changed from a comparative backwater to the most powerful and prosperous region in the world. A series of costly wars stretching from the seventeenth century to the twentieth shaped the modern state. The industrial *market economy* emerged in Protestant Europe and America. It has transformed these and other societies, with their class structures and patterns of social interaction, and sown the seeds of the democratic impulses of the nineteenth and twentieth centuries. The *industrial revolution*, which originated in Britain around 1770, has vastly changed the working lives and improved the standards of living of billions of people around the world. Representative democracy traces its modern origins to the British struggle starting in the seventeenth century to democratize parliament and contain the arbitrary power of the king, and to the American and French Revolutions of 1776 and 1789. The first wave of democratization in the modern world was confined to Europe and a few of Europe's former colonies, but subsequent waves have affected more and more countries around the world.

Europe is a relatively small continent. Its influence on the contemporary world has been far out of proportion to its size and its earlier history. In the Middle Ages and early Renaissance, Europe was relatively backward and defensive, divided into a number of kingdoms, principalities, dukedoms, baronies, and independent cities. Much of Europe was in the thrall of a hierarchical and often corrupt Roman Catholic Church establishment.

Yet, in three fateful centuries the Renaissance, the Protestant Reformation, the Enlightenment, and the Industrial Revolution transformed Europe in fundamental ways—in its aspirations and ideas, its technology, its social structure, and in its political organization. Europe became concentrated into a small number of expansive, bureaucratically centralized states. These states drew upon a growing industry and commercial agriculture, and possessed professional and technologically sophisticated armies and navies. Between the sixteenth and the nineteenth centuries, Europe became the proactive continent, with the rest of the world increasingly reactive. Yet, while Europe was outwardly expansive, it was inwardly divided between states that were almost constantly at war with one another. Only after the fall of Napoleon in 1814 and with the emergence of British dominance did Europe experience a long spell of relative peace ("Pax Britanica") and unprecedented economic and technological progress. In the twentieth century, however, Europe's divisions and rivalries culminated in the two world wars. Since the end of World War II, Europe has tamed its national rivalries and relaxed its imperial ambitions, but not without leaving its values and institutions implanted on the rest of the world, where they have combined and interacted with indigenous forms and practices.

THE PURPOSE AND ORGANIZATION OF THIS BOOK

This book celebrates a new Europe. The progress of European integration after World War II, the end of the Cold War, and the demise of totalitarian governments have, we hope, altered Europe's historic pattern of division and conflict. Democratic in reality or in aspiration, and committed to market exchange and freedoms, the 39 states of this new Europe are no longer divided ideologically or pitted against each other in unremitting war. Large parts of this new Europe, including many countries of the former Soviet orbit, have begun the process of merging sovereignties in a European Union.

European Politics Today is about Europe, not just about Western Europe or Eastern Europe. Our first goal is to introduce Europe as a cultural and political region. The nations of Europe have different histories, but they all have been shaped by common social, economic, and political experiences. They were all affected in differing degrees by the Renaissance, the Reformation, the *Enlightenment*, and the Industrial Revolution. They shared actively or passively in the rising nationalism of the nineteenth century, and in the Communism, Fascism, and the terrible wars of the twentieth century. The European experience is also relevant to Americans who live in a modern democracy that originated as a transplanted fragment of Europe. America has not been able to avoid involvement in Europe's politics and wars, and has hosted successive generations of European exiles and refugees.

Our second goal is to use the political experience of Europe to introduce important concepts and theories in political science. Modern political science was formed in the attempt to grasp and explain the workings of the political and economic structures that originated in Europe: the bureaucratic state, the industrial market economy, and representative democratic government. Thus the unique European experience is relevant to anyone trying to understand and utilize modern political science. We use the concepts and tools of political science to examine the rich and varied democratic experience, its values, institutions, and processes, in well-established as well as in new democracies.

European Politics Today contains four introductory chapters and eight chapters presenting individual European political systems. The four introductory chapters set the stage for understanding today's political Europe. This first chapter places the European nations geographically and historically by tracing the emergence of contemporary nations through centuries of conflict and consolidation. Relations between European nations are an important part of the politics of each nation, and the importance of these relations has been heightened by the rapid and radical changes in Eastern Europe and by the increasing integration of the European Union (EU). This chapter also discusses two critical features of each country's domestic environment that help create different problems and possibilities for its politics: national economic conditions and ethnic division or unity. In conclusion, the chapter introduces a continuing theme of this book: Europe's special relationship with democracy and democratization.

Concerns about the nature, bases, and varieties of democracy in Europe also help shape the subsequent chapters. Chapter 2 provides an overview of how Europeans think and act politically. It focuses especially on what democracy expects of its citizens and what citizens in old and new democracies expect of their governments. Chapter 3 offers a similar overview of the interest group and political parties that Europeans use to participate in political decision making. Finally, Chapter 4 presents the main features of European constitutions, government institutions, and policymaking processes.

Chapters 5 through 11 apply these general themes to specific European political systems, including some well-established democracies (England and France), some that have made the transition to democracy after World War II (Germany and Spain), and some that have only in the last 15 years grappled with the transition to democratic politics (Russia, Poland, and Hungary). The chapters on specific political systems conclude in Chapter 12 with an analysis of the European Union, which since 2004 comprises 25 of Europe's countries, including 8 from Eastern Europe. Of the countries covered in Chapters 5 through 11, only Russia is not a member of the EU. The European Union is an in-creasingly important, though sometimes complex and inscrutable, supranational political system. It influences political decisions in all European countries, including those states that are not members.

The Appendix outlines the framework of specific topics that are discussed in the introductory chapters and in each country study, indicating the pages where these topics are treated. This appendix makes it possible to compare general topics from the introductory chapters across the political systems examined in the book.

THE EMERGENCE OF TODAY'S EUROPE

Europe is a large peninsula extending out of the Eurasian landmass, with its eastern border in the Ural Mountains and its western border on the Atlantic. It ranges from the Arctic Ocean in the north, to the Mediterranean Sea on the south, almost touching Africa at the Straits of Gibraltar. It is the next to smallest of the seven continents, larger than Australia, but smaller than Antarctica—roughly 4 million square miles in extent, with some three-quarters of a billion inhabitants.

The major changes in the political map of Europe over the past several centuries and up until the most recent years, have been formalized in a series of treaties following major European wars. The *Peace of Westphalia* terminated the "Thirty Years War" of religion (1618–1648), triggered by the *Protestant Reformation*. The Treaty of Westphalia tried to solve these conflicts by dividing Europe into Catholic countries (mainly in the South) and Protestant ones (mainly in the North and West). This peace settlement also established the principle of national sovereignty, which meant that each country would have the right to determine internal affairs, including religion, as it saw fit. Figure 1.1 presents Europe as it was organized following the Peace of Westphalia (1648). The whole of southeastern Europe lived within the Ottoman Empire, the domain of the Turkish sultanate. Central Europe, in the form of Austria, Prussia, Switzerland, and Poland, was just beginning to take shape out of the mist of the Holy Roman Empire. Northern Europe was dominated by Sweden, which was at the peak of its power after its

FIGURE 1.1   Europe in 1648

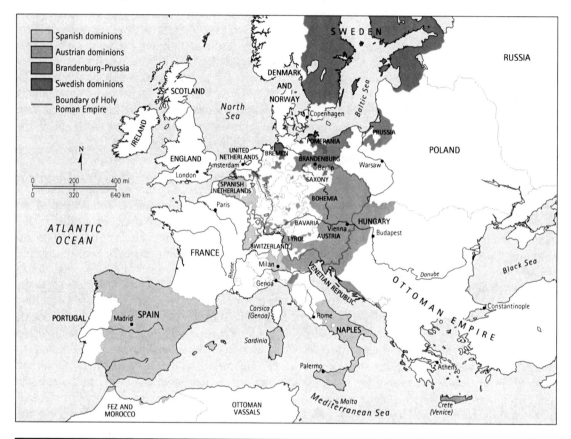

victories in the religious wars. But more than any-thing else, Europe's future was foreshadowed in a tier of countries bordering on the Atlantic Ocean with maritime access to the rest of the world—Spain, Portugal, England, the Netherlands, and France. This part of Europe evolved into a set of powerful states much earlier than other parts of Europe. In Italy and Germany, for example, control was split up between loose and ineffective empires and a patchwork of city-states and small principalities. Their size, seafaring capacity, and ability to mobilize resources enabled the Atlantic states to become the architects of world imperialism from the seventeenth to the nineteenth centuries. For two centuries after the Treaty of Westphalia, France and England became the leading European powers.

The next great European wars followed after France had gone through a political revolution and seen the rise to power of a brilliant general, Napoleon Bonaparte. However, Napolean's expansionist policies eventually led to military defeat. The *Treaty of Vienna* terminated the Napoleonic Wars that followed the French Revolution (1796–1815). The Europe that emerged after the Napoleonic Wars reflected the dissolution of the Holy Roman Empire and the retreat of the Ottoman Empire toward its roots in Asia Minor. Prussia was on its way to becoming a powerful state. Poland and Finland were gobbled up by Russia, as that enormous empire moved westward. Europe of the early nineteenth century was dominated by a "Holy Alliance" of conservative monarchs who sought to preserve their power and to prevent further social revolutions. Later in the nineteenth century, Europe became more concerned with an increasingly powerful and expansive Germany, which was unified in 1871 under Prussian leadership, and a united Italian state that emerged at about the same time. In the East, the Ottoman Empire gradually weakened and thus earned its reputation as the "sick man of Europe." It lost a part of Greece in the early nineteenth century, and Bulgaria in the early twentieth.

World War I (1914–1918) was the disastrous result of the great power rivalries of the late nineteenth and early twentieth centuries. The postwar *Treaty of Versailles* (1919) established the national right to self-determination. Each nation (a people with a common self-defined identity) sharing a common territory should have the right to determine whether they want to form their own state. The military results of World War I were hard on empires, and the Treaty of Versailles was not friendly to them, either. The defeated Ottoman Empire was driven back to its Turkish base, and the multiethnic Austro-Hungarian Empire was split into Austria, Hungary, Yugoslavia, and Czechoslovakia. The German Empire crumbled at the end of the war and was replaced by a fragile republic. The Russian Empire collapsed in 1917, and the ensuing revolution led to a radical, Bolshevik Russia, which became the Soviet Union. Devastated by war and treated with hostility by its neighbors, Russia gave up its control of Finland, Estonia, Latvia, Lithuania, and Poland. The map of Europe "between the wars" was much like contemporary Europe, except that Ukraine, Belarus, and Moldova were still parts of the Soviet Union. But the Treaty of Versailles failed to solve Europe's national tensions or to provide an umbrella of collective security.

World War II was brought on by the aggressions of the *Axis* powers (*Nazi [National Socialist]* Germany, Fascist Italy, and authoritarian Japan), which were countries that had largely been left behind in the age of imperial conquest. Within the first years of World War II, almost all of Western Europe, with the notable exception of the United Kingdom (Britain), was overpowered, brutalized, and "coordinated" by Nazi armies. Eventually the hold of Nazi Germany on Europe was broken by

1945, by the bloodied troops of the Soviet Union from the east, and the armed forces of the United States, Britain, and their allies from the west. World War II led to the formation of the United Nations in 1945 and to the proclamation of the Universal Declaration of Human Rights three years later.

Yet, the 1948 Communist coup in Czechoslovakia and the Soviet blockade of Berlin during the same year soon dashed hopes for a peaceful Europe of low tensions. The line separating the Soviet and the Anglo-American forces in the middle of Germany in 1945 became the *Iron Curtain* of the next generation. Figure 1.2 depicts the Europe of the *Cold War*—a sharply divided continent with its eastern part under Soviet political control and military occupation, and with a western part tightly drawn together under American leadership. Europe was frozen in what seemed like a permanent confrontation.

The most recent remaking of the European map resulted from the collapse of the Soviet Union and Yugoslavia. In 1989, communist governments all over Eastern Europe collapsed or were forced from power. The hated Berlin Wall, which for almost 30 years had separated East and West Germany, was torn down by ordinary people on both sides, while armed border guards stood by and watched. The Soviet Union acquiesced and withdrew from Eastern Europe and in 1991 split into 15 independent political entities, 7 of which are commonly counted as European. Four of these (Russia, Belarus, Ukraine, and Moldova) have retained close ties to one another, and the Soviet heritage has remained fairly strong and democratization uncertain. In contrast, the Baltic countries that had been independent between the two world wars—Estonia, Latvia, and Lithuania—quickly reasserted their independence and sought collaboration with Western Europe. Five countries emerged from the dissolution of Yugoslavia in 1991–1992: Slovenia, Croatia, Macedonia, Bosnia-Herzegovina, and Serbia and Montenegro. The latter contained a predominantly Albanian and deeply conflicted province of Kosovo. Except for Slovenia, all the former components of Yugoslavia have had a troubled and more or less violent history since the breakup of the larger country. Two nations emerged from the peaceful breakup of the former

FIGURE 1.2   Europe in the Cold War

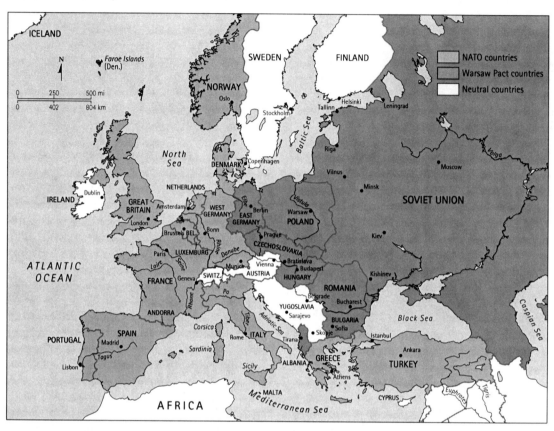

Czechoslovakia in 1993: the Czech Republic and Slovakia. Figure 1.3 presents a map of contemporary Europe after the end of the Cold War.

It is still common to think of Europe as divided into Western and Eastern parts, a view surviving from the Cold War. From this perspective, 19 of the 39 countries of contemporary Europe are the Eastern successors to the old Communist bloc: the 7 European successor states to the Soviet Union, the 5 components of the former Yugoslavia, plus Albania, Bulgaria, the Czech Republic, Hungary, Poland, Romania, and Slovakia. The remaining 20 countries that are considered Western include the 15 states that made up the European Union until its expansion in 2004: Austria,

Belgium, Denmark, Finland, France, Great Britain, Germany, Greece, Ireland, Italy, Luxembourg, the Netherlands, Portugal, Spain, and Sweden. In addition, there are two smaller Western countries, Cyprus and Malta, that only joined the EU in 2004, and three that have chosen to remain outside that organization: Iceland, Norway, and Switzerland. With patience, you should be able to count 39 countries in Figure 1.3.

When you consult that map, it is immediately obvious that Western Europe includes considerable parts that are not geographically "western." In longitudinal terms, for example, Greece is more "eastern" than Poland and the Czech Republic, and Cyprus even more so. Similarly, the northern Euro-

FIGURE 1.3   Europe Today

pean countries of Finland and Sweden are as far east as Hungary and Croatia. In this book, however, we most frequently refer to "Eastern" versus "Western" Europe, because of the important legacies of economic conditions, political histories, and international alliances.

EUROPEAN INTEGRATION

The history of state- and nation-building in Europe would not be complete without recent important trends toward integration. Since World War II, the industrialized countries of Western Europe found that the peaceful and free exchange of ideas, products, and persons across national boundaries greatly enhances productivity. Step by step since the 1950s,

Western Europeans have created a *common market economy* of ever-growing political integration.

The *European Economic Community (EEC)* was formed in 1957 and originally consisted of six countries: France, Germany, Italy, Belgium, the Netherlands, and Luxembourg.[2] The European Community expanded in the 1970s and 1980s to include Britain, Ireland, Denmark, Greece, Spain, and Portugal. The organization expanded again in 1995 to include Austria, Finland, and Sweden, and renamed itself the *European Union (EU)*.[3] In 2004 the European Union admitted ten new states. These included eight Eastern European countries: Estonia, Latvia, Lithuania, Poland, the Czech Republic, Slovakia, Hungary, and Slovenia. Also admitted were two smaller

Mediterranean island states: Cyprus and Malta. In the same year, EU leaders proposed a new "constitutional treaty," which each member states will have to ratify. The process of integration creates regional institutions with limited policymaking power and with resources to address common policy goals. The European Union might be called a "confederated state" in which the governing institutions have policymaking authority, but they must rely on the member governments for enforcement, implementation, and revenue. (See Chapter 12 for a more complete account of the European Union.)

Another change in the international structure involves security policy. The international security arrangements put in place during the Cold War no longer fit the contemporary geopolitical situation. The *North Atlantic Treaty Organization (NATO)* was formed early in the Cold War (1949) under American leadership in order to mobilize Western European countries against the communist threat. The Soviet bloc formed the *Warsaw Pact* (1955) to counter NATO; the *Council for Mutual Economic Assistance (COMECON)*, formed in 1959, coordinated the Eastern economies in response to the European Union. Both the Warsaw Pact and COMECON dissolved with the end of the Cold War.

The EU and NATO are still in operation and expanding in membership, but they are also searching for new equilibria in scope and function. The European Union in 2004 admitted eight Eastern European countries as members. Likewise, NATO has added ten Eastern European nations. Yet, while NATO has continued to expand, its role in the new Europe is uneasy. Russia opposes NATO expansion to the east, viewing it as a threat to isolate Russia internationally. And while NATO is still playing an important role in the former Yugoslavia, some of its functions in that area are being taken over by the EU. Thus, NATO's security functions in the new Europe are unclear. The close Cold War security relationship between the United States and Europe is no longer justified by a Soviet threat, even though some of the Eastern European countries still worry about their Russian neighbor. Thus, while substantial parts of the former East are now peacefully incorporated into a greater Europe of democracy and relative prosper-ity, there are still areas of internal and international instability.

DESCRIBING EUROPE: LARGE AND SMALL COUNTRIES

The variation in the size of European countries is enormous. Table 1.1 describes the differences in population for the Western and Eastern European countries in this book. Russia with over 140 million inhabitants is the European giant. Some 30 million Russians live east of the Urals, in the Asian part of the country. Even if we deduct these eastern residents, European Russia still dominates Europe with a population almost 50 percent larger than that of Germany, the second most populous European country. The population of European Russia is almost 400 times that of Iceland, which has fewer than 300,000 inhabitants. France is third in population size with close to 60 million residents. The United Kingdom is very close behind; Spain and Poland are next among the countries covered in this book, although Ukraine is larger than either. Hungary is a relatively small nation, with around 10 million inhabitants.

Grouping all 39 European countries according to population, we have 9 large European countries with populations of 20 million or more. Six of them are covered in this book; the remaining ones are Ukraine, Italy, and Romania. There are 15 medium-sized countries ranging from 5 million to about 15 million, 9 of these in Western Europe and the remaining 6 in Eastern Europe. The 15 smallest European countries have populations that range from fewer than 5 million inhabitants to under 1 million each for Cyprus, Luxembourg, Malta, and Iceland.[4]

When we compare European countries according to their geographic area (the second column in Table 1.1), we get a somewhat different pattern. European Russia comes out on top even more dramatically in geographic size; the ratio of its area to the second largest country is even greater than that of its population. Although European Russia is only half again as populous as Germany, it has seven times the area of Ukraine, the next largest European state, and eight times that of France, which is the largest country in Western Europe. The other West-

TABLE 1.1   Aspects of Economic Development for Selected European Countries

	Population (millions)	Average Inflation (%) 1998–2002	Per Capita GNP 2003	P.C. GDP Growth (%) 1998–2002	Per Capita PPP 2003	Percent of Labor Force in Agriculture (%)
Germany	82.6	1.4	$25,250	1.4	$27,460	3
France	59.7	1.3	24,770	2.3	27,460	2
United Kingdom	59.3	2.3	28,350	2.2	27,650	1
Spain	41.1	2.8	16,990	2.9	22,020	6
Russia	143.4	34.3	2,610	4.5	8,920	12
Hungary	10.1	9.7	6,330	4.3	13,780	6
Poland	38.2	7.3	5,270	3.1	11,450	19

Source: World Bank, *World Development Indicators 2004,* retrieved August 10, 2004 from https://publications.worldbank.org/subscriptions/WDI/. The inflation measure is the change in the consumer price index (CPI). World Bank, *Quick Reference Tables,* retrieved December 1, 2004 from http://www.worldbank.org/data/databytopic/GNIPC.pdf.

ern European countries with areas exceeding 100,000 square miles (about the size of Oregon) include Spain, Sweden, Norway, Germany, Finland, and Italy. The United Kingdom is slightly under the hundred thousand mark. The Eastern giants include Russia, Ukraine, and Poland, whereas Romania is just below the hundred thousand mark.

Magnitudes of population and area do not in themselves explain the politics of European states. The biggest ones in territory or population are not necessarily the richest or most powerful ones. Thus, the small country of Switzerland has been an independent, free, and prosperous country for centuries, whereas Ukraine is large but comparatively poor and has only recently gained its independence. Size, of course, does make a difference in warfare, as Napoleon and Hitler discovered on the wintry steppes of Russia. It also makes a difference in the availability of resources, in problems of governmental centralization, and the like. Similarly, the relation between area and population is important. America had a frontier for growth and expansion. Asian Russia (Siberia) has been a frontier for that country. The Netherlands and other densely populated European countries have very different and powerful geographic constraints on their economic development.

One of the most important population questions is the rate of increase, a fact that has important implications for economic growth. Recently, Europe

has had the smallest population growth rate of all the world regions. Between 1965 and 1998, Europe had only a 0.4 percent average annual increase, in comparison with the Middle East and North Africa (2.8), Sub-Saharan Africa (2.7), South Asia (2.2), and Latin America and the Caribbean (2.1).[5] This means that Europe does not have to worry about some of the issues that plague many developing countries with rapidly growing populations. However, the low European birthrates are raising serious concerns about the sustainability of that continent's welfare states, as their populations will age dramatically over the next few decades.

The sheer magnitude of a country's economy is also important. Thus we can think of large and small countries in terms of economic as well as population size. Germany is at the top among the European countries with close to a $2,000 billion economy as of 2001, contrasted with an Albanian economy of around $4.2 billion. The economic output of Germany is thus close to 500 times that of Albania. The other large Western European economies—France, the United Kingdom, and Italy—generate well over $1,000 billion each year, while the larger Eastern European economies range from the $250 billion mark for Russia, $163 billion for Poland, to around $50 billion for Hungary. By this measure the German economy in 2001 was about eight times the size of the Russian one, with only a little more than half the population.

DESCRIBING EUROPE: RICH AND POOR COUNTRIES

The economic measures most vital to internal politics are expressed in relationship to population size: what occupations divide the citizens in the labor force; how productive are their efforts; how is their collective income to be divided? Table 1.1 presents a comparison of the economic performance of those Western and Eastern European countries that are treated in depth in this book.

As a starting point, the last column in the table underscores the fact that the economies of Eastern Europe still have substantial agricultural sectors in comparison with the heavily industrialized and urbanized societies of Western Europe. In Germany, France, and the United Kingdom, the agricultural percentage of the labor force is well below 5 percent. Even in Spain only about 6 percent of the labor force is now employed in agriculture, a figure matched only by the most developed Eastern European economies, such as Hungary. In contrast, close to a fifth of Poland's labor force works in agriculture. The relative size of the agricultural labor force is significant for two reasons. For one thing, a large agricultural labor force usually indicates low economic development and productivity. Highly productive modern economies manage their agricultural needs with small farm populations, even if the nature of their land and skills make this sector valuable. Secondly, a large agricultural sector usually means strong interest groups that promote the farm sector, and these interests often resist economic modernization policies and international integration.

There are two measures of income and productivity in Table 1.1: per capita *Gross National Product (GNP)* based on prevailing currency exchange rates (columns 3 and 4) and *Purchasing Power Parities (PPP)* (column 5). Both of these measures take statistics in national currencies and recalculate them to allow for international comparisons. The first measure converts per capita GNP based on the exchange rates that are used in the international financial markets. This is the simplest and most common way to compare eco-

nomic output across countries, but it has two important problems. First, exchange rates sometimes fluctuate quite strongly. For example, as some of you may have noticed to your dismay, between 2001 and 2004 the U.S. dollar lost about one-third of its value against most Western European currencies. In comparative economic statistics, it may thus appear as if the U.S. economy shrunk dramatically compared to the European ones over that period, even though growth rates were generally higher in the United States than in most Western European countries.

Second, currency exchange rates are not necessarily accurate representations of what a given currency can purchase in food, shelter, clothing, and other amenities. For example, any international tourist who has visited both Bolivia and Switzerland will know that while both countries have spectacular mountains, one's money goes a lot further in the former country than in the latter. Purchasing power parities (PPP) are an attempt to measure the "true" values of different currencies, based on their respective capacities to purchase goods and services in the domestic market. These estimates can then be used to measure the comparative outputs of different economies. Most economists consider GNP per capita measures based on PPP equivalents to be a more appropriate estimate of personal income, although they are more difficult to measure.[6]

Table 1.1 clearly shows that the choice of measure can make a difference. If we use the exchange rate version of GNP to measure personal income, the ratio between Britain at the top and Russia at the bottom is more than 10 to 1. If we instead use the PPP indicator, the contrast between these two countries is less than 4 to 1. The PPP figure is closer to the reality of economic welfare in Europe today. The PPP statistics indicate that the economic contrasts between Eastern and Western Europe are striking, although less formidable than implied by the exchange rate-based statistics. The average PPP-based GNP per capita among the nations of Western Europe in 2003 was close to $30,000, while in Eastern Europe it was about $10,000. Hungary's average personal income is a little less than one-half that of Germany and France, and roughly two-thirds that of

Spain. Russia and Poland have economies yielding about one-third per capita of those of Britain, Germany, and France. These differences, while large, are within the range of what can be overcome in time through human effort, political organization and will, and constructive policies.

In terms of economic growth, the gap between Western and most Eastern European economies was growing, not diminishing, in the 1990s.[7] All the Western European countries had positive economic growth rates for the 1990s; the average country grew annually at about 2 percent. In contrast, most Eastern European countries struggled with the very difficult problems of transition from communist "command control" economies to market economies. The average Eastern country declined nearly 2.5 percent a year. By the late 1990s, however, this pattern changed and since 1998 the Eastern European countries have generally had stronger growth than those in the West.

The Eastern European average conceals great differences, moreover, in success in managing the economic transition. Poland and Hungary are among the most successful Eastern European economies, and their average gains of 3 to 5 percent per year are larger than those of most Western European countries. Russia, whose economy was greatly affected by the collapse of its military sector and the obsolescence of much of its heavy industry, experienced disastrous economic performance in the 1990s, as its economy lost an average of 7 percent a year. Fortunately, around 1998 the Russian economy began to turn around, and it has in recent years produced robust economic growth, even though drastic poverty persists.

Inflation was a major problem in Western Europe from the 1960s to about the 1980s. In recent years, however, the countries of the West have worried much less about this problem, as Table 1.1 indicates. But in Eastern Europe, inflation was a serious, and largely unfamiliar, phenomenon in the 1990s. For the period 1990–1998, Russia averaged an *annual* rate of inflation of 137 percent, Romania 118 percent, Poland about 30 percent, and Hungary 23 percent. The bulk of these price increases directly followed from the economic transitions of the late 1980s and early 1990s, and in many countries they have come down in recent years. But Eastern inflation rates are still troubling, as Russia and Romania continue to experience inflation rates of 30 to 40 percent. Governments confronted with inflation problems of this magnitude can easily encounter serious discontent, which can undermine support for democratic politics and market economies.

SOCIAL DEVELOPMENT AND WELFARE IN EUROPE

Gross economic statistics on economic production and inflation are far from the whole story on the economic and social realities facing Europeans today. Economic conditions and public policies jointly shape the welfare of citizens and, in turn, their satisfactions or frustrations with democratic politics. Table 1.2 presents four measures of social development and welfare in European countries: education, computer ownership, income distribution, and infant mortality. These measures reflect different aspects of wealth and resource abundance, but also the past performance of national governments. As shown in the first column of the table, most European countries, East and West, are successful in keeping their teenagers in school. There also seems to be gender equality in access to secondary education in both the West and the East. High levels of literacy are consistent with these education figures. The percentage of young people enrolled in colleges and universities, as shown in column 2, tells a similar story. All over Europe, and including most Eastern countries, about half of all young adults attend some level of college or university. In some countries, including Russia, the percentage is even higher. Even in the poorer European countries, college education is far more widespread than in many low-income countries in other parts of the world. Public expenditures on education are also relatively similar across these eight nations. In 1997 West Germany spent 4.8 percent of its GNP on education, the United Kingdom, 5.3 percent, compared with Russia's 3.5 percent and Poland's 7.5 percent. If, however, we consider that the GNP of the Western countries is several times larger than that of some Eastern countries, the effort converts

TABLE 1.2   Aspects of Social Development for Selected European Countries

	Percentage in School as Percentage of Age Group (secondary)	(college)	Computers per 1000	Percentage of Income to Lower 20%	Percentage of Income to Upper 20%	Infant Mortality per 1000 Births
Germany	88	46	431	8.5	36.9	4
France	92	54	347	7.2	40.2	4
United Kingdom	95	59	406	6.1	44.0	5
Spain	93	57	196	7.5	40.3	5
Russia	na	68	89	4.9	51.3	18
Hungary	87	40	108	7.7	37.2	8
Poland	88	55	106	7.3	42.5	8

Source: World Bank, *World Development Indicators 2004,* retrieved August 10, 2004 from https://publications.worldbank.org/ subscriptions/WDI/. Secondary school enrollment is percent net enrollment and Tertiary school enrollment is percent gross enrollment. The income share numbers for Spain date back to 1990 and for France to 1995. All other income share numbers are from 1999 and 2000.

into substantially larger Western European spending on such things as construction and maintenance of schools, teacher salaries, educational equipment, and the like.

Table 1.2 also shows computer ownership. In this respect, the richer Western European countries are significantly ahead of Spain as well as the Eastern European states. Yet, computer access is growing rapidly in all parts of Europe. As an indicator of public health, we include the infant mortality per thousand live births. Here again, the main difference runs not so much between East and West as between the poorest countries of the East and the rest. Thus, Russia has significantly higher infant death rates than any other country. Differences between the various Western European countries are almost nonexistent.

The distribution of income reported in Table 1.2 for Western and Eastern countries reflects an ironic situation: Only a few years after the introduction of a market economy, Russia, which for 75 years had a government ostensibly committed to social equality and the eradication of class differences, has the most unequal distribution of income among all the countries listed. More than half of Russia's total income goes to the top 20 percent of income recipients, and less than 5 percent goes to the bottom fifth. Although not as severe as the discrepancies in some South American countries and South Africa, it is among the world's least egalitar-

ian distributions, which contributes to its political tensions (see Chapter 9). This situation is exacerbated by the fact that many recent fortunes have been gained quickly and often through shady deals involving the sell-off of former government assets. In contrast, Hungary and Poland are much more egalitarian, with around 40 percent of income going to the top fifth and 7 to 8 percent going to the bottom fifth. Distributions in most of Western Europe are fairly similar to these.

DEVELOPMENT, MODERNIZATION, AND DEMOCRACY

Statistical comparisons of Western and Eastern Europe thus yield substantial differences in economic levels and welfare provisions. If we take purchasing power parity as a measure of economic productivity, the Eastern European economies produce somewhat more than a third of the per capita level of the richer Western European economies. The Eastern countries have larger rural, agricultural sectors, and there are significant differences in the provision of higher education and health services. By these purely economic and social measures, most of our Eastern European countries fall into the World Bank classification of "middle income countries," ranging from "lower middle income" (e.g., Albania, Ukraine, Romania, and Russia) to "upper middle income" (e.g., Poland and Hungary).[8] Statistical measures also suggest that most Eastern Europeans are educated and literate people, exposed to the "world culture." They have the makings of "civil societies"; although long stultified by communist control, interest groups, voluntary associations, and competitive media of communication are growing (see Chapter 3).

On the troubling side, high rates of inflation and slow rates of growth in many Eastern states show that they are experiencing serious developmental difficulties. While some countries are making substantial progress, others continue to have great difficulty (see Table 1.1). They are involved in "dual transitions"—simultaneous efforts to replace collectivist with market economies, and to replace centralized, authoritarian regimes with pluralistic, democratic ones.[9]

Students of democratization have long debated the relationship between economic development and democratization. Indeed, the great ideological struggles of the nineteenth and twentieth centuries turned on these issues. Karl Marx anticipated that the development of the capitalist economy and the rise of the *"bourgeoisie"* would signal the decline of feudalism, and the introduction of bourgeois democracy, which would in turn be supplanted by socialist democracy after the working class ousts the bourgeoisie.

Modern political science replaced the Marxist view of the relationship between economics and politics with more limited observations and forecasts. Many leading political scientists drew attention to a strong statistical association between economic development, social and political mobilization, and democracy.[10] These "social mobilization" studies of the 1950s and 1960s pointed out that economic growth and industrialization were associated with urbanization, the spread of education and literacy, and exposure to the mass media of communication. They argued that these conditions would result in greater political awareness and activity ("mobilization"), the formation of voluntary associations and competitive political parties, and the attainment of what came to be called *civil society* (see Chapter 2). These elements of a civil society would both demand and support more democratic political systems.

Contrary to early hopes, democracy proved fragile. All the Eastern European countries were forcefully assimilated into the Communist orbit at the onset of the postwar period. Efforts to break free in Hungary in 1956 (see Chapter 11) and Czechoslovakia in 1968 were repressed by Soviet troops. Spain and Portugal came through World War II as authoritarian regimes; Greece also fell under military control in the 1960s. It became evident that the road to economic development could be long and hard—and that at least in the short run, economic development could be politically destabilizing.[11]

However, development theory seemed to "kick in," so to speak, in the late 1970s and 1980s; rapid and sustained economic growth in authoritarian Spain (see Chapter 8), Portugal, Greece, and other nations around the world weakened the legitimacy of authoritarian regimes. The culmination of these events came with the dramatic collapse of the Soviet Union and the establishment of new democracies in the newly free countries of Eastern Europe. The dominant political ideas of the 1990s were democracy and the market economy.

In view of the experiences of the last decades, as well as the European historical experience, we have a better understanding of the complexity of the interaction of economic, social, and political institutions and forces.[12] There is no doubt that stable or "consolidated" democracy is strongly associated statistically with economic development. But the relationship occurs over the long run. It is shaped by the more dispersed resources for power and coercion in a complex economy, by the more participatory values, perceptions, and demands of an educated and organized citizenry, and by the presence of greater resources to meet human needs.[13] A whole set of connecting relationships—structural discontinuities, breakdowns and synergies, interventions of chance, and failures and triumphs of leaders—weaken or strengthen the connection between a growing economy and a democratic polity.

As we write of Europe in the early years of the third millennium, there is a division of realities and prospects. Western European countries—

economically developed, democratically consolidated, and largely organized in a confederation—have well-established democracies. A substantial group of Eastern European countries are approaching their economic level, and many of these have joined the European Union. A substantial set of Eastern European nations are far less economically productive, often plagued by inflation and economic stagnation, and struggling with democratic ways of coping with change and conflict. With such a short experience of political independence and such limited and fragile socioeconomic bases, we would expect substantial difficulty in sustaining stable democratic government in some parts of Eastern Europe.

Sadly enough, these forecasts seem to be accurate, with democratic freedoms under pressure in nearly half of Eastern Europe, especially in the countries with lower levels of economic development. Figure 1.4, depicts the relationship between economic development and political freedom for the nations of Europe. The *Freedom Scores* in the figure are taken from the 2003 report of Freedom House, a nonprofit organization that provides an-nual ratings of political rights and civil liberties in each country. The economic development measure—expressed as purchasing power parity (PPP)—is taken from the World Bank's *World Development Report* for 2003.[14] Each circle or square dot in the figure represents a single country, with circles representing countries in Eastern Europe and squares countries in Western Europe.

Toward the top right of Figure 1.4, indicated by the small squares, we see the Western European countries. All have economic productivity levels higher than most of the Eastern European countries and all receive the top or next to top Freedom Score. The poorest Western European countries, Portugal and Malta, have PPP levels only slightly below the richest Eastern European country (Slovenia). Spain is somewhat better off than Slovenia and notably more economically developed than the Czech Republic and Hungary, the next most developed Eastern countries, with which it shares a similarly high Freedom Score.

Freedom House considers any country with a score of 10 or more to be "Free." All eight Eastern Eu-

FIGURE 1.4   Population of Selected European Countries in 2003

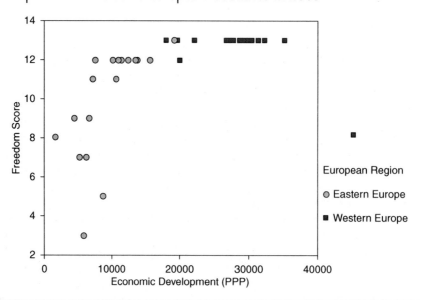

Source: World Bank, World Development Report 2005; Table 1.

ropean countries with a PPP/capita over $10,500 achieve that designation (including Poland and Hungary). In the middle left of Figure 1.4 are five dually troubled Eastern European countries— Albania, Macedonia, Bosnia, Moldova, Russia, and Ukraine—which have PPP/capitas under $9,000 and all of which are rated only "Partly Free" by Freedom House. While each country has its own story, Freedom House's observers reported various pressures and constraints on the mass media, limited rights for minorities, and problems in establishing the rule of law as frequent themes. (See the discussion of the difficulties in establishing the rule of law generally in Chapter 4 and in Russia in particular in Chapter 9.) At the bottom left of the figure is Belarus, dominated by an increasingly powerful president, as the only European country scored as completely not free.

Another way of looking at Figure 1.4 is to observe that of the 15 Eastern European countries whose PPP per capita had been less than Hungary's $13,780, slightly less than half of them were fully free democracies on January 1, 2004. The rest were, at best, only "partly free." In a statistical sense, this suggests that some of these nations will succeed in sustaining democracy, but that others may falter or fail. In a human sense it means that good leadership may play a particularly critical role in these poorer nations. It also means that it is important that the lagging Eastern European countries begin to overcome the difficulties of economic transition and move toward growth and economic development, as Poland seems to have done (see Chapter 10).

Of course, in considering the prospects for democracy, economic development and modernization are not the only considerations. On the one hand, international norms and institutions may help support democracy as a political system. On the other, religious and ethnic cleavages create additional problems in many of the newly independent Eastern European countries. Democracy can arouse new expectations from suppressed minorities, and the absence of resources in the poorer nations can make accommodation of these particularly difficult. This consideration brings us to the troubling prospects of religious and ethnic conflict in Europe.

ETHNIC AND RELIGIOUS CONFLICT IN EUROPE

In the long course of European history, through the forces of population growth and decline, migration, warfare, famine, and disease, an ethno-religious distribution of great complexity has taken shape. There is evidence of a Celtic past, still surviving on the European periphery and in remote mountain valleys. Traces of a long Roman domination can still be seen. There is evidence of great migrations of Goths, Vandals, and Huns from the Asian steppes; Moors, Berbers, and Ottoman Turks from the Middle East; and Vikings and Norsemen from the North. These peoples brought their languages and religions with them. Over time these languages and beliefs combined and differentiated, partly through long-term processes of intermittent fighting, trading, and intermarrying, and partly through the deliberate actions of political and military elites seeking effective ways of extracting resources and recruiting military forces. Populations sharing the same beliefs and speaking in the same tongue could be mobilized and exploited more effectively.

Religion provided one central basis of differentiation. The great religions of the world offer coherent systems of values and standards of behavior beyond local customs and memories to their adherents. Periodically, they have swept across tribes and peoples to create, by force or example, more unified cultural systems. Before the Reformation, the Catholic Church had provided much of the cultural unity for the extremely fragmented political systems in Christian Europe. The birth of modern Europe in the *Renaissance* and the *Reformation* was associated with the shattering of religious unity. The religious wars of the sixteenth and seventeenth centuries created, at the cost of dreadful suffering, lines of religious cleavage that shaped the formation of the European nation-states and continue to influence their politics today.[15]

When the struggle between Catholicism and the forces of Protestant dissent stabilized, religious minorities within each state had largely been expelled or converted. This produced relatively homogeneous religious groupings in most countries. National governments dominated Protestant churches in northwest Europe, usually without much internal religious conflict. In much of Eastern Europe, too, secular governments established dominance over and collaboration with the Eastern Orthodox Church.

In southwestern Europe, the Catholic Church prevailed. The Counterreformation regained France and some German states from Protestantism, held Italy and the Austro-Hungarian empire (including Belgium and Spain), and reclaimed some ground from Islam to the East. The French Revolution of 1789 then unleashed a secular rebellion against the Catholic Church that left its mark on politics and party systems, as a "secular-clerical" divide, for two centuries. The emergence of democracy and the development of mass education resulted in intense internal conflict over the role of the Church in politics and public policy.

Along the fault line between North and South lay a series of states with both Catholic and Protestant populations—the Netherlands, Germany and Switzerland. In these states political conflict between Catholics and Protestants, as well as between clericalism and secularism, has been a fact of political life. This tension has endured through today, with a new focus on education, abortion, and the rights of women—areas in which religious identities and values have been particularly divisive. Apart from the religious issues as such, the followers of the faiths have been historically organized into separate communities with distinct social and political organizations.

A decline in church attendance and other religious practices throughout most of Western Europe since World War II has shifted the political balance in secular directions and decreased the sense of conflict associated with religious division. Nonetheless, at least until very recently a voter's frequency of church attendance was usually the best single predictor of his or her vote choice in most Western European nations with substantial Catholic populations.

Ethnicity may sometimes be associated with religion, but in the modern world it is additionally or even primarily associated with language, custom, and historical memories. Max Weber, in his (classic) introduction to sociological theory *Economy and Society*, defined ethnic groups as "those human groups that entertain a subjective belief in their common descent because of similarities of physical type or of customs or both, or because of memories of colonization and migration. . . . (I)t does not matter whether or not an objective blood relationship exists."[16]

Ethnicity can be a powerful force in politics. It provides an important basis for mobilization of common interests and deeply felt personal identities. It can be especially potent where allied with *nationalism*, a belief that a common ethnic group should be the basis of a geographically defined independent state. The formation of large nation-states between the sixteenth and the nineteenth centuries suppressed many of the lessor customs and dialects in favor of a few relatively dominant ones. The spread of printing and literacy replaced Latin as the international language of the educated and substituted national languages linked to larger independent states. The rise of mass education and mass media in the nineteenth and twentieth centuries obscured and devalued the surviving parochialisms. People identified themselves with some larger "nationality," and according to their social conditions and new ideological beliefs. They were the French, the Spaniards, the English, and the Germans; they were members of the working class or the bourgeoisie; they were conservatives, liberals, or socialists of one kind or another. Nation-states became both the foci of local political activity and, with enormous human costs, the actors in catastrophic international conflict. In the aftermath of World War II under the ideological pressure of the Cold War, ethnic particularisms within the nation-states were even further subordinated.

In Eastern Europe the implications of the withdrawal of Soviet control were, of course, very dramatic. As a matter of ideology, the political aspirations of ethnic minorities had been ruthlessly repressed. Yet, the bureaucratic and even party organizations in the Soviet Union, Czechoslovakia, and Yugoslavia were constructed to recognize and even encourage local ethnic cultures based on language and history, even while religion was generally suppressed. This duality in Soviet policy, dating back to Lenin's initial understanding of the problems created by ethnic nationalism, greatly facilitated the breakup of the Soviet Union, Yugoslavia, and later Czechoslo-

Box 1.1   Ethnicity Defined

The point that ethnicity is based on subjective belief in common descent, rather than a necessary physical reality, is stressed by Donald Horowitz, the leading contemporary authority on ethnicity and politics. Horowitz points out that the concept of ethnicity has to be elastic, since groups physically quite similar but differing in language, religion, customs, marriage patterns, and historical memories may consider themselves to be "ethnically" different. For example, the Serbs, Croats, and Muslim Bosnians (of the same physical stock) may believe themselves to be de-scended from different ancestors. Here, following Gurr and his associates, we use the term "ethnicity" even more generally to refer to all groups "whose core members share a distinctive and enduring collective identity based on cultural traits and lifeways that matter to them and to others with whom they interact."

Sources: Donald Horowitz, *Ethnic Groups in Conflict* (Berkeley: University of California Press, 1985), pp. 52–53. T. Robert Gurr, *Minorities at Risk: A Global View of Ethnopolitical Conflicts* (Washington: U.S. Institute of Peace Press, 1993), p. 3.

vakia, when central controls were removed. The overthrow of most of these authoritarian political systems and the introduction of free discussion and mass media, especially in the absence of well-entrenched democratic party systems, created political space for ethnic and religious particularisms to maneuver within the newly independent political systems.

Of all the countries in Europe, few are free of ethnic diversity, but in many countries there is little or no serious conflict. Table 1.3 provides a sense of the diversity, dangers, and promises of ethno-religious conflicts in Europe. There are several recent "hot spots," where conflict has taken the most violent form in recent years. Casualties in Bosnia, Cyprus, Chechnya, and Kosovo have numbered in the tens of thousands. While less deadly than all-out civil war, terrorism in Northern Ireland in the United Kingdom, in Basque Spain, and French Corsica has taken many lives and shattered the peace of these countries for many decades. These confrontations all involve efforts by one or more ethnic or religious groups to change the boundaries of existing states or to form new ones. Disputes over nation-state boundaries find no simple solution through democratic procedures. If the conflict comes to violence, the struggle can quickly degenerate into "ethnic cleansing," the forcible eviction or destruction of local minorities. Ethnic differences and historic grievances have this capacity to justify dehumanization of the "ethnically" different and cruelties of unimaginable proportions.

While ethnic conflict can inflict terrible costs, it need not. Table 1.3 also contains examples of ethno-religious conflicts that still retain sharp communal awareness, but there is now a stable and constitutionally protected status for group relations. Austria, Belgium (in its religious dispute), the Netherlands, and Switzerland are examples of this situation. A system of power-sharing offers security to communal groups at the cost of the efficiency and redistributive possibilities of majority rule. Austria, for example, used elaborate arrangements for sharing power between the Socialists and the Catholics in the 1950s and 1960s to prevent recurrence of the community conflicts that led to civil war in the early 1930s. The Netherlands and Belgium handled explosive religious conflicts in the same fashion.

While these more or less successful "solutions" to ethnic conflict indicate the possibilities for containing violence, they are each bought at substantial cost and require some tolerance from leaders and followers on all sides. Russia seems to have created a successful federal relationship with the Tatars. The Russian suspension of Chechnyan federal autonomy and the continuance of Chechnyan terrorism and guerrilla warfare illustrate failure, however. The more militant Chechnyans have been unwilling to lay down arms in a situation short of secession and the Russian central government has refused to allow this (see Chapter 9).

In addition to the current "hot spots" mentioned earlier, many of the successor countries in the territory of the former Soviet bloc have potential ethno-religious conflicts (even to the point of

TABLE 1.3   Examples of Ethno-Religious Conflict in Contemporary Europe

	Groups	Bases of Conflict
Austria	Catholics v. Socialists	Religion
Belarus	Belarussians v. Russians	Religion
Belgium	Flemings v. Walloons	Language
Bosnia	Serbs v. Muslims	Language, Religion
Bulgaria	Bulgarian v. Turks	Language, Religion
Croatia	Croats v. Serbs	Language, Religion
Cyprus	Greeks v. Turks	Language, Religion
Estonia	Estonians v. Russians	Language, Religion
France	French v. Corsicans	Language
Hungary	Hungarians v. Roma	Language, Religion
Latvia	Latvians v. Russians	Language, Religion
Macedonia	Macedonians v. Albanians	Language, Religion
Netherlands	Catholics v. Protestant v. Secular	Religion
Russia	Russians v. Muslims	Language, Religion
Serbia	Serbs v. Albanians	Language, Religion
Spain	Spanish v. Basque	Language
Switzerland	Germans v. French v. Italians	Language
	Catholics v. Protestants	Religion
Ukraine	Ukrainians v. Russians	Religion
United Kingdom	British v. Irish	Religion

violence). The breakup of the Soviet Union, Czechoslovakia, and Yugoslavia still left mixed ethnic populations in many states. Moreover, although religion was sharply suppressed under communist control, Eastern Europe is distinctive for the extent to which religion and language simultaneously divide many of the same groups. The substantial Russian populations left in most of the bordering countries after the breakup of the Soviet Union involve both domestic relationships with the host ethnic majority and an international relationship with Russia. For example, Russian minorities constitute around a third of the population of Estonia and Latvia, and a quarter in Ukraine. This situation has already created severe tensions, both domestic and "international," as was exemplified in the struggle over the Ukrainian "stolen election" in November–December 2004, which pitted the Russian-dominated east of the country (backed by Russia) against the Ukrainian-dominated west.

The states of the former Yugoslavia, with the exception of Slovenia, face a variety of complex ethnic pulls. Macedonia, for example, was on the verge of civil war in 2001–2002. Strife spilling over from the war in Kosovo pitted a guerrilla movement based in the Albanian minority against the central government. International intervention and NATO peacekeepers, as well as guarantees of minority rights, were needed to dampen the conflict.

Another source of ethnic conflict is the rapidly growing presence of recent immigrants and foreign workers, primarily in Western Europe. During previous periods of economic boom, a several Western European countries invited foreign workers to fill vacancies in the labor force. Many came, and their families often followed. Germany has almost 2 million Turks and Kurds; in Switzerland, nonresidents account for over 10 percent of the population. Although many do not have formal citizenship, these workers and their families have become long-term residents. The economic difficulties and political conflict in Eastern Europe since the breakdown of Soviet control, produced new waves of immigrants to Western European countries that would accept them. Moreover, Western European countries whose former colonial empires created special relationships with now independent nations in Africa, Asia, and the Caribbean have had substantial numbers of immigrants from those areas. For instance, 3 million Algerian Muslims now reside in France. Immigrants surged from 1 percent of the Spanish population in 1990 to a current 6 percent.

The presence of these groups, especially when coupled with high unemployment and other economic tensions, has stimulated expressions of ethnic nationalism by majority groups. Some members of ethnic majorities feel that their cultural and religious customs, as well as long-standing policies regulating church-state relations, are threatened. The minorities have been the target of rising, though still sporadic, ethnic violence in a number of countries. For example, there were numerous attacks and several foreigners were killed in Germany in the early 1990s. Although the situation has quieted as the economy has improved, German leaders have taken firmer antiviolence stands, and immigration has been curtailed. Immigrant groups have become a rallying point for disruptive nationalist parties calling for strong limits on immigration (adopted in many countries), the immediate expulsion of the groups, or worse (see Chapter 3).

In the euphoria of the 1989–1991 collapse of Communism and the Soviet Union, historian Francis Fukuyama forecasted that we would soon witness "the end of history" as secular democratic enlightenment and the market economy would come to dominate all over the world.[17] Since then, however, more pessimistic voices have also been heard. Samuel Huntington argues in "The Clash of Civilizations" that the political future will be dominated by clashing ethno-religious civilizations: the Judeo-Christian, the Eastern Orthodox Christian, the Islamic, the Chinese, the Japanese, the Hindu, and others.[18] He challenges the optimistic belief in the emergence of a unified, rational-secular *world culture*. Since the September 11, 2001 terrorist attacks in the United States, consciousness of international fundamentalist terrorism has increased. On March 11, 2004, the deadly terrorist attack on the Madrid train station brought the destructive dangers home to Europeans.

The EU has begun to move to strengthen anti-terrorism cooperation. These events have intensified European concerns about immigrants and given credence to Huntington's projection.

The starkly contrasting predictions of Fukuyama and Huntington capture the conflict between, on the one hand, an emerging democratic-market civilization, with its base in science, technology, secular education, mass communication, and the market, and on the other hand a world of persistent and intensely felt religious and ethnic identities that are often locally, nationally, or regionally based. Fukuyama may underestimate the perceived threats to the sense of identity and safety that many people derive from familiar beliefs, tongues, and historical experiences. However, Huntington may not properly recognize the powerful material and spiritual incentives of productivity, welfare, and participation that underlie the unifying trends. Only by considering both of these powerful messages can we begin to understand the future of political development, identity, and democracy.

FURTHER DEMOCRATIZATION?

Modern *democracy*, as Samuel Huntington points out, has emerged in *"three waves."*[19] The first began in the aftermath of the American and French revolutions and continued for more than a century through World War I, the "war to make the world safe for democracy." In this first wave successful democracy was largely a phenomenon of Europe and its colonial offspring, but it foundered on the Great Depression and then receded to form the "reverse wave" of *fascist* and *communist* authoritarianism in the 1930s. These disasters, above all the terrible replacement of Germany's democratic Weimar Republic by Hitler's brutal and aggressive Nazi dictatorship, are also a critical part of the European experience.

The second wave, which Huntington calls the "short wave," lasted from the defeat of Fascism in World War II and the breakup of the European colonial empires afterward, until approximately the mid-1960s. While a large number of countries in Europe, East Asia, Africa, and Latin America became formally democratic in these post–World War II years, most of them collapsed quickly into authoritarian regimes of one kind or another. The interwar democracies of Eastern Europe, like their authoritarian counterparts, were repressed by Soviet military force and replaced with Communist authoritarianism. The overthrow of democracy in Greece by military coup in 1967 represents Western Europe's contributions to the reversal of the second wave.

The third wave began in Southern Europe in the mid-1970s, with democratic transformations in Portugal, Spain (see Chapter 8), and Greece, and then quickly spread into Latin America, East Asia, and Africa. In the late 1980s, to the surprise of the rest of the world, it engulfed the Eastern European satellites of the Soviet Union. Then in the early 1990s the Soviet Union itself collapsed into its ethno-national components. Without warning from the worlds of scholarship and the media, democracy, now the formal regime in more than three-quarters of the independent countries in the world had become the "only game in town." It had no expansive, ideological rivals, with the possible exception of the theocratic Islamic regimes of the Middle East.

Given this history, Europe has been a primary laboratory of natural experiments with politics. The modern bureaucratic state, representative parliamentary institutions, various electoral systems, political parties and party systems, interest groups, specialized media of communication—the whole modern political apparatus—emerged first in Europe and its colonies. They emerged at different times, in different parts of the continent, in differing degrees and sequences, and as a consequence of different conditions and events. Most of the rest of the planet has now assimilated these institutions and practices and is in the process of combining them (sometimes more and sometimes less successfully) with indigenous cultures and institutions. Hence, when we study Europe we are observing the origins of modern politics and describing most of the political models for political institutions and theories in the rest of the world. We are also observing some of the greatest triumphs and greatest disasters of democratic politics.

Juan Linz and Alfred Stepan have cautioned that although we are currently in an era of democra-

tization, we should avoid the assumption that all countries of the world will move toward a stable *democratic consolidation*.[20] There are still totalitarian, and "post-totalitarian" regimes in the world, and several varieties and large numbers of authoritarian ones. Many formally democratic regimes in many parts of the world are teetering at the point of economic, social, and political breakdown.[21]

In addition, regimes that seem to be in *democratic transition* may not be moving ahead on some inevitable course toward "completing" the process, but may instead be pausing in "halfway houses." The last 25 years also have seen the growth of "electoral authoritarianism, in which a façade of democracy provides some space for political opposition, independent media, and social organizations that do not seriously criticize or challenge the regime."[22] There is serious concern that Russia (Chapter 9) and some other Eastern European regimes may follow that path and fail to complete or even backslide on the democratization process. Moreover, political corruption is an obstacle to democratic consolidation and performance that has proved to be very difficult to eradicate (see Chapter 4).

As the third wave of democracy seems to be reaching its peak and showing signs of reversal in some parts of the world, the 19 Eastern European countries are a crucial battleground in the long human struggle for freedom and welfare. Nothing would affect the balance of this struggle more than rapid economic growth and consolidated democratization in such countries as the Russian Federation, Ukraine, Belarus, and Romania. Moreover, the consolidated democracies of Western Europe can still go much further to achieve a more fully realized democratization that bases responsive public policies on a participating and confident citizenry.

These then are some of the major challenges of European political studies to which this book is an introduction. How can scholars draw effectively from the great fund of experience and knowledge, most richly based on Western European political and economic studies, in order to illuminate, interpret, and forecast the issues and prospects of a larger and unified democratic Europe?

Key Terms

Axis
bourgeoisie
bureaucratic state
civil society
Cold War
Council for Mutual
    Economic
    Assistance
    (COMECON)
democracy, three
    waves of
democratic transition

Enlightenment
ethnicity
European Economic
    Community (EEC)
European Union (EU)
fascist authoritarianism
Freedom Score
Gross National Product
    (GNP)/Gross
    Domestic Product
    (GDP)

industrial revolution
industrialization
Iron Curtain
market economy
nationalism
Nazism-National
    Socialism
North Atlantic Treaty
    Organization
    (NATO)
Peace of Westphalia

perestroika
Protestant Reformation
Purchasing Power
    Parity (PPP)
Reformation
Renaissance
Treaty of Versailles
Treaty of Vienna
Warsaw Pact
world culture

Suggested Readings

Budge, Ian, and Kenneth Newton, et al. *The Politics of the New Europe.* New York: Addison Wesley Longman, 1997.

Dahl, Robert A. *Democracy and Its Critics.* New Haven: Yale University Press, 1989.

———. *Polyarchy: Participation and Opposition.* New Haven: Yale University Press, 1971.

Diamond, Larry. *Developing Democracy: Toward Consolidation.* Baltimore: Johns Hopkins University Press, 1999.

Fukuyama, Francis. *The End of History and the Last Man.* New York: Avon Books, 1992.

Hall, Peter, and David Soskice. *Varieties of Capitalism: The Institutional Foundations of Comparative Advantage.* Oxford: Oxford University Press, 2001.

Horowitz, Donald. *Ethnic Groups in Conflict.* Berkeley: University of California Press, 1985.

Huntington, Samuel. *The Clash of Civilizations and the Remaking of the World Order.* New York: Simon and Schuster, 1996.

———. *The Third Wave: Democratization in the Late Twentieth Century.* Norman, OK: University of Oklahoma University Press, 1991.

Linz, Juan, and Alfred Stepan. *Problems of Democratic Transition and Consolidation.* Baltimore: Johns Hopkins University Press, 1996.

Sbragia, Alberta, ed. *Europolitics: Institutions, and Policymaking in the "New" European Community.* Washington: Brookings Institution, 1992.

Endnotes

1. Mikhail Gorbachev, *Perestroika: New Thinking for Our Country and the World* (New York: Harper and Row, 1987), pp. 190, 197.

2. See Chapter 12; also Leon Lindberg, *The Political Dynamics of European Economic Integration* (Stanford: Stanford University Press, 1963).

3. See Chapter 12; also Alberta Sbragia, *Europolitics: Institutions and Policymaking in the "New" European Community* (Washington: Brookings, 1992); Desmond Dian, *Ever Closer Union? An Introduction to the European Community* (Boulder: Lynne Rienner, 1994).

4. We excluded from our analysis the interesting "microstates" of Andorra, Liechtenstein, Monaco, San Marino, and Vatican City, all of them with populations of less than 50,000 permanent residents.

5. World Bank, *World Development Indicators 2000*; retrieved May 3, 2000 from http://www.worldbank.org/data/wdi2000/pdfs/tab1_4.pdf.

6. Goods generally cost less in agricultural societies than in urbanized, industrial societies; thus the PPP adjustments in Eastern Europe are greater because living costs are lower in these societies. At the same time, agricultural societies are also likely to generate lower living standards, as seen in Table 1.1.

7. Economic growth figures are based on Gross Domestic Product (GDP), which is similar to GNP, but (roughly speaking) excludes income sent home from nonresidents.

8. Moldova is clearly the poorest nation in Eastern Europe, falling into an international "lower income" category. Albania also seems to be substantially less economically developed than the rest of Eastern Europe.

9. Omar G. Encarnacion, "The Politics of Dual Transitions," *Comparative Politics* 28 (July 1996): 477–92.

10. Daniel Lerner, *The Passing of Traditional Society* (New York: Free Press, 1958); Karl Deutsch, "Social Mobilization and Political Development," *American Political Science Review* (September 1961): 493 ff.; Seymour Martin Lipset, "Some Social Requisites of Democracy," *American Political Science Review* (September 1959); James Coleman, "Conclusion: The Political Systems of the Developing Areas" in Almond and Coleman, *The Politics of the Developing Areas* (Princeton, NJ: the Princeton University Press, 1960), pp. 532–77.

11. A "dependency" school of political economy gained substantial headway among American, European, Latin American, African, and Asian intellectuals. The dependency movement argued that the idea of "developmentalism" was a sham that concealed the essential international exploitation by the leading capitalist powers. Dependency theorists saw the global political reality as control of the third world periphery by American and European "multinational" capitalist corporations, backed up by first-world military force, and also by the international capitalists' indigenous henchmen. These theorists believed that the authoritarian regimes instituted in many developing countries in the 1960s and 1970s were intended to enforce this systematic exploitation of "peripheral" economies. The dependency school gradually lost support among social scientists during the 1980s and has generated little scholarly research since then.

12. For a careful review and update of development theory, see Larry Diamond, "Economic Development and Democracy Reconsidered," in G. Marks and L. Diamond, eds., *Reexamining Democracy* (Newbury Park, CA: Sage, 1992); see also Seymour Martin Lipset, "Second Thoughts and Recent Findings," in Lipset, *Political Man*, rev. ed. (Baltimore: Johns Hopkins University Press, 1981).

13. On the theme of the dispersion of potential political resources in modernized societies, see especially Tatu Vanhanen, *Prospects of Democracy: A Study of 172 Countries* (New York: Routledge, 1997) and Robert E. Dahl, *Democracy and Its Critics* (New Haven: Yale University Press, 1989), pp. 251–54. Also, from a different but not unrelated point of view, see the "class" analyses of Dietrich Rueschemeyer, Evelyne Huber Stephens, and John D. Stephens, *Capitalist Development and Democracy* (Chicago: University of Chicago Press, 1992), pp. 75–78 ff. On the connections between modernization, citizen attitudes of trust and participation, and democracy, see especially Gabriel A. Almond and Sidney Verba, *The Civic Culture: Political Attitudes and Democracy in Five Nations* (Princeton: Princeton University Press, 1963) and Ronald Inglehart, and *Christian Welzel, Modernization, Cultural Change and Democracy* (New York: Cambridge University Press, 2005).

14. Freedom House ratings are taken from their website, http://www.freedomhouse.org/research/freeworld/2003/countries.htm, retrieved December 1, 2003. World Bank, Quick Reference Tables, retrieved December 1, 2004 from http://www.worldbank.org/data/databytopic/GNIPC.pdf. Comparative economic data were not available for Serbia and Montenegro (Yugoslavia) so it is not included in the figure.

15. Seymour Martin Lipset and Stein Rokkan, "Cleavage Structures, Party Systems and Voter Alignments: An Introduction," in Lipset and Rokkan, eds., *Party Systems and Voter Alignments* (New York: Free Press, 1967).

16. Max Weber, *Economy and Society: An Outline of Interpretive Sociology*, edited by Guenther Roth and Claus Wittich (Berkeley: University of California Press, 1978), p. 389.

17. Francis Fukuyama, *The End of History and the Last Man* (New York: Avon Books, 1992).

18. Samuel Huntington, *The Clash of Civilizations and the Remaking of the World Order* (New York: Simon and Schuster, 1996).

19. Samuel Huntington, *The Third Wave: Democratization in the Late Twentieth Century* (Norman, OK: University of Oklahoma Press, 1991).

20. Juan Linz and Alfred Stepan, *Problems of Democratic Transition and Consolidation: Southern Europe, South America, and Post-Communist Europe* (Baltimore: Johns Hopkins University Press, 1996).

21. Ibid. For a generally sober account of democratic prospects in the contemporary world, see Larry Diamond, *Is the Third Wave of Democratization Over?* (Baltimore: Johns Hopkins University Press, 1998). For accounts of earlier overthrows of democracies, see Juan Linz and Alfred Stepan, *The Breakdown of Democratic Regimes* (Baltimore: Johns Hopkins University Press, 1978).

22. Larry Diamond, "Thinking about Hybrid Regimes," *Journal of Democracy* 13 (2002): 26. In general see the articles by Diamond; Andreas Schedler; Steven Levitsky and Lucian Way; and Nicholas van de Valle, *Journal of Democracy* 13 (2002): pp. 21–80.

Chapter 2

Democratic Political Culture and Political Action

Virtually all the nations of today's Europe—east and west, north and south—have converged on a single political destiny: They are all democratic or claim to be. This is a radical change from Europe's modern history when world wars and political divisions wracked the continent. Now as the twenty-first century has begun, the nations of Western Europe and the 19 independent European nations carved out of the territories of the former Soviet Union all claim to follow the democratic model.

There is wide variation, however, in the institutions and practice of democracy (see Chapters 3 and 4). For instance, Britain has had organized and competitive political parties for well over a century and a half, while the Bulgarian party system is still developing. West Europeans are more likely to turn out to vote and to be engaged in other electoral activities. Western European nations have complex civil societies where individuals join organizations and participate in social and political affairs. These institutions and behaviors are just beginning to develop in the East.

Beyond institutional structures, political systems also differ because their citizens vary in how they think and act politically. People in the West have a long experience with democratic elections and autonomous social groups to represent their interests. These experiences have nurtured attachments to democratic values and an understanding of how the democratic process functions. Even within Western Europe, moreover, people emphasize different aspects of the democratic model. The French are more likely to engage in protest because of their revolutionary traditions; the British favor more conventional politics. Such variations in political norms shape the nature of a nation's politics.

The question of political norms has special relevance to the study of Eastern Europe. To what extent have democratic values and norms become consolidated in the new democracies of the East? Furthermore, East Europeans may have different expectations about the democratic process and their role within this new political system. What has been the legacy of their communist histories? Democracy requires that its citizens share its fundamental values, and the development of such values in the East remains one of the important questions in the study of European politics.

By examining citizen attitudes and behavior, this chapter should help us understand what democracy expects of its citizens, what citizens expect of their government, and the variations in how Europeans can participate in the political process.

THE CULTURAL FOUNDATIONS OF DEMOCRACY

As the democratization wave swept across Eastern Europe in the early 1990s, the key questions were whether, where, and how it might succeed. The answers not only determined the political fate of the East; they directly affected the peace and stability of Western Europe. Would the political values inherited from the prior communist regimes be congruent with the new democratic institutions they were building? Could the nations of Eastern Europe be successfully integrated into the democratic, capitalist system of the West? These questions repeated those that were posed by the earlier democratic transitions of Spain, Portugal, and Greece in the 1970s, and Germany and Italy in the 1950s.

Eastern Europe has made remarkable democratic progress over the past decade. Despite severe economic problems, struggles with new democratic procedures, and a host of social problems, most of these nations have maintained their democratic course. But beyond the institutional changes, there is a deeper question of whether East Europeans accept democratic principles and their rights and responsibilities under a democratic system. The futures of these new democracies partially depend on the values and beliefs of their citizens. If the people share the values of the political system, then it is more likely that they and the system can function more effectively. If the people reject the values of the system, it can lead to revolts like those that swept across Eastern Europe in the early 1990s,

when one communist regime after another fell in a series of revolutions.

These shared attitudes constitute the *political culture* of a nation.[1] The political culture includes what the people think and feel about politics, attitudes that have evolved from history and traditions. During times of regime change, the agreement between the public's political norms and the institutions and procedures of the new political system is especially important. For example, most scholars believe that the Weimar Republic collapsed in the 1930s because many Germans did not believe in democracy. Prior experiences had taught these Germans to accept authoritarian and ethnocentric values, attitudes that made them susceptible to Hitler's demagogic appeals. Thus post–World War II West Germany again faced the question of whether the new institutions of democracy could succeed if Germans lacked democratic values. Fortunately, military defeat and a postwar economic growth led to a transformation of the West German political culture (see Chapter 7). The Spanish transition to democracy generated similar questions, and fortunately a similarly positive answer (see Chapter 8).

Now we face the same question for Eastern Europe. What are the enduring historical, political, and cultural legacies of the communist regimes of Eastern Europe? Do Poles, Czechs, Russians, and the other nationalities of Eastern European hold political values that support the democratic process? Or, has prior communist rule created undemocratic and authoritarian values that may produce a fragile new political order?

These questions become all the more important as the nations of East Europe join the institutions of the West. The security net of the North Atlantic Treaty Organization now includes 10 nations from Eastern Europe. In addition, in 2004 18 new East European states joined the European Union. Will the incorporation of these new nations transform the institutions of Europe?

Political culture is not only important for predicting the viability of a new political system; it also influences the style of politics within a political system. The style of Italian politics, for example, differs from Dutch politics, although both are democracies with multiparty systems, parliamentary structures, and coalition governments. When Czechoslovakia divided in 1993 into the Czech and Slovak Republics, it was immediately apparent that citizen expectations varied in these two new nations despite their common political heritage. Institutional structures can explain a portion of these cross-national differences, but a substantial part of the explanation depends on how the public and the elites envision the political process.

The Congruence Principle

What does it take to become a democratic polity? The literature on democracy maintains that the political institutions of a nation must be congruent with the political culture of the public. A stable democracy thus requires a democratic social and political culture. Tocqueville, for instance, wrote that democracy should develop as a habit of the heart reflecting basic values and patterns of social relations: "The manners of the people may be considered as one of the great general causes to which the maintenance of a democratic republic in the United States is attributable."[2] The first president of Czechoslovakia, Tomas Masaryk, similarly argued that democracy is not only a form of government, it is not only what is written in constitutions; democracy is a view of life, rests on faith in man, in humanity, and in human nature.

Research on modern democracies shows that tolerance and patterns of cooperative social relationships are the wellsprings of the democratic process.[3] A society such as Norway, with its tolerance and social trust, provides a fertile ground for developing a democratic political culture and a democratic polity.[4] Other research suggests that social trust and cooperative social relations improve one's health, lower crime rates, improve child welfare, lessen social inequality, and generally improve the quality of life—a seeming panacea for societal needs.[5] Authoritarian political systems, such as Nazi Germany or Spain under Franco, often built upon (or fostered) societies in which interpersonal trust and cooperation were absent, and therefore democratic discourse was difficult to maintain.

This congruence theory about the cultural basis of democracy leads to speculation about the potential social base for democracy in Eastern Europe. On

the one hand, the collectivism of communism sought to develop feelings of mutual solidarity among the public. Communist systems created parts of a civil society that might serve as a training ground for democratic social norms to develop. Worker collectives addressed employment-related problems, neighborhood collectives handled residential issues, and the state encouraged collective action. On the other hand, communist systems ultimately sustained themselves through force and coercion. The government told the public to be obedient to the state, and security police ensured conformity to the regime's directives. Collective action was allowed, but only under direction of the monopolistic Communist Party and the state. The type of spontaneous and autonomous social life that Tocqueville admired in America could not flourish in the East.

A recent survey illustrates the link between social relations and democratic politics. Researchers asked people in 37 European nations whether they trust their fellow citizens. Figure 2.1 illustrates how the levels of interpersonal trust vary across European nations (and the United States).[6] The nations with continuous democratic histories during this century display relatively high levels of interpersonal trust. In nations that experienced authoritarian disruption in mid-century, such as Germany, Italy, Spain, and Portugal, people are slightly less trustful.

Even a decade after the end of communism, levels of interpersonal trust are generally lower for Eastern Europe and the former states of the Soviet Union (Russia, Belarus, and the Baltic States). Communism did not create a trusting and tolerant citizenry and these patterns have carried over to the present. At the same time, the levels of social trust in Eastern Europe are not markedly different from the situation in the postwar transitional democracies in the West. But theory would suggest that social trust should develop if democracy is to grow deeper roots in these societies.

One may ask whether democracies create a trustful and tolerant society, or whether a trustful society leads to a democratic political system. Obviously, it works both ways. For example, West Germans became more trustful as the nation democratized following World War II. This may have been a

FIGURE 2.1   National Scores on Personal Trust and Democratic History

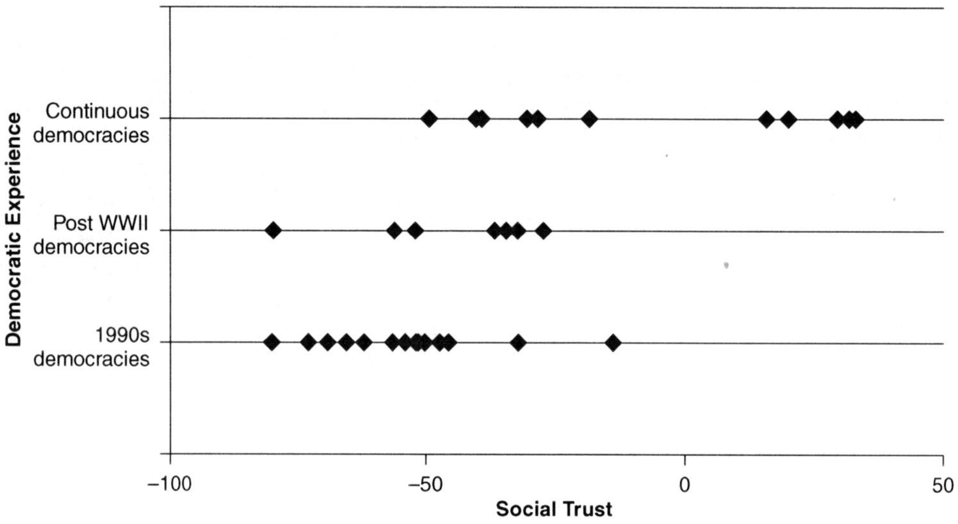

Source: Personal trust from the 1999–2000 European Values Survey and World Values Survey. The figure presents the difference between trustful and distrustful responses.

result of Westerners living in a democratic system as well as democracy encouraging this aspect of the culture. Trend data also suggest that East Germans are becoming more trustful since the democratic transition in 1990. The important conclusion is that there is a congruence between social and political life. It is difficult for democracy to endure when people lack trust and respect for each other. When these values exist, a democratic government must reinforce them; when they are lacking, an aspiring democracy must create them. The hope is that democratization will gradually change these norms among the publics of Eastern Europe.

The political culture begins with social relations, but it develops into more specific political attitudes. These elements of the political culture determine the viability of a democratic political system and the style of politics within the existing institutional structure.

THE LEVELS OF A POLITICAL CULTURE

Beyond social norms, the political culture embodies citizen orientations toward three areas: (1) the political system, (2) the political and policymaking

TABLE 2.1   The Aspects of Political Culture

Aspects of Political Culture	Examples
System	Pride in nation
	National identity
	Legitimacy of government
Process	Role of citizens
	Perceptions of political rights
	Norms of political process
Policy	Role of government
	Governmental policy priorities

process, and (3) policy outputs (Table 2.1). The *system* level involves public orientations toward the political community and the values and organizations that comprise the political system. Does the public identify with the nation and generally accept the political system?

The *process* level taps expectations of how politics should function and individuals' relationship to the political process. For instance, public attitudes toward the procedures of government and political institutions, such as the principles of pluralist democracy and support for parliamentary government, are important in defining how politics actually functions.

The *policy* level deals with what citizens expect from the government. What are the government's policy goals and how are they to be achieved?

The System Level

Attitudes toward the nation and the political system are an important component of a political culture. These sentiments are often acquired early in life, taught by parents and the educational system. Therefore, these are fairly stable beliefs that are relatively independent of attitudes on more specific political matters.

Public acceptance of the legitimacy of the political system provides a foundation for a successful, or at least enduring, polity. When citizens believe that they ought to obey the laws, then legitimacy is high. If they question the authority of the state, or if they comply only from fear, then legitimacy is low. A new political system often faces a challenge in convincing the people that the new government is legitimate, and thus its directives should be followed voluntarily.

A strong emotional tie to the nation also can provide a basis of support that reinforces acceptance of the polity and can maintain a political system through temporary periods of political stress. The deep sense of national pride and national destiny voiced by Winston Churchill during World War II struck a responsive chord with the British public, thus enabling Britain to endure in the midst of an intense military conflict. In contrast, most Germans did not identify with the democratic institutions of the Weimar Republic; and thus when they faced political and economic crisis, they shifted their loyalties to a new system.

A similar question now faces many of the nations of Eastern Europe. Some nations, such as Poland, have a strong national identity, but many others are relatively new political constructs that lack public identifications. Virtually all East European nations have new constitutions written during

FIGURE 2.2 Feelings of National Pride (percent "Very Proud" and "Proud")

West		East
Ireland United States	100	Poland
Denmark		Albania
Austria Britain/France/Spain Norway/Greece Sweden	90	Hungary Romania
Netherlands	80	Czech Republic
Germany	70	Russia Bosnia/Bugaria
	60	Ukraine Montenegro

Source: Selected nations from the 1999–2001 European Values Survey and World Values Survey. Figure presents the percent "very proud" and "proud"; missing data is not included in the calculation of percentages.

the 1990s, and most have existed as independent nations for barely a decade. There has also been considerable tumult and political debate in many Western European states in recent years. Thus, we might ask whether European publics—in West and East—have a strong sense of national identity.

Feelings of pride in one's nation are a revealing example of this aspect of the political culture, as shown in Figure 2.2. At the end of the 1990s, the worst upheavals of the political transition were past in most of Eastern Europe, and enduring national traits are more apparent. Most nations enjoy widespread feelings of pride among their citizens. Americans are noted for their expressions of national pride, but the Poles, the Irish, and other nationalities around the world, display equal enthusiasm. Strong feelings about the nation exist in both Western and Eastern Europe—the Danes express as much pride as the Albanians, for example. National pride is not a function of the longevity or past political form of the nation.

More problematic are the cases where the populace does not identify with the nation; this raises warning signals for the political system. For example, national pride was relatively low in Czechoslovakia in a 1990 survey—within three years, the nation had split in two. German political leaders have consciously avoided the nationalism of the past, and it shows. National pride is also relatively restrained in several Eastern nations that have struggled throughout the 1990s: Russia, Bulgaria, and the Ukraine. And in two regions trying to develop a national identity—Bosnia and Montenegro—these orientations are still in short supply.

Most Europeans, however, express pride in their nation virtually regardless of its historical traditions or national status. Like pride in a sports team, true fans are supportive regardless of what occurs on the field.

The Process Level

The second level of the political culture involves what the public expects of the political process. What do Hungarians think is expected of them as citizens, and what do they expect of their government? Are their views different from those of British or Spanish citizens?

Political theorists generally stress three norms as the basis of the Western democratic process. The first is the Lockean emphasis on popular sovereignty as the basis of governmental authority and the final arbiter of politics. Democracy must, above all, be based on the rule of the people. The second is a commitment to the equality of citizens based on the arguments of Jefferson, Bentham, and Paine. The third is the principle of majoritarian decision making, with adequate protection of minority rights. These principles lead to specific procedures by which democratic processes are ensured, such as formulated in Robert Dahl's "conditions of polyarchy."[7] In short, the congruence principle also holds that democracies can survive only when the public endorses the values of a democratic regime.

Research on West European countries generally finds broad public support for *democratic values*.[8] Citizens and elites accept the principle of organizing political institutions based on popular control through regular elections, as well as party competition and the turnover of leadership through elections. Most Western Europeans recognize the legitimacy of conflict over political means and ends, while opposing violence as a political tool. Europeans also broadly endorse the right of individual participation and majority rule, paired with the protection of minority rights.

At the same time, we cannot become complacent about public support for democracy in the West. Often there is a gap between public support for these democratic principles and their application in specific cases. Many people say they support free speech, but they are less willing to actually grant this right to groups that challenge their values. Still, most citizens in the established democracies of the West accept the principles upon which their democratic system was founded and functions today.

Prior European transitions from authoritarianism to democracy show how a previous authoritarian state could leave a negative cultural heritage. Postwar Italy began with a cultural legacy of fascist attitudes that was not conducive to the workings of democracy. But the Italian culture was transformed and democratic values became the norm.[9] The postwar Germans held broadly undemocratic views, and the remaking of the political culture over the next generation was quite remarkable. Postwar Austria struggled to overcome a similar cultural inheritance from Fascism. The more recent democratic transitions in Spain and Portugal reflected this same pattern. The Francoist regime was an antidemocratic movement based on authoritarian norms. With Franco's failing health and Spain's efforts to integrate itself into Western Europe, the Spanish process of cultural transformation created a new political

---

Box 2.1   A Persistent Political Culture

Although Britain follows democratic procedures, it remains a constitutional monarchy and its traditions underscore the importance attached to the Crown. For example, the Queen of England presides over the opening of the new Parliament following the general elections. The Lords and Ladies assemble in the House of Lords, along with the Bishops of the Church, foreign ambassadors, members of the royal family, and other dignitaries. When the Queen arrives from the palace, the members of the House of Commons are summoned by Blackrod following a centuries old tradition. When both houses of parliament are assembled, the Queen delivers an address outlining the policies of "her" government during the next legislative session.

(The opening of Parliament, as well as weekly Question Hour in the House of Commons, are broadcast on C-SPAN by many U.S. cable television systems.)

---

culture that was more conducive to democracy (see Chapter 8).

In short, in several Western European nations the antidemocratic values of a prior right-wing authoritarian state created hostility toward pluralism and democratic procedures among the citizenry. The subsequent democratic regime inherited a public that was critical of its institutions and unsupportive of its norms. The new regime had to remold citizen beliefs into a culture compatible with democratic processes.

Communism raises a similar question of the cultural legacy of Eastern Europe. In the early 1990s, it was difficult to know whether these nations would face the same cultural problems as the previous authoritarian/democratic transitions in Western Europe. Democracy illustrated the internal contradictions of the communist system. Although the Soviet Union and other Eastern European states suppressed dissent and prohibited meaningful forms of representative democracy, the official rhetoric of these regimes often endorsed democratic principles. Elections were regularly held, and turnout routinely topped 90 percent of the eligible electorate. Many of these governments also mobilized people into an array of political organizations, ranging from labor unions to women's federations and state-sanctioned environmental groups. While some communist regimes were openly authoritarian, others displayed examples of a nascent form of democracy. Gorbachev's reforms of *perestroika* and *glasnost* built upon these tendencies, and some reform movements existed within Eastern Europe.[10]

Almost as soon as the Berlin Wall fell, survey researchers moved eastward, quickly assembling a wealth of findings on the attitudes of Russians and East Europeans toward democratic institutions and procedures. Researchers found surprisingly high levels of support for basic democratic principles in the former Soviet Union and other East European nations.[11] Figure 2.3 compares the opinions of Westerners and Easterners on two examples of democratic values: willingness to allow a revolutionary to publish a book and belief that elections make government responsive. Almost two-thirds of Western Europeans would allow even a revolutionary the opportunity to publish a book, and East Europeans average only a few percentage points lower. Similarly, most Westerners believe that elections make government pay attention to the people, and these opinions are only slightly lower in the East. Indeed, since the earliest surveys after the collapse of communism, East Europeans have displayed surprising support for democratic values. One should also note that democratic sentiments are among the lowest in Russia. This reflects the economic and social tumult that accompanied the transition toward democracy in Russia, as well as the deeper impact of a long authoritarian experience.

The support for democratic principles in Eastern Europe is somewhat surprising given the attempts of the prior regimes to instill communist values among the citizenry. To many Eastern Europeans, however, these democratic rights represent a new reality for which they had fought the old regime. The Solidarity demonstrations in Poland,

FIGURE 2.3   Democratic Values in Western and Eastern Europe, 1996

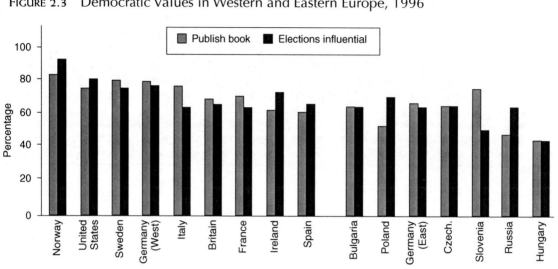

Note: Percentages indicate agreement with the statements "revolutionaries should be allowed to publish books expressing their views" and "elections are a good way of making governments pay attention to the important political issues facing our country." Missing data are excluded from the calculations of percentages.

Source: International Social Survey Program, 1996.

the protests in central Prague, the candlelight marches in Leipzig, and the public response to the August 1991 Russian coup demonstrate this commitment. Having newly won these freedoms, Eastern Europeans openly endorse them.

After half a century or more of communism, how did these publics come to express such support for democratic norms? There is no single answer, and researchers point to several factors. The limited empirical evidence suggests that support for the prior communist system eroded sharply during the 1980s. Eastern Europeans saw their living standards decline during the decade, and the government seemed unwilling or unable to respond. This eroded popular support for the communist system and its values. And, ironically, the old regimes had voiced support for democratic principles, even if the reality of the communist system was much different. These democratic sentiments were further encouraged by *perestroika* and *glasnost* reforms—albeit with different consequences than Gorbachev had

envisioned. The positive model of the West also appealed to many Easterners, as seen in the mass exodus from East Germany in 1989. Furthermore, the euphoria of the democratization wave in 1989–1991 undoubtedly boosted support for the new political creed. Even with these explanations, the broad support for democratic principles in Eastern Europe is still a surprising starting point for these democratic transitions.

Although democratic principles appear fairly similar in East and West, more striking differences often appear in how people evaluate the actual functioning of democracy in their nation. In some Eastern European nations there is a widening gap between the public's support for democratic principles and their views of the present political process. For instance, a recent poll found that three-fifths of the public in 10 Eastern European nations was dissatisfied with the way that democracy works in their nation.[12] People are frustrated by the inability of the new political institutions to deal with the economic and social problems existing in Eastern Europe, which may eventually carry over to public support for the democratic process itself.[13] Furthermore, events such as the Bosnian and Kosovo conflicts, the rise of an authoritarian government in Belarus, and the increasingly autocratic government in Russia constantly remind us that the prospects for democracy remain uncertain in many Eastern European states.

In the end, we should be cautious in reaching conclusions from Eastern European public opinion surveys as democracy is still developing in these nations. It is difficult to evaluate the depth of Easterners' feelings about democracy, whether these are enduring cultural norms or the temporary response to traumatic political events. Still, even if public expressions of democratic values cannot yet be described as an enduring political culture, the widespread expression of such values is a positive signal for democratic prospects in the East. The people in most post-communist states espouse strong support for democratic principles, which facilitates the democratization process. As two of the nations in this volume demonstrate, Poland and Hungary have made impressive progress in developing competitive elections, ensuring the rule of law, and protecting democratic liberties. Democratic development in Russia is less certain. Most Russians value democracy and freedom—although a significant minority still longs for a less democratic state. Rather than the apathy or hostility that greeted democracy after transitions from right-wing authoritarian states in Western Europe, the cultural legacy of communism in Eastern Europe appears to be more supportive of democratization.

By comparison, most Western Europeans broadly endorse democratic values and principles. However, dissatisfaction with the incumbents of office and the current governing parties is growing in the West.[14] For instance, the French political system recently has experienced a series of political scandals reaching up to the highest political officials. Criticisms of the political parties have become commonplace in many Western party systems, and public identification with political parties has generally eroded. Up to this point, the dissatisfaction with the holders of democratic of-fice has not generalized into disaffection with the democratic process. Indeed, the goal of democratic politics is to give the public an institutionalized way to express their dissatisfaction by electing new public officials and changing the policies of government.

The Policy Expectations Level

A third level of the political culture is the public's expectations of what government should achieve. In part, these expectations involve specific policy demands. When Soviet mineworkers protest the government's privatization programs or British farmers lobby the European Union on agricultural policy, they are testing the democratic process. More broadly, public views about policy—the legitimate scope of government, the needs and wants that government should address, and the areas that should remain in the private sphere—define the parameters for government action.

The history of Western democracies records great conflict over just these questions. Industrialization raised issues about the government's role in providing the infrastructure for modern commerce. The labor and social democratic movements of the nineteenth century focused debate on the government's rightful role in the provision of basic social services and the management of the economy. The urbanization process created new demands on municipal governments, and new questions of urban development and redevelopment. More recently, the environmental movement is demanding that governments address the environmental costs of economic activity and ensure environmental quality. Other social interests press the government to be active in everything from training rock bands to preserving the nation's historic sites.

Indeed, nearly all Western European democracies have seen government activity grow during the latter half of the twentieth century (see Chapter 1). The various branches of government in the United States spend roughly a third of the GNP, but many European governments account for half (or more!) of the GNP. Governments are now responsible for a variety of social and personal conditions that were once outside the domain of government activity. Analysts attribute at least a portion of this growth to the expanding public expectations.[15] People demand more of their government and they are promised more by politicians; thus government has expanded to meet these expectations. As Anthony King has written: "Once upon a time, man looked to God to order the world. Then he looked to the market. Now he looks to government."[16]

These public expectations have several important implications for contemporary European politics. Although most Westerners expect more of their government, there are still sharp cross-national and domestic differences in exactly what is expected. Labor unions want government to expand the benefits given to workers; businesses want government to provide tax incentives and subsidies to spur economic growth. Environmentalists want the government to spend more on protecting the environment; commuters want the government to build more roads and expand public transportation. The essence of democratic politics is to find the balance between these competing interests.

As Western European governments grew over the past generation, some people began to complain against high taxation and the excess of government action. Some political analysts claim that excessive policy demands overload contemporary governments.[17] They argue that people are demanding more than what democratic government can provide in an effective and efficient way. Others maintain that government is usurping individual freedom and private initiative. Public opinion surveys show a renewed skepticism of government action as many Europeans began to question the government's appropriate role in society. Margaret Thatcher championed a neoconservative campaign in Britain in the 1980s that scaled back government by privatizing government-owned businesses and reducing the government's policy responsibilities. Conservative governments in the Netherlands, Scandinavia, Germany, and the United States have echoed these statements. Thus, in many Western European societies the debate about the appropriate role of government is continuing.

GOVERNMENT AND THE ECONOMY   Just as Western Europeans began questioning the appropriate role of government in the 1980s, the political changes in

Eastern Europe and the Soviet Union added a new theme to this discussion. State corporations and government agencies almost exclusively controlled the command economies of Eastern Europe. The government set both wages and prices as well as directing the economy. It was also responsible for providing for individual needs, ranging from guaranteed employment to the provision of housing and health care. "Cradle to grave socialism" was more than just a slogan in Eastern Europe.

The collapse of these systems created new questions. The lack of popular support for the communist political system weakened support for the socialist economic system. This clearly occurred in Eastern Europe, as non-communist governments and their citizens rushed to privatize their economies. This partially reflected the economic failures of the old regime. The Eastern European economies could provide the basic needs of their citizens, but they were uncompetitive in the world market and fell steadily behind the economic progress of the West. Thus, the democratization of Eastern European political systems was paralleled by a privatization of their economies.

To what extent do Eastern Europeans carry forward their expectations for government activities from the experiences of the prior regimes? Similarly, do Germans in the West and East have similar expectations about what services government should provide, or has unification created a public with sharply contrasting views of the government's appropriate role? The collapse of communism does not necessarily mean that Eastern Europeans reject the socialist principles of their former systems—principles that could often conflict with their new market economies.

We can describe the present policy norms of Europeans by comparing opinions in several areas. At the heart of the debate on the government's role is the question of government management of the economy. This separates both conservatives and liberals in the West, as well as forms a potential East-West divide. Comparative research shows that levels of economic development are one influence on these opinions; the citizens of less-affluent nations are generally more in favor of government action as a strategy for economic development.[18] In addition, we want to compare the nations with established market economies in the West with the new market economies in Eastern Europe.

Figure 2.4 shows how various groups of nations differ in their support for government control of wages and prices as examples of government management of the economy. The more-affluent countries of Northern Europe (for example, Germany, France, Britain, Sweden, and Denmark) are less likely to favor government management of the economy. Resistance to government management has grown over the past few decades, paralleling the privatization of government-owned businesses and the sell-off of government monopolies. The less-affluent nations of Western Europe (Ireland, Spain, and Italy) are more supportive of government management of the economy.

Equally interesting are the results for Eastern Europe. The dismantling of the socialist economies in the East was accompanied by popular endorse-ment of a greater role for a market economy. But East Europeans still favor a greater role for government in the economy, especially in Russia. A full 90 percent of the Russian public feel the government should control prices—partially a reaction to the runaway inflation that plagued Russia in the 1990s—and 68 percent of Russians also believe the government should control wages. More generally, Russians remain relatively supportive of a socialist economy because the experience with capitalism has fallen far short of the experience in the West.[19]

It is illuminating to compare support for a government managed economy in the various social strata in Eastern Europe. The better-educated are the "carriers of the creed" in most societies.[20] These are the individuals who normally occupy positions of status and influence; they are the operators of the existing economic and political systems. In addition, accepting the regime norms was often required to gain access to higher education. One could not

FIGURE 2.4   Support for Government Management of the Economy

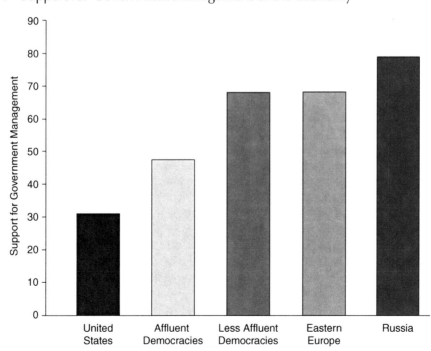

Source: *International Social Survey Program, 1996.* The figure averages support for government control of wages and control of prices.

attend the university without being a member in the correct communist youth groups, or without a good family record of regime support. Thus we would expect the better educated to espouse the values of the communist and socialist systems of pre-1989. In fact, just the opposite occurs. When the old regimes were just ending in the early 1990s, the better-educated Eastern Europeans showed little affection for socialism.[21] Instead of adhering to the values of the old regime, as is normally the case, the better educated advocated a privatized economy. In some ways this is not surprising; the intelligentsia of the communist society led the protests in East Berlin or Prague, and the faces of young university students were prominent in these crowds. Perhaps communism fell as rapidly as it did because it had lost the support of the managers and technicians of the old regime.

The communist regimes were better able to socialize the less educated into believing in government management of the economy. This pattern holds in most of the nations in Eastern Europe. Think of the irony: these regimes claimed to represent workers and peasants, and the less educated actually adhered to these socialist principles. The true beneficiaries of these regimes—the better educated and upper social status—doubted their value. Possibly the better educated were more aware of the superior productivity of the market systems of the West.

In contrast to the generally steady political progress that has been made over the past decade, Eastern Europeans have had a tumultuous economic experience (see Chapter 1). Living standards declined precipitously in many nations after the collapse of communism, and the economic shocks of capitalist market forces were unsettling to many. Yet, support for market principles still exists. A 1996 survey by the European Union found that market reforms received majority support among Eastern Europeans, although 65 percent of Russians said it was wrong for their nation.[22]

The 1998 *New Democracies Barometer* clearly illustrates the juxtaposition of economic and political images.[23] The survey asked residents in Central and Eastern Europe to judge the past, present, and future economic and political systems. Figure 2.5 shows that most Eastern Europeans, even in 1998,

FIGURE 2.5   Public Approval of the Economic and Political Systems in Central and Eastern Europe, 1998

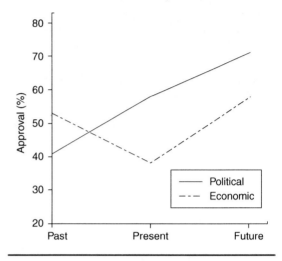

Source: Richard Rose and Christian Haerfer, *New Democracies Barometer V* (Strathclyde: Center for the Study of Public Policy, 1998): 17, 25; combined results from representative surveys in Bulgaria, the Czech Republic, Hungary, Poland, Romania, Slovakia, and Slovenia.

expressed greater approval for the pre-1989 socialist economy than for the contemporary economic system. Russian images show an even greater contrast: in 1996, 83 percent of Russians approved of the former economic system, versus only 18 percent for the present system.[24] This is a clear signal of the disaffection that has resulted from the drop in living standards and the economic insecurities that have accompanied the restructuring of these economies.

At the same time, there are several positive indicators in these opinion surveys. Approval of the present economic system has improved between 1991 and 1998. Furthermore, Eastern Europeans remain optimistic that the economic system in five years time will be much better. In addition, there is a significant juxtaposition of economic and political images. The citizens of Eastern Europe are more positive about their present political system than the pre-1989 system, and these impressions have improved since 1991. Political expectations for the future are optimistic, although most Eastern Europeans expect that it will require several more years to deal with the problems inherited from the communists.

The Government's Policy Responsibilities

Government management of the economy is one of the state's most basic policy activities. Governments are also involved in a great many other areas, from deterring crime to protecting the quality of the environment. Recent public opinion surveys show that many people believe the government is responsible for promoting individual well-being and guaranteeing the quality of life for its citizens—and both Westerners and Easterners share these expectations.

Table 2.2 displays the percentage of the public in several European nations (and the United States) who think the government is "definitely responsible" for dealing with specific social problems. East Europeans, who were conditioned by their former regimes to expect big government, have high expectations of their democratic governments. Most citizens in East Germany, Hungary, Poland, and Russia believe the government is definitely responsible for providing for health care, providing a decent standard of living for the elderly, protecting the environment, and lessening unemployment. Expectations of the state are especially high among Russians.

Many West Europeans share these high expectations of government. Thus support for government action to resolve social needs is a core element of the European political culture, even if there are significant cross-national differences in exactly what is expected.

In comparison to most Europeans, Americans are more reserved in accepting government action. Even in areas where the government is a primary actor, such as care of the elderly and unemployment, only a minority of Americans view these problems as definite government responsibilities. Analysts often explain the conservative socioeconomic attitudes of Americans by the individualist nature of American political culture and the absence of a socialist working-class party.

The public sentiments may partially explain why the scope of government has grown so large in Europe over the past generation. Other scholars claim that these opinions result from the growth of government activism, which conditions the public

to expect even more from government.[25] In either case, these expectations are another example of how political culture and political outcomes tend to converge. Governments can grow more easily when the public accepts (and expects) that they will grow. Governments are more likely to shrink when public support for government activism wanes. Thus it is more than a coincidence that the expansion of the welfare state in Scandinavian countries coincided with broad public support for social programs, while Margaret Thatcher's program of privatizing government-owned industries in Britain coincided with decreasing public support for nationalized industry.

Debates about the proper role of government will be a continuing feature of contemporary politics. However, it is clear that most Europeans expect their government to protect social welfare, help the economy, and guarantee the quality of life. The question is not whether government should act, but how it should manage the diverse demands the public makes upon it.

PARTICIPATION AND DEMOCRACY

Democracy empowers its citizens to affect the course of government and to influence policy. The history of modern democracies, however, is marked by the slow and often conflictual expansion of the public's participation in politics. The growth of democracy can be measured by the public's broadening access to politics and the government's responsiveness to public demands.

Modern democracy is *representative democracy*. It enshrines elections as the main institution of democracy and the primary vehicle for public participation and democratic governance. Through elections, the public controls the selection of political leaders, which determines the formation of government and the policies the government will likely implement.

Although *election turnout* is now a standard part of democratic participation, the expansion of the franchise in Europe occurred only during the past century. At the start of the twentieth century most European democracies severely restricted the franchise. Britain, for instance, limited election rolls

TABLE 2.2   Government Responsibility for Dealing with Social Issues (in %)

	United States	Britain	France	Spain	Italy	Sweden	Norway	West Germany	East Germany	Hungary	Poland	Russia
Provide health care for sick	39	82	53	81	81	71	87	51	66	71	69	82
Provide decent living standard for the elderly	38	73	51	80	76	69	86	48	64	63	68	87
Strict environmental laws	46	63	67	69	69	58	56	58	72	56	60	71
Give aid to needy college students	35	38	59	75	59	36	34	27	43	37	48	63
Keep prices under control	25	44	42	59	59	45	53	23	43	38	41	68
Provide job for everyone who wants one	14	29	40	61	41	35	48	28	57	47	58	71
Reduce income differences between rich and poor	17	36	49	57	41	43	41	25	48	41	48	49
Provide housing for those who need it	20	37	44	70	45	27	22	20	38	22	39	52
Provide a decent living standard for the unemployed	13	29	34	59	30	39	41	17	38	16	31	39
Provide industry with help	17	41	36	64	28	33	23	16	27	35	39	51
Average	26	47	48	68	53	46	49	31	50	43	50	63

Source: *1996 International Social Survey Program.* Table entries are the percentage who say that each area should definitely be the government's responsibility. Missing data were excluded in the calculation of percentages.

through residency and financial restrictions, and by allowing multiple votes for business owners and university graduates. In 1900 only 14 percent of the British adult population was eligible to vote. Similarly, Prussia used a weighted voting rule that gave a triple vote to the landed aristocracy and a single vote to laborers. Almost without exception, governments denied women the right to vote.

During the twentieth century, governments gradually extended suffrage rights to the adult population. Property restrictions were steadily rolled back. Most nations acknowledged the right of women to vote early in the century, but some countries delayed—most notably France until 1944 and Switzerland until 1970. During the 1970s, most nations also reduced the minimum voting age to 18. By the later half of this century, voting rights were essentially universal among the adult populations in Western Europe.

Even though the communist parties of Eastern Europe did not permit open competition, these nations also held regular elections, sometimes with multiple parties or a unified slate of candidates. Voting turnout routinely exceeded 90 percent of the eligible electorate; the last Soviet-era election of 1984 had an official turnout rate of 99.9 percent. Elections were not a method of popular influence, however; they were a means for the government to mobilize and indoctrinate the populace. Nonvoting signified opposition to the regime, which might jeopardize the nonvoter (and local officials who were responsible for ensuring a large turnout). Thus voting levels were consistently high even if some ballots had to be cast by election officials themselves. Nevertheless, elections were held and the public learned the mechanics of campaigns and the voting process.

Today, most eligible Europeans vote in national elections. Moreover, voting is a significant method of citizen influence because it selects political elites and determines the composition of the government. Elections also provide an opportunity for political activists to participate in the selection of party candidates and to try to influence the political views of others. In some countries as many as a tenth to a fifth of the electorate attend a campaign meeting, work for a party, or participate in other campaign activities. Elections are national civics lessons in which voters learn about the past and future programs of the parties, participate in the democratic process, and decide about the issues facing their nation.

Figure 2.6 displays the distribution of election turnout in Western and Eastern Europe in the most recent national election for which data are available. What is most striking is the large range in voting turnout across these nations. The lowest level of

FIGURE 2.6   Levels of Election Turnout in Western and Eastern Europe

West Europe	East Europe
Belgium — 100	
Cyprus — 90	
Denmark	
Luxembourg	
Italy/Austria	
Sweden/Netherlands — 80	
Germany	
	Croatia
Greece/Norway	Hungary/Macedonia
	Latvia/Ukraine
— 70	Slovakia/Slovenia
Spain	Georgia
Finland	Bulgaria
Ireland/Portugal	Romania
France — 60	Russia/Belarus
Britain	Estonia/Lithuania
	Czech Republic
— 50	
Switzerland	Poland

Source: Institute for Democracy and Electoral Systems (www.idea.int). Figure plots percentage of registered voters who cast a ballot.
* Voting is compulsory in Belgium.

involvement is in a well-established democracy, Switzerland, where less than half of the eligible electorate (43 percent) actually voted in 1999. Voting rates are consistently higher in most other European nations; in two nations where voting is still compulsory, turnout tops 90 percent (Belgium and Cyprus). Turnout rates in Eastern Europe were often quite high in the first elections after the democratic transition. Now turnout in the East is a bit lower than the average levels of the established democracies in the West.

Cross-national research has identified a range of factors that affect levels of voting turnout.[26] Analysts find that laws and institutions, such as the type of electoral system or registration regulations, directly affect participation rates. In addition, political competition and the structure of party choices strongly influence turnout levels. For example, turnout in American elections is significantly below the norm for European democracies, and this can largely be explained by such uniquely American characteristics as complicated registration requirements and the frequency of elections.[27]

Voting is the most common form of political action and the basis of representative democracy. Thus it is somewhat worrisome that electoral participation has gradually declined in most of Western Europe over the last few decades.[28] Furthermore, participation in campaign activities beyond voting is also declining. Fewer citizens, even in established democracies, attend a campaign rally or display their partisan support during a campaign. Similarly, high turnout levels in the first democratic elections in Eastern Europe often were followed by a drop-off in later elections. If elections are the celebration of democratic politics, fewer individuals seem to be joining in these celebrations.

The decrease of electoral participation is even more surprising when compared with the socioeconomic development of Europe described in the previous chapter. Contemporary electorates are better educated, better informed, and more interested in politics than their predecessors. Europeans are also more democratic in their values than was the public a generation ago. Nevertheless, electoral participation has decreased. Richard Brody refers to this as "the puzzle of political participation."[29] Why is elec-toral participation limited and decreasing, if the public's political skills and resources are increasing?

At the core of this question is a concern with the vitality of the democratic process. This view holds that higher levels of voting turnout are a positive feature for democracy. In general this is correct; democratic nations with high levels of turnout in elections are more successful in involving their citizens in the political process. Consequently, the decrease in turnout is often attributed to growing alienation from politics or a more general decline in civic life.[30]

Another explanation for reduced levels of electoral participation is the development of a new style of *participatory democracy* among Western European publics. Instead of indirect influence through elected officials, a growing share of the public now tries to influence politics directly. People seem more interested in contacting politicians or in participating in direct-action methods. Citizen-action groups and public interest groups are pressing for greater citizen input in policy formation and administration.[31]

The situation, of course, is different in Eastern Europe. These prior communist regimes involved the public in mass membership groups and state-sponsored political organizations.[32] In East Germany, for example, there were millions of members in the labor unions, the women's federation, and the German-Soviet Friendship Society. These were so-called "*civil society*" groups, except they were not autonomous and were controlled by the Communist Party and state agencies.

This situation changed with the democratic revolutions of the 1990s. The political demonstrations of Solidarity, the mass protests in Leipzig and East Berlin, and the public demonstrations in the streets of Prague toppled communist regimes across Eastern Europe. These were "people power" revolutions where public pressures brought down the old regimes and created democracies in their place. The Eastern Europeans very quickly became involved in democratic politics.

The extent of participatory democracy among Europeans can be estimated by the public's involvement in various non-electoral forms of participation. As Table 2.3 shows, many Europeans have signed a petition within the previous year, a mild form of participatory democracy. One can hardly

TABLE 2.3   Cross-National Levels of Non-Electoral Participation (in %)

Nation	Signed Petition	Lawful Demonstration	Contact Official	Boycott Product
Britain	40	4	18	26
Denmark	28	8	18	23
Germany	31	11	13	25
Finland	24	2	24	27
Greece	5	4	15	9
Ireland	27	7	22	13
Italy	19	11	12	8
Luxembourg	27	20	18	15
Netherlands	23	3	14	11
Norway	37	9	24	20
Portugal	7	4	11	3
Spain	22	16	12	23
Sweden	41	6	17	33
Switzerland	40	8	17	34
West Europe Average	27	8	17	18
Czech Republic	15	4	21	11
Hungary	4	4	15	5
Poland	7	1	10	4
Slovenia	12	3	12	5
East Europe Average	10	3	15	6

Source: 2002 *European Social Survey*. Respondents engaged in the activity during the previous 12 months.

enter a Marks & Spencer in Britain or a Kaufhof in Germany without being asked to sign a petition. For some people, this form of direct action is more common than voting in elections. Signing petitions is less common among Eastern Europeans, especially in the successor states of the Soviet Union (Russia, Ukraine, and Belarus).

Political protest is an even stronger measure of direct political action. The second column in Table 2.3 shows that participation in a demonstration is fairly common. Such unconventional action now often matches or exceeds normal involvement in campaign activities among Western Europeans.[33] Many West European publics are as likely to engage in protest activities as they are to participate in an election campaign beyond voting. Protest is now the extension of conventional politics used by the full range of societal interests (see Box 2.2). The level of protest activity is generally lower across Eastern Europe, and in most all of these nations

protest has declined as the tumultuous events of 1990–1991 have passed into history.

The third column of the table lists the percentage of the public who have directly contacted a politician or government official in the previous year. To an increasing degree, citizens are willing to be advocates for their own interests. And the expanded role of government more often brings them into contact with government. Again, participation levels are highest in the affluent advanced industrial democracies of Northern Europe, with lower participation levels in the South and East.

Perhaps the most interesting set of statistics come from the rightmost column in the table. This displays the percentage of people who say they have boycotted a product for a political or ethical reason. This form of economic participation is surprisingly common, especially in the established market economies of the West. Another question from the survey (not shown) indicates that Euro-

Box 2.2   Protest in Action

Coal miners in several Eastern European nations had been active in organizing protests against the communist regimes during the democratic transitions, and have become one of the more assertive participants under the new democratic system. In Russia, for example, miners organized a series of strikes in the mid-1990s to protest their unpaid back wages and government plans to close down several mines. The unions claimed that up to a fourth of their members went without a paycheck each week. In the spring of 1998, Siberian coal miners went on strike and blockaded the Trans-Siberian railway for more than a week. There were sporadic actions of violence, and some spouses went on a hunger strike. Hundreds of union members set up a camp outside of Moscow for the summer to continue their protests. The government eventually persuaded the miners to return to work by taking emergency measures to pay off wage arrears and promising to investigate the reasons that wages were chronically going unpaid. Coal miners had been the first group of workers to mobilize independently under the Soviet regime when they launched a massive strike under Gorbachev in 1989, and they continue to demonstrate their political influence in the post-communist period.

peans are even more likely to say they bought certain products for political or ethical reasons.

Thus, European political participation has changed in two significant ways over the last two decades. First, the public's involvement and interest in political matters is now widespread. Many Europeans turn out at the polls, others work on political campaigns, many individuals contact their representative directly, many people belong to local community organizations, and large numbers are members of public interest groups.[34] Therefore some analysts describe the last two decades as a *participatory revolution*, during which public involvement in the democratic process grew. Now, the expansion of democracy to Eastern Europe gives additional meaning to this term—although participation levels are generally lower in the East.

Second, the patterns of political participation have changed in qualitative terms. The methods of representative democracy—voting and campaign work—are important activities because they determine the control of government. However, these are relatively blunt democratic tools since the typical election involves many issues and candidates. And participation in elections and campaigns have decreased.

Participatory democracy produces a qualitatively different form of citizen input. Involvement in a citizen action group or direct contact with policymakers allows people to focus attention on a specific policy concern. The voice of the public is also louder when the citizens express their views themselves. Direct action gives citizens greater control over the timing and methods of participation, compared with the institutionalized framework of elections. Therefore the growing use of citizen-initiated participation increases popular control of political elites.

These developments may permanently change the style of political participation in advanced industrial democracies. *New social movements* have created an infrastructure for continued citizen involvement in the policy process. For instance, in Germany administrative law now gives the public more say in policy administration; in Italy new legislation gives the public legal standing in defending the environment in court, and the use of initiatives and referendums is generally increasing. Citizen groups such as these have legitimated direct-action methods of participation for other citizen groups. Today, Gray Panthers protest for senior citizen rights, consumers are active monitors of industry, and citizen groups of all kinds are proliferating.

Research finds that different kinds of people engage in these various forms of participation.[35] Because voting places the least demands upon its participants, it is the most common form of political action and involves a diverse mix of people. By comparison, direct-action methods require greater personal initiative and more sophisticated political skills. It is much more demanding to organize a letter-writing campaign or participate in a public interest group than to cast a ballot at the next election. Consequently, participation in direct forms of action often varies considerably by social status. While voting is spread across the electorate, direct action is now disproportionately used by the affluent and better educated. Similarly, only those with strong political beliefs are likely to become active in single-issue groups. This situation increases the participation gap between lower-status and higher-status individuals. As the better educated expand their political influence through direct-action methods, less-educated citizens might be unable to compete on the same terms. Ironically, overall increases in political involvement may mask growing inequalities in citizen participation and influence, which run counter to democratic ideals.

The strength of the democratic process is its ability to adapt, evolve, and become more democratic. In recent years the political systems in most Western European states have adopted forms of participatory democracy and given their citizenry new methods to participate in the decisions affecting their lives. The nations of Western Europe vary in their emphasis on representative and participatory democracy, but nearly all are now characterized by a mix of these styles.

As they are learning about democracy, many Eastern Europeans have ambivalent feelings toward both of these styles of democratic participation. They recognize elections and representative democracy as essential elements of the modern democratic process. At the same time, many Easterners are disillusioned by the competitive style of electoral politics as practiced in the West. Many people are drawn to the principles of participatory democracy, albeit with a plebiscitarian emphasis. The conditions of affluence and civil society that nurture participatory democracy in the West are underdeveloped in the East; therefore participation in citizen-action groups and direct-action methods is relatively low in Eastern Europe. Ray Taras's discussion of Polish participation patterns illustrates their ambivalence to both representative and participatory styles of action

(Chapter 10). Many Eastern Europeans still seem unsure about how best to participate in democratic politics, even if they support the principles of democracy.

The challenge for established and emerging democracies is to expand the opportunities for citizens to participate in the political process. To meet this challenge also means ensuring an equality of political rights and opportunities that will be even more difficult to guarantee with these new participation forms.

THE PUBLIC AND DEMOCRACY

In many ways, the citizenry defines the essence of democratic politics. In its practice, democracy is a German at the polls casting a vote for her preferred party, a French farmer driving his tractor to Paris to protest the government's agricultural policy, a Hungarian writing a letter to the Budapest *People's Freedom* to criticize government policy, or Russian mine workers protesting a cut in government benefits.

Public wants and needs set the priorities that democratic governments strive to address. Citizen expectations of the political process influence the ways in which that process works and the kinds of policies it produces. Citizen participation in the political process presses a democracy to match its lofty ideals.

This chapter's emphasis on the citizenry does not presume that political culture and citizen action determine policy outcomes. Other parts of the process—interest groups, political parties, and political leaders—act as intermediaries between the public and policy outcomes, and their direct impact is often greater in the short term. Similarly, if we want to predict the success of democracy in Eastern Europe, it is much more important in the short term to study the actions and values of elites and the role of institutions.

Thus, citizen politics does not primarily explain the daily outcomes of politics, but it determines the broad boundaries of the political system. One political scientist described public opinion as a set of dikes, channeling the course of democratic politics and defining its boundaries. The public's policy preferences influence policy outcomes in a democratic system—but this is through a complex and sometimes circuitous route.[36] In the same way, the public's expectations of politics and support for the political system determine the long-term functioning of the system. The immediate success of the new Eastern European democracies may depend on elite actions, but their long-term success depends on creating a democratic political culture among both the public and the elites. Democracy cannot endure in a nation without democrats.

There are nearly two dozen established democracies in the West and nearly an equal number of new democracies in the East. The citizens in these nations generally share a common democratic creed, and these political systems are built upon common principles. Most Europeans express support for their political system and a sense of national identity; expectations about an activist government are also common.

Where these publics differ is in their conceptions about *how* the democratic process should function. People in some nations display a more participatory style of democracy, with high levels of conventional and unconventional political action. The Dutch and the Danes, for example, are activist publics with institutional structures that encourage the representation of diverse political interests. Other Europeans, such as the British, accept a more representative style of democracy, placing greater reliance on elites and the role of elections as instruments of popular control. The French seem to follow a more conflictual style of politics, where protest and political strife are almost routine. Democracy follows a single set of principles, but it takes life in many forms.

The nations of Eastern Europe are now making choices about how to practice democracy as the new system becomes institutionalized and these nations join Western organizations such as the European Union and NATO. Communists ruled these nations for half a century, and these nations must surmount the legacy of this experience. Many Eastern European nations have suffered from violence and political corruption. Chapter 1 showed that several nations still merit poor scores for political rights and civil liberties. Some political experts argue that another form of authoritarian state lies in the future for some of these nations, and political progress in Russia remains uncertain.

We do not overlook these difficulties, but we also note that these democratic transitions generally began with a majority of the people and elites supporting democratic principles. Moreover, the international community is actively working to encourage freedom and political liberties in Eastern Europe. If democracy successfully takes root, Eastern Europeans will search for democratic forms that meet their particular histories and their expectations. Political debates over representative and participatory democracy, and over various institutional choices for democratic politics, are especially real in Eastern Europe as these systems are now taking shape. Thus the evolution of democracy continues with new trends among the consolidated democracies in the West and still unclear trends developing among the nations in Eastern Europe. How these two democratization processes develop will define the political fate of Europe in the next century.

 Key Terms

civil society	new social movements	participatory revolution	representative
democratic values	participatory democracy	political culture	democracy
election turnout			

Internet Sources

The World Values Survey website has information on this global survey of values: www.worldvaluessurvey.org

The Eurobarometer website of the European Union has information on their latest citizen and elite surveys: europa.eu.int/comm/dg10/epo/

The Institute for Democracy and Electoral Assistance (IDEA) has data on election turnout around the globe: http://www.idea.int/

The International Social Survey Program (ISSP) website has additional information on these surveys: www.issp.org

Suggested Readings

Almond, Gabriel, and Sidney Verba. *The Civic Culture.* Princeton: Princeton University Press, 1963.

———, eds. *The Civic Culture Revisited.* Boston: Little Brown, 1980.

Blais, Andre. *To Vote or Not? The Merits and Limits of Rational Choice Theory.* Pittsburgh: University of Pittsburgh Press, 2000.

Borre, Ole, and Elinor Scarbrough, eds. *The Scope of Government.* Oxford: Oxford University Press, 1995.

Dalton, Russell. *Citizen Politics: Public Opinion and Political Parties in Advanced Industrial Democracies.* 4th ed. Washington, DC: CQ Press, 2005.

———. *Democratic Challenges, Democratic Choices: The Erosion of Political Support in Western Democracies.* Oxford: Oxford University Press, 2004.

Eckstein, Harry, Frederic Fleron, Erik Hoffman, and William Reisinger, eds. *Can Democracy Take Root in Post-Soviet Russia? Explorations in State-Society Relations.* Latham, MD: Rowman & Littlefield, 1998.

Franklin, Mark. 2004. *Voter Turnout and the Dynamics of Electoral Competition in Established Democracies since 1945.* New York: Cambridge University Press.

Inglehart, Ronald. *Culture Shift in Advanced Industrial Society.* Princeton: Princeton University Press, 1990.

Inglehart, Ronald, and Christian Welzel. *The Human Development Model and Value Change.* New York: Cambridge University Press, 2005.

Jennings, M. Kent, and Jan van Deth, eds. *Continuities in Political Action.* Berlin: deGruyter, 1990.

Kaase, Max, and Ken Newton. *Beliefs in Government.* Oxford: Oxford University Press, 1995.

Klingemann, Hans-Dieter, and Dieter Fuchs, eds. *Citizens and the State.* Oxford: Oxford University Press, 1995.

Niemi, Richard, Lawrence LeDuc, and Pippa Norris, eds. *Comparing Democracies 2: New Challenges in the Study of Elections and Voting.* Newbury Park, CA: Sage, 2002.

Norris, Pippa. *Democratic Phoenix: Reinventing Political Activism.* New York: Cambridge University Press, 2002.

Petro, Nicholai. *The Rebirth of Russian Democracy: An Interpretation of Political Culture.* Cambridge: Harvard University Press, 1995.

Pharr, Susan, and Robert Putnam, eds. *Discontented Democracies: What's Troubling the Trilateral Countries?* Princeton, Princeton University Press, 2000.

Putnam, Robert. *Bowling Alone: The Collapse and Revival of American Community.* New York: Simon and Schuster, 2000.

Putnam, Robert, ed. *Democracies in Flux: The Evolution of Social Capital in Contemporary Society.* Oxford: Oxford University Press, 2002.

Rose, Richard, William Mishler, and Christian Haerpfer. *Democracy and Its Alternatives: Understanding Post-Communist Societies.* Johns Hopkins University Press, 1998.

Verba, Sidney, Kay Schlozman, and Henry Brady. 1995. *Voice and Equality: Civic Volunteerism in American Politics.* Cambridge: Harvard University Press.

White, Stephen, Richard Rose, and Ian McAllister. *How Russia Votes.* Chatham, NJ: Chatham House Publishers, 1996.

Endnotes

1. Gabriel Almond and Sidney Verba, *The Civic Culture* (Princeton: Princeton University Press, 1963); Almond and Verba, eds., *The Civic Culture Revisited* (Boston: Little Brown, 1980).

2. Alexis de Tocqueville, *Democracy in America* (New York: Knopf, 1945), p. 299.

3. Almond and Verba, *The Civic Culture,* Ch. 10; Harry Eckstein, "Authority Relations and Government Performance," *Comparative Political Studies* 2 (1969): 269–325; Robert Putnam, *Making Democracy Work* (Cambridge: Harvard University Press, 1993).

4. Harry Eckstein, *Division and Cohesion in Democracy* (Princeton: Princeton University Press, 1966).

5. Robert Putnam, *Bowling Alone: The Collapse and Revival of American Community* (New York: Simon and Schuster, 2000).

6. For an interesting comparison, earlier editions of *European Politics Today* include the same figure based on 1990-1991 and then 1995-1998 survey data, and the same pattern is apparent. The survey asks: "Can most people be trusted, or can't you be too careful when dealing with people?" Also see Ronald Inglehart, *Culture Shift in Advanced Industrial Society* (Princeton: Princeton University Press, 1990), Ch. 1; Ronald Inglehart, *Modernism and Postmodernism* (Princeton: Princeton University Press, 1997).

7. Robert Dahl, *Polyarchy* (New Haven: Yale University Press, 1971).

8. Russell J. Dalton, *Democratic Challenges, Democratic Choices* (Oxford: Oxford University Press, 2004); Hans-Dieter Klingemann and Dieter Fuchs, eds., *Citizens and the State* (Oxford: Oxford University Press, 1995).

9. Giacamo Sani, "The Political Culture of Italy," in Almond and Verba, eds., *The Civic Culture Revisited*.

10. Nicholai Petro provocatively argues that there are strong currents of democracy and civil society that predate the communist era, in *The Rebirth of Russian Democracy: An Interpretation of Political Culture* (Cambridge: Harvard University Press, 1995); for a counterview see Harry Eckstein et al., *Can Democracy Take Root in Post-Soviet Russia?* (Lanham, MD: Rowman & Littlefield, 1998).

11. Richard Rose, William Mishler, and Christian Haerpfer, *Democracy and Its Alternatives: Understanding Post-Communist Societies* (Johns Hopkins University Press, 1998); William Reisinger, Arthur Miller, and Vicki Hesli, "Political Values in Russia, Ukraine, and Lithuania," *British Journal of Political Science* 24 (1994): 183-223; James Gibson et al., "Emerging Democratic Values in Soviet Political Culture," in A. Miller, W. Reisinger, and V. Hesli, eds., *Public Opinion and Regime Change* (Boulder, CO: Westview Press, 1993); Russell Dalton, "Communists and Democrats: Attitudes Toward Democracy in the Two Germanies," *British Journal of Political Science* 24 (1994): 469-93. Compare with Robert Rohrschneider, *Learning Democracy: Democratic and Economic Values in Unified Germany* (New York: Oxford University Press, 1999).

12. Richard Rose, "Advancing into Europe: Contrasting Goals of Post-Communist Countries," in *Nations in Transition 2002* (New York: Freedom House, 2002).

13. G. Evans and S. Whitefield, "The Politics and Economics of Democratic Commitment," *British Journal of Political Science* 25 (1995): 485-514; Arthur Miller, Vicki Hesli, and William Reisinger, "Reassessing Mass Support for Political and Economic Change in the Former USSR," *American Political Science Review* 88 (1994): 399-411; Stephen White, Richard Rose, and Ian McAllister, *How Russia Votes* (Chatham, NJ: Chatham House, 1996).

14. Dalton, *Democratic Challenges, Democratic Choices*; Susan Pharr and Robert Putnam, eds., *Discontented Democracies* (Princeton: Princeton University Press, 2000).

15. Ole Borre and Elinor Scarbrough, eds., *The Scope of Government* (Oxford: Oxford University Press, 1995).

16. Anthony King, "Overload: Problems of Governing in the 1970s," *Political Studies* 23 (1975): 166.

17. Richard Rose and Guy Peters, *Can Government Go Bankrupt?* (New York: Basic Books, 1978); Crozier, Huntington, and Watanuki, *The Crisis of Democracy*; Samuel Brittan, "The Economic Contradictions of Democracy," *British Journal of Political Science* 5 (1975): 129-59.

18. Inglehart, *Culture Shift*, Ch. 8; Ole Borre and Jose Manuel Viega, "Government Intervention in the Economy," in Borre and Scarborough, *The Scope of Government*.

19. See also Raymond Duch, "Tolerating Economic Reform," *American Political Science Review* 87 (1993): 590-608; Richard Rose, *New Democracies Barometer V: A Twelve Nation Survey* (Glasgow: University of Strathclyde, 1998).

20. For instance, the better educated are more likely to espouse democratic values if they live in a democratic system, and German public opinion surveys immediately after the collapse of the Third Reich found that the better educated were more likely to support the tenets of Fascism. This point is, however, debated for post-communist societies. See Ada Finifter, "Attitudes Toward Individual Responsibility and Political Reform in the Former Soviet Union," *American Political Science Review* 90 (1996): 138-52; Arthur Miller, William Reisinger, and Vicki Hesli, "Understanding Political Change in Post-Soviet Societies," *American Political Science Review* 90 (1996): 153-66.

21. See, for example, Figure 2.6 in the first edition of *European Politics Today*, p. 45.

22. Central and East European Eurobarometer 6.

23. Rose and Haerpfer, *New Democracies Barometer V*; more recent data suggest that East Europeans are still more positive about the present and the future than they are about the communist regimes. But images of the old regime had improved by 2001. See Rose, "Advancing into Europe."

24. Stephen White, Richard Rose, and Ian McAllister, *How Russia Votes* (Chatham, NJ: Chatham House, 1996), p.12.

25. Ole Borre, "Beliefs and the Scope of Government," in Borre and Scarbrough, *The Scope of Government*.

26. Mark Franklin, *Voter Turnout and the Dynamics of Electoral Competition in Established Democracies since 1945* (New York: Cambridge University Press, 2004); Andre Blais, *To Vote or Not to Vote? The Merits and Limits of Rational Choice Theory* (Pittsburgh: University of Pittsburgh Press, 2000).

27. G. Bingham Powell, "American Turnout in Comparative Perspective," *American Political Science Review* 80 (1986): 17-44; Ray Wolfinger and Steve Rosenstone, *Who Votes?* (New Haven: Yale University Press, 1980).

28. Mark Gray and Miki Caul, "The Decline of Election Turnout in Advanced Industrial Democracies," *Comparative Political Studies* 33 (2000); Andre Blais, *To Vote or Not?*

29. Richard Brody, "The Puzzle of Participation in America," in A. King, ed., *The New American Political System* (Washington: American Enterprise Institute, 1978).

30. Robert Putnam, ed., *Democracies in Flux: The Evolution of Social Capital in Contemporary Societies* (Oxford: Oxford University Press, 2002).

31. Pippa Norris, *The Democratic Phoenix* (New York: Cambridge University Press, 2000); Bruce Cain, Russell Dalton, and Susan Scarrow, eds., *Democracy Transformed? Expanding Citizen Access in Advanced Industrial Democracies* (Oxford: Oxford University Press, 2003).

32. Donald Schulz and Jan Adams, eds., *Political Participation in Communist Systems* (New York: Pergamon Press, 1981).

33. Dalton, *Citizen Politics*, Chs. 3, 4; Norris, *The Democratic Phoenix*, Ch. 2.

34. Klingemann and Fuchs, *Citizens and the State*, Chs. 2, 3; Norris, *The Democratic Phoenix*.

35. Sidney Verba, Norman Nie, and Jae-on Kim, *Participation and Political Equality* (Cambridge: Cambridge University Press, 1978); Dalton, *Citizen Politics*, Chs. 3, 4.

36. Benjamin Page and Robert Shapiro, *The Rational Public* (Chicago: University of Chicago Press, 1992); Christopher Wlezien, "Patterns of Representation: Dynamics of Public Preferences and Policy," *Journal of Politics* 66 (2004): 1–24.

Section 2
European Union Politics

Chapter 12

Politics in the European Union

ALBERTA SBRAGIA

European Union Bio

POPULATION: 453.7 Million

TERRITORY: 2,372 sq. mi

YEAR OF LEGAL CREATION: 1958

PRESIDENT: Rotates among member-states

LANGUAGES: German 19.8%, French 14.2%, English 13.7%, Italian 12.7%, Spanish 8.7%, Polish 8.5%, Other 22.4%

RELIGION: Roman Catholic 58%, Protestant 20%, Jewish 0.2%, Muslim 2%, Orthodox 3%, Other & unaffiliated 16.8%

The *European Union (EU)* represents a remarkable attempt by the nation-states of Europe to construct a framework of governance in which together they make collective decisions about a broad range of issues. As an organization, the EU is far more legally authoritative and institutionally sophisticated than any other international body. The 25 member nations have not, however, renounced the vigorous pursuit of their "national interest" in any policy area. Yet, by agreeing to pursue that interest within an organization as constraining as the European Union, the member-states have recognized the ultimate superiority of multilateral, as opposed to unilateral, decision making and action in a variety of policy arenas.

The term European Union is often used interchangeably with the term European Community. The original European Economic Community (EEC) established with the Treaty of Rome in 1958 gradually came to be known as the European Community (EC). The Treaty of Maastricht changed the name of the EC to the European Union. In certain legal contexts, however, the term European Community is still used. In this chapter, we determine usage by what seems most appropriate given the historical period being discussed.

Although the European Union resembles an international organization in certain ways, it is in fact very different. To begin with, it includes institutions that are not directly controlled by the member-states and that exercise real policymaking power. Although the EU has similarities to a traditional national political system, it is clearly distinct from the other political systems discussed in this book. For example, it does not have its own military or its own police force, and it does not belong to the United Nations. It is not a sovereign entity in the way that traditional nation-states are sovereign in international affairs. Furthermore, it is governed without a prime minister and a cabinet as found in traditional parliamentary democracies. Rather than being governed by an elected government, a group of institutions collectively makes EU policy. Although the EU produces binding laws, the fact that it does so without having a traditional "government" is perhaps the EU's most confusing feature.

National governments believe that by becoming members of the Union, they can achieve both peace and prosperity for themselves and for Europe. The Union is an experiment in "pooling sovereignty." National governments have over time agreed to restrict their own ability to make decisions unilaterally; they have agreed to make decisions in concert with other member governments and with institutions that are not under their control. In many policy areas, a national government, when outvoted by other governments, is legally required to comply with the decision it opposed. This process does not cover all policy areas, but it does cover many. Unilateral decision making by national governments has become less frequent as the EU's policy agenda has gradually expanded.

The consequences of belonging to the European Union are serious for member-states. In fact, some analysts have calculated that "today only 20 to 25 percent of the legal texts applicable in France are produced by the [French] parliament or the government in complete autonomy, that is, without any previous consultation in Brussels."[1] Membership in the Union is not to be taken lightly, for it changes the policy processes and the policy outcomes of national political systems. Membership carries with it serious and binding economic and political commitments. Individual nations belonging to the Union can be increasingly thought of as member-states of a larger collectivity that shapes their policy options. However, membership does not change the culture of a country—the same language is spoken before and after accession, for example, and its "way of life" goes on after accession as it did before. A country makes a serious political and economic commitment when it joins the European Union but it does not commit to changing its culture.

Why "Europe"?

Why have the individual nation-states of Europe—among the oldest in the world—decided to "pool their sovereignty"? Why have they accepted the sharing of power with institutions not directly controlled by the member-states? After all, political scientists tend to argue that the protection and maintenance of sovereignty is the top priority of governments throughout the world. Why did the process of European integration begin in the first place?

National leaders initiated the drive for European integration out of fear—fear that the history of European warfare would repeat itself unless they found a new way in which to live together. At its core, the Union is rooted in the desire to transcend European history, a history filled with "rivers of blood" to use Winston Churchill's famous phrase. European integration is an attempt to change the geopolitics of Europe. By entangling the domestic institutions of individual nation-states within the institutions of the European Union, integration has changed (hopefully forever) the relations between European states. Such a change in international relations, however, has "fed back" into national political systems. Domestic policies, institutions, and modes of governance have been changed by virtue of belonging to the Union.[2]

The integration effort was initially anchored in the belief that it represents the best answer to what is known as "the German Question." That is, integration (rather than confrontation) was the best way to keep Germany firmly in the company of peaceful democratic nations and to keep it from playing a destructive role in European geopolitics. The attempt to ensure that Germany was a cooperative rather than a threatening neighbor led to a historic restructuring of relations among European states. This has also had a significant impact on domestic politics and policy.

Although the fear of potential German aggression was an initial motive for European integration, other important spurs to integration have more recently come into play. European business firms' fear of losing competitiveness relative to American and Japanese firms is one such spur. A growing acceptance that international problems such as environmental pollution, illegal immigration, and organized crime require transnational solutions is another. The less than stellar European role in dealing with the various Balkan crises, including Kosovo, has pushed governments to increase their coordination in the defense area.

The enlargement of the Union from 15 to 25 members in May 2004 led national leaders to agree on a constitutional treaty (commonly referred to as a "constitution for Europe") that will be either ratified or rejected by national parliaments or referenda in the next few years.

Government leaders have acknowledged, sometimes reluctantly, that together they can have a much greater impact on problems than through individual action. Essentially, they have had to decide whether they wanted to exercise "a share of more effective power or [have] exclusive control over a less effective or wholly ineffective power."[3] Old-fashioned sovereignty—that is exclusive control over policymaking—is associated with "naive sovereignty."[4] The result is that Brussels, the city that symbolizes the European Union, has gradually come to supplement, constrain, lead, and at times supplant national capitals.

The international (European) relations and the domestic politics of the members of the European Union are increasingly intertwined. While the Union is not a traditional state and cannot be viewed as the "United States of Europe," it is an extremely important form of governance. A complete analysis of politics, policymaking, and economics in any member-state must consider the impact of the Union.

National governments have sometimes led this effort at integration. At other times, they have acquiesced in accepting it, or they have resisted it. Whatever their stance toward European integration, however, national governments play a key role in shaping and directing it. The institutions of the Community not controlled by the member-states, including the European Court of Justice, also play a role in keeping the process of integration moving, especially when the member-states do not exercise leadership.

The European Union is now so important that much of what happens in national capitals cannot be understood without considering Brussels. However, neither can one understand what happens in Brussels without taking national capitals into account.[5] Brussels is not nearly as divorced from national politics as is Washington from the politics of state capitals in the United States.[6]

The European Union's political system is entangled with the politics of its constituent member-states while simultaneously having its own separate institutional identity and political dynamics. That balance between entanglement and autonomy makes it both complex and fascinating. The "separateness" of the Union's political dynamics is rooted in the role of the various institutions involved in the policymaking process at the Union level, institutions that form a highly sophisticated and complex policymaking machinery. Most of those institutions do not strictly represent the interests of national governments. This means that national governments operating within the Union need to accommodate, respond to, and compromise with institutions representing the "supranational" interest.

HISTORICAL ORIGINS

Precisely because of the linkage between national systems and the European Union discussed earlier, the Union is considered to be *sui generis*. Although it is recognizable to students of federal systems such as the United States, Canada, and the Federal Republic of Germany, it is also recognizable to students of international organizations such as the United Nations. In fact, the Union as a political system stands somewhere between a federal system and an international organization. To understand why—and why it is still moving along that continuum—it is important to understand its historical origins.

Those origins have shaped subsequent developments much as the historical underpinnings of the American Constitution have shaped American politics. Its historical origins help explain why the Union does not look more like a traditional state, why the electorate often plays an indirect role, and why the national governments play such an important role in a framework that does have strong supranational elements to it.

The European Union is the most important institutional manifestation of the process of European integration. It has succeeded in moving toward an integrated Europe, whereas other European institutions (such as the completely separate Council of Europe) have not. The desire for integration is rooted in European history, much of it the result of the numerous and bloody centuries-old conflicts between France and Germany (see Chapters 6 and 7).

Recent history makes it clear why so many in postwar Europe were afraid that the past would continue to haunt Europe's future. Between 1870 (the Franco-Prussian War) and 1945, France and Germany had fought three times, twice in conflicts so vast that they were known as "world" wars. Only 21 years separated the end of World War I (1918) from the beginning of World War II (1939). Both France and Germany had also been involved in the traumatic Spanish Civil War (1933–1936), which foreshadowed the world war to come.

European integration is linked to the creation of institutions that have some autonomy apart from the member governments. While member governments continue to be pivotal, they are not the only important actors. Institutions that have some independence from the member governments are also important. The existence of such independent institutions—cohabiting with institutions that are more tightly controlled by member governments—is known as "supranationality." Intergovernmentalism, by contrast, refers to institutional arrangements in which only national governments matter in the making of policy. European integration therefore is symbolized by a supranational component existing alongside an intergovernmental one. The

symbiotic relationship between the two makes the politics of European integration so intriguing.

Supranational Integration: Schuman, Monnet, and the European Coal and Steel Community

The effort toward European integration—understood as having a supranational component—dates from May 9, 1950 and the *Schuman Plan* (see Figure 12.1). On that day, French Foreign Minister Robert Schuman proposed the creation of an international organization to coordinate activity in the coal and steel industries. Designed to ensure Franco-German reconciliation and representing "a first step in the federation of Europe," Schuman's proposal represented a reversal of French foreign policy toward Germany. France changed from a policy of unremitting hostility to one of reconciliation. Rather than viewing Russia/USSR as the key to constraining German power (the view historically taken by France), Schuman envisioned a Germany embedded in an integrated framework as the way to constrain German might. That view was a radical break with the past and helps explain why today's European Union represents such an extraordinary development. At its core, the Union has attempted to break the underlying dynamics of European geopolitical history.

Above all, the Schuman Plan was, in Schuman's own words, "a leap into the unknown."[7] France declared its willingness to restrict its own sovereignty in the fields of coal and steel in order to ensure that German sovereignty would be equally limited. Reconciliation was tried as an alternative to the "balance of power" international game that had brought so much death and destruction to Europe. Schuman hoped that war would become "politically unthinkable and economically impossible."[8]

That "leap into the unknown" had been designed by Jean Monnet, then general commissary for the French Plan of Modernization and Equipment. Monnet developed the plan in an atmosphere of tremendous secrecy. Monnet was to play a critical role in the process of European integration throughout the following decade and beyond, so much so that he is sometimes referred to as "Mr. Europe." Monnet underscored the strategic impor-

Figure 12.1   The Timetable for European Integration

May 1950	Schuman Plan
1952	Treaty of Paris (European Coal and Steel Community) (ECSC)
1954	European Defense Community defeated
1958	Treaty of Rome—European Economic Community (EEC)
1966	Luxembourg Compromise (Legitimated use of national veto)
1973	Britain, Denmark, and Ireland join the EC
1979	Direct election of European Parliament
1981	Greece joins the EC
1986	Spain and Portugal join the EC
1987	Single European Act (SEA)
1993	Maastricht Treaty
1995	Austria, Sweden, and Finland join the EU
1999	Introduction of euro as a "virtual" currency, Treaty of Amsterdam
2002	The euro is introduced into daily use
2003	Treaty of Nice
2004	The EU enlarges to 10 new countries: Cyprus, Czech Republic, Estonia, Hungary, Latvia, Lithuania, Malta, Poland, Slovakia, Slovenia
2004	Member-states agree on the European constitution

tance of having a "supranational" component in any initiative designed to achieve integration. In his view, supranationality was necessary to prevent the old interstate balance of power dynamics from becoming preeminent. His role in articulating the importance of supranationality in European integration was so important that many consider Monnet to be "the most important single architect of the European Community."[9]

The Franco-German relationship lay at the core of the Schuman Plan, and that relationship remains the central one within the process of European integration. France is Germany's key interlocutor in Europe, and Germany is France's key referent. When they agree on the need for further integration, France and Germany provide the political energy, the driving force, and the momentum for achieving further integration.

In addition to reversing French foreign policy toward Germany, the Schuman Plan invited democratic nations in Europe to join in forming an organization that would implement the vision outlined in the plan. Germany, Italy, Belgium, Luxembourg, and the Netherlands (the latter three known as the Benelux countries) responded. Negotiations began a month later, and these nations signed the Treaty of Paris, which established the European Coal and Steel Community (ECSC), on April 18, 1951. Although the ECSC was overshadowed by future developments in integration, it represented the first key step in overcoming the ancient divisions of continental Europe.

Negotiating Europe

The European Coal and Steel Community focused on economics as the most appropriate arena for integration. In particular, interstate trade and the prosperity that was thought to flow from such trade was to be fostered by integration. In turn, integration would be fostered by the results of such trade. This view has shaped the evolution of European integration and its substantive policy core: economics, economic policy, and trade in the pursuit of economic prosperity.

Underlying this concern with prosperity was the notion that prosperity facilitates peace. Because

the interwar years (1918–1939) had seen economic tumult throughout much of Europe and the simultaneous rise of fascism and Nazism, economic prosperity was considered necessary for both democracy and peace.

The negotiations over the Schuman Plan did not involve only economic issues, however. Both domestic and foreign policy were major considerations. Foreign affairs—closely intertwined with domestic politics—emerged as a critical concern for all heads of state after World War II.

Why Join Europe?

It is useful to consider why these other countries accepted Schuman's invitation to discuss integration. We find an often entangled combination of political/economic and geopolitical reasons—the Siamese twins of Europe. Economics played an important role in the first attempt at integration and has remained as a critical factor. It might be argued that integration proceeds fastest when the political/economic and geopolitical reasons reinforce one another.

European integration was not inevitable. It represented a political choice. If different leaders had been in power, it might well not have occurred. While integration addressed the needs of the political leaders who accepted Schuman's invitation, these leaders were also predisposed to the idea. All of the leaders who decided to accept Schuman's invitation were from the Christian Democratic Party. (Schuman was a Christian Democrat as well.) Their party affiliation gave them a common bond and a set of ideological referents and beliefs that provided a basis for similar views of the world. Their ideology was a cognitive lens through which leaders and followers could define problems and choose solutions. The leaders who agreed had a great deal in common.

Schuman's own life experience encouraged him to shape "French foreign policy to his vision of a Europe in which France and Germany were reconciled and the suffering of the border provinces ended."[10] (See Box 12.1). For Konrad Adenauer, who became German Chancellor in 1949, the proposed community represented a way for Germany to become an accepted and respectable member of

Box 12.1   Robert Schuman: A True "European" (1886–1963)

Born in Luxembourg and raised in German-speaking part of Lorraine	Escaped in 1942 and became active in French Resistance
Attended German universities	Helped to found Christian Democratic Party (MRP) in 1944
Drafted into German Army in World War I	
Became French citizen in 1919 when Alsace-Lorraine was restored to France under Treaty of Versailles	November 1947–December 1952–Served as either premier or foreign minister of France
Elected to French Parliament	November 1950–Proposed the Schuman Plan, the catalyst for European integration
Refused to serve under Vichy Regime	1958–1963–Served as a member of the European Assembly, the forerunner of the European Parliament
Imprisoned by Gestapo for condemning expulsions of French population of Lorraine	

both Europe and the international system. Personally, he anxiously sought closer ties with France. He was also confident that the German coal and steel producers were in a strong enough position that their interests would be safeguarded. In both strategic and personal terms, therefore, Schuman's proposal was attractive. By contrast, Kurt Schumacher, the leader of the German Social Democratic Party, opposed integration with France. Although other key members of the Social Democrats supported European integration and the European Coal and Steel Community, he strongly opposed both. He saw the ECSC as both too capitalist and too dominated by the Christian Democratic Party.[11] The fact that Adenauer rather than Schumacher was chancellor when Schuman made his proposal was undoubtedly significant in shaping the history of European integration.

For the Benelux countries, dependent on trade with their neighbors, Schuman's proposal represented an attractive way of solving the German Question. The Dutch Foreign Ministry saw the Schuman Plan as creating "the capability for Europe to profit by Germany's strength without being threatened by it."[12] Once Belgium was able to obtain special treatment of its coal mines, the Benelux countries were on board.

The Italian Christian Democratic premier Alcide de Gasperi made a different calculus.[13] He viewed integration as a way both to escape Italy's fascist past and to keep the strong Soviet-linked Ital-

ian Communist Party from coming to power. (The Communist Party opposed the Schuman Plan, viewing it as increasing American domination in Europe.) Eventually, European integration also represented a way to modernize the country, partially by ensuring export markets and partially by ensuring that millions of Italians could emigrate and work in the rest of Europe.

Although in 2004 most of Europe was in the European Union, in 1950 the governments of only six countries saw European integration as being in their interest.

Why Stay Out of Europe?

The countries that did not join in 1951 made their decisions on a variety of grounds. Spain and Portugal were under dictatorships and thus did not qualify for membership, while Greece was experiencing a civil war. The Scandinavians were uninterested in "supranational" schemes: the Nordic Union was based on intergovernmental cooperation rather than integration through supranationality. The Eastern European countries were in the Soviet sphere of influence and were simply unable even to consider answering Schuman's invitation. All of these countries were to join the drive toward European integration much later. The United Kingdom, the most important country to absent itself from the ECSC, did not join for a variety of reasons. Perhaps the most important, Britain saw itself as a world power, the leader of an empire, rather than as a state that needed to be concerned with its "European" role. The British rejection of the French government's invitation to participate in the ECSC negotiations was to be a defining moment for the future relationship of Britain with an integrated Europe.[14]

The Cold War, the United States, and European Integration

American influence on European integration in the 1950s was expressed in a number of ways. The United States, the "maker" of the international system, decisively shaped global institutions so as to break down trade barriers, protectionism, and imperial preferences and thereby create a liberal international economic system.[15]

The United States also influenced Europe more directly. The postwar period, especially between 1947 and 1950, was a crucial one for institutionally linking the United States to Europe. On June 5, 1947, the United States announced the outlines for the *Marshall Plan* (1948–1951). By insisting that Europe coordinate requests for Marshall Plan aid rather than allow each recipient country to deal bilaterally with the United States, the plan helped set the stage for European integration, "not least in the fostering of new modes of thinking."[16] Later, the United States provided strong support for both the Schuman Plan and the European Economic Community.[17]

While the Marshall Plan linked the United States and Europe economically, the Americans also became involved militarily. In April 1949, the Atlantic Pact was signed and the *North Atlantic Treaty Organization (NATO)* was born. Through NATO, the United States and Canada committed themselves militarily to European defense.

Six weeks after Schuman made his historic announcement on May 9, 1950, war broke out when North Korea invaded South Korea. The Korean War was a pivotal event in the American relationship to Europe and thereby for the future of European integration. The American government feared that the Soviet Union would invade Western Europe via Germany. The United States therefore backed German rearmament, announced (in

September 1950) that American troops would be incorporated into the NATO defense force, and that German divisions would be put under NATO command.

The European Defense Community (EDC) emerged as a counterproposal, which called for a European army incorporating all German forces. However, the French parliament definitively rejected the proposal on August 30, 1954. Although the EDC was dead, German rearmament was still on the agenda. In May 1955 Germany was recognized as a sovereign state and accepted as a member of NATO. The dream of a European army was stillborn. In a similar vein, the possibility of an independent European role in international politics was remote. "The European state system was, for the first time since the seventeenth century, firmly embedded in an international order dominated by others."[18]

The incorporation of both American troops and Germany in NATO within the context of the Cold War set the framework within which security and defense issues would be considered even after the end of the Cold War. Those issues were essentially taken off the agenda of European integration.[19] The Bretton Woods system had taken international monetary policy off the agenda. The path of integration was profoundly shaped by the fact that European integration took place within the "NATO-Bretton Woods system" in which the United States exercised hegemony in the West.[20]

It was not until the 1980s (in response to the breakdown of the Bretton Woods system) that the Community seriously addressed the issue of international finance (in the form of exchange rates) from an integrationist perspective. And the issue of security and defense policy remained within a transatlantic arena of discussion.[21]

It was not until 1999 that Europe began seriously discussing the creation of a separate European military force to be used for crisis management and even that would be linked to NATO. The process of European integration, therefore, has until very recently incorporated only selected issues rather than concerning itself with all those issues traditionally considered "high politics." The exclusion of such issues ensured that European integration would not lead to the establishment of a European state in the traditional sense.

The European Economic Community

In May 1955, the Assembly of the ECSC asked the foreign ministers of the Six to draft new treaties to further European integration. The *Treaty of Rome* established the *European Economic Community (EEC)* and came into force on January 1, 1958. One of the French negotiators, Robert Marjolin, articulated the hopes and symbolism attached to the signing of the Treaty of Rome:

> I do not believe it is an exaggeration to say that this date [March 25, 1957] represents one of the greatest moments of Europe's history. Who would have thought during the 1930s, and even during the ten years that followed the war, that European states which had been tearing one another apart for so many centuries and some of which, like France and Italy, still had very closed economies, would form a common market intended eventually to become an economic area that could be linked to one great dynamic market?[22]

The Treaty of Rome included a much wider range of economic arenas and modified the institutional structure of the ECSC in important ways. Unlike the superseded ECSC, the European Economic Community has remained at the core of the integration process. The close working relationship that gradually developed among the six countries operating within the ECSC transferred over into the EEC. The Treaty of Rome called for the creation of a common market—the free movement of people, goods, services, and labor—among the six signatories. It called for a common agricultural policy (the latter provision had been included in order to convince the French parliament to ratify the treaty). It also called for measures to move the EEC beyond a mere common market. It embodied both economic and political objectives: "Whilst the Treaty of Rome is virtually exclusively concerned with economic cooperation, there was (and remains) an underlying

political agenda. There is no doubt that its architects saw it . . . as another step on the road to political union."[23]

The Expansion of Europe

Two models of "Europe" developed during the 1960s. The EEC, with its supranational dimension, symbolized the first. The *European Free Trade Association (EFTA)* symbolized the second. EFTA was established in 1960 with Britain playing a leading role in its birth and Norway, Sweden, Denmark, Switzerland, Austria, and Portugal joining the British-led initiative. It was entirely intergovernmental, lacked any supranational element, and was concerned only with free trade. Whereas EFTA did not compromise sovereignty, the ECC created an entanglement and a fusion between national and community powers.[24]

Over time, the supranational model eclipsed the intergovernmental. Only Iceland, Norway, and Switzerland remain in EFTA. The decline of EFTA was presaged by the UK's decision to apply for membership in the EEC. After two vetoes by President De Gaulle of France, the British, along with Ireland and Denmark (for whom the UK was a key trading partner), finally joined in 1973 when Georges Pompidou replaced De Gaulle as President of France. Norway had also applied and been accepted, but its electorate rejected membership in a referendum in 1972.

In 1981 Greece joined and in 1986 Spain and Portugal did the same. The accession of all three was viewed as consolidating their transition to democracy and as widening European integration to the Mediterranean. In 1995, Austria, Sweden, and Finland joined; Norway's electorate again refused accession in a referendum. On May 1, 2004, ten new countries joined the Union, in what is referred to as the "big bang enlargement": Czech Republic, Cyprus, Estonia, Hungary, Latvia, Lithuania, Malta, Poland, Slovakia, and Slovenia. Bulgaria and Romania have been promised accession for 2007, and it is likely that Croatia will join in 2007 as well. In addition, the EU has made it clear that the map of the EU would not be completed without all the Balkan countries. More controversially, Turkey was

Box 12.2   Candidate Countries for Membership in the European Union as of 2004

Countries seeking to enter the EU must first be officially accepted as candidate countries by the current 25 member-states. The second stage in the process of accession involves entering into complex negotiations during which the candidate countries must demonstrate that they satisfy criteria laid down by the EU. Once negotiations are completed both the European Parliament and all 25 national parliaments must approve the accession of the candidate countries.

Bulgaria and Romania—Negotiations began 2000—set to join in 2007.
Croatia—Negotiations will start in early 2005.
Turkey—It was recognized as a candidate country at the Helsinki Summit in December 1999—member-states decided in December 2004 that negotiations will start in October 2005

---

also recognized as a candidate country at the Helsinki Summit of December 1999, but accession negotiations have not yet begun (see Box 12.2). Of the four poorest countries included in the enlargements before 2004, Ireland, Spain, and Portugal are typically viewed as "success" stories. Greece, in contrast, has been far more problematic for the Union. Its internal politics have been such that the fit between Brussels and Athens has been far from an easy one.[25]

Most of the countries included in the 2004 enlargement are much less prosperous than are the 15 "old" member-states. Many believe that with EU membership, the kind of assistance which the EU has provided Italy, Spain, Ireland, Portugal, and Greece will help the new entrants progress economically. Many in the "old" EU hope that the "newcomers" will do as well as Portugal, Spain, and Ireland, all of whom have become prosperous and active supporters of European integration.

Beyond the Treaty of Rome

The dismantling of tariffs within the Community did indeed increase trade among the six signatories of the Treaty of Rome. However, the increased volatility of financial markets, rooted in the breakdown of the Bretton Woods economic system, threatened the expansion of trade. In 1979 the Six supported a Franco-German initiative designed to minimize the fluctuations in exchange rates. They

established the European Monetary System (EMS), which served as the foundation for a common currency and Economic and Monetary Union (EMU). Britain, however, declined to join the EMS's key mechanism, the exchange rate mechanism. Again, the Six had taken the process of European integration one step further, but without British participation. Britain remained outside until October 1990, just before Margaret Thatcher was forced out of office by her own political party.

While the British government did not want to tie the British pound to the currencies of the Six, it was concerned with the declining competitiveness of European industry with its American and Japanese counterparts. Beginning with the election of Margaret Thatcher as prime minister in 1979, political elites in Europe gradually became more sympathetic to the idea that the opening of markets was necessary both to spur economic growth and to improve the competitiveness of European firms in the emerging global economy. The election of Christian Democratic Chancellor Kohl in Germany in 1982 and the ill-fated fortunes of the French Socialist government's policies from 1981 to 1983 led to an emerging consensus that Europe needed to establish a true common market, one in which so-called nontariff barriers were dismantled. Experts increasingly saw markets as promoters of economic growth rather than simply as a mechanism from which workers needed extensive protection.

The new president of the European Commission, Jacques Delors, crystallized the emerging consensus. Delors' own father was left for dead by German troops in World War I, but he played a key role in the movement toward European integration. Appointed in 1985, Delors seized on the idea for an internal market (the new name given to the "common market" with the connotation of removing nontariff barriers). The internal market project revitalized the Community, ensured Delors' place in the history of European integration, and gave the Community a much higher profile than it had previously had.

The process led to the Single European Act, a major amendment to the Treaty of Rome. For Delors, the single-market project was a way to use economics to pursue a political agenda. As he explained in a radio interview in 1993, "If this job was about making a single market I wouldn't have come here in 1985. We're not here just to make a single market—that doesn't interest me—but to make a political union."[26]

The Single European Act

The decision to amend the Treaty of Rome was made in 1985, and the *Single European Act (SEA)* came into force in 1987. The SEA changed the decision rules for legislation designed to create the internal market in that qualified majority voting rather than unanimity was to apply to such legislation. (A qualified majority requires more votes for approval than does a simple majority.) A national government could not veto legislation introduced for the explicit purpose of creating the market (the veto had been legitimated in January 1966 in the Luxembourg Compromise). Furthermore, the SEA increased the powers of the European Parliament and increased the Community's powers in the area of environmental protection.

The drive for the single market came to be known as the "1992" Project—1992 was the deadline for the adoption of Community legislation needed to remove nontariff barriers. The adoption of a single market represented a milestone in the history of European integration. It was analogous in importance to the "interstate commerce clause" in the American constitution. Just as that clause undergirded the growth of federal power in nineteenth-century America, the single market represented a

major step in the integration of Europe and the power of the Community institutions.

A single market minimizes nontariff barriers. Such barriers accumulate over time and are often closely tied to cultural traditions, which means that overriding them can be politically sensitive. For that very reason, the single market has been so important. By examining barriers from the perspective of whether they inhibit the possibilities open to an exporter to a certain country, the single market opens to scrutiny many institutional arrangements in both the public and private sectors which have been accepted over time. Germany could not exclude beer made in an "unGerman" way, Italy could not exclude pasta made with "foreign" wheat, and so forth.

The 1992 Project was above all a project of regulatory reform—national deregulation combined with re-regulation at the Community level. Market forces were strengthened in order to improve the ability of European firms to compete globally. Regulation was implemented in Brussels rather than the national level. The European Community began setting up regulatory agencies—such as the European Agency for the Evaluation of Medicinal Products to regulate pharmaceuticals—that have complemented national regulatory frameworks. Although national economic systems were deregulated, re-regulation occurred in Brussels. Furthermore, environmental regulation was increasingly concentrated at the Community level. Finally, the Commission began exercising its powers in the area of competition policy (which covers antitrust and state aids) much more aggressively.[27] Protected markets, such as those in the telecommunications and air transport sectors, were gradually liberalized (so that phone calls and intra-European air travel became far cheaper than they had been). The protectionist policies which economic integration was meant to overturn were gradually eroded or eliminated. By the late 1990s, the Community's regulatory reach was so important that some analysts considered it a "regulatory state."[28]

The Maastricht Treaty

The single market of the late 1980s was largely viewed as a success. Business investment climbed, and Europe enjoyed a new sense of economic optimism. Under these circumstances, an initiative to move to a European central bank and a common currency as an extension of the single market began to attract support. Central bank governors, under the chairmanship of Jacques Delors, began to lay out a framework for achieving a common currency.

While that effort was underway, the Berlin Wall fell in November 1989. German unification, once barely considered, now became a reality (see Chapter 7). A new Germany was on the scene. Would it continue to face westward—to Brussels—or would it face toward the East? What role would the new Germany play in a Europe fundamentally changed by the end of the Cold War? How could Europe "contain" this economic powerhouse that had just added more than 16 million inhabitants? These questions were especially pressing, as the problems—and especially the huge costs—associated with German unification were still unacknowledged by most observers.

One response to a new version of the old "German Question" was to move toward a new treaty that would bind Germany even more firmly to the West by further tying German institutions to those of the Community. The purpose was to ensure that a "European Germany" would not be supplanted by a "German Europe." Helmut Kohl, the chancellor of Germany, for whom memories of World War II were still keen, strongly supported embedding Germany in a more deeply integrated European Community. The result was the *Treaty of European Union (TEU)*, usually referred to as the *Maastricht Treaty* after the small Dutch town in which the final negotiations took place in December 1991.

The Maastricht Treaty came into effect in November 1993. It represented another milestone in the history of European integration, moving the process of European integration into two critical new arenas as well as entrenching the Community's jurisdiction over the pivotal area of monetary policy. The treaty is complex. It changed the name of the European Community to that of the European Union (EU). Most importantly, it changed the structure of the Community by establishing three "pillars" in which the Community institutions played different roles. That same structure was retained in the subsequent Treaty of Amsterdam and the Treaty of Nice which that came into effect in 1999 and in 2003 respectively.

In the Maastricht, Amsterdam, and Nice treaties, the European Council and the Council of Ministers were important in all three pillars, whereas the other Community institutions were central only in pillar one. The more federally inclined members of the Union saw the pillar structure as a transition phase, one that would ultimately lead to all three areas of policy being brought under the Community's institutions. The more intergovernmentalist members viewed the pillar structure as a safeguard against precisely that kind of evolutionary development.

Pillar One: The Extension of the Treaty of Rome

Pillar one as defined by Maastricht encompassed the creation of the *Economic and Monetary Union (EMU)*—including a new European Central Bank and a common currency (the euro) as well as incorporation of all the policy areas previously falling under the Community's jurisdiction. The *acquis communautaire*—all the accumulated laws and judicial decisions adopted since the signing of Treaty of Rome—belonged to the first pillar. For example, the single market, agriculture, environmental policy, regional policy, research and technological development, consumer protection, trade policy, fisheries policy, competition policy, and transportation policy all fell under pillar one.

Decision-making procedures within pillar one were firmly rooted within the traditional European Community institutions while expanding the Parliament's decision-making power. Policy areas that were designated as falling under the jurisdiction of pillar one were dealt with within the institutional machinery of the Commission, the Parliament, the Council of Ministers, the presidency, the European Court of Justice, the European Council, and the new European Central Bank. Under Maastricht, however, the UK and Denmark were allowed to "opt out" of the common currency as well as several other provisions if they so wished. In September 2000, the Danish public voted against joining the euro and in 2003 Swedish voters also rejected the euro in a referendum. In general, pillar one under Maastricht includes everything that the "old" European Community included plus the new European Central Bank and the euro for those countries that joined the Eurozone.

Pillars Two and Three: An Intergovernmental Compromise

Pillars two and three expanded the scope of what became renamed the European Union by encompassing policy areas that had been outside the scope of European integration. The institutional structures that governed pillars two and three differed from those found in pillar one. Pillar two referred to the area of the *Common Foreign and Security Policy (CFSP)* and pillar three referred to what is known as *Justice and Home Affairs (JHA)* (internal security). In both pillars, the Council of Ministers rather than the Commission was primarily responsible for action, unanimous voting was required, the Parliament was largely excluded, and the European Court of Justice did not exercise jurisdiction.

The fact that the Council of Ministers rather than the European Commission was established as the key institution represented a compromise. On one side were those countries that favored a more "federal" model of integration and therefore supported giving the Commission its traditional powers in these areas. On the other side were those governments (Britain and France) that were worried about sovereignty. Pillars two and three therefore were brought within the process of integration but were governed by the European Council and the Council of Ministers, the most intergovernmental institutions within the Community's institutional framework.

Treaty of Amsterdam

The *Treaty of Amsterdam* came into effect in 1999 and significantly changed the policy and institutional landscape established by the Maastricht Treaty. First of all, most issues of pillar three under Maastricht were now placed within pillar one, significantly strengthening the policy reach of the Commission and the influence of the European Court of

Justice. Along with that expansion, the treaty enhanced the power of the Commission president vis à vis the other commissioners. Second, the treaty increased the power of the European Parliament by both simplifying and expanding the use of codecision in a wide range of issue areas. Third, the powers of the EU in several policy areas, including public health (critical to the European welfare state) and CFSP, both of which are very sensitive for national sovereignty, were enhanced. Public health is firmly under the Union's institutions in pillar one, while CFSP is firmly in the intergovernmental pillar two.

The transfer of most policy areas within the "old" pillar three to pillar one represented a very significant step in the process of European integration. Internal security is traditionally viewed as absolutely central to national sovereignty. In the post-Amsterdam period, issues such as asylum, immigration, and judicial cooperation in civil matters came within the policy remit of the Commission and, with some restrictions, the jurisdiction of the European Court of Justice. In Maastricht, the member-states had given up their sovereignty in the area of monetary policy by accepting the euro, but they had been very reluctant to "Europeanize" internal security. The Treaty of Amsterdam represented their new willingness to "pool" their sovereignty in the area of Justice and Home Affairs. (In the United States, the Department of Justice is concerned with most of the same issue areas.) The intergovernmental pillar three of the Maastricht Treaty was widely viewed as having been a failure so that the Treaty of Amsterdam signaled the new willingness of the member-states to try to make it more effective by bringing it under the Commission's umbrella.

In a similar vein, in October 1999 the member-states met at a special summit in Tampere, Finland, and agreed to numerous initiatives that mark a major turning point in the member-states' willingness to accept further integration in this extremely sensitive area (see Box 12.3). Only two policy areas remain within the "new" pillar three after Amsterdam police cooperation (including the European Police Office known as EUROPOL which under Amsterdam was given stronger powers and a more operational role) and judicial cooperation in criminal matters. Even here, the member-states were

> ### Box 12.3   Justice and Home Affairs (JHA) Pillars 1 and 3
>
> The Treaty of Amsterdam, the 1999 European Council Summit in Tampere, Finland, and responses to terrorist attacks in the United States and Spain resulted in much deeper integration in the sensitive area of internal security. The EU increased the level of intergovernmental cooperation and the powers of the Commission and the European Court of Justice were broadened so that Justice and Home Affairs is now viewed as a key component of an integrating Europe. Included among the important new initiatives in this area were:
>
> EUROPOL given significant new powers to initiate criminal investigations
> Police and immigration officials given cross-national legal powers in all EU member-states
> Network of Union public prosecutors (Eurojust)
> European Police College to train law enforcement officials
> European Arrest Warrant (EAW) created to make process of arrest and extradition of fugitives within the EU more efficient
>
> Antiterrorism czar appointed to coordinate counterterrorism efforts among the member states
> Joint investigative teams to combat terrorism and drug trafficking
> Task force of senior police officers
> Development of
> - Common EU asylum and immigration policy
> - Harmonized approach to dealing with refugees (including a European refugee fund)
> - Standardized methods of combating illegal immigration
> - Tougher laws against money-laundering
> - Policies to ensure that court judgments issued in one country are enforceable throughout the Union

willing to be less intergovernmental. The European Court of Justice was completely excluded in the old pillar three, but it was given a limited role in the post-Amsterdam pillar three. Furthermore, the Commission as well as the member-states have the right of initiative in all matters falling under pillar three. This is an expansion of the role of the Commission. Some convergence of criminal legislation is now possible, so that Amsterdam is viewed by some as contributing "towards creating a common European criminal law."[29]

Finally, the EU's reaction to the September 11, 2001 terrorist attack on the United States and the March 11, 2004 terrorist attack on a Madrid train station further strengthened the EU's role in the area of Justice and Home Affairs. The member-states accepted the creation of a "European arrest warrant" and the appointment of an EU antiterrorism "czar." However, the EU has not created a European version of the Central Intelligence Agency (CIA). Intelligence gathering remains a strictly national function; however, with much greater cooperation and coordination among national intelligence agencies than had been the case before 2001.

With regard to pillar two of the Maastricht Treaty, Amsterdam enhanced the powers of the Union in the area of a common foreign and security policy. Institutionally, the Secretary-General of the Council of Ministers was also appointed as the High Representative for the EU Common Foreign and Security Policy ("Mr. CFSP"). Javier Solana, widely respected in his previous posts as NATO Secretary-General and Spanish Foreign Affairs Minister was appointed to that position when the Treaty of Amsterdam came into effect in 1999.

The Treaty of Nice

The *Treaty of Nice*, the fourth revision of the Rome Treaties entered into force on February 1, 2003. The treaty attempted to prepare the EU for its enlargement to Central and Eastern Europe. In particular, the treaty sought to streamline decision making in the EU's institutions. Making decisions with 25 countries would be much more difficult than with 15 countries. Streamlining decision making, however, necessarily changes the distribution of power within the institutions concerned. In particular, the small states, which had historically been overrepresented in the EU's institutions, fought to keep their privileged position. The large member-states argued that since enlargement would add so many small states to the Union, maintaining the privileges of small states would lead to an unbalanced Union in which the populous member-states would be deprived of their appropriate role. The final deal was reached in the early morning of the last day of the Nice European Council in December 2000.

In addition to finding a compromise between the demands of the small and large member-states (in which the small states did relatively well), the Treaty of Nice also introduced some important changes. Institutionally, it allowed each member-state to appoint only one commissioner (previously, the larger member-states had appointed two commissioners). Second, the Treaty of Nice introduced qualified majority voting to choose the president of the Commission and increased his power vis à vis other commissioners. Third, a new weighting of votes was accepted in the Council of Ministers (that weighting represented the concrete results of the compromise between the large and small states). Fourth, qualified majority voting (as opposed to unanimity) was extended to roughly 30 new policy areas. It strengthened the EU's role in the area of security and defense, and created a new *Political and Security Committee (PSC)*.

The Nice Treaty was rejected by Irish voters in a referendum held in 2001, but it was subsequently accepted in a referendum in 2002. Many interpreted the initial defeat as an indication that European publics were uneasy about the changes to the Union that the enlargement to the East would inevitably bring.

THE INSTITUTIONS

The institutional structure of the European Union is based on the complex divisions represented by different institutions in different policy areas (see Figure 12.2). The sophisticated policymaking process normally associated with the Community resides in pillar one—including key policymaking institutions such as the European Commission, the Council of Ministers, the European Parliament, the European Council, European Court of Justice, and the European Central Bank.

Whereas the other institutions all interact with one another, the European Central Bank (located in Frankfurt, Germany) is very independent from all the other institutions. However, Justice and Home Affairs within pillar one still excludes the Parliament. The Commission and the Council are the central policymaking actors in areas such as immigration, visa policy, and asylum policy. In pillars two and three, the European Council and the Council of Ministers are the key institutional actors.

The European Commission

The *European Commission*, located in Brussels, is the Community's most visible institution in day-to-day policymaking. Its institutional mission within the Community is to promote integration. Toward that end, the Commission is made up of the College of Commissioners, the decision-making body within the Commission, and civil servants that do the important technocratic work typical of all bureaucracies. The College of Commissioners is the political (although not in a partisan sense) component of the Commission while the civil servants are the administrative sector. The term "Commission" is used in the press to refer either to the civil servants, the College, or both.

The Commission is composed of 25 commissioners who collectively make up the College of Commissioners. Each commissioner is appointed by the head of a member-state, but once appointed the commissioner is able to act independently of his country's national government. A commissioner does not take instructions from the national government and can operate quite autonomously. That independence gives the Commission as a whole its "supranational" authority and power.

Each commissioner serves for a five-year term, and can be reappointed if the national government so wishes. Each has one vote. And each is in charge of certain policy areas (environment, trade, external relations, agriculture, research and technology, transport, or telecommunications, for example). When they meet collectively every Wednesday, they are known as the College of Commissioners.

FIGURE 12.2 The Structure of the European Union

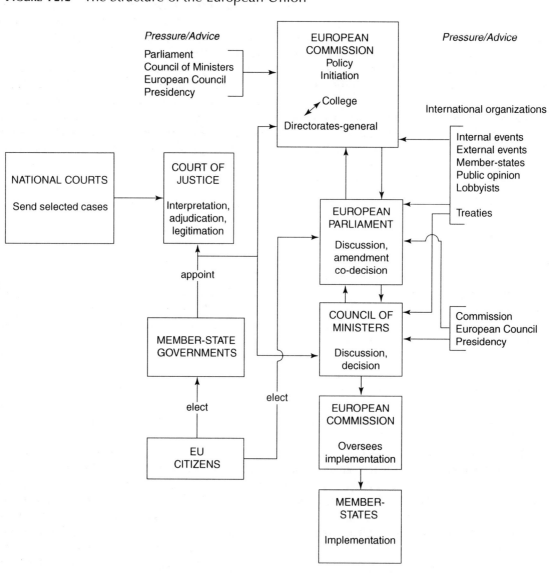

Source: Taken from John McCormick, *European Union: Politics and Policies* (Boulder, CO: Westview Press, 1996), p. 207.

The president of the Commission is the most important commissioner; the Treaty of Amsterdam and the Treaty of Nice enhanced his influence within the Commission. In the post-Nice era, the European Council nominally chose the president by qualified majority voting. However, the current Commission president, the Portuguese Jose Manuel Barroso, was selected by the European Council in June 2004 by consensus. The reliance on consensus rather than qualified majority voting acknowledged the political reality that a Commission president would be ineffective if one of the large member-states opposed his appointment. (In fact, Barroso was selected after other proposed candidates were in effect vetoed by one or more of the large member-states.) The European Council's nomination then must be approved by the European Parliament. Typically a president from a large country is succeeded by a president from a small country. (Barroso is from Portugal, a small country, while his predecessor Romano Prodi was from Italy, a large country.) Strong Commission presidents leave an imprint: Walter Hallstein, the first president, and Jacques Delors (1985–1995) both led the Commission in ways that increased its profile and prestige. Commission presidents, however, are constrained by the fact that they do not appoint their fellow commissioners and have relatively little formal control over them. Even Jacques Delors at the height of his power and prestige was unable to convince some governments to reappoint commissioners he would have liked to have returned to the Commission.

The Treaty of Nice, however, did strengthen the president's hand to some extent. For example, the president may now request a member of the Commission to resign after obtaining the approval of the College. Jose Barroso, the first Commission president in the post-Nice era, took advantage of his newly strengthened position to allocate desirable portfolios to small countries. The fact that France, traditionally a very influential country in the EU, was given responsibility for transport rather than a more presitigious assignment was taken as a sign that President Barroso would not be shy about using the new powers of the Commission president.

Nonetheless, the role of the president of the Commission is not similar to that of a prime minister. The president is not accountable to Parliament in the way that a national prime minister is and does not become president of the Commission through an election. He is appointed by the national governments rather than being elected, as are prime ministers. In a similar vein, the Commission is not a "government" in that it is not selected by either the voters (as is the president of France) or the legislature (as are prime ministers).

The Commission has a number of important powers, but its most pivotal power is contained in pillar one: it is the only institution that can propose legislation in pillar one. Neither the Council of Ministers nor the European Parliament can initiate legislation. The monopoly exercised by the Commission over policy initiation is one of its most important formal powers. Although the initiation power is limited by the Parliament's power to ask for a legislative proposal, the fact that it must be the Commission which drafts the proposal gives the Commission important leverage in the legislative process. This power thus enables the Commission to shape the policy agenda. The Commission also manages the Community's budget, is involved in external relations, monitors the application of Community law in the member-states, and generally is expected to make the arguments and proposals necessary to promote further integration.

The College of Commissioners decides by majority vote which proposals for legislation to send to the Council of Ministers and the European Parliament. The College can also decide to take antitrust action (without the approval of the Council of Ministers) and can argue cases before the European Court of Justice.

The Commission's bureaucracy, although very small in comparison to national bureaucracies, is the most important administrative component of the entire Community and is key to the Commission's ability to promote the process of integration. Sometimes known as Eurocrats, officials who work for the Commission are multilingual and highly educated. They typically receive their position after passing a competitive examination. They do the initial drafting of the legislation (which is then approved by the College) and are present at the negotiations within the Council of Ministers on all proposals from the College of Commissioners. Commission officials are emphatically not the functional equivalents of international civil servants, such as officials who work for global international organizations such as the United Nations. Commission officials are viewed as having much more authority when dealing with national officials than are traditional international civil servants.[30]

The operations of its civil servants allow the Commission to play a complex role. Commission officials often operate very effectively behind the scenes. They consult with a wide variety of interest groups and often receive complaints about non-compliance with Community laws from citizens in the member-states.

Fundamentally, the Commission promotes European integration and provides the administrative resources absolutely essential for policymaking in a system as complex as the European Union. Without the Commission, the European Union would not have an administrative apparatus.

Because of its centrality in the definition of problems and the formulation of policy, its access to significant administrative resources, and its links to a variety of groups throughout the Community, the Commission plays a key role in policymaking. It is at the heart of the European Union.[31] The fact that the European Union has a policymaking body not directly controlled by the member-states and able to wield important influence clearly distinguishes the organization as different from all other international bodies. The Commission as an institution symbolizes that supranational dimension within European integration that was so vigorously promoted by Jean Monnet.

The Council of the European Union (Council of Ministers)

The Council of the EU is usually referred to as the *Council of Ministers*. It adopts Community legislation and develops the budget along with the Commission and the Parliament. It is the top decision-making body. Its decisions, often taken in conjunction with the European Parliament in pillar one, become Community law. Its members are ministers from national governments. If a national government loses an election, the ministers from the new government immediately participate in the Council's decision-making process.

The Council of Ministers, as the Union's main legislature, is a more powerful decision maker than either the Commission or the Parliament. It, rather than the Parliament, formulates the EU's trade policy and is the dominant actor in the area of Justice and Home Affairs. Above all, it adopts Community legislation that is then incorporated into national legal codes. It does not, however, participate in the formation of the Commission and cannot dismiss it.

Technically speaking, there are nine Councils of Ministers and the term "Council of Ministers" is applied to each sectoral council (see Box 12.4). Each Council is composed of the relevant ministers from each of the member-state governments (or someone delegated to represent them).

Hierarchically, the most important configuration is the General Affairs and External Relations Council (GAERC), which brings together the foreign affairs ministers. The GAERC deals with external relations, but also with horizontal matters, such as the coordination of decisions, the preparation and follow-up of the European Council, as well as institutional and administrative questions. The GAERC meets at least once a month. Other councils also meet frequently reflecting the fact that the Community is more active in certain policy areas. For example, the Council of Agriculture and Fisheries meets at least once a month, whereas the Council of Environment Ministers meets once formally and once informally within every three-month period.

All ministers operating within a Council do not carry the same weight as they have unequal voting power (see Table 12.1). In a similar vein, not all Councils are equal in significance. Although the most important is the GAERC, finance ministers are constantly competing with foreign ministers for influence, and in pillar one the Council of Economic and Finance Ministers (especially the Euro-Group) comes next in the hierarchy of influence.[32] The Justice and Home Affairs Council became important after the Maastricht Treaty came into effect and is now a key council in both pillar one and pillar three.

The Council of Ministers is the EU institution in which national interests are represented, defended, and ultimately compromised in the interests of reaching agreement. It is a "club" in the sense that the participants understand that ultimately compromises will have to be made by everyone and because its participants acknowledge that the Council is not a traditional international organization. Although the Council zealously guards its prerogatives and keeps a close eye on activities to ensure that the Commission does not encroach on the Council's territory, it must be emphasized that the

Box 12.4   The Nine Councils of Ministers

There are nine sectoral Councils, each of which is referred to as the "Council of Ministers." The nine sectoral Council configurations are:

GAERC (General Affairs and External Relations Council)
Economy and Finances
Justice and Home Affairs
Employment, Social Policy, Health, and Consumer Affairs

Competitiveness
Transport, Telecommunications, and Energy
Agriculture and Fisheries
Environment
Education, Youth, and Culture

Each Council is composed of the relevant ministers from each of the member-state governments (or someone delegated to represent them).

TABLE 12.1   Distribution of Power Before and After the Treaty of Nice

Member-State	Number of Commissioners		Number of Votes in Council of Ministers Under QMV		Number of Members of European Parliament (MEPs)	
	Before Nice Treaty	After Nice Treaty (2004)	Before Nice Treaty	After Nice Treaty (2004)	Before Nice Treaty	After Nice Treaty (2004)
Germany	2	1	10	29	99	99
UK	2	1	10	29	87	78
France	2	1	10	29	87	78
Italy	2	1	10	29	87	78
Spain	2	1	8	27	64	54
Poland	—	1	—	27	—	54
Netherlands	1	1	5	12	31	27
Greece	1	1	5	12	25	24
Czech Republic	—	1	—	12	—	24
Belgium	1	1	5	12	25	24
Hungary	—	1	—	12	—	24
Portugal	1	1	5	12	25	24
Sweden	1	1	4	10	22	19
Austria	1	1	4	10	21	18
Slovakia	—	1	—	7	—	14
Denmark	1	1	3	7	16	14
Finland	1	1	3	7	16	14
Ireland	1	1	3	7	15	13
Lithuania	—	1	—	7	—	13
Latvia	—	1	—	4	—	9
Slovenia	—	1	—	4	—	7
Estonia	—	1	—	4	—	6
Cyprus	—	1	—	4	—	6
Luxembourg	1	1	2	4	6	6
Malta	—	1	—	3	—	5

Source: Population figures from *Eurostat Yearbook 2004*, published October 1, 2004.

Council is very much an EU institution. While it represents national interests, it does so within the framework of European integration.[33] Member-states, by operating within the framework of the Council, accept an institutional framework that leads to a collective—rather than a unilateral—decision. By participating in the Council, national governments give up the maneuverability and autonomy that is implicit in national (unilateral) decision making. It is for that reason that "Euroskeptics" argue that participation in the Union means giving up sovereignty—defined as the ability to make unilateral decisions.

In contrast, the power of the Council of Ministers ensures that the Union always adopts legislation that meets with the approval of most or all of the member-state governments. The Community does not impose legislation on national governments—they adopt the legislation themselves in the Council of Ministers (and in many areas in partnership with the European Parliament). Opposition parties in national parliaments, however, do not have access to Council of Ministers meetings. So the EU does in fact enhance the power of those political parties that are in government at the national level.

The Council of Ministers plays a stronger role in pillars two and three than it does in pillar one. In pillar one, the policymaking process gives an important role to both the Commission and the Parliament (the latter, however, is excluded from Justice and Home Affairs even in pillar one), and the European Court of Justice can be central. The Commission plays a smaller role, and the Parliament no role, in the policymaking process within pillars two and three.

The culture of the Council is based on negotiation and is predisposed toward finding agreement:

> The whole system depends on a crucial assumption that there is give and take between the positions of the member-states and that, whatever the starting positions of the members, there is *both* scope for those positions to evolve *and* a predisposition to find agreement. Thus atmospherics, mutual confidence and trust are important ingredients.[34]

The member governments, acting within the Council of Ministers, are engaged in an institu-tional process that is unlike that of any other legislative body in the world. Multinational, bound by Community rather than international law, and (in pillar one) engaged in important relationships with the Commission and the European Parliament, the Council of Ministers "locks" national ministers into an ongoing cooperative venture that includes a shared and enlarging policy agenda. It is that "locking" effect that helps ensure that national officials do not decide to act unilaterally rather than multilaterally.

Although some analysts view the Council as blocking further integration, comparison with other attempts at regional integration throughout the world highlights the importance of having national ministers involved in the nitty-gritty of policymaking at the European level. The Council of Ministers, in essence, is the guarantor of European integration in that national governments must participate in it and cannot ignore it. Without the Council, the actions of the Commission and the Parliament could conceivably be ignored by national governments, but their membership in the Council helps ensure that national governments address the issues proposed by the Commission.

The European Council

The key strategic institution within the Union is clearly the *European Council*. Strictly speaking, it does not form part of the Council of Ministers hierarchy, but it is closely linked to it. The European Council does not adopt legislation, leaving that to the Council of Ministers. It does, however, set out the key guidelines for action and future development. The European Council is attended by prime ministers (the president in the case of Cyprus, France, and Finland), foreign ministers, the Commission president and another designated commissioner. The foreign ministers provide the institutional continuity between the Council of Ministers and the European Council.

The Council meets formally four times a year in "summits" held in Brussels since the 2004 enlargement. (If a presidency decides to organize an informal summit, it can organize it wherever it wants.) These meetings receive far more publicity than do meetings of the various sectoral Councils and may well symbolize the European Union for the average citizen.

The European Council usually operates through unanimity even when it is not required to do so. The European Council now "occupies a position at the apex of the EU's institutional system, overseeing the work of each of the three pillars, and the specialized sectoral Councils which operate therein. It monitors their work, sets framework principles to guide their future deliberations, takes or clears major political decisions, and frequently engages in trouble-shooting."[35] It is the European Council, for example, that has decided key issues such as whether enlargement to Eastern Europe would occur, when it would occur, and whether Turkey could begin accession negotiations.

The European Council, as well as the Council of Ministers, is chaired by representatives of the member-state government holding the *Presidency of the European Council and the Council of Ministers*. Every six months the presidency of the European Union rotates, so that each member government exercises the powers of the presidency in both the European Council and the Council of Ministers. The head of state or government of the country holding the presidency, along with the Commission president and the High Representative for Foreign and Security Policy of the Council of Ministers (Javier Solana), represents the Union at summit meetings with non-EU leaders. For example, in June 2004 Irish Prime Minister Ahern represented the presidency at a U.S.-EU summit. Most burdensome perhaps is the fact that officials representing the member-state government holding the presidency chair all of the hundreds of meetings that go on in the Council of Ministers.

Finally, the European Council controls the agenda and negotiations of the *Intergovernmental Conference (IGC)* which is called to revise treaties. The most difficult compromises made at the IGC—the Single European Act, the Maastricht Treaty, the Treaty of Amsterdam, the Treaty of Nice, and the proposed constitutional treaty which is currently being debated across Europe—were all made at the end of the negotiations by the European Council. Only prime ministers (accompanied by their for-

eign ministers) or heads of state have the political power necessary to make concessions that are very difficult for national governments to accept but which are critical for the success of negotiations.

The European Parliament

The *European Parliament* is the only supranational assembly in the world whose members are chosen by voters rather than by governments. Its 732 members serve five-year terms congruent with the commissioners' five-year terms. *Members of the European Parliament (MEPs)* are elected at the same time across the Community, but each country uses its own electoral system. (A uniform European Community electoral system does not yet exist.) Because of the disproportionate influence of small countries (discussed later) in the Community, members represent constituencies vastly different in size (see Table 12.1).

Turnover is very high after each parliamentary election. After the 1999 parliamentary election, over half of all the MEPS were new rather than returning incumbents. Some MEPs continue on to distinguished careers in national politics, especially in France (where 10 of the 16 prime ministers and 4 of the 6 presidents in the Fifth Republic were MEPs). In reverse, six former prime ministers were elected as MEPs in the 1999 elections, and over 10 percent of MEPs have been ministers in national governments. Roughly 30 percent of the MEPs in the 1999–2004 Parliament were women, with the highest proportion in the Finnish delegation and the lowest in the Italian.[36] In the 2004—2009 Parliament, 222 MEPS were women.

The Parliament argues that it is the only directly elected European institution (it became directly elected in 1979) and is therefore closer to the citizens of Europe than either the Commission or the Council. Thus, the Parliament has pressured, coaxed, threatened, and in general become an important presence on the political scene. It is not yet an equal partner with the other institutions across the board. For example, it cannot decide the total size of the EU's budget nor formulate the EU's trade policy; it is excluded from spending on agriculture, foreign policy issues other than enlargement, and is largely excluded from the area of Justice and Home Affairs.

Nonetheless, since the Treaty of Amsterdam went into effect in 1999, its influence is very strong on most legislation falling under pillar one. The Treaty of Nice further reinforced the Parliament's power of being a co-legislator with the Council of Ministers. The Parliament can only ask the Commission to draft proposals rather than initiating its own draft proposals. However, the Parliament, in those areas in which it has jurisdiction, is able to offer amendments which can substantially change the proposal offered by both the Commission and the Council of Ministers. In the year after Amsterdam went into effect, the Parliament had 81 percent of its amendments accepted by the Council of Ministers. This indicates that it is effective in shaping legislation.[37]

The Parliament has control (within limits) of so-called "noncompulsory" spending. This includes spending not directed toward agricultural support (the largest single portion of the budget) or based on international agreements with third countries. Over time, the proportion of noncompulsory spending as a percentage of the total budget has increased. Currently, it is over 50 percent and in 1999, the Parliament and the Council of Ministers agreed that 10 percent of spending in agriculture traditionally classified as compulsory would be reclassified as noncompulsory.[38] In fact, the granting of budgetary authority to the Parliament in 1975 could be seen as a key step that has undergirded the subsequent increases in the parliamentary power.

The Parliament's formal powers were strengthened by the Treaty of Maastricht and strengthened still further by Amsterdam and Nice which extended the use of the co-decision procedure in the adoption of legislation. The Parliament's power of co-decision allows it to stop legislation which it does not want, even if the Council of Ministers unanimously supports it. In cases in which the Parliament and Council approve different versions of a piece of legislation, conciliation talks are held to try to agree on a compromise. If such talks fail, the legislation dies. Now that co-decision is so frequently used within pillar one, the Council and the Parliament contact each other early in the legislative process so that conciliation talks will not be necessary. Between November 1993 and April 1999, 165 directives requiring co-decision were dealt with and

40 percent required conciliation talks (three of the proposed directives considered were killed as no agreement could be reached). However, in the year after Amsterdam, 65 pieces of legislation were addressed and only 25 percent required conciliation talks.[39]

Parliament also exercises the right to approve the president of the Commission as well as giving a formal vote of approval of the College of Commissioners as a whole. Finally, it also approves the president of the European Central Bank. The Parliament must also assent to certain international agreements, including accession treaties and association agreements.

Most of the Parliament's work is done in committee. Each committee can decide whether its work will be done in public view or in closed session. Whereas committees in most national parliaments work in closed session, most European parliamentary committees now work in public. Each MEP is a full member of at least one committee. Final parliamentary approval however has to be granted in plenary sessions, and at times committee recommendations are overridden in the plenary.

The European Court of Justice

The *European Court of Justice*, located in Luxembourg, is a powerful "supranational" institution making what is in effect judicial law. The Court is composed of one judge from each member-state (chosen by the national government). Judges serve a six-year term of office that can be renewed. They elect one of the sitting judges as president. The ECJ established the Court of First Instance, which began operating in November 1989. That court has a more limited jurisdiction and cannot hear what might be termed constitutionally important cases.

The European Court of Justice is often the arbiter in disputes between an individual member-state and the Commission. It also handles interinstitutional disputes—for example, between the Commission and the Council of Ministers. Individual citizens can bring cases before the Courts only if a Community action has directly harmed them. It is typically easier for a firm to argue such harm than a noneconomic actor. Non-governmental groups such as environmental organizations do not have easy access to the Court. Since the Nice Treaty, the European Parliament can also bring a case to court. The Court has jurisdiction over issue areas falling within pillar one as well as very limited jurisdiction in pillar three.

Most of the Court's cases come from national courts asking for a preliminary ruling. The national court then takes the ECJ's preliminary ruling and delivers it as its own opinion. National judges therefore are an important factor in developing the effectiveness of the Community's legal order.

Initially established as an international court operating under the constraints of international law, the Court rather quickly began to represent the "European interest" in its own right. After the Treaty of Rome went into effect, the Court "constitutionalized" that international law under which it had been operating. Rather than simply becoming an international court with limited impact, it gradually evolved into a powerful body resembling, in some striking albeit limited ways, the U.S. Supreme Court. Its influence in the policymaking process is such that one scholar has concluded that "for many areas of European and national policy, knowing the position of the ECJ is as important as knowing the position of the member-states and national interest groups."[40] The Court performs an important role in the policymaking process as we discuss later.

The Single Currency and the European Central Bank

Although Economic and Monetary Union (EMU) had been discussed since the late 1960s, it was not until the Maastricht Treaty that a timetable was established and a serious commitment made to move ahead to that milestone of integration. A *single currency* and a *European Central Bank* were established in 1999, and citizens began using the common currency (the euro) in January 2002.

The political dynamics behind EMU were clear to political elites but difficult to explain to the general public. Under the previous European Monetary System (EMS) established in 1979, currencies were allowed to fluctuate only within an agreed-upon range. The German Bundesbank was the dominant decision maker. The German currency, the Deutsche mark, became the "anchor currency." That is, when the Bundesbank raised interest rates, the other EMS members were forced to follow in order to keep their currencies within the range to which they had agreed. When such a need arose during a recession, this had a harmful impact on national economies. The high interest rates in a recession exacerbated high unemployment and therefore were very painful.

The high cost of German unification led the German Bundesbank to raise interest rates while many other EMS members were in a recession. The French and the Italians in particular realized that they needed to gain a voice in European monetary policy. To do so, they had to give up their own monetary sovereignty (largely illusory in any case because of the dynamics of the EMS) and convince the Germans to give up their own monetary sovereignty. This would occur within the framework of a European Central Bank in which each central bank would have equal representation.

Although the Bundesbank was reluctant to embrace EMU, Chancellor Kohl, anxious to show that unification was not leading Germany away from the European Community, agreed to economic and monetary union. The decision over EMU fell within the "Chancellor's prerogative."[41] That is, the ultimate decision about EMU was the Chancellor's. The Maastricht Treaty embodied that agreement. The German government, however, insisted on certain conditions in order to ensure that the new *euro-currency* would be as "strong" a currency as the deutsche mark that the Germans were to give up. In particular, the European Central Bank was to have price stability (rather than, for example, low unemployment or high rates of economic growth) as its primary objective. Countries were not allowed to join EMU unless their deficits were at 3 percent of GDP or lower.

Years of brutal budget cutting were required for many countries (such as Italy) to qualify. In 1999, 11 countries joined what became known as the Eurozone; Britain, Sweden, and Denmark stayed out. Greece was allowed to join in 2001.

The European Central Bank, established in Frankfurt, is composed of the governors of the national central banks. It is extremely independent of all the other EU institutions as well as of the member-state governments. It is arguably the most independent central bank in the world. In fact, that independence has been criticized, but the ECB believes it is necessary to convince the financial markets that it will not pursue a monetary policy that would allow inflation. Price stability is its policy mantra.

NATIONAL GOVERNMENTS AS ACTORS

As already indicated in our discussion of the Community's institutions, national governments play a key role in the Community's policymaking process. Their influence is felt directly in the Council of Ministers and through the power of appointment in the Commission and the European Court of Justice. Typically, the focus on understanding how and why national governments operate as they do within the European Union highlights the role of ruling parties and bureaucracies. National governments are able to defend their national interest in all the Union's institutions in one fashion or another. The opportunity to defend one's national interest has lubricated the path of integration for the member-states.

The need to prepare the Union's institutions for enlargement, however, highlighted the disproportionate power of the small member-states. This feature of the Union had not been the subject of controversy since the Treaty of Rome. As the negotiations proceeded for the Treaty of Nice, the disproportionality of size became the object of intense political conflict among the current member-states. Simply put, the negotiations for the Treaty of Nice forced the question of *which* governments could adequately defend their national interests in the future. In addition to wielding disproportionate power within the EU as indicated by Table 12.1, small countries have a status largely equal to that of the large countries in the European Court of Justice, the European Council, and the governing council of the European Central Bank. Given that many new small countries would join the EU once enlargement occurred,

the large member-states in 2000 sought to redress the balance in the negotiations leading to the Treaty of Nice.

The small states, however, feared being "pushed around" by the large states and rejected many of the demands made by the four large states (France, Germany, Italy, and the UK). The last half of 2000 was filled with acrimony as the small states accused the large of trying to weaken the Commission (which the small states view as an ally) in the name of efficient decision making, of trying to make the EU more intergovernmental so that the large states would have more influence, and of being insensitive to the national interests of the small states. The large states, for their part, were adamant that they needed more power within the Council of Ministers (through a reallocation of voting weights) and were likely to want more representation in the European Parliament. Furthermore, they viewed their proposals for the Commission as strengthening it by making it more effective. In brief, the large states wanted to ensure that the next enlargement did not privilege small countries even further. The small member-states worried that if the large member-states were allowed to gain too much power, the EU was going to become more like an international organization (in which small countries fare very badly) and less like a federation (in which small subfederal units exercise disproportionate power as they do in the United States). The small countries wanted the policymaking process to respect their wishes as it has since the Treaty of Rome. The final compromise gave the large states less power than they had desired, but nonetheless gave them more than they had in the pre-Nice period. Poland and Spain (through exploiting their position as "medium-size" countries as well as through very tough bargaining) gained an especially privileged position.

The issue of the appropriate balance between large and small states reemerged during the negotiations over what is known as the Constitution for Europe (but is actually a constitutional treaty). The final compromise, obtained in June 2004 after months of bitter negotiations, gave the big member-states more power than they had had under the Treaty of Nice but less than they had desired. It is not clear whether that compromise will satisfy the parliaments and electorates that need to accept it.

POLITICAL PARTIES

Political parties do not play the same role in European Union politics as they do in the national politics of the European countries described in this book. On the one hand, political parties in Europe generally do not offer alternative policies and analyses at the European level. In almost every member-state the focus of party competition throughout the development of the EU has continued to be domestic politics.[42] Thus, while national elections may determine which party controls the government that chooses representatives to the Commission and the Council of Ministers, the electoral debate has seldom focused on the policies of those representatives. Even direct elections to the European Parliament have tended to operate primarily as referenda on the domestic achievements and promises of the competing parties.

On the other hand, this inattention is encouraged by the fact that election outcomes do not directly determine the control of the EU's governing institutions.

Politics in the European Union revolves around broad territorial (national) divisions rather than the socioeconomic divisions that characterize politics at the national level. The "left-right" division so pivotal in structuring political party positions at the national level manifests itself less often and in different ways in Brussels. Political conflict at the European Union level is characterized by "the dominance of national, cultural, and territorial differences over socio-economic divisions."[43] Whereas differences related to class have shaped political conflict in Europe throughout the postwar period, those differences have been muted in Brussels where national differences are more significant. "It is, therefore, essentially via governments that political parties influence European affairs."[44]

The histories of national political parties are not rooted in conflicts over European integration. Until voters in some member-states became concerned with the impact of integration, parties had not addressed policy issues dealt with in Brussels.

Even when integration became more politicized, major parties did not take clear positions on the issues they would face in the Council of Ministers. On the contrary, they cloaked their actions in the garb of national interest:

> Instead of defending their participation in European regulatory decision-making on the grounds of fulfilling an electoral mandate, ruling parties have consistently defended such actions on the grounds that they have done their best to protect national interests, thus casting European politics as a zero-sum game between the member-states.[45]

In spite of not offering European-level policy alternatives, parties have nonetheless begun to organize a bit more extensively on the European level than they have in the past. In 1992 and 1993, all the major transnational party federations began institutionalizing themselves to a greater degree. Furthermore, the transnational federations have begun meeting right before the European Council meetings, so that prime ministers and other leading politicians as well as members of the European Parliament and commissioners from each of the leading political families gather to discuss EU issues.[46] Whether and how quickly transnational parties will evolve, however, is still an open question.

The issues with which the Community deals typically have a strong economic component that often manifests itself in technical issues not usually the subject of political discourse. That economic component is shaped by the Treaty of Rome and the Single European Act, both of which embodied a certain model of economics. Expanding cross-border trade and competition, as well as opening economies and markets, are the Union's key economic objectives. That model does not easily address political problems in the way that parties have traditionally done so in national contexts. Finally, much national party competition revolves around issues related to the welfare state. The Community does not directly legislate on welfare state issues, which means that a central element of national political party conflict is not even on the Community agenda.[47]

Parliamentary Elections

Elections to the European Parliament differ from national parliamentary elections in a variety of ways. Most centrally, they do not set in motion a process of government formation in the same way as do national elections in the member-states. Turnout is higher in national (and sometimes even in subnational) elections. The big parties typically do better in national elections, while small parties do better in elections to the European Parliament. Worrisome for those concerned about the "democratic deficit" (discussed later in this chapter), in most countries the turnout for parliamentary elections has declined since the elections of 1979 (see Table 12.2). The lowest turnout was in the 2004 elections.

European elections are described as "pale reflections of national elections."[48] The electoral campaign does not highlight choices to be made at the European level, but rather emphasizes the kinds of issues typically debated within the voters' "habitual national party context."[49]

National elections are often viewed as "first-order" elections. Elections to the European Parliament are "second-order" elections because no actual

TABLE 12.2   Turnout in the European Parliament Elections, 1979–2004

	1979	1981	1984	1987	1989	1994	1995	1996	1999	2004
EU	63.0	—	61.0	—	58.5	56.8	—	—	49.4	45.7
Belgium	91.6	—	92.2	—	90.7	90.7	—	—	90.0	90.8
Luxembourg	88.9	—	87.0	—	87.4	88.5	—	—	85.8	89.0
Malta	—	—	—	—	—	—	—	—	—	82.4
Italy	85.5	—	83.9	—	81.5	74.8	—	—	70.8	73.1
Cyprus	—	—	—	—	—	—	—	—	—	71.2
Greece	—	78.6	77.2	—	79.9	71.2	—	—	70.2	63.4
Ireland	63.6	—	47.6	—	68.3	44.0	—	—	50.5	58.8
Lithuania	—	—	—	—	—	—	—	—	—	48.4
Denmark	47.1	—	52.3	—	46.1	52.9	—	—	50.4	47.9
Spain	—	—	—	68.9	54.8	59.1	—	—	64.4	45.1
Germany	65.7	—	56.8	—	62.4	60.0	—	—	45.2	43.0
France	60.7	—	56.7	—	48.7	52.7	—	—	47.0	42.8
Austria	—	—	—	—	—	—	—	67.7	49.0	42.4
Latvia	—	—	—	—	—	—	—	—	—	41.3
Finland	—	—	—	—	—	—	—	60.3	30.1	39.4
Netherlands	57.8	—	50.5	—	47.2	35.7	—	—	29.9	39.3
Portugal	—	—	—	72.2	51.1	35.5	—	—	40.4	38.6
Hungary	—	—	—	—	—	—	—	—	—	38.5
United Kingdom	31.6	—	32.6	—	36.2	36.4	—	—	24.0	38.3
Sweden	—	—	—	—	—	—	41.6	—	38.3	37.8
Czech Republic	—	—	—	—	—	—	—	—	—	28.3
Slovenia	—	—	—	—	—	—	—	—	—	28.3
Estonia	—	—	—	—	—	—	——	—	—	26.8
Poland	—	—	—	—	—	—	—	—	—	20.9
Slovakia	—	—	—	—	—	—	—	—	—	17.0

Source: Francis Jacobs, Richard Corbett, and Michael Shackleton, *The European Parliament*, 4th ed. (London: John Harper, 2000), p. 25. Information regarding 2004 elections from European Parliament website: http://1www.elections2004.eu.int/ep-election/sites/en/results1306/turnout_ep/turnout_table.html

executive power is at stake. Rather than focusing on European issues, elections to the Parliament provide a forum for voters to express their support of, or discontent with, national parties. National cues, rather than the specific policies of the European Union, are paramount in shaping how voters cast their ballots.[50]

Parties in the European Parliament

Within the Community's institutions, political parties are most visible in the European Parliament. Europe's extraordinary cultural and political diversity is demonstrated by the fact that over 164 parties are represented in the European Parliament. These in turn are combined in Political Groups which are the centers of power within the Parliament (see Table 12.3). After the 2004 parliamentary elections, seven Political Groups emerged. Each party group includes MEPs with a political affinity and from at least two member-states. The groups set the parliamentary

agenda and de facto choose the president and 14 vice-presidents of the Parliament as well as the chairs, vice-chairs, and rapporteurs of the various parliamentary committees. The groups each have staffs.

Political Groups in the European Parliament do not perform the same role as do parties in national parliaments. The appointment of the executive—that is the Commission—is not formally determined by the Parliament. However, in 2004, Commission President Barroso was chosen from the political family (center-right) that had the largest number of seats in the European Parliament. Neither do the groups influence the portfolios that the individual commissioners receive. The groups do not have any influence on the partisan coloring of the ministers in the Council of Ministers. National governments choose both the commissioners and the ministers in the Council of Ministers. To understand the difference between a party in a national parliament and a Political Group in the European Parliament, it is important to remember that

TABLE 12.3   Political Groups in the European Parliament (2004–2009)

Group	Number of Political Parties in Group	Number of Member-States Represented	Number of Seats (732 Total)
European People's Party (Christian Democrats) and European Democrats (EPP-ED)	44	25	268
Party of European Socialists (PES)	27	23	200
Alliance for Liberals and Democrats for Europe (ALDE)	30	19	88
Greens/European Free Alliance (Greens/EFA)	19	13	42
European United Left/Nordic Green Left (EUL/NGL)	18	14	41
Union for a Europe of Nations (UEN)	7	6	27
Independence/Democracy (IND/DEM)	8	10	37
Nonattached	11	8	29

Source: "Chronique Élections 2004, Édition Spéciale: Composition du Parlement Européen au 20/07/04," Parlement Européen, Direction Générale de l'Information et des Relations Publiques, July 20, 2004.

"European elections do not initiate a process of government formation, as they do in most parliamentary democracies."[51]

The Political Groups provide an important channel of information for national parties. They are also important in organizing meetings, typically held before European Council meetings. At these sessions, heads of government and commissioners from that particular party, party leaders, and the chair of the Political Group meet to try to achieve a consensus on certain key issues affecting European integration.

The two largest Political Groups are the center-right European People's Party (previously named the Christian Democrats) and the center-left Socialist Group. Until the parliamentary elections of 1999, the Socialists had the most seats and were the dominant party within the Parliament. However, in 1999, much to the shock of the Socialists, the European People's Party (EPP) won 233 seats while the Socialists won only 180. The trend was repeated in 2004 when the EPP won 278 seats and the Socialists won 199 seats. Whereas previously the Socialists and the EPP had engaged in a kind of "grand coalition" and shared the committee chairmanships and the presidency of the Parliament amongst themselves, the EPP decided to pursue a different strategy. It concluded an informal alliance with the third largest party, the Liberals (with 51 seats) and agreed to share the presidency of the Parliament with the Liberals rather than with the Socialists. Most importantly, however, it began to stress the left-right division within the Parliament and the Commission. The Parliament became more "politicized." Rather than subordinating partisan conflict to the desire to increase the Parliament's power vis à vis the Commission and the Council of Ministers, the EPP highlighted the policy differences between the Socialists and the center-right parties. The EPP views government intervention in the market less favorably than do the Socialists. In fact, the Parliament voted in ways that were more pro-business and less environmentally friendly than had been the case in the past. After the 2004 elections, the EPP and the Socialist Group again decided to share the committees chairmanship and the presidency of the EP among themselves so that the "grand coalition" has reemerged.

It is important to note, however, that the party families (especially the EPP and the Socialists) have traditionally cooperated with one another. The EPP, the Socialists, and the Liberals still need to cooperate because neither one alone can mobilize the majorities needed under parliamentary procedures. Given the necessity to cooperate, the Parliament is not the forum for the kinds of partisan clashes found in the British House of Commons (see Chapter 5).[52] Nonetheless, adversarialism is now present in the Parliament to a greater degree, especially since the 1999 elections. Partisanship which divides tends to dilute the Parliament's power when dealing with the other institutions. For example, when the partisan divisions between right and left are highlighted on an issue, the Parliament is in a weaker position when entering conciliation talks with the Council than when there is a unitary parliamentary position. In general, politics within the Parliament is now less predictable and more fluid than had been the case in the past. The EPP is itself divided between members from the Christian Democrats who have traditionally been very strongly in favor of European integration and Euroskeptics. This means that the political dynamics of the Parliament are very complex. They are less structured than in the past. At times partisanship is subordinated so that the Parliament can act in a unified manner vis à vis the other institutions. At other times, however, partisanship is so strong that the Parliament is internally divided and therefore weakened when dealing with the Council or the Commission.[53]

The 2004 elections were marked by a low turnout (in the 10 new countries, overall participation was only at 26 percent, with notable exception in Malta and Cyprus). The elections also showed a clear gain for smaller, Euroskeptic, or populist parties compared to more traditional parties. In the UK, for instance, the UK Independence Party (UKIP), whose agenda calls for complete withdrawal of the UK from the EU, placed third after the Conservatives and the Labor Party with 17 percent of the votes. In Sweden, Poland, and Denmark, Euroskeptic parties also gained ground. Voters punished their government either because of their support to the Iraq war (in the UK), or because of poor economic performances (in France and Germany).

INTEREST GROUPS

As the Community has expanded the range of policies about which it can legislate, a "seemingly endless increase in interest group mobilization at the European level" has occurred.[54] Their number has grown so rapidly that scholars better understand the role of interest groups in national systems than in the Community. Research is still trying to catch up with the growth and activity of groups. What is clear is that the system of policymaking within the Union is so open that interest groups can participate at some point in the process of making public policy.

Interest groups interact with the Community's institutions in relatively unpredictable ways and at different points in the policy process. They lobby the Parliament for favorable amendments to Commission and Council of Ministers proposals as well as the relevant Commission officials. They are an integral part of the policy process in Brussels much as they are in Britain, Germany, The Netherlands, Denmark, and Sweden. Although groups representing a variety of interests are ever more numerous in Brussels, the structure of interest group interaction is not "corporatist," as it is in several European nations (see Chapter 3). That is, business and labor groups do not work with government officials in a structured way to make policy.

Interest groups are so numerous (in 2000, there were about 900 interest groups operating at the EU level in the Commission directory) that both the Commission and the Parliament feel the need to regularize their activities. The Parliament in 1996 decided to establish a register of interest groups. Once registered, each interest group receives a one-year pass for access to the Parliament after they have accepted a code of conduct. The Commission also developed some guidelines to help guide Commission officials in their dealings with representatives of interest groups and to improve transparency.[55] The Commission, which is the object of most of the lobbying, found it particularly difficult to maintain access to its relatively small staff while not being overwhelmed by the demands on its time and attention. Although regulation exists, there are no uniform rules across EU institutions on the participation of interest groups in the EU decision-making process.

Since political parties are not the key actors in Brussels that they are in national political systems and due to the absence of a "government" in the traditional sense, the Commission is the key target of interest groups because of its role in initiating legislation. The Commission encourages European-level groups, which it sees as a way to support further integration. Such groups are transnational actors—that is, they bring together national associations to form a European group. Transnational groups are not, however, as important as many had assumed, at least partially because national associations often find it difficult to agree on a common position. Many groups are much weaker than their national counterparts. National organizations, rather than the European federations of such organizations, often possess the information that is the interest group's chief asset and the resource most valuable to the Commission as it attempts to formulate policy. Thus the Commission "unwittingly undermine[s] the development of effective European-level groups by frequently consulting directly with national groups and individual firms."[56]

Although it is difficult to gauge the relative power and influence of diverse groups, many analysts argue that business interests have the most access and are the most influential.[57] Trade unions, although members of the European Trade Union Conference, have been unable to organize as effectively. In general, labor representatives are less visible in policy debates. Environmental and consumer groups, although nurtured and supported by the Commission, are still much weaker in general than are business groups.

In spite of the number of interest groups operating in Brussels and their varied activities, it is important not to overestimate their influence. As indicated earlier, the Economic and Monetary Union represents a historic milestone for European integration. The new European Central Bank and the euro are key changes in the economic landscape of the Union. Yet interest groups were not involved at key decision-making points. Business groups, labor representatives, and associations representing banks were all excluded. Heads of state and government and finance ministers along with their advisers and civil servants were the key actors in negotiations about EMU, not interest groups. The same general argument can be made about the decision in the Treaty of Amsterdam to Europeanize pillar three—interest groups were not relevant.

Although interest groups are not necessarily included in the "historic" decisions, they are typically woven into the Community's policy process. In particular, sophisticated groups lobby at both the national and European level. They lobby the Commission when it is drafting the legislation, the Parliament for favorable amendments, and national officials who will be involved when the issue reaches the Council of Ministers. The European Union has many access points for groups or individual actors, and they are increasingly taking advantage of all of them. A large business firm's lobbying effort may therefore use its national association—which has an office in the national capital as well as an office in Brussels, a Euro-association that brings together national associations, and the firm's own office in Brussels. It can thus lobby a variety of officials using a variety of venues and strategies. To be effective, lobby groups also need to coordinate across European, subnational, and national levels, as EU laws need to be transposed into national laws.

PUBLIC OPINION—DOES IT MATTER?

The European Community is different from the national systems which constitute it in that mass politics plays a different role. It is also an ambiguous role, and scholars are still in the process of delineating how public opinion intersects with the Community's policymaking process. In the Community, the wishes of voters are transmitted primarily through national governments. In national systems, the voters directly choose those in power. Because the Community involves negotiations among governments, similar in that sense to international relations, governments can pursue policies somewhat independently from the wishes of voters.

Governments, once in power, have more discretion on issues related to integration than they do on national issues centrally identified with their political party. The question of "Europe" is not clearly positioned within national political systems. It tends to divide political parties internally rather than to distinguish one party from another. A prime minister therefore tends to exercise considerable discretion when deciding broad issues of European integration. In countries where referenda are common (Denmark and Sweden, for example), voters can express their views more directly and have them be more binding than can voters in countries without referenda (such as Germany). In some cases, where referenda are possible but infrequent (France), the results can be surprising. This was evident when President Mitterrand, assuming that the French would support the Maastricht Treaty, called for a referendum—only to see the treaty supported by the thinnest of margins. Even when referenda are used, the substantive results can be somewhat surprising. Norwegian voters rejected membership in the Community (having rejected it already once before) in a 1995 referendum. Still, Norwegian governments have tried to pass legislation and pursue economic policies compatible with those being adopted by the European Union. If one examines selected aspects of Norwegian public policy, it would not be immediately obvious that Norway is not a member of the Union. In addition, the initial rejection of the Nice Treaty in a 2001 Irish referendum left many in the EU astonished, considering how much Ireland benefited economically from the process of integration.

That discretion has implications for the role of public opinion, which emerges as a factor that does not constrain political leaders as directly as it does in national, strictly domestic, politics. That is not to say that it does not constrain them at all. However, the type of constraint exercised is more subtle and diffuse. Public opinion as expressed in the elections to the European Parliament is again diluted as the Parliament does not form the government.

Although compromise is a normal part of the democratic process, especially in systems with coalition governments, national politicians do not feel comfortable explaining the policy positions they take in Brussels to their mass electorate. While political elites understand the necessity for compromise, the Community's decision-making process is often presented to mass publics as one in which countries lose or win. Depending on the circumstances, ministers either claim to have "won" (when carrying out popular policies) or to have been "forced" by the Community to take an (unpopular) action.

When taking unpopular actions, it is quite likely that the national government voted in favor of the unpopular action, but the government conveniently does not mention that fact. The process of "scapegoating" Brussels is made easier because the legislation approved by the Council of Ministers often does not actually take effect until several years later. Only the most sophisticated newspaper reporter is likely to track the legislative history of an EU law which, when it goes into effect, is criticized by national politicians.

The lack of a direct transmission belt between public opinion and voting and the EU executive has led many to argue that a "democratic deficit" exists. Some argue that a much stronger European Parliament is necessary for the deficit to be remedied. Others argue that national parliaments need to be given a stronger role in the Community policy process. Yet neither of these two positions confronts the fact that the Union is not a state. As long as the policy process involves bargaining among legally constituted national governments, the influence of public opinion will face many of the same constraints they have faced in the making of foreign policy. Multilateral decision making that requires bargaining with foreigners is not the same as decision making within national systems in which foreigners do not play a role. That difference raises difficult issues in trying to remedy the democratic deficit.

The Council of Ministers operates in a great deal of secrecy, and that secrecy helps political leaders operate in Brussels with less scrutiny than they receive in their national capitals. Minutes of Council meetings, even when accessible to the public, are often not very revealing of the political dynamics which led to the decision being reported in the minutes.[58] The deals made between ministers are often not revealed to the press. Each minister may well claim "victory" for his or her position, but what is typically not revealed is what concessions were made by that same minister. Even though the Council could not reach a decision without each national government being willing to compromise, ministers do not publicize their role in reaching a compromise.

The secrecy accompanying Council of Ministers decision making has led many critics to identify such secrecy as a contributor to the democratic deficit. The fact that citizens do not know what kinds of concessions their national government made or even how their government voted on a particular piece of legislation leads to a lack of "transparency" in the Community's operations, which is seen by many as intrinsically undemocratic.

Again, secrecy in decision making is more characteristic of international relations than of domestic politics. Many international "deals" are made away from public scrutiny. The making of foreign policy is one of the least transparent policy arenas within national systems. International diplomacy has historically been rooted in secrecy, partially so that negotiators can protect their negotiating flexibility and thereby arrive at a compromise. Negotiations with foreign states differ in important ways from negotiations carried on by domestic actors within a national system. Although the European Union exhibits a great deal of integration, and negotiations within the Council of Ministers differ in significant ways from those in other international forums, such negotiations are nonetheless different from their domestic counterparts.[59] The Union is composed of states that still regard each other as foreign. That basic fact affects the dynamics of negotiation and raises difficult questions about whether such a system can be democratized without paralyzing its decision-making capacity.

However, as Brussels has come to penetrate more and more deeply into domestic political systems and as it has come to wield greater power in policy areas traditionally seen as domestic, the lack of openness in its decision making has become increasingly problematic. Given the lack of strong European transnational parties that could claim some legitimacy in the tradition of "party government" and the lack of oversight by national parliaments over the EU's executive levels, the Council of Ministers is open to the charge that it is "undemocratic." But can multilateral decision making involving foreign governments be democratic in the same way in which national systems are? Can public opinion be as influential?

The current policy process does not allow public opinion, defined either ideologically or nationally, to be directly transmitted into decision making. The relative absence of transnational political parties and the discretion exercised by national ministers both dilute the impact of public opinion. It is therefore difficult to predict the position a national government will take by looking at the state of public opinion. Chancellor Helmut Kohl, for example, strongly supported the drive for a single currency even though at times a majority of Germans opposed it. While elections that bring in new political parties can certainly change a government's position on integration, such change is not automatic.

In spite of the relative insulation policymaking has enjoyed, public opinion became far more important during the ratification of the Maastricht Treaty.[60] That ratification process politicized the issue of European integration, so much so that elites negotiating the Treaty of Amsterdam in 1997 had to keep public opinion in the forefront of their calculations. (That is particularly true for political leaders in countries that use referenda for ratification.) Such politicization did not, however, lead to a political debate in any country about the desirability of the common currency in the campaign for the 1994 European Parliament elections. Most probably the issue would have divided political parties internally and therefore was kept off the agenda by those same parties.[61]

Although it can be argued that adverse public opinion has mainly slowed down the progress of integration rather than changed its orientation in any fundamental way, there is no doubt that political leaders now take it into account tactically if not strategically. However, outside of a referendum, public opinion becomes most influential when it is mobilized by political parties. European political parties are divided by religion, the proper role of government in the economy, and the limits of social welfare rather than by issues linked to European integration. Thus they have not capitalized on different opinions about integration within the mass electorate. In addition, they have not engaged in a sustained debate about the policy choices presented by integration. Consequently, public opinion has less impact on the European arena than it does on

the national, except when referenda are involved. As we will see in the conclusions, several member-states will hold a referendum on the new constitutional treaty. One of the challenges for national governments is thus now to sell the new treaty to their population.

Cross-National Differences

Support for European integration typically varies cross-nationally. It is important to remember that there is no "European" public opinion; there is instead only public opinion within 25 different national political discourses. Such segmentation is reinforced by the lack of a "European" media; nationally based newspapers and television reporting strengthen the notion of national opinion, national electorates, and national victories and losses within the Community. In a similar vein, the notion of a "European identity" gains more support in some member-states than others, but is secondary to national identity. Public support for "Europe" generally rose until 1989, went into decline subsequently, and in late 1994 began to stabilize at a lower level of support than had been found in the pre-1989 period.[62]

In general, the citizens of the founding six members are more supportive of European integration than are the citizens of Britain and Denmark. The latter show far more ambivalence than do others. The citizens of Sweden, Finland, and Austria seem to share such ambivalence. In mid-2004, only 8 percent of the Irish and 7 percent of the Luxembourghese and Greeks thought EU membership was a bad thing while 20 percent of the Danes, 33 percent of the Swedes, 29 percent of the Austrians, and 29 percent of the British judged membership negatively. If we examine only the original big member-states, we find that in early 2004 only 13 percent of the Italians, 18 percent of the French, and 14 percent of the Germans thought EU membership was a "bad thing."[63] (See Figure 12.3.)

In the countries that joined in 2004, Estonian citizens were the most skeptical of integration with only 38 percent seeing EU membership as a good thing (although only 16 percent saw it as a bad thing and 37 percent were neutral). Support for membership was greatest in Cyprus with 59 percent

FIGURE 12.3   Public Support for European Integration

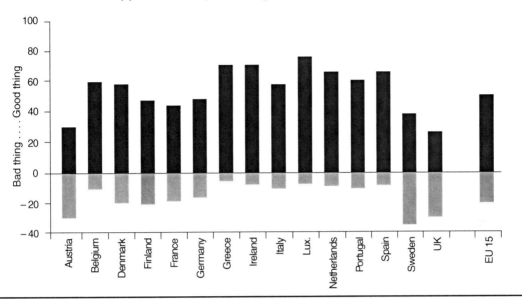

Source: Eurobarometer 61, Spring 2004. The figure plots the percent of the public in each nation that say member in the European Union is a "bad thing" or a "good thing."

FIGURE 12.4   Who is Pro-European?

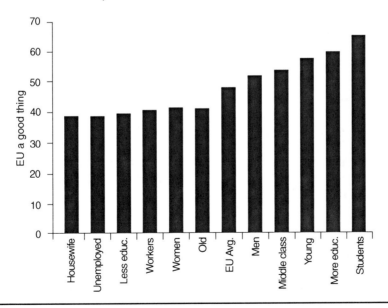

Source: Eurobarometer 61, Spring 2004. Figure presents the percentage in EU 15 who say membership is a good thing.

of Cypriots saying EU membership was a good thing. Support for the euro was generally high, with Estonia (46 percent) and Malta (48 percent) showing the least support. The common security and defense policy was the policy that received the highest rate of approval among the 10 new countries (76 percent).[64] In the 10 new member countries, 62 percent of the citizens supported their country's membership in the fall of 2003.[65]

Support for the euro has also been volatile and has generally been lower than has support for EU membership. Support peaked (64 percent in favor) in autumn 1998, and then fell after it was introduced as a "virtual" currency on January 1, 1999. Support varies cross-nationally, however. In mid-2000, only 14 percent of Italians opposed the euro while 29 percent of the French and 39 percent of Germans did so and 61 percent of the British. In September 2000, 53 percent of Danes voting in a referendum on the euro voted against Danish membership. Three years later, 56 percent of Swedes also rejected the adoption of the euro. By contrast, most Europeans favor a common foreign and security policy.

The citizens of states that joined in 1981 and 1986 (Greece, Spain, and Portugal) have consistently been favorable, far more favorable than the attitudes of the Danes and the British. For members such as the Irish, the Spanish, and the Portuguese, favorable attitudes may be rooted in the view that the modernization of the economic and political system is inextricably entangled with admission to the Union. Modern Spain or modern Ireland are viewed as intrinsically "European" while the traditional Spain was outside of the European mainstream. In general, attitudes in Greece, Spain, Portugal, and Ireland are now as favorable toward integration as are attitudes in the original Six.[66]

Public opinion became especially salient during the process of ratifying the Maastricht Treaty. Given the broad consensus among all the key political parties in the member-states, the leaders meeting in Maastricht in December 1991 expected no trouble during ratification of the treaty. Much to the surprise of political elites, however, the Danish electorate voted "no" on Maastricht on June 1992. The Danes only voted "yes" in May 1993 after the Dan-

ish government had obtained key "opt-outs" from central provisions of Maastricht. Even more troubling was the French reaction to Maastricht. In October 1992, the French barely approved the ratification of Maastricht. The shock waves from the Danish and French results obscured the fact that the Irish electorate approved the treaty by a substantial margin. Denmark and France became the symbols of a troubled European integration whereas the Irish results were largely discounted. However in 2001, the Irish rejected the Nice Treaty and only accepted it in a second referendum.

Most analysts interpreted the results of the Maastricht referenda as a warning light that mass electorates were either hostile to or deeply skeptical about further European integration. Within the Commission itself, a new sense of caution and circumspection emerged. National politicians clearly interpreted the referenda as a vote on integration, and the importance of public opinion in setting the parameters for elite action increased.

In sum, the role of public opinion concerning integration is still ambiguous. How to mobilize public opinion in a system of multilateral decision making involving foreigners is still an open question. The issues linked to European integration, although nearly 50 years old, have not yet found their place on the national political agenda as shaped by national political parties.

THE POLICYMAKING PROCESS

Given the institutional complexity of the European Union—its unusual institutions, its differing decision-making procedures across pillars—the policymaking process is more varied, segmented, and less uniform than in nation-states. The system itself is in flux while the cast of political characters is often unpredictable. Nonetheless, certain key characteristics of the Community make that process more understandable.

First, small states wield a surprising amount of power within the Union (see Table 12.1). The large countries have more administrative resources to bring to bear in the Union's policymaking process, but small member-states typically focus on issues of particular concern to them and do extraordinarily well in defending their national interests in those areas. Especially in pillar one, where the small member-states tend to view the Commission as an ally that can help protect them from overly aggressive big country pressure, officials representing small member-state governments can be quite important in the policymaking process.

Second, Germany has made disproportionate net financial contributions to the Union, as Table 12.4 indicates. If Germany refuses to support a new initiative that would require new expenditure, its opposition is particularly important because of Germany's role as paymaster.

As it stands, the Union's budget is very small compared to the member-states. In 1997 the Community spent under 1.2 percent of the Community's gross national product. In 2003, it only spent 1.02 percent, while the ceiling is at 1.27 percent. The lack of money encourages the Union to use reg-

TABLE 12.4   Member-States' Shares in EU Financing and in EU$_{15}$ GNP (percent of total, data for 1997), including UK

Country	Share in EU GNP	Share in Financing of EU Budget
Austria	2.6	2.8
Belgium	3.1	3.9
Denmark	1.9	2.0
Finland	1.4	1.4
France	17.2	17.5
Germany	26.0	28.2
Greece	1.5	1.6
Ireland	0.8	0.9
Italy	14.2	11.5
Luxembourg	0.2	0.2
Netherlands	4.5	6.4
Portugal	1.2	1.4
Spain	6.6	7.1
Sweden	2.7	3.1
UK	16.1	11.9

Source: European Commission, *Agenda 2000: Financing the European Union* (1998).
In Bridge Laffan and Michael Shackleton, "The Budget," *Policy-Making in the European Union*, Helen Wallace and William Wallace, eds. (Oxford, England: Oxford University Press, 2000), Ch. 8, p. 234.

ulation rather than expenditure as an instrument of policy. Expenditures are comparatively small; however, they are very important for the smaller, poorer countries. Between 1994 and 1999, Community funds (known as structural funds) accounted for 3.67 percent of Greek GDP, 2.8 percent of Irish GDP, 4 percent of Portuguese GDP, and 1.7 percent of Spanish GDP.[67]

Third, questions about expenditure and financial resources invariably run up into the compulsory expenditure for the Common Agricultural Policy (CAP), which has dominated the Community's budget. Although CAP spending has declined significantly—from roughly 70 percent of the budget in 1984 to under 45 percent—it still represents the single largest expenditure. Designed as a key element of the European postwar welfare state, it maintains the incomes of farmers by keeping food prices high and cheaper agricultural products out of the European Community's market. International actors (the United States especially) as well as some member-states, the United Kingdom in particular, have consistently criticized CAP. The GATT Agreement on Agriculture and reforms which the Commission successfully promoted in 1992 reduced the budgetary burden of agriculture. However, a great deal more change is needed if the accession of the post-Communist applicant countries with their large agricultural sectors are not to intolerably strain the Union's finances. Although the Commission had hoped for more reform, the Berlin European Council meeting of 1999 agreed on only relatively modest changes. In essence, Germany, facing very strong French resistance to major changes in the financing of the CAP, agreed to continue its role as paymaster of the Union. Even though Germany is the largest contributor because it pays (in 1997 figures) 28.2 percent of the total EU budget, it agreed to receive only 14.2 percent of CAP monies, while France receives 22.5 percent of the CAP while only contributing 17.5 percent of the EU's budget.[68] (See Table 12.4.)

Fourth, the policy process is rooted in a culture in which consensus building is highly valued. Even when qualified majority voting is permissible, the Commission as well as member-states try to agree on legislation that is acceptable to all 25 member-states.

The consensual style of decision making reflects the style in many of the member-states, but is clearly different from the more adversarial political cultures found in Britain and France.

Finally, the Community is characterized by such diversity of interests, administrative and political cultures, and regulatory arrangements that the policy outcomes tend to show the influence of several models. No national government can impose its own framework on others, and no national government consistently accepts models alien to its own traditions. In the field of regulation, analysts describe the outcome as a "patchwork" that incorporates aspects of varied traditions.[69] In a similar vein, no national government consistently loses in terms of policy outcomes.

Policy Initiation

The European Commission formally initiates all policy in pillar one. In the process of following its proposals through the policy process it interacts closely with both the Council of Ministers and the European Parliament. The Commission can be viewed as the spoke in the wheel, with constant and routine contacts with both the Parliament and the Council. The Commission is the focal point of attention in the policymaking system because it is instrumental in shaping the agenda of the other institutions. The Commission's "work in progress" is an excellent predictor of the issues that the Council and the Parliament will be debating in the future.

The Commission is represented at all meetings within the Council of Ministers and the Parliament but neither the Council nor the Parliament is represented at Commission meetings. The role of the Commission in the Council is so visible that it is sometimes referred to as the "twenty-sixth member state." The Commission plays such a powerful role in various stages of the policymaking process that it can be described as a "co-player" with the Council of Ministers: "neither institution can act without the other."[70] In many policy areas now, however, the European Parliament has become a "third co-player."

THE COMMISSION PRESIDENT The *President of the Commission* plays a critical role in the policy process (in pillar one) because of the visibility and the in-

tensely political nature of the position. He is appointed as a commissioner by his home country, but he is chosen (in practice) as president by consensus by the 25 heads of state and government and has to be approved by the European Parliament. Jacques Delors, the president from 1985 to 1995, was a commissioner from France (having served as the French Minister of Finance) and the longest-serving Commission president in the Community's history. He was followed by Jacques Santer, appointed in 1995, the former prime minister of Luxembourg, who was forced to resign along with the entire Commission in March 1999. Romano Prodi, the former prime minister of Italy, was his successor. In June 2004, Jose Manuel Barroso, the prime minister of Portugal, was designated as the next president and took office in November 2004.

Choosing a president of the Commission is a delicate, intensely political task carried out by the chief executives of the member governments when meeting in the European Council. Delors was chosen because another Frenchman, Claude Cheysson, was opposed by British Prime Minister Margaret Thatcher and German Chancellor Helmut Kohl. His successor, Jacques Santer, was chosen because the choice of the French and Germans was vetoed by John Major (the British prime minister). Santer then became the candidate who could receive unanimous support. Barroso was chosen because the Franco-German choice was considered too federalist by the UK. Jean-Claude Juncker, the popular prime minister of Luxembourg refused to be a candidate, and Chris Patten, the British choice, did not speak good French and did not come from a country that participates in the Eurozone (those being France's requirements for the new president).

Jacques Delors was especially important in increasing the prestige and political weight of the Commission, both within the Community and in the international arena. Described by his admirers as strategic, brilliant, intellectual, and visionary, he was, critics argued, arrogant and too much of a centralizer, and did not give enough consideration to the wishes of national governments or the other commissioners. Both his critics and admirers would agree, however, that under his leadership the Community made some of its most important steps toward further integration. His advocacy and implementation of the *1992 Project*, the initiative to create a single market, will undoubtedly give him a firm place in the history of European integration. It is possible that future histories of the Community will identify Monnet and Delors as the two most important individuals associated with the project of European integration in the twentieth century.

CIVIL SERVICE   The Commission's civil service is organized by Directorate-General (DG) rather than by ministry, as in national executives. The Commission's Secretary-General plays an important albeit discreet role in coordinating the work of the various directorate-generals. He is responsible for the relations between the Commission and the Parliament and the Council of Ministers and is the only non-commissioner who sits with the commissioners when the College meets.

NATIONAL GOVERNMENTS   The relationship between the Commission and the national governments is critical. Delors' success in Brussels made him a potential candidate for the French presidency, which in fact strengthened his political power in Brussels.[71] His close friendship with German Chancellor Kohl throughout Delors' tenure was also an important political resource. When Romano Prodi faced problems, the fact that he did not receive support from the Italian government (whose prime minister was Prodi's arch-rival in Italian domestic politics) added to his travails. Thus are the politics of Brussels and the politics of key national capitals entangled. Power in a national political system, especially within the French or German system, is a tremendous asset when operating within the Community's policymaking system.

The Commission is in constant contact with national executives during the routine of policy initiation. The commissioners have political contacts at the highest national level while Commission officials have frequent contact with their national counterparts. In fact, the Commission often introduces proposals at the behest of a national government.

The national governments must be dealt with by the Commission president as soon as the appointments process begins in national capitals. Prodi was in a stronger position to bargain with the national governments because of the increased

powers given to the president by the Treaty of Amsterdam and Barroso was in an even stronger position. However, there were definitely limits to their ability to persuade the national governments to appoint the people they preferred. Barroso was pleased that more women were appointed to his Commission than had been the case previously (there are 8 out of 25), but he could not himself appoint any female commissioners. After negotiations between the Commission president and national governments, each commissioner is given a portfolio—a specific policy area for which he or she is primarily responsible. For example, one commissioner is in charge of environmental policy while another is responsible for the internal market and still another for transportation programs. As in a national cabinet, some portfolios are more attractive and prestigious than others. Those dealing with external relations are always desirable, as are those dealing with economic matters. At the beginning of each new term, the president assigns portfolios with an eye to seniority, national government pressure, expertise, and political clout back home. In assigning a policy area to each commissioner, President Barroso has seemingly acted more independently from the member-states than many had expected. Even though the big states now have only one commissioner, he has not given the big member-states the posts they sought for their commissioners. For instance, France was pushing for the competition post, but was given the transport post.

The policy initiation process, broadly defined, is complex because commissioners must deal with their national governments, other national governments in the areas of their policy responsibilities, and with the institutions of the Community. Given that the Commission is involved in nearly all phases of the policy process in pillar one, officials contact an innumerable range of actors as a proposal is drafted, refined, accepted by the College of Commissioners, and then shepherded through the Community's institutional process.

Although commissioners are required formally to represent the European interest, they need to keep their prime ministers at home happy if they want to be reappointed. In general, commissioners try to represent both the European and the national interest within certain boundaries. While they do not accept instructions from their government, they typically do put forth policy positions (especially in areas such as industrial, competition [antitrust], and environmental policy) that are recognizable as "national" positions.

Keeping a political master minimally satisfied without sacrificing one's European credentials can be a difficult tightrope to walk. Typically, an effective commissioner informs his colleagues in Brussels when a proposed piece of legislation will run into severe political trouble with his national government. Conversely, he will keep his capital well informed about developments within the Commission so that the national capital is not surprised. Finally, he will mobilize his colleagues in the College of Commissioners to support the positions he advocates, positions that his national government is likely to support.

Legislating Policy

Once the College of Commissioners approves draft legislation by majority vote, it goes to the Council of Ministers and often the Parliament. In both cases, the Commission's proposal will undergo amendments although usually the main lines of the Commission's proposal are accepted. Depending on the subject matter, the Council can legislate by itself or more often needs to approve a draft of the legislation which then will be amended by the Parliament under what is known as the "co-decision" procedure. In the latter case, both the Council and the Parliament need to agree in order for a bill to become a law. If the Council agrees on a piece of legislation but the Parliament and the Council cannot jointly come to an agreement, the legislation dies and is not enacted.

The Commission does not have the political clout in relation to the Council of Ministers that, say, the German chancellor or the U.S. president has in relation to the Bundesrat or the Senate. The Commission's leverage over the collectivity of national governments comes more from the power that accompanies the setting of the policy agenda and the definition of problems than from the formal powers typically associated with a cabinet or executive branch.

COREPER When ministers fly into Brussels for Council of Ministers meetings, they consider only the most difficult issues, those that need compromise at the high political level of a minister. The *Committee of Permanent Representatives* (known as *COREPER*, its French acronym) has already negotiated most of the other issues.

COREPER is critical to the successful functioning of the Council of Ministers as an institution. Some analysts view it as "the contemporary battlefield on which the nations of Europe settle their differences."[72] This group, made up of the ambassadors to the European Union from each of the member-states, resolves all but the most politically sensitive issues embedded in the legislation passed by the Council of Ministers. The group meets every Thursday morning, with the Commission and the Secretariat of the Council of Ministers both represented. At least once a month, they have a very private lunch at which time no interpreters and no note takers are present; English and French are the only languages spoken. That kind of privacy allows the real deals to be made, as both the Commission representatives and the ambassadors can select what they report back to their superiors. In the words of one participant, "It's very simple, there are no spies."[73]

COREPER represents the views of national capitals in Brussels and gives officials in those same capitals a sense of which arguments are likely to be accepted by the other national governments within the Council of Ministers. COREPER officials play a key role in the entanglement of the "European" and the "national." They are taken seriously by both national and Community officials.[74] COREPER operates in pillar one while the Political and Security Committee (PSC) plays a similar function in security-related issues of pillar two. According to the Nice Treaty, the PSC monitors the international situation covered by the areas of the second pillar. It also contributes to the definition of the CFSP by giving opinions to the Council. The PSC is composed of senior ambassadors from the national permanent representations to the EU.

The Parliament has become a much more important legislative actor in many policy arenas. The triangular relationship between the Commission, the Council, and the Parliament is one in which the Commission and the Parliament have typically been allies. Increasingly, the Council and the Parliament are participating in direct relations as the co-decision procedure forces the Council to take the Parliament seriously. Given the Parliament's significant budgetary powers, the three institutions are inextricably linked when fashioning budgetary policy.[75]

Policy Implementation

The Commission is the "motor" of European integration, but it is not the implementor of Community legislation. That function falls to the member-states. The Commission's civil service is too small to carry out the duties of monitoring that a national bureaucracy naturally assumes. Furthermore, the Commission does not have all the enforcement powers of a national bureaucracy.

The Commission is largely restricted to the use of legal instruments in its efforts to oversee implementation. In particular, it can bring a member-state government before the European Court of Justice if a directive passed by the Council of Ministers has not been appropriately "transposed" into national law. It can also bring a member-state before the Court if the implementation of a Community directive is not properly pursued. Such an action is difficult, however, because the Commission does not have the power physically to enter a member-state to gather the kind of evidence it would need to persuade the European Court of Justice. Non-governmental groups (NGOs) and private citizens do, however, write to the Commission with complaints of infringements of Community law. The Commission often uses informal pressure on a national government to improve the execution of directives on the ground.

Judicial Review

The European Court of Justice has evolved in a way that the member-states did not expect. Established to ensure that the Commission did not overstep its authority, the Court, however, expanded the scope of Community authority in several ways. Most importantly, it declared that Community law was supreme—that is, superior to

member-state law.[76] It also ruled that the Community gained powers in external relations in those areas in which it approved intra-Community legislation, thereby giving the Community a much greater international profile than had been anticipated.

The sweep and direction of the Court's decisions have been so important that the Court has been viewed by some as the "motor" of European integration at times when national governments were reluctant to move integration forward. Although its power is limited by the constraints that affect all courts, it has also gradually obtained the unique legitimacy enjoyed by courts. The process of integration would have proceeded much more slowly, and in some areas might not have proceeded at all, without the Court's activism. Martin Shapiro offers this explanation:

> The European Court of Justice has played a crucial role in shaping the European Community. In a sense, the Court created the present-day Community; it declared the Treaty of Rome to be not just a treaty but a constitutional instrument that obliged individual citizens and national government officials to abide by those provisions that were enforceable through their normal judicial processes.[77]

Several factors have helped the Court in its integrationist project. First, the use of legal reasoning and argument seems apolitical. In that sense, the very language and procedures of the judiciary and the legal profession help "mask" the political consequences of legal decisions.[78] Second, it is very difficult for the member-states to agree among themselves to pass legislation overriding Court decisions. In fact, the supranational institutions in general benefit from the fact that each one typically has allies on any issue among at least several states. Dissenting states therefore find it difficult to reverse "integrationist" decisions or processes once they are established.[79]

Third, the Court has benefited from the use of national courts (through what is known as the preliminary ruling system) in implementing Community law. Once national judges accepted the legitimacy of the rulings of the European Court of Justice, the maneuverability available to national governments that disagreed with the Court's decisions narrowed considerably. It is difficult for national governments to ignore the decisions of their own national courts so the Court's use of national judges has given the Court powerful allies within the member-states themselves.

The Court has been a powerful instrument of integration. Until very recently, it typically promoted further integration through its decisions and has been viewed as a powerful ally of the Commission as well as of the Parliament. In policy terms, it set the stage for the single market with groundbreaking decisions, granted the Commission external power in those areas in which the Community was allowed to legislate internally, decided the boundaries within which environmental protection could act as a nontariff barrier, and promoted gender equality in the workplace.

In general, the Court has "constitutionalized" the treaties that underpin the Community and has evolved into "a vertically integrated legal regime conferring judicially enforceable rights and obligations on all legal persons and entities, public and private, within EC territory."[80] The Court therefore provides the Community with a legal order in which EC law is supreme to national law, a supremacy accepted by national judges. The Court, in the words of one of its distinguished judges, has sought "to fashion a constitutional framework for a quasi-federal structure in Europe."[81]

EXTERNAL RELATIONS

The powers of the Commission in the field of external relations have been growing. The Treaty of Rome specifically identified the Commission as representing the Community in organizations such as the Organization for Economic Cooperation and Development (OECD) and the United Nations Economic Commission for Europe (UNECE): the Commission was thus granted an external role very early. Furthermore, the fact that the Commission was the sole negotiator for the Community in the various rounds of the General Agreement on Tariffs and Trade (GATT) enhanced the Community's presence in the field of international economic relations. It, along with the member-states, became a contracting party to the World Trade Organization (WTO).

The EU (whether represented by the Commission or the Commission and the Presidency of the Council of Ministers) has struggled to be granted recognition in the United Nations. While it has the status of an observer, it has pressed very hard to be treated as an equal partner in, for example, international environmental negotiations. In the case of global agreements (such as the Montreal Protocol limiting CFCs), for example, the Commission bargained hard and long to be recognized as a signatory.[82] Generally, outside of the trade area, the member-states regard treaties as "mixed" agreements in which the Commission signs on behalf of the Community and the member-states sign as well.

ENTANGLEMENT OF THE "NATIONAL" AND THE "EUROPEAN"

The coexistence of "intergovernmental" and "supranational" elements within the Community makes the Community clearly distinct from any of the nation-states that belong to the Community. The institutions are in a delicate balance. Some (the Council of Ministers) are intended to ensure that the views of national governments are respected and that integration does not proceed further than that permitted by the "permissive consensus" within which national governments have operated. The functions of other institutions (the Commission, the European Court of Justice, and the Parliament) are to push the goal of integration, to set the agenda, raise issues, and keep the pressure on to further integrate. These institutions might test the boundaries of the "permissive consensus." They project a broad strategic "European" perspective that does not match the views of any of the national governments per se but represents the interest of the collectivity rather than that of any specific member government. They are the "supranational" component of the Community. Proponents of a more "federal" Europe see the Court, the Parliament, and the Commission as the institutions that should be given more power, while the proponents of an "intergovernmental" Europe wish to increase the power of the Council of Ministers and the European Council.

Because political parties have much less power than they do at the national level and because the key institutions are not directly elected, the Community's institutions qua institutions are more important than at the national level. The Union is above all its institutions. There is not a European Union political culture, media, party system, electoral system, welfare state, or society. National diversity in all those areas is so great that the Union is identified more by its institutions than by those societal and cultural factors so important in shaping national polities.[83] In brief, there is no European Union "public" or "culture" as such.

Given the delicate balance between institutions and the still evolving nature of the European Union, it is not surprising that much of the "politics" observed in Brussels involves the various institutions jockeying for institutional power. The Council of Ministers, the Commission, and the Parliament are constantly trying to maximize their institutional reach and influence as they collectively struggle to construct a consensus on proposed legislation. The Commission tries to protect itself from encroachments from both the Parliament and the Council of Ministers, and the Council and the Parliament eye each other warily. Rather than being based on some kind of balance of power between the executive and the legislative branches as in the United States, the Community's political system is based on a balance between the representation of national interests and of "European" interests. The (national) governmental interest and the supranational interest coexist, but are in constant tension. In that sense, the Community is more recognizable to students of federal systems than of unitary systems, for in federal systems the states and the federal government are typically struggling to maximize their own power.

In a parallel vein, those institutions representing national governments are "Europeanized" so that national governments when operating within them are enmeshed in a decision-making machinery that is significantly different from that of a traditional international organization and from decision making at the national level. A national government operating within the Council of Ministers is a "co-decision maker," rather than a "decision maker," as it is when operating unilaterally at the national level.[84]

The member governments of the Community collectively work together so that each individual national government has submitted to the "European" collectivity in the foregoing of unilateral decision making. A national government operates within the boundaries of the Community's institutional structure in a qualitatively different manner from the way it operates unilaterally in other international forums or at home. In brief, France in the European Union acts differently from France in the rest of the world, as does Paris acting as the sole decision maker in French national politics.

The *supranational* and the *intergovernmental* institutions are both integral to the project of European integration. The Council of Ministers, the main intergovernmental body, is there to bring the member-states to a collective view in contrast to the unilateral national decision making that would take place if the European Union did not exist. A national government participating in the Council of Ministers is not acting unilaterally. The Union's institutions, whether representing national governments or the "European" interest, all implicitly reject the exercise of unilateral national power.

The rejection of unilateral national power across a broad range of issues makes the European Union so distinctive when viewed from the outside. Even when the member-states decide to cooperate within the Council of Ministers, downgrade the Commission's role, and exclude the European Court of Justice, the degree of integration that they accept is far greater than that found in other parts of the world. Even when an arrangement is considered to be "intergovernmental" by Europeans, it would be considered far too integrationist for a country such as the United States to accept. The debate between the "intergovernmental" states (such as the United Kingdom and Denmark) and the "federalist" states (such as the Benelux states, Germany, and Italy) takes place within a context in which the rejection of the exercise of unilateral national decision making is much more commonly accepted than it is anywhere else in the world. In brief, an "intergovernmental" posture within the European Union would typically be considered as radically "integrationist" or "federalist" in Asia, North America, or Latin America.[85]

POLICY PERFORMANCE

National governments provide social services; the European Union makes laws, but it does not engage, with a few exceptions (such as agriculture and regional policy) in activities that involve large public expenditure. The Union's comparatively small budget keeps it from engaging in the kinds of activities traditionally the province of national governments.

The Union does engage in regulation, for the costs of regulation are borne by the objects of regulation rather than the regulators.[86] The creation of the single market led to the Union's emergence as an important regulator of economic activity. Its role consisted of removing national regulations that impeded cross-border trade and re-regulating at the EU level to ensure that safety standards, for example, were instituted. The processs of regulatory reform therefore empowered the EU while eliminating many national nontariff barriers to trade.

The Single-Market Program

As already mentioned, the Single European Act allowed the member-states to create a true single market. The single-market program involved the removal of nontariff barriers from the Community's economy. Regulatory barriers that protected national markets from competition, as well as from goods and services produced in other EU countries, have been largely dismantled. The 1992 Project (the goal was to approve nearly 300 pieces of single-market legislation in Brussels by 1992, a goal largely achieved) was the foundation stone of the more integrated European economy with which Europe entered the twenty-first century. Its effects in both the economic and the political spheres were huge. Once firms no longer benefited from protected national markets, they realized they had to become global rather than simply European players to survive the competition from American firms. These same American firms were attracted to the single market, invested huge sums in building production facilities in Europe, and bought promising European firms. European firms therefore entered the American market in a sustained fashion, set up production facilities in the United States, and bought promising American firms. Interestingly, the relationship be-

came quite symmetrical—the number of Americans working for European firms roughly equaled the number of Europeans working for American firms.[87]

There are still a few areas in which agreement has not been reached, but the Community's legislative program for the single market is largely finished. Whereas in 1980, a citizen from one EU country was stopped when crossing the border into another EU state, by 2004 the frontiers within the EU were usually crossed without any interruption. Capital can now move freely without national governments imposing capital controls. Firms based in one country can acquire firms in other member-states, and banks can set up offices outside their home country. Airlines, previously protected from each other, now compete with one another, and low-cost carriers have emerged (symbolized by Ryanair). The telecommunications sector is now open to fierce competition; previously it had been a monopoly run by the state. As a result of the competitive forces unleashed by the single market, nationalized industries have increasingly been privatized throughout the member-states thereby transforming the European economy. The single-market program was such a pivotal program for the process of European integration that the proponents of the single currency argued that a single market required a single currency—"one market, one currency."

External Relations

Since the implementation of the single-market program, the EU has become far more active in the area of external relations. The EU has been involved in external relations since the Rome Treaties, through the role of the Commission in trade negotiations, as well as through the EU role in development policy. The EU is the world's biggest donor of humanitarian aid. The EU's development policy dates from the special relationship (primarily in the area of trade) which France insisted should exist between the EU and France's colonies and overseas territories. The special relationship was strengthened when Britain joined the Community as its former colonies also benefited from that relationship. The first Lome Convention of 1975 established the cooperative framework within which the then Community and the developing world with links to Europe developed. The EU also strengthened its relations with countries of the Maghreb and the Masreq.

Today, the European Union is the world's leading development partner, in terms of aid, trade, and direct investment. Together, the EU and its member-states provide 55 percent of all official international development aid.

In foreign policy, the EU has been slower in acquiring a role, first because foreign policy and international security touch the core of national sovereignty, and second because the defense of Europe was left to the North Atlantic Treaty Organization (NATO). Since the 1970s however, member-states have coordinated their positions on foreign policy issues through the European Political Cooperation (EPC). EPC, however, represented a nonbinding commitment and thus did not yield substantive policy outcomes. The end of the Cold War and the uncertainty of a continued U.S. military involvement in Europe, along with the poor military performance of member-states (particularly France) during the first Gulf war led to the creation of the second pillar of the EU during the Maastricht negotiations. Known as the Common Foreign and Security Policy of the EU (CFSP), the second pillar is mainly intergovernmental in that the Commission has only a shared right of initiative (rather than the monopoly of initiative which it enjoys in pillar one) with the member-states. The EP and the ECJ have no role at all. As defined in the Maastricht Treaty, the CFSP also entails the eventual creation of a genuine EU defense policy, not however in competition with NATO. The first test of the EU's new CFSP was the Yugoslav wars of the early 1990s, in which the EU did not fare well, except in the area of humanitarian aid. The wars only ended when the United States and NATO became involved. The Treaty of Amsterdam strengthened the commitment of the member-states to CFSP, but it did not become a major area of Union policy until the British and French, the two major actors in European defense, came to an agreement at a Franco-British summit at St. Malo, France, in December 1998.

Essentially, the UK, a traditional supporter of NATO and concerned that a European defense policy would weaken NATO, agreed to cooperate with European efforts to develop a European capability in security and defense policy. The French, who had traditionally supported a European defense posture independent of NATO, agreed that such efforts should not weaken NATO. The EU would develop a common defense policy within the framework of the CFSP through summit meetings among the fifteen's foreign ministers and defense ministers. For the first time, defense ministers, who previously had operated solely within NATO, would be brought under the EU's umbrella, although still meeting informally.

Once the Franco-British bargain had been struck—the UK willing to become more European in its defense policy in return for the French accepting NATO's crucial role in Europe's collective defense—movement came quickly. The Helsinki European Council in December 1999 agreed to develop by 2003 a collective European capability to deploy a rapid-reaction force of 60,000 troops for crisis management operations. These troops would be capable of deployment at 60 days' notice and remain operational for 1 year. They would intervene in humanitarian and rescue tasks as well as in peacekeeping and crisis management (what is referred to in the EU jargon as the Petersberg tasks). Since March 2000 a Political and Security Committee meets weekly at the ambassadorial level and a military committee (MC) and a military staff within the Council's structures provide the Council of Ministers with military expertise. The year 2001 also saw the inclusion of the Western European Union (WEU) in the EU—the WEU only keeping its collective defense role through its Article V.

The major challenge to the European Security and Defense Policy (ESDP) is in the area of military capabilities. The Europeans, with the exception of France and the United Kingdom, are extremely weak in what is called C3I (control, command, communication, and intelligence).

Since the goal of the ESDP is not to create a European army, EU-NATO relations are critical. Yet these two organizations have had no relationship with each other throughout the entire postwar period (see Box 12.5). Although France initially wanted to keep NATO at arm's length from the ESDP, it reversed its position in April 2000 and at

Box 12.5   European Integration and Transatlantic Security Meet at Last

Since 1949 responsibility for European defense policy has been in the hands of individual governments and the North Atlantic Treaty Organization, an intergovernmental body involving (and relying heavily upon) the United States. In 1999 the member-states of the European Union finally agreed to take important steps in the direction of more integrated defense and security policies, by cooperating with NATO, rather than replacing it.

	EU	NATO
Membership:	European member-states only	Transatlantic membership (most EU states, Norway, Turkey, U.S., and Canada)
Main Objective:	Political & economic integration	Collective defense and peacekeeping (out-of-area) operations
Key Officials:	Foreign Ministers and, after 1999, Defense Ministers and the High Representative for Common Foreign and Security Policy	Foreign and Defense Ministers
Headquarters:	Headquartered in Brussels	Headquartered in Brussels
Type of Organization:	Supranational organization	Intergovernmental organization
Role of U.S.:	U.S. does not have a "seat at the table"	U.S. has the most important "seat at the table"
EU-NATO Relationship:	No relationship with NATO until 2000— relationship formalized in the Copenhagen Agreement of December 2002	No relationship with EU until 2000

the Feira European Council Summit in June 2000 agreed to the establishment of four ad-hoc EU/NATO working groups. In September 2000, for the first time, the Interim Political and Security Committee and NATO's Permanent Council met—the first formal high-level contact between the EU and NATO. In December 2002 at the Copenhagen Summit, the EU and NATO reached an agreement about the EU's use of NATO military assets in operations in which NATO as a whole is not involved. Assurances were given that the ESDP would not affect any vital interest of a non-EU NATO member.

The agreement allowed the EU to launch its first military operation April 1, 2003, when it took over from NATO in Macedonia. A second military operation, without the use of NATO assets, was launched in June 2003 in the Republic of Congo. At

the end of 2004, the EU was also poised to take over the bigger NATO peacekeeping operation in Bosnia.

Does the European Union Make a Difference?

The European Union now affects a great many people, some of them more directly than others. It makes the most difference for the farmer whose prices and subsidies are largely dependent on the decisions made by the Council of Agricultural Ministers and the Commission. Fishermen's catches and allotments are significantly influenced by Brussels. Businesspeople are affected by the provisions of the single market (especially the mobility of capital and the liberalization of numerous once-protected markets), the move to the euro, the robust antitrust policy implemented by the Commission (and coordinated with the antitrust policy of the United States in relevant cases), and the Union's environmental policy. Bankers and investors are affected by the policies of the European Central Bank and the move to a common currency. Environmentalists want to increase environmental protection. Consumers are worried about the safety of the food they eat; soccer players now enjoy "free agency" because of the EU. Women seek equal pay for equal work. Airline passengers benefit from airline deregulation. Retirees can decide to live in another member-state. Regional government officials receive funds from Brussels to help their region develop roads and jobs. Patients benefit from more rapid approval of new medicinal drugs now that they fall under the jurisdiction of the EU. Telephone users have benefited enormously in terms of both price and level of service from the deregulation of the telecommunications sector pushed through by the Commission. In 2002, everyone living in the 12 member-states that have accepted the euro became accustomed to paying their bills by using a new currency and relinquishing their old familiar national currency.

By contrast, in areas such as the provision of health care, education, urban policies, social security, and unemployment compensation, national governments have retained the right to unilaterally make policy. These policy areas are only indirectly affected by the European Union. The "welfare state" is largely still under the unilateral control of national policymakers (although its financing is affected by the policies of the European Central Bank). In areas related to economic activity and social regulation (consumer and environmental protection, for example), rather than social services, the European Union is particularly relevant. Thus, the European Union does not legislate the health benefits that any citizen of any member-state is entitled to enjoy. However, the fact that the doctor chosen by a patient may be of a different nationality from the patient occurs because EU regulations recognize medical degrees across borders. The drugs that the doctor prescribes are under EU regulations if they are new to the market, and the competition among firms selling that drug is shaped by EU rules.

Countries outside of the EU are also particularly aware of the European Union. The United States must bargain with the Union in important global forums such as the World Trade Organization; poor developing world countries are given preferential access to EU markets as institutionalized in the Cotonou Agreement. Countries such as Turkey and Israel and in the Mediterranean have negotiated special trade agreements with the Union.[88] Although at this point in time the EU is not yet a true "military" power, its economic reach and power make it an important international actor.

From the beginning, the external economic role that "Europe" would play if organized into a relatively integrated unit has been an important consideration for European policymakers. In the field of agriculture, for example, the Common Agricultural Policy allowed the Community to ward off strong American pressure to open up the European agricultural market.[89] This external role was particularly important given that the states initially involved in European integration were not "self-confident" states. Their capacities were not in any way similar to those enjoyed by the United States, a superpower with enormous resources and global power.[90] European integration allowed these states to have much greater influence in the international environment than if they had exercised traditional sovereignty. Public opinion attitudes among mass electorates, in fact, show high degrees of support for Union activity regarding the international environment in all policy arenas, not simply those having to do with economics. "European elites may emphasize the difficulties of coordinating foreign and defense policies among the European states, but European publics see this as a natural area of joint action."[91] In fact, as we have seen, the leaders of the EU member-states are following the lead of public opinion in cooperating more extensively in the field of foreign and security policy.

POLICY CHALLENGES

The European Union faces three key challenges in the years ahead—all extremely difficult. How to digest the May 2004 enlargement to Eastern and

Central Europe without undermining the process of integration is one. The second involves having the recently agreed upon European Constitutional Treaty accepted by the 25 member-states, some of them through a referendum. The third requires creating a balance between integration and the protection of cultural diversity so that ordinary citizens of very diverse member-states do not feel they are being culturally "homogenized" and blame European integration for that threat to their identity.

The Challenge of Enlargement

How can the European Union digest the enlargement to 10 new member countries? Having recently regained their independence, support for EU membership in the 10 candidate countries was at a steady level of 52 percent in 2003. The highest level of support was in Cyprus (59 percent), Slovakia (58 percent), and Hungary (56 percent). The lowest level was in Estonia (38 percent) and Latvia (46 percent). In addition, the 2004 enlargement (plus the prospective 2007 enlargement to Bulgaria, Romania, and Croatia and the commitment to eventually accept all the Balkan countries) has left the question as to where the borders of the EU will finally come to rest.

The new entrants from the East and the South are primarily small states (with the exception of Poland) with large agricultural populations. These nations will all be net gainers under present distributive policies within the Union. Funds that previously helped the poorer member-states—Spain, Portugal, Ireland, and Greece—will either need to be expanded, eliminated, or redirected toward the new entrants. In 2002, for example, even Slovenia, the wealthiest of the 10, had a per capita GDP that was only 70 percent of the EU average; the Czech Republic and Hungary had 57 percent and 50 percent respectively. Latvia had a per capita GDP that was only 35 percent of the EU's GDP per capita.

Perhaps the key question, however, is how to restructure the policymaking institutions of the European Union. Should each member-state be allowed one commissioner or should there be a rotation of countries with a commissioner? If the latter

option were chosen, would the Commission have the legitimacy required to offend the big member-states? How should votes in the Council of Ministers be allocated? Small countries are by far the majority of the 10 states, with only Poland (with a population of 39 million) having a population of more than 10 million. Enlargement will change the dynamics of coalitions within the Council, especially if the use of qualified majority voting expands so as to avoid decision-making paralysis. The big member-states have opposed maintaining the disproportionate power of small countries, but the small member-states have been determined to protect their role in the decision-making process. In December 2000, some of these issues were addressed in the negotiations for the Treaty of Nice, which incorporated very difficult compromises. The Nice Treaty decided to adopt a system of re-weighting of votes within the Council (a total of 237 votes were allocated to the 15 member-states, with a qualified majority threshold set at 169 votes). As from November 1, 2004 and taking into consideration the 2004 enlargement, a Council decision is adopted when it receives at least 232 votes out of 321, reflecting the majority of the members of the Council (subject to the demographic clause), combined with a double or even triple majority. While the re-weighting of votes favors the large member-states, the qualified majority must also be a majority of the member-states. This is combined with a system known as the "demographic safety net," which means that each member-state can request verification of whether the qualified majority represents at least 62 percent of the population of the Union. If this condition is not fulfilled, the decision cannot be adopted.

The Central and Eastern European countries viewed admission to the Union as a necessary component of their road toward democratization, a market economy, and a "return to Europe" (that Europe of which they were a part before the Cold War). From the point of view of the previous EU member-states, admitting the countries of Central and Eastern Europe involved a whole series of decisions with profound implications for the future governance of the Union. Whereas Germany favored enlargement, that federalist perspective was countered by the United Kingdom, which favored enlargement but thought it would lead toward a more "intergovernmental" Community with fewer inroads on national sovereignty. Countries that have benefited from the EU's special programs for poorer countries—Greece, Spain, Portugal, and Ireland—view the "newcomers" as competitors for funds that have accelerated their own economic modernization.[92]

As the Union faces eastward, therefore, it has to answer questions about where its final external frontier will be. Will it be the eastern border of Poland? Or beyond? It has to answer questions about whether it will become more integrated or less integrated, as the current stage of integration is likely to lead to paralysis if extended to a Union with many more countries. It will have to consider whether it must become more integrated in the area of foreign and security policy. Or does NATO enlargement to admit Central European countries imply that those countries will not favor the further development of a European (rather than transatlantic) defense identity even if the "old" EU members desire it? As Europe enters the next century, it is striking that an organization rooted in the geopolitics of the past is the arbiter of "the challenge of continental order."[93] The European Union has succeeded to such an extent that it now has the responsibility of drawing the political and economic map of Europe. Yet the average man in the street is not certain that he wants to accept that responsibility.

The EU Constitution

The questions raised earlier about decision making, the avoidance of paralysis, and a more coherent European Union in international affairs have occupied both EU and national politicians since the Treaty of Nice was signed in 2000. The answers to many of those questions were finally given in June 2004. The 25 heads of state and of government meeting in Brussels agreed on a new constitutional treaty. It is hoped that this treaty will bring stability to the decision-making procedures and institutional design of the Union and end the cycle of treaty-making which began with the 1986 Single European Act.

A constitutional convention that met for one and a half years under the chairmanship of former French President Valery Giscard d'Estaing prepared the reforms. The constitutional convention was as an alternative to the Intergovernmental Conferences (IGC) that had traditionally revised treaties. In an IGC, representatives of member-states met and negotiated often hard-fought bargains among themselves. The European Union resembled a traditional international organization when it was engaged in negotiating an IGC. The constitutional convention was convened in order to make the process of treaty revision more transparent, democratic, and open to more actors than just national representatives. The convention, besides including national government representatives from the 25, included representatives from the European Commission, the European Parliament, and national parliaments. The convention also met with representatives from civil society.

The members of the convention agreed on a draft constitution in July 2003. It presented the draft to the member-states who started renegotiating various points of contention. It took another year for the national representatives to agree on the new treaty.

The provisions that led to the bitter negotiations were the ones that already proved contentious during the Amsterdam and Nice negotiations: the size of the Commission, the number of seats in the European Parliament, and the weighting of votes in the Council of Ministers. These key questions pitted big member-states against small member-states and emphasized the dual nature of the EU: a supranational organization where member-states still are key power-holders.

If the new constitutional treaty passes the test of ratification and referendum (it is not expected to enter into force until 2007), the key changes to the EU decision-making process would be the following:

- A president of the EU: chosen by the EU heads of state and of government for 2.5 years (renewable once) to chair the European Council and represent the EU abroad.
- An EU foreign affairs minister (who will become vice-president of the European Commission): chosen by the member-states to chair

meetings of EU foreign affairs ministers; formulate policies on issues from terrorism to peace-keeping; and represent the EU abroad with the EU president.

- The definition of a new Qualified Majority Vote (QMV): 55 percent of member-states (representing at least 15 countries) and 65 percent of the EU population. The voting minority must comprise at least 4 states.
- The size of the Commission: starting in 2014, the Commission's size will be equal to two-thirds of the member-states.

Cultural Diversity

As of 2004, the European Union was composed of 25 member-states, including most of Scandinavia, key Mediterranean countries, and former Soviet satellites. The Union's gross national product and population are larger than that of the United States, and today it is the largest market in the industrialized world. As the Union has expanded, what has become more striking is its cultural diversity. As the economies of the 25 are more intertwined and as more policy areas are included in an integrated Europe's policy portfolio, questions of national identity are more salient. Diverse European cultures have emerged out of many centuries of disparate historical experiences, and the current economic convergence is proceeding far more quickly than is any type of cultural (or linguistic) convergence. Although the EU is firmly committed to protecting cultural diversity, the tension between culture, economics, policy, and identity are more pronounced now that the European Union includes nearly all of Western Europe and a big part of Eastern Europe. How far will the average person accept being made into a "European" in political and economic terms without feeling that his or her identity is being fundamentally threatened? That question has not yet been answered.

The question of a "European" identity is further complicated by whether Turkey actually belongs in the European Union. The need to decide whether accession negotiations should begin with Turkey (which had been officially accepted as a candidate country in 1999) divides mass electorates (which generally opposed Turkish membership) from their elected leaders (many of which supported it) as well as the political class itself. The very difficult history that has shaped the relationship between Christian Europe and Muslim Turkey (and its predecessor the Ottoman Empire) has brought issues of identity, previously of secondary importance, to the fore as the debate over Turkish accession has developed. The consequence of such a debate over "European" identity is unpredictable. Ironically, the debate over Turkey may make "the 25" feel more European than they did before the issue of Turkey came onto the political agenda. The history that binds the 25 together and separates them from Turkey is much discussed and debated. Yet the question of Turkish accession also presents an opportunity for the EU. Given the capabilities of the Turkish military, an EU with Turkey as a member could play a major role in geopolitics. The Turkish question may well force the EU to choose between cultural affinity and a major geopolitical role.

 Key Terms

Council of Ministers (Council of the European Union)	Economic and Monetary Union (EMU)	European Economic Community (EEC)	Intergovernmental Conference (IGC)
Committee of Permanent Representatives (COREPER)	European Central Bank European Commission European Council European Court of Justice	European Free Trade Association (EFTA) European Parliament European Union (EU) intergovernmental	Justice and Home Affairs (JHA) Maastricht Treaty (Treaty of European Union)

Marshall Plan
Members of the
    European
    Parliament (MEPs)
North Atlantic Treaty
    Organization
    (NATO)

Political and Security
    Committee (PSC)
Presidency of the
    European Council
    and the Council of
    Ministers

President of the
    Commission
Schuman Plan
single currency (euro)
Single European Act
    (SEA)
supranational

Treaty of Amsterdam
Treaty of Nice
Treaty of Rome
1992 Project

 Internet Resources

The European Commission:
The European Parliament:
The Council of the EU:

Commission Delegation in Washington, DC:
EU-Related News:
EU-Related News: www.eupolitix.com

 Suggested Readings

Bomberg, Elizabeth, and Alexander Stubb, eds. *The European Union: How Does It Work?* New York: Oxford University Press, 2003.

Cini, Michelle, ed. *European Union Politics.* Oxford: Oxford University Press, 2002.

Corbett, Richard, Francis Jacobs, and Michael Shackleton. *The European Parliament,* 4th ed. London: John Harper, 2000.

Cowles, Maria, Thomas Risse, and James Caporaso, eds. *Transforming Europe.* Ithaca, NY: Cornell University Press, 2001.

Dinan, Desmond. *Europe Recast: A History of European Union.* New York: Palgrave Macmillan, 2004.

Dinan, Desmond, ed. *Encyclopedia of the European Union.* Boulder, CO: Lynne Rienner, 2000.

Gillingham, John. *European Integration 1950–2003: Superstate or New Market Economy?* New York: Cambridge University Press, 2003.

Hayes-Renshaw, Fiona, and Helen Wallace. *The Council of Ministers.* London: Macmillan, 1997.

Gilbert, Mark. *Surpassing Realism—The Politics of European Integration Since 1945.* Lanham, MD: Rowman and Littlefield, 2003.

Keohane, Robert O., and Stanley Hoffmann, eds. *The New European Community: Decisionmaking and Institutional Change.* Boulder, CO: Westview, 1991.

Moravcsik, Andrew. *The Choice for Europe: Social Purpose & State Power from Messina to Maastricht.* Ithaca, NY: Cornell University Press, 1998.

Parsons, Craig. *A Certain Idea of Europe.* Ithaca: Cornell University Press, 2003.

Peterson, John, and Michael Shackleton, eds. *The Institutions of the European Union.* New York: Oxford University Press, 2002.

Rosamond, Ben. *Theories of European Integration.* New York: St Martin's, 2000.

Ross, George. *Jacques Delors and European Integration.* Oxford, England: Oxford University Press, 1995.

Sbragia, Alberta M. *Euro-Politics: Institutions and Policy-Making in the "New" European Community.* Washington: Brookings Institution, 1992.

Sbragia, Alberta M. "The Treaty of Nice, Institutional Balance, and Uncertainty." *Governance: An International Journal of Policy, Administration and Institutions,* Vol. 15, No. 3, July 2002, pp. 393–410.

Smith, Michael E. *Europe's Foreign and Security Policy: The Institutionalization of Cooperation.* New York: Cambridge University Press, 2004.

Trachtenberg, Marc. *A Constructed Peace: The Making of the European Settlement 1945–63.* Princeton: Princeton University Press, 1999.

Wallace, Helen, and William Wallace, eds. *Policy-Making in the European Union,* 4th ed. Oxford, England: Oxford University Press, 2000.

Winand, Pascaline. *Eisenhower, Kennedy, and the United States of Europe.* New York: St. Martin's, 1993.

Endnotes

1. Giandomenico Majone, "The Rise of Statutory Regulation in Europe," in Giandomenico Majone, ed., *Regulating Europe* (New York: Routledge, 1996), p. 57.

2. Beate Kohler-Koch, "Catching Up with Change: The Transformation of Governance in the European Union," *Journal of European Public Policy* 3, No. 3 (September 1996): 359-80.

3. Jack Hayward, "Populist Challenge to Elitist Democracy in Europe," in Jack Hayward, ed., *Elitism, Populism, and European Politics* (Oxford, England: Clarendon, 1996), p. 29.

4. Wolfgang Wessels, "The EC Council: The Community's Decisionmaking Center," in Robert O. Keohane and Stanley Hoffman, eds. *The New European Community: Decisionmaking and Institutional Change*, (Boulder, CO: Westview, 1991), p. 136.

5. Many scholars have debated whether national governments are the only real decision makers in the Union, with the Community institutions which do not represent state interests being in fact agents of the national governments, or whether national governments share their decision-making power with those other "non-state-centric" institutions. For example, see Andrew Moravcsik, *The Choice for Europe* (Ithaca, NY: Cornell University Press, 1998); Gary Marks, Liesbet Hooghe, and Kermit Blank, "European Integration from the 1980s: State-Centric v. Multi-Level Governance," *Journal of Common Market Studies* 34, No. 3 (September 1996): 341-78; James A. Caporaso and John T. S. Keeler, "The European Union and Regional Integration Theory," in Carolyn Rhodes and Sonia Mazey, ed., *Building a European Polity?* (Boulder, CO: Lynne Rienner, 1995), pp. 29-62.

6. Alberta M. Sbragia, "Introduction," in Alberta M. Sbragia, ed., *Euro-Politics: Institutions and Policymaking in the "New" European Community* (Washington: Brookings Institution, 1992), pp. 1-22.

7. Cited in Edmund Dell, *The Schuman Plan and the British Abdication of Leadership in Europe* (New York: Oxford University Press, 1995), p. 22.

8. John Gillingham, *Coal, Steel, and the Rebirth of Europe, 1945-1955: The Germans and French from Ruhr Conflict to Economic Community* (Cambridge, England: Cambridge University Press, 1991), p. xi.

9. George Ross, *Jacques Delors and European Integration* (New York: Oxford University Press, 1995), p. 1.

10. F. Roy Willis, "Schuman Breaks the Deadlock," in F. Roy Willis, ed., *European Integration* (New York: New Viewpoints, 1975), p. 27.

11. For a sophisticated study of Kurt Schumacher and his attitude toward France and European integration, see Lewis J. Edinger, *Kurt Schumacher: A Study in Personality and Political Behavior* (Stanford, CA: Stanford University Press, 1965), pp. 144-89.

12. Albert Kersten, "A Welcome Surprise? The Netherlands and the Schuman Plan Negotiations," in Klaus Schwabe, ed., *Die Anfange des Schuman-Plans 1950/51; The Beginnings of the Schuman Plan*, contributions to the Symposium in Aachen, May 28-30, 1986 (Baden-Baden, Germany: Nomosverlag, 1988), p. 287.

13. See F. Roy Willis, *Italy Chooses Europe* (New York: Oxford University Press, 1971), pp. 1-52.

14. Dell, *The Schuman Plan and the British Abdication of Leadership in Europe*, p. 4.

15. Stephen D. Krasner, "United States Commercial and Monetary Policy: Unraveling the Paradox of External Strength and Internal Weakness," in Peter Katzenstein, ed., *Between Power and Plenty: Foreign Economic Policies of Advanced Industrial States* (Madison: University of Wisconsin Press, 1978), p. 52.

16. Derek W. Urwin, The Community of Europe: A History of European Integration since 1945, 2nd ed. (New York: Longman, 1995), p. 21.

17. Pascaline Winand, *Eisenhower, Kennedy, and the United States of Europe* (New York: St. Martin's, 1993).

18. Miles Kahler, "The Survival of the State in European International Relations," in Charles Maier, ed., *Changing Boundaries of the Political* (Cambridge, England: Cambridge University Press, 1987), p. 289.

19. William Wallace, *Regional Integration: The West European Experience* (Washington: Brookings Institution, 1994), p. 11. See also David Armstrong, Lorna Lloyd, and John Redmond, *From Versailles to Maastricht: International Organization in the Twentieth Century* (New York: St. Martin's, 1996), p. 148.

20. Peter Ludlow, "The European Commission," in Keohane and Hoffman, eds., *The New European Community*, p. 111.

21. I have drawn heavily from Winand, *Eisenhower, Kennedy, and the United States of Europe*, pp. 24-73.

22. Cited in Desmond Dinan, *Ever Closer Union? An Introduction to the European Community* (Boulder, CO: Lynne Rienner, 1994), p. 34.

23. David Armstrong, Lorna Lloyd, and John Redmond, *From Versailles to Maastricht: International Organization in the Twentieth Century* (New York: St. Martin's, 1996), p. 159.

24. Wolfgang Wessels, "Institutions of the EU System: Models of Explanation," in Dietrich Rometsch and Wolfgang Wessels, eds., *The European Union and Member States: Towards Institutional Fusion?* (New York: Manchester University Press, 1996), pp. 20-36.

25. Graham T. Allison and Kalypso Nicolaidis, eds., *The Greek Paradox: Promise vs. Performance* (Cambridge, MA: MIT Press, 1997).

26. Cited in Charles Grant, *Delors: Inside the House That Jacques Built* (London: Nicholas Brealey, 1994), p. 70.

27. David Allen, "Competition Policy: Policing the Single Market," in Helen Wallace and William Wallace, eds., *Policy-Making in the European Union*, 3rd ed. (Oxford, England: Oxford University Press, 1996), pp. 157-84.

28. Giandomenico Majone, "The Rise of the Regulatory State in Europe," *West European Politics* 17, No. 3 (July 1994): 77–101; see also Majone, *Regulating Europe*.

29. Damian Chalmers and Erika Szyszczak, *European Union Law: Towards a European Polity?* Volume II, Brookfield, VT: Ashgate, 1998, 146–47.

30. Wallace, *Regional Integration: The West European Experience*, p. 34.

31. Neill Nugent, ed., *At the Heart of the Union: Studies of the European Commission*, 2nd ed. (New York: St. Martin's Press, 2000); Alberta Sbragia, "The European Union as Coxswain: Governance by Steering," in Jon Pierre, ed., *Debating Governance: Authority, Steering, and Democracy* (Oxford: Oxford University Press, 2000), pp. 219–40.

32. Dinan, *Ever Closer Union*, pp. 247–49; Hayes-Renshaw and Wallace, *The Council of Ministers*, pp. 7, 29–32.

33. Alberta Sbragia, "The Community: A Balancing Act," *Publius* 23 (Summer 1993): 23–38; Wolfgang Wessels, "The EC Council: The Community's Decisionmaking Center," in Keohane and Hoffmann, eds., *The New European Community* (Boulder, CO: Westview, 1991), pp. 133–54.

34. Hayes-Renshaw and Wallace, *The Council of Ministers*, p. 18.

35. Hayes-Renshaw and Wallace, *The Council of Ministers*, p. 163.

36. Richard Corbett, Francis Jacobs, and Michael Shackleton, *The European Parliament*, 4th ed. (London: John Harper, 2000), pp. 49–54.

37. Rory Watson, "MEPs win 81% of tussles over new EU laws," *European Voice* 19–25 (October 2000): p. 5.

38. Richard Corbett, Francis Jacobs, and Michael Shackleton, *The European Parliament*, 4th ed. (London: John Harper, 2000), p. 226.

39. Rory Watson, "MEPs win 81% of tussles over new EU laws," *European Voice* 19–25 (October 2000), p. 5; Michael Shackleton, "The Politics of Codecision," *Journal of Common Market Studies* 38 (June 2000): 327.

40. Karen J. Alter, "The European Court's Political Power," *West European Politics* 19, No. 3 (July 1996): 458.

41. Beate Kohler-Koch, "Germany: Fragmented but Strong Lobbying," in M.P.C.M. van Schendelen, ed., *National Public and Private EC Lobbying* (Brookfield, England: Dartmouth, 1993), p. 32.

42. Denmark is an exception: the People's Movement against the European Community competes in European parliamentary elections—but not in domestic elections—on an anti-integration platform. Vernon Bogdanor, "The European Union, the Political Class, and the People," in Jack Hayward, ed., *Elitism, Populism, and European Politics* (Oxford, England: Clarendon, 1996), p. 110.

43. Simon Hix, "Parties at the European Level and the Legitimacy of EU Socio-Economic Policy," *Journal of Common Market Studies* 33, No. 4 (December 1995): 534.

44. John Gaffney, "Introduction: Political Parties and the European Union," in John Gaffney, ed., *Political Parties and the European Union* (London: Routledge, 1996), p. 13.

45. Mark Franklin and Cees van der Eijk, "The Problem: Representation and Democracy in the European Union," in Cees van der Eijk and Mark N. Franklin, eds., *Choosing Europe? The European Electorate and National Politics in the Face of Union* (Ann Arbor: University of Michigan Press, 1996), p. 8.

46. Simon Hix, "Parties at the European Level and the Legitimacy of EU Socio-Economic Policy," *Journal of Common Market Studies* 33, No. 4 (December 1995): 545; Robert Ladrech, "Partisanship and Party Formation in European Union Politics," *Comparative Politics* (January 1997): 176.

47. For an analysis of how the Community's policies indirectly affect various aspects of welfare state provision, see Stephen Leibried and Paul Pierson, eds., *European Social Policy: Between Fragmentation and Integration* (Washington: Brookings Institution, 1995).

48. Mark Franklin, "European Elections and the European Voter," in Jeremy J. Richardson, ed., *European Union: Power and Policymaking* (London: Routledge, 1996), p. 187.

49. Michael Marsh and Mark Franklin, "The Foundations: Unanswered Questions from the Study of European Elections, 1979–1994," in Cees van der Eijk and Mark N. Franklin, ed., *Choosing Europe? The European Electorate and National Politics in the Face of Union* (Ann Arbor: University of Michigan Press, 1996), p. 11.

50. Cees van der Eijk and Mark Franklin, "The Research: Studying the Elections of 1989 and 1994," in van der Eijk and Franklin, *Choosing Europe*, p. 42.

51. Mark Franklin and Cees van der Eijk, "The Problem: Representation and Democracy in the European Union," in van der Eijk and Franklin, *Choosing Europe*, p. 5.

52. For a good description of the differences between the British House of Commons and the European Parliament, see Bogdanor, "Britain," pp. 211–15.

53. Gareth Harding, "Winds of Change Blow Through Parliament," *European Voice* 8–14 (June 2000): p. 18; "Breaking New Ground in Euro-politics," *European Voice* 10–17 (November 1999): 22.

54. Sonia Mazey and Jeremy Richardson, "The Logic of Organization," in Jeremy J. Richardson, ed., *European Union: Power and Policy-Making* (London: Routledge, 1996), p. 204.

55. Sonia Mazey and Jeremy Richardson, "Promiscuous Policymaking: The European Policy Style?" in Carolyn Rhodes and Sonia Mazey, eds., *Building a European Polity? The State of the European Union*, Vol. 3 (Boulder, CO: Lynne Rienner, 1995), p. 342; Andrew M. McLaughlin and Justin Greenwood, "The Management of Interest Representation in the European Union," *Journal of Common Market Studies* 33, No. 1 (March 1995): 143–56.

56. Mazey and Richardson, "Promiscuous Policymaking," p. 350.

57. For a discussion of a powerful business group, see Maria Green Cowles, "Setting the Agenda for a New Europe: The ERT and EC 1992," *Journal of Common Market Studies* 33 (December 1995): 501–26.

58. See EC regulation no. 1049/2001 of the European Parliament and of the Council of 30 May 2001 regarding public access to European Parliament, Council, and Commission documents; Council decision of 29 November 2001

amending the Council's Rules of procedure (2001/840/EC); Council Decision of 22 March 2004 adopting the Council's Rules of procedure (2004/338/EC).

59. For a sophisticated discussion of how bargaining and negotiations proceed within the Council of Ministers, see Hayes-Renshaw and Wallace, *The Council of Ministers*, pp. 244–73.

60. Russell J. Dalton and Richard Eichenberg, "Citizen Support for Policy Integration," in Wayne Sandholtz and Alec Stone Sweet, eds., *European Integration and Supranational Governance* (Oxford: Oxford University Press, 1998), pp. 250–82.

61. Mark Franklin, Cees van der Eijk, and Michael Marsh, "Conclusions: The Electoral Connection and the Democratic Deficit," in van der Eijk and Franklin, *Choosing Europe*, p. 370.

62. European Commission, *Eurobarometer* 43 (Autumn 1995): xi.

63. European Commission, Eurobarometer: Public Opinion in the European Union 61 (Spring 2004): p. 8.

64. European Commission, Eurobarometer 2003.4: Public Opinion in the Candidate Countries (February 2004): 78, 130, 136.

65. European Commission, Eurobarometer 2003.4: Public Opinion in the Candidate Countries (February 2003): 78.

66. Oskar Niedermayer, "Trends and Contrasts," in Oskar Niedermayer and Richard Sinnott, eds., *Public Opinion and Internationalized Governance* (Oxford: Oxford University Press, 1995), pp. 59–62; Christopher Anderson, "Economic Uncertainty and European Solidarity Revisited: Trends in Public Support for European Integration," in Rhodes and Mazey, eds., *Building a European Polity*, pp. 111–33.

67. Brigid Laffan and Michael Shackleton, "The Budget: Who Gets What, When, and How," in *Policy-Making in the European Union*, 4th ed. (Oxford, England: Oxford University Press, 2000), pp. 213–14.

68. Elmar Rieger, "The Common Agricultural Policy: Politics Against Markets," in Helen Wallace and William Wallace, eds., *Policy-Making in the European Union*, 4th ed. (Oxford: Oxford University Press, 2000), pp. 202–203.

69. A. Heritier, "The Accommodation of Diversity in European Policy-Making and Its Outcomes: Regulatory Policy as a Patchwork," *Journal of European Public Policy* 3, 2 (1996): 149–67.

70. Dietrich Rometsch and Wolfgang Wessels, "The Commission and the Council of Ministers," in Geoffrey Edwards and David Spence, eds., *The European Commission* (Essex: Longman, 1994), p. 221.

71. He was widely considered a major presidential contender, and in November 1994 the Socialist Party Conference announced that it would support Delors if he decided to run for the French presidency. However, on December 11, 1994, Delors announced that he would not be a candidate after all. Colete Ysmal, "France," *European Journal of Political Research* 28, No. 3, 4 (December 1995): 337.

72. Lionel Barber, "The Men Who Run Europe," *Financial Times*, March 11–12, 1995, sect. 2, p. I.

73. Barber, "The Men Who Run Europe," p. II.

74. Hayes-Renshaw and Wallace, *The Council of Ministers*, p. 76.

75. Martin Westlake, *The Commission and the Parliament: Partners and Rivals in the European Policy-Making Process* (London: Butterworths, 1994), p. 10; Brigid Laffan, *The Finances of the European Union* (New York: St. Martin's, 1997).

76. See Joseph Weiler, "The Transformation of Europe," *Yale Law Journal* 100 (1991): 2403–83 and "A Quiet Revolution: The European Court of Justice and Its Interlocutors," *Comparative Political Studies* 26, No. 4 (January 1994): 510–34; Eric Stein, "Lawyers, Judges and the Making of a Transnational Constitution," *American Journal of International Law* 75/1 (1981); Anne-Marie Slaughter Burley and Walter Mattli, "Europe Before the Court: A Political Theory of Legal Integration," *International Organization* 47 (1993): 41–76; Martin Shapiro, "The European Court of Justice," in Sbragia, *Euro-Politics*, pp. 123–56; Alter, "The European Court's Political Power," pp. 458–87.

77. Shapiro, "The European Court of Justice," p. 123.

78. Burley and Mattli, "Europe Before the Court," pp. 72–73.

79. Karen Alter, "Who Are the 'Masters of the Treaty'? European Governments and the European Court of Justice," *International Organization* 52, No. 1 (Winter 1998): 121–48; Alec Stone Sweet and Thomas L. Brunell, "Constructing a Supranational Constitution: Dispute Resolution and Governance in the European Community," *American Political Science Review* 92, No. 1 (March 1998): 63–81.

80. Alec Stone Sweet and Thomas L. Brunell, "Constructing a Supranational Constitution: Dispute, Resolution and Governance in the European Community," *American Political Science Review* 92, No. 1 (March 1998): 63–82.

81. C. Federico Mancini, "The Making of a Constitution for Europe," in Keohand and Hoffmann, *The New European Community*, p. 178.

82. Alberta Sbragia, "Institution-Building from Above and from Below: The European Community in Global Environmental Politics," in Wayne Sandholtz and Alec Stone, eds., *European Integration and Supranational Governance*.

83. For instance, even the imported titles on best-seller book lists differ in the various member-states. In a similar vein, even though the inhabitants of Freiburg, Germany, and of Strasbourg, France, are close geographically, they do not buy each other's newspapers. Ralf Dahrendorf, "Mediocre Elites Elected by Mediocre Peoples," in Jack Hayward, ed., *Elitism, Populism, and European Politics* (Oxford, England: Clarendon, 1996), p. 7.

84. Wolfgang Wessels, "The EC Council," p. 136.

85. For example, see Miles Kahler, *Regional Futures and Transatlantic Economic Relations* (New York: Council on Foreign Relations Press, 1995).

86. Majone, *Regulating Europe*.

87. Alberta Sbragia, "The Transatlantic Relationship: A Case of Deepening and Broadening," in Carolyn Rhodes, ed., *The European Union in the World Community* (Boulder, CO: Lynne Rienner, 1998), pp. 147–64.

88. To get a sense of the policy areas in which the Union is most important, see Wallace and Wallace, *Policy-Making in the European Union*, 4th ed; Calingaert, *European Integration Revisited;* Dinan, *Ever Closer Union*, 2nd ed. Part III.

89. Elmar Rieger, "The Common Agricultural Policy: External and Internal Dimensions," in Wallace and Wallace, *Policy-Making in the European Union*, 3rd ed. pp. 102–106.

90. William Wallace, "Government Without Statehood: The Unstable Equilibrium," in Wallace and Wallace, *Policy-Making in the European Union*, 3rd ed., p. 453.

91. Dalton and Eichenberg, "Citizen Support for Policy Integration," p. 260.

92. Anna Michalski and Helen Wallace, *The European Community: The Challenge of Enlargement* (London: Royal Institute of International Affairs, 1992), p. 55.

93. Brigid Laffan, "The Intergovernmental Conference and the Challenge of Governance in the European Union," European Community Studies Association Conference, Brock University, Ontario Canada, May 31–June 2, 1996, p. 29.

Section 3
Russian Politics

POLITICS IN RUSSIA

Thomas F. Remington

REBUILDING THE RUSSIAN STATE

Russian President Vladimir Putin hosted the annual summit of the leaders of the world's major industrial democracies, the Group of Eight, in his native city of St. Petersburg from July 15 to 17, 2006. Inclusion of Russia in this group, bringing it from the Group of Seven to the Group of Eight, was controversial, but the United States and its allies hoped that by making Russia a full partner in this body they would strengthen Russia's integration into the international community. For his part, Putin used the occasion of the G-8 meeting to showcase Russia's importance as a great power. The summit represented a symbolic victory for Putin's consistent efforts to rebuild Russian power at home and abroad following nearly two decades of political upheaval. Over that period, Russia's political and economic institutions collapsed; the Soviet federal state fell apart into its constituent parts; bloody ethnic conflicts erupted in several regions on Russia's periphery; and people's high expectations for a smooth transition to democracy and capitalism were dashed. Putin took understandable

satisfaction from the fact that during his presidency, political order in Russia had been restored, economic output was growing steadily, and Russia's role as a major oil and gas exporter gave it significant international leverage. The other members of the G-8, recognizing that too much was at stake to allow a new Cold War between Russia and the West to develop, implicitly endorsed Russia's claim to membership in the club of major powers.

The sustainability of Russia's great-power status is tenuous, however. Indeed, in several respects Russia's transformation from a communist state into a stable capitalist democracy has gone into reverse. Putin's policies are far from reestablishing a communist state, but they harken back to an older Russian political pattern in which Russia's rulers seek to restore the power of a weakened state by diminishing the realm of free association outside the state. Moreover, Russia's dependence on oil and gas revenues to fuel its economy leaves it vulnerable to the "resource curse," characteristic of states that become dependent on their abundant natural resources for their exports. Such states typically exhibit high levels of corruption, low accountability, and low investment in human capital. Finally, Russia continues to experience a severe demographic crisis. Mortality rates, particularly among adult males, shot up in the early 1990s and have improved little since then. High mortality combined with low birthrates are resulting in a net loss of close to a million people per year, posing a grave threat to Russia's national security and economic viability. In view of these deeper structural dilemmas, the long-term viability of Russia's political and economic recovery will require far-reaching institutional reform.

CURRENT POLICY CHALLENGES

Vladimir Putin took office as president in dramatic fashion. His predecessor, Boris Yeltsin, had served as president of Russia since 1991. On December 31, 1999, Yeltsin appeared on national television to announce that, as of midnight, he was resigning as president. Although his term was not due to expire until June 2000, he had decided to resign early to allow his chosen successor, Vladimir Putin, to take over. Putin was Yeltsin's prime minister and enjoyed Yeltsin's confidence, as well as strong public support. As acting president, Putin had a substantial advantage in the presidential elections, which under the constitution had to be held within three months of the president's departure. Putin's first move was to issue a decree guaranteeing Yeltsin and his family lifetime immunity from criminal prosecution. Although the manner in which the succession occurred was not illegal, it appeared to reflect an unseemly bargain: Yeltsin gave the presidency to Putin in return for security for himself.

Putin went on to win election as president in his own right in March 2000 and to exercise the powers of the presidential office forcefully. Enjoying a strong base of popular confidence, Putin undertook a steady effort to rebuild state power. He attacked the power of the so-called **oligarchs**—the small group of extremely wealthy figures who held controlling shares of Russia's major natural resource, manufacturing, financial, and media companies and exercised disproportionate influence over government—through prosecutions of two particularly prominent ones. He systematically weakened the independence of the chief executives of the country's regions—the **governors**—by establishing new federal districts

overseen by presidentially appointed representatives, securing the power to dismiss governors for violations of the law, and removing them as ex-officio members of the upper chamber of parliament. He placed people whom he had worked with closely in the past into positions of responsibility in the government and the presidential administration.

Putin has continued to enjoy exceptionally high levels of public approval. This has given him considerable latitude in choosing policies to achieve his goals. Although Putin was not well known to the Russian public or to the international community at the point he assumed the presidency, with time, his general objectives have become clearer (see Box 12.1). In foreign policy, he seeks to restore Russia to its place as a major world power, a status it lost with the collapse of the Soviet Union. In the economy, he wants to achieve high, sustained growth by attracting substantial private investment, both domestic and foreign. At the same time he seeks direct state ownership and control of strategically important sectors, especially oil and gas. In politics, he seeks to preserve a framework of democratic institutions but to control the exercise of power through them. Elections are held, but their outcomes are predetermined; civil society is allowed to exist within certain highly restricted limits; individual rights are honored to the extent they do not conflict with the prerogatives of the state.

Many have termed Putin's model of political order "managed democracy," but more recently, Putin's associates have taken to using the slogan "sovereign democracy." Putin seeks to integrate Russia into the international economic system but at the same time to maintain a wide sphere of control for the state in the polity and economy. A strong state, for Putin, is one with an unbroken chain of executive authority stretching from the president down to the head of each region and district, with accountability running upward to the center rather than downward to the citizenry or society. He sees the president as the central figure directing the flow of power within the state. Putin accepts that Russia forms part of Europe and European civilization, but regards democratic principles as subordinate to, and potentially at odds with, the principle of state sovereignty. Possibly he believes that in a generation or two, Russia will be ready for a system featuring democratic accountability and separation of powers. For now, however, he appears to believe that the capacity and sovereignty of the state

BOX 12.1

Who Is Mister Putin?

Vladimir Putin's rise to power was so rapid that when he succeeded to the presidency, he was virtually unknown. A question often asked by Russians and foreigners alike was: "Who is Mr. Putin?"

Vladimir Vladimirovich Putin was born on October 7, 1952, in Leningrad (called St. Petersburg since 1991), and grew up in an ordinary apartment. From early on, he took an interest in martial arts and became expert at judo. Inspired by heroic tales of the secret world of espionage, at age 16 he visited the local headquarters of the KGB, hoping to become an agent. There he was told that he needed to go to university first. In 1970, he entered Leningrad State University and specialized in civil law. Upon graduation in 1975, Putin went to work for the KGB and was first assigned to work in counterintelligence, and then in its foreign intelligence division. Proficient in the German language, he was sent to East Germany in 1985. In 1990, after the Berlin Wall fell, Putin went back to Leningrad, working at the university but in the employ of the KGB. When a former law professor of his, Anatolii Sobchak, became mayor of Leningrad in 1991, he went to work for Sobchak. In the mayor's office he handled external relations, dealing extensively with foreign companies interested in investing in the city, and rose to become deputy mayor.

In 1996, Putin took a position in Yeltsin's presidential administration. He made a rapid career. In 1998, Yeltsin named Putin head of the FSB (the Federal Security Service—successor to the KGB), and in March 1999, secretary of the Security Council as well. In August 1999, President Yeltsin appointed him prime minister. Thanks to his decisive handling of the military operation in Chechnya, Putin's popularity ratings quickly rose. On December 31, 1999, Yeltsin resigned, making Putin acting president. Putin ran for the presidency and, on March 26, 2000, won with an outright majority of the votes.

Over time, Putin's political persona has become somewhat clearer. Uncomfortable with the give and take of public politics, he prefers the hierarchical style of organization used in the military and police. He is a pragmatist with no particular affection for either the Soviet or tsarist order. He recognizes that Russia must participate in the contemporary world economy rather than burden itself with new international conflicts. Skilled at projecting an affable, relaxed demeanor, he is also self-possessed and disciplined, and reveals little of himself in dealing with others. Like many previous Russian rulers, he has made the consolidation of his own political power his first priority.

require the centralization of executive authority, with the president as the linchpin of the entire political system.

Putin has only been partially successful in realizing his goals. Much of the credit for Russia's economic recovery goes to the high world market prices for oil and gas. Most of the ambitious fiscal and administrative reforms he has introduced have been blunted in implementation. Some of Putin's actions—such as the suppression of independent media and the state's takeover of the assets of the oil company **Yukos**— have discouraged business investment and fueled capital flight. Putin's heavy reliance on the country's "power structures" (the interior ministry with its police and security troops, the regular armed forces, the law enforcement system, and the secret services) to remove or intimidate his rivals has chilled open public discourse. This makes it harder for the center to monitor bureaucratic performance. Actual improvements in

the quality of governance under Putin have been modest. Putin has been much more successful in undercutting democratic checks and balances on central power than in making the new authoritarian system work effectively. However, history suggests that administrative over-centralization usually ends up not strengthening but weakening state capacity.

HISTORICAL LEGACIES

The Tsarist Regime

The Russian state traces its origins to the princely state that arose around Kiev (today the capital of independent Ukraine) in the ninth century. For nearly a thousand years, the Russian state was autocratic. That is, it was ruled by a hereditary monarch whose power was unlimited by any constitution. Only in the first decade of the twentieth century did the Russian tsar agree to grant a constitution calling for an elected legislature—and even then, the tsar soon dissolved the legislature and arbitrarily revised the constitution. In addition to autocracy, the historical legacy of Russian statehood includes *absolutism, patrimonialism,* and *Orthodox Christianity.* Absolutism meant that the tsar aspired to wield absolute power over the subjects of the realm. *Patrimonialism* refers to the idea that the ruler treated his realm as property that he owned rather than as a society with its own legitimate rights and interests.[1] This concept of power continues to influence state rulers today.

Finally, the tsarist state identified itself with the Russian Orthodox Church. In Russia, as in other countries where it is the dominant religious tradition, the Orthodox Church ties itself closely to the state, considering itself a national church. Traditionally, it has exhorted its adherents to show loyalty and obedience to the state in worldly matters, in return for which the state treated it as the state church. This legacy is still manifested in the postcommunist rulers' efforts to associate themselves with the heritage of Russia's church, and in many Russians' impulse to identify their state with a higher spiritual mission.

Absolutism, patrimonialism, and orthodoxy have been recurring elements of Russian political culture. But alternative motifs have been influential as well. At some points in Russian history, the country's rulers—have sought to modernize its economy and society. Russia imported Western practices in technology, law, state organization, and education in order to make the state competitive with other great powers. Modernizing rulers—such as Peter the Great (who ruled from 1682–1725) and Catherine the Great (1762–1796) had a powerful impact on Russian society, bringing it closer to West European models. The imperative of building Russia's military and economic potential was all the more pressing because of Russia's constant expansion through conquest and annexation of neighboring territories, and the ever-present need to defend its borders. The state's role in controlling and mobilizing society rose with the need to govern a vast territory. By the end of the seventeenth century, Russia was territorially the largest state in the world. But for most of its history, Russia's imperial reach exceeded its actual grasp.

Compared with other major powers of Europe, Russia's economic institutions remained backward well into the twentieth century. However, the trajectory of its development, especially in the nineteenth century, was toward that of a modern industrial society. By the time the tsarist order fell in 1917, Russia had a large industrial sector, although it was concentrated in a few cities. The country had a sizable middle class, although it was greatly outnumbered by the vast and impoverished peasantry and the radicalized industrial working class. As a result, the social basis for a peaceful democratic transition was too weak to prevent the Communists from seizing power in 1917.

The thousand-year tsarist era left a contradictory legacy. The tsars attempted to legitimate their absolute power by appealing to tradition, empire, and divine right. They treated law as an instrument of rule rather than a source of authority. The doctrines that rulers should be accountable to the ruled and that sovereignty resides in the will of the people were alien to Russian state tradition. Throughout Russian history, state and society have been more distant from each other than in Western societies. Rulers and populace regarded one another with mistrust and suspicion. This gap has been overcome at times of great national trials, such as the war against Napoleon and later World War II. Russia celebrated victory in those wars as a triumphant demonstration of the unity of state and people. But Russia's political traditions also include a yearning for equality, solidarity, and community, as well as for moral purity and sympathy for the downtrodden. And throughout the Russian heritage runs a deep strain of pride in the greatness of the country and the endurance of its people.

The Communist Revolution and the Soviet Order

The tsarist regime proved unable to meet the overwhelming demands of national mobilization in World War I. Tsar Nicholas II abdicated in February 1917 (March 1917, by the Western calendar). He was replaced by a short-lived provisional government, which in turn fell when the Russian Communists—Bolsheviks, as they called themselves—took power in October 1917 (November, by our calendar). Their aim was to create a socialist society in Russia and, eventually, to spread revolutionary socialism throughout the world. Socialism, the Russian Communist Party believed, meant a society without private ownership of the means of production, where the state owned and controlled all important economic assets, and where political power was exercised in the name of the working people. **Vladimir Ilyich Lenin** was the leader of the Russian Communist Party and the first head of the Soviet Russian government. (Figure 12.1 lists the Soviet and post-Soviet leaders since 1917.)

Under Lenin's system of rule, the Communist Party controlled all levels of government. At each level of the territorial hierarchy of the country, full-time Communist Party officials supervised government. At the top, final power to decide policy rested in the CPSU (Communist Party of the Soviet Union) Politburo. Under **Joseph Stalin,** who took power after Lenin's death in 1924, power was even further centralized. Stalin instituted a totalitarian regime intent on building up Russia's industrial and military might. The state survived the terrible test of World War II, ultimately pushing back the German army all the way to Berlin. But the combined cost of war and terror under Stalin was staggering. The institutions of rule that Stalin left behind when he died in 1953 eventually crippled the Soviet state. They included personalistic rule, insecurity for rulers and ruled alike, heavy reliance on the secret police, and a militarized economy. None of Stalin's successors could reform the system without undermining communist rule itself.

As vast as the Soviet state's powers were, they were frustrated by bureaucratic immobilism. As in any organization, overcentralization undermined the leaders' actual power to enact significant policy change—or even to recognize when serious policy change was needed. The center's ability to coordinate bureaucratic agencies in order to execute its initiatives was frequently undermined by tacit resistance to the center's orders by officials at lower levels, distortions in the flow of information up and down the hierarchy, and the force of inertia. Bureaucratic officials were generally more devoted to protecting and advancing their own personal and career interests than in serving the public interest. By the time **Mikhail Gorbachev** was elected General Secretary of the CPSU in 1985, the political system of the Soviet Union had grown top heavy, unresponsive, and corrupt. The regime had more than enough power to crush any political opposition. However, it was unable to modernize the economy or improve living standards for the population. By the early 1980s, the economy had stopped growing, and the country was unable to compete militarily or economically with the advanced countries of the West.

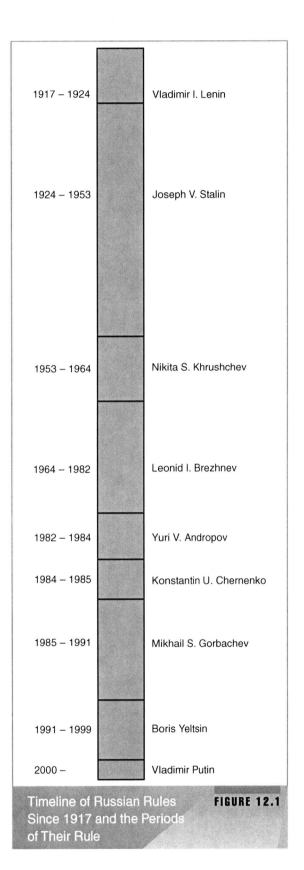

Timeline of Russian Rules Since 1917 and the Periods of Their Rule **FIGURE 12.1**

The youngest member of the Politburo at the time he was named party leader—he was age 54—Gorbachev quickly grasped the levers of power that the system granted the General Secretary. He moved both to strengthen his own political base, and to carry out a program of reform.[2] Emphasizing the need for greater openness—**glasnost**—in society, Gorbachev stressed that the ultimate test of the party's effectiveness lay in improving the economic well-being of the country and its people. By highlighting such themes as the need for market relations, pragmatism in economic policy, and less secretiveness in government, he identified himself as a champion of reform. Gorbachev not only called for political democratization, but he pushed through a reform bringing about the first contested elections for local soviets in many decades. He legalized private enterprise for individual and cooperative businesses and encouraged them to fill the many gaps in the economy left by the inefficiency of the state sector. He called for a "law-governed state" (*pravovoe gosudarstvo*) in which state power—including the power of the Communist Party—would be subordinate to law. He welcomed the explosion of informal social and political associations that were formed. He made major concessions to the United States in the sphere of arms control, which resulted in a treaty which, for the first time in history, called for the destruction of entire classes of nuclear missiles.

Gorbachev's early initiatives in the economic sphere failed to generate improvements in either competitiveness or living standards, and instead began fueling inflation. In 1988 he therefore turned to the political realm, hoping that democratization—a more open and competitive political arena—would unleash pressures for better bureaucratic performance. Using to the full the General Secretary's authoritarian powers, Gorbachev railroaded his proposals for democratization through the legislature. In 1989 and 1990, Gorbachev's plan for free elections and a working parliament was realized as elections were held and new deputies were elected at the center and in every region and locality. When nearly half a million coal miners went on strike in the summer of 1989, Gorbachev declared himself sympathetic to their demands.

Gorbachev's radicalism received its most dramatic confirmation through the astonishing developments of 1989 in Eastern Europe. All the regimes making up the Socialist bloc collapsed and gave way to multiparty parliamentary regimes in virtually bloodless popular revolutions. The Soviet Union stood by and supported the revolutions. The overnight dismantling of communism in Eastern Europe meant that the elaborate structure of party ties, police cooperation, economic trade, and military alliance that had developed with Eastern Europe after World War II vanished. Divided Germany was allowed to reunite.

In the Soviet Union itself, meantime, the Communist Party faced a critical loss of authority. The newly elected governments of the national republics making up the Soviet state one by one declared that they were sovereign. The three Baltic republics declared their intention to secede from the union. Between 1989 and 1990, throughout the Soviet Union and Eastern Europe, Communist Party rule crumbled.

Political Institutions of the Transition Period: Demise of the USSR

Gorbachev's reforms had consequences he did not intend. The 1990 elections of deputies to the Supreme Soviets in all fifteen republics and for local soviets stimulated popular nationalist and democratic movements in most republics. In the core republic—Russia itself—Gorbachev's rival Boris Yeltsin won election as chairman of the Russian Supreme Soviet in June 1990. As chief of state in the Russian Republic, Yeltsin was well positioned to challenge Gorbachev for preeminence.

Yeltsin's rise forced Gorbachev to alter his strategy. Beginning in March 1991, Gorbachev sought terms for a new federal or confederal union that would be acceptable to Yeltsin and the Russian leadership, as well as to the leaders of the other republics. In April 1991, he reached an agreement on the outlines of a new treaty of union with nine of the fifteen republics, including Russia. A weak central government would manage basic coordinating functions. But the republics would gain the power to control the economies of their territories.

Gorbachev had underestimated the strength of his opposition. On August 19, 1991, his own vice president, prime minister, defense minister, head of the security police, and other senior officials preempted the signing ceremony of the treaty by placing Gorbachev under house arrest and seizing state power. This was a fateful moment for Russia. In Moscow and St. Petersburg, thousands of citizens rallied to the cause of democracy and Russian sovereignty. The coup collapsed on the third day and Gorbachev returned to office again as president. But his power had become fatally weakened. Neither union nor Russian power structures heeded his commands. Through the fall of 1991, the Russian government took over the union government, ministry by ministry. In November 1991, President Yeltsin issued a decree formally outlawing the Communist Party of the Soviet Union. By December, Gorbachev was president without a country. On December 25, 1991, he resigned as president and turned the powers of his office over to Boris Yeltsin.[3]

Political Institutions of the Transition Period: Russia 1990–1993

The Russian Republic followed the example of the Soviet Union and adopted its own constitutional amendments creating the Congress of People's Deputies and Supreme Soviet, and soon after, a state presidency.

Boris Yeltsin was elected president of the Russian Federation in June 1991. Unlike Gorbachev, Yeltsin was elected in a direct, popular, competitive election, which gave him a considerable advantage in mobilizing public support against Gorbachev and the central Soviet Union government (see Box 12.2).

Like Gorbachev before him, Yeltsin demanded extraordinary powers from parliament to cope with the country's economic problems. Following the August 1991 coup attempt, he sought from the Russian Congress of People's Deputies, and was given, the power to carry out a program of radical market-oriented reform by decree. Yeltsin named himself acting prime minister and formed a government led by a group of young, Western-oriented leaders determined to carry out a decisive economic transformation. The new government's economic reforms took effect on January 2, 1992. Their first results were felt immediately as prices skyrocketed. Quickly many politicians

---

Boris Yeltsin: Russia's First President

BOX 12.2

Boris Yeltsin, born in 1931, graduated from the Urals Polytechnical Institute in 1955 with a diploma in civil engineering, and worked for a long time in construction. From 1976 to 1985, he served as first secretary of the *Sverdlovsk oblast* (provincial) Communist Party organization.

Early in 1986 Yeltsin became first secretary of the Moscow city party organization, but he was removed in November 1987 for speaking out against Mikhail Gorbachev. Positioning himself as a victim of the party establishment, Yeltsin made a remarkable political comeback. In the 1989 elections to the Congress of People's Deputies, he won a Moscow at-large seat with almost 90 percent of the vote. The following year he was elected to the Russian republic's parliament with over 80 percent of the vote. He was then elected its chairman in June 1990. In 1991, he was elected president of Russia, receiving 57 percent of the vote. Thus, he had won three major races in three successive years. He was reelected as president in 1996 in a dramatic, come-from-behind race against the leader of the Communist Party.

Yeltsin's last years in office were notable for his lengthy spells of illness, and for the carousel of prime ministerial appointments he made. The entourage of family members and advisers around him, dubbed colloquially "the Family," seemed to exercise undue influence over him. Yet, infirm as he was, he judged that Russia's interests and his own would be safe in Vladimir Putin's hands. Instead of turning against Putin when Putin gained in power and popularity, Yeltsin chose to resign and turn the presidency over to Putin. His resignation speech was full of contrition for his failure to bring a better life to Russians. After retiring, Yeltsin stayed out of the public eye. He died of heart failure on April 23, 2007, and was buried in Moscow with full honors.

Yeltsin's legacy is mixed. He was most effective when engaged in political battle, whether he was fighting for supremacy against Gorbachev or fighting against the communists. Impulsive and undisciplined, he was gifted with exceptionally keen political intuition. He regarded economic reform as an instrument in his political war with the communist opposition, and used privatization to make it impossible for any future rulers to return to state socialism. Imperious and willful, he also regarded the adoption of the 1993 constitution as a major achievement and willingly accepted the limits on his presidential power that it imposed.

began to distance themselves from the program: even Yeltsin's vice president denounced the program as "economic genocide." Through 1992, opposition to the reforms grew stronger and more intransigent. Increasingly, the political confrontation between Yeltsin and the reformers on the one side, and the opposition to radical economic reform on the other, became centered in the two branches of government. President Yeltsin demanded broad powers to carry out the reform program, but parliament refused to adopt a new constitution that would give him the powers he demanded. In March 1993, a motion to remove the president through impeachment nearly passed in the parliament.

On September 21, 1993, Yeltsin declared the parliament dissolved, and called for elections to a new parliament. Yeltsin's enemies barricaded themselves inside the parliament building. After a ten-day standoff, the dissidents joined with some loosely organized paramilitary units outside the building and attacked the Moscow mayor's offices adjacent to the Russian White House. They even called on their followers to "seize the Kremlin." Finally, the army agreed to back Yeltsin and suppress the uprising by force.

The circumstances of the December 1993 parliamentary elections were hardly auspicious. Yeltsin's decree meant that national elections were to be held for a legislature that did not, constitutionally, exist, since the constitution establishing these institutions was to be voted on in a referendum held in parallel with the parliamentary elections. Yet for all the violence surrounding its inception, the constitution approved in the December referendum has stayed in force since then.

THE CONTEMPORARY CONSTITUTIONAL ORDER

The Presidency

The 1993 constitution combined elements of presidentialism and parliamentarism. (See Figure 12.2 for a schematic overview of the Russian constitutional structure.) Although it provided for the separation of executive, legislative, and judicial branches and for a federal division of power between the central and

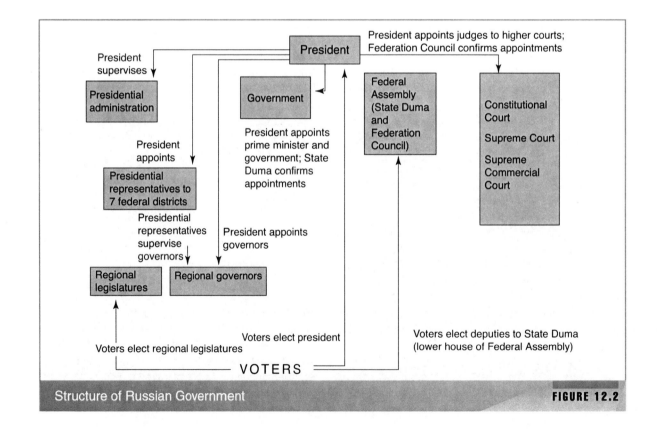

Structure of Russian Government   **FIGURE 12.2**

regional levels of government, it gave the president wide power. The president is directly elected for a four-year term and may not serve more than two consecutive terms. The president names the prime minister to head the government. Yet the government must have the confidence of parliament to remain in power. Although the constitution does not call the president the head of the executive branch, he is so in fact by virtue of his power to appoint the prime minister and the rest of the government and his right to issue **presidential decrees** with the force of law. (The decree power is somewhat limited in that decrees may not violate existing law and can be superseded by legislation.)

Over the decade since the constitution was approved, some informal practices have come to govern the exercise of central power. For example, the president and government divide executive responsibility. The government, headed by the prime minister, is primarily responsible for economic and social policy. The president directly oversees the ministries and other bodies directly concerned with coercion, law enforcement, and state security—the "power ministries." These include the Foreign Ministry, Defense Ministry, Ministry of Internal Affairs (which controls the regular police and security troops), Federal Security Service (FSB—formerly the KGB), and several other security and intelligence agencies. The president and his staff set overall policy in foreign and domestic domains, and the government develops the specific proposals and rules carrying out this policy. In practice, the government answers to the president, not parliament. The government's base of support is the president rather than a particular coalition of political forces in parliament.

Despite the asymmetrical constitutional balance, the parliament does have some power. Its ability to exercise this power, however, depends on the composition of political forces represented in parliament and the cohesiveness of the majority. Parliament's approval is required for any bill to become law. The State Duma (the lower house of parliament) must confirm the president's nominee for prime minister. If, upon three successive votes, the Duma refuses to confirm the nomination, the president must dissolve the Duma and call new elections. Likewise, the Duma may vote to deny confidence in the government. If a motion of no confidence carries twice, the president must either dissolve parliament or dismiss the government. During

Yeltsin's tenure as president, the Duma was able to block some of Yeltsin's legislative initiatives. Under Putin, however, it has largely been a rubber stamp. Conceivably, future presidents may have less of a free hand in their dealings with parliament than Putin has. The constitution allows for wide ranging of types of relationships among the president, government, and parliament, depending on the degree to which the president dominates the political system.

In addition to these powers, the president has a large array of other formal and informal powers in his constitutional capacity as "head of state," "guarantor of the constitution," and commander-in-chief of the armed forces. He oversees a large presidential administration, which supervises the federal government and keeps tabs on regional governments. Informally, the administration also manages relations with the parliament, the courts, big business, the media, political parties, and major interest groups.

The president also oversees many official and quasi-official supervisory and advisory commissions, which he forms and regulates by presidential decree. One of the most important is the **Security Council,** chaired by the president. The Security Council consists of a permanent secretary, the heads of the power ministries and other security-related agencies, the prime minister, and chairs of the two chambers of parliament. Its powers are broad but shadowy. Putin has used it to formulate policy proposals not only in matters of foreign and defense policy, but also on selected issues having to do with the organization of the executive branch.

Another prominent advisory body is the **State Council,** which comprises the heads of regional governments and thus parallels the Federation Council. In 2005 Putin created the **Public Chamber,** which is made up of 126 members from selected civic, sports, artistic, and other nongovernmental organizations (NGOs). Its purpose is to deliberate on matters of public policy, make recommendations to parliament and the government on pending policy issues, and link civil society with the state. Like the State Council, it is a quasi-parliamentary deliberative body that the president can consult at will. All three bodies duplicate some of the deliberative and representative functions of parliament, and therefore weaken parliament's role. They illustrate the tendency, under both Yeltsin and Putin, for the president to create and dissolve new structures answering directly to the president. These improvised structures can be politically useful for the president as counterweights to constitutionally mandated bodies (such as parliament), as well as providing policy advice and feedback. They help ensure that the president is always the dominant institution in the political system, but they undermine the authority of other formal institutions.

The Government

The *government* refers to the senior echelon of leadership in the executive branch. It is charged with formulating the main lines of national policy (especially in the economic and social realms) and overseeing its implementation. (The president oversees the formulation and execution of foreign and national security policy.) Here, the government corresponds to the Cabinet in Western parliamentary systems. But in contrast to most parliamentary systems, the makeup of the Russian government is not directly determined by the party composition of the parliament. Indeed, there is scarcely any relationship between the distribution of party forces in the Duma and the political balance of the government. Nearly all members of the government are career managers and administrators rather than party politicians. Overall, the government is not a party government, but reflects the president's calculations about how to balance certain considerations, such as personal loyalty, professional competence, and the relative strength of major bureaucratic factions. When President Putin chose Mikhail Fradkov to be prime minister on March 1, 2004—two weeks *ahead* of presidential elections—the political establishment was taken by surprise. Fradkov was a relatively obscure figure who had headed the Federal Tax Police for two years. His very lack of independent political clout underscored the fact that Putin would be the main source of policy direction for the country.

A major restructuring in 2004 reduced the number of ministries to sixteen. The goal was to simplify and rationalize the organization of the government by cutting down the number of ministries and state committees that were responsible for specific governmental functions and economic sectors and instead giving the ministries broader authority to oversee specialized agencies and services. However, although the aim was to streamline the structure of government, the total number of federal-level executive bodies rose from fifty-seven to seventy-two.[4]

The Parliament

The parliament—called the Federal Assembly—is bicameral. The lower house is called the **State Duma,** and the upper house, the **Federation Council.** Legislation originates in the Duma. As Figure 12.3 shows, upon passage in the State Duma, a bill goes to the Federation Council for consideration. The Federation Council can only pass it, reject it, or reject it and call for the formation of an agreement commission (consisting of members of both houses) to iron out differences. If the Duma rejects the upper house's changes, it can override the Federation Council by a two-thirds vote and send the bill directly to the president.

When the bill has cleared parliament, it goes to the president for signature. If the president refuses to sign the bill, it returns to the Duma. The Duma may pass it with his amendments by a simple absolute majority or it may override the president's veto, for which a two-thirds vote is required. The Federation Council must then also approve the bill, by a simple majority if the president's amendments are accepted or by a two-thirds vote if it chooses to override the president. On rare occasions, the Duma has overridden the president's veto; it has overridden the Federation Council rejections more frequently. In other cases, the Duma has passed bills rejected by the president after accepting the president's amendments. Under President Yeltsin, political forces opposed to Yeltsin, particularly communists and nationalists, held the majority in the Duma. But parliament and the president generally worked to head off major confrontations.

Until recently, the Duma's 450 members were equally divided between deputies elected in 225 single-member districts under a first-past-the-post (plurality) rule, and 225 deputies elected through proportional representation (PR) in a single national electoral district. A party receiving at least 5 percent of the vote on the party-list ballot is entitled to as many of the party-list seats in the Duma as its share of the party-list vote. As in other PR systems, votes cast for parties that fail to clear the 5 percent threshold are redistributed to winning parties. The electoral system has been reformed, however. Starting with the 2007 election, all 450 deputies will be elected proportionally from party lists in a single nationwide district, and the threshold for winning seats has been raised to 7 percent.[5]

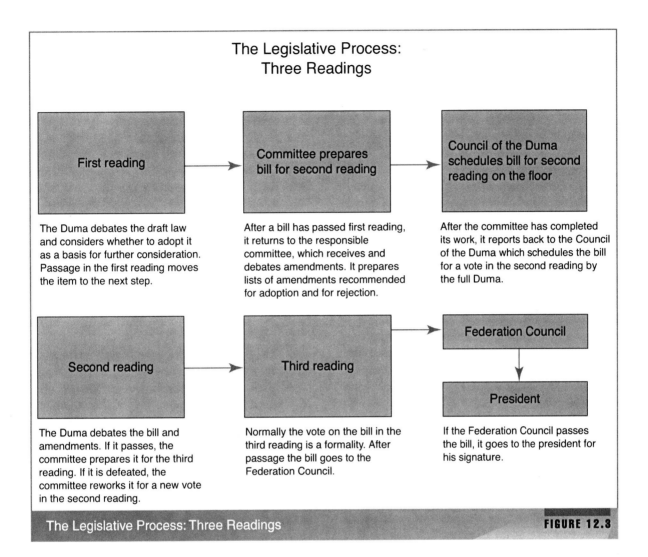

The Legislative Process: Three Readings

First reading

The Duma debates the draft law and considers whether to adopt it as a basis for further consideration. Passage in the first reading moves the item to the next step.

Committee prepares bill for second reading

After a bill has passed first reading, it returns to the responsible committee, which receives and debates amendments. It prepares lists of amendments recommended for adoption and for rejection.

Council of the Duma schedules bill for second reading on the floor

After the committee has completed its work, it reports back to the Council of the Duma which schedules the bill for a vote in the second reading by the full Duma.

Second reading

The Duma debates the bill and amendments. If it passes, the committee prepares it for the third reading. If it is defeated, the committee reworks it for a new vote in the second reading.

Third reading

Normally the vote on the bill in the third reading is a formality. After passage the bill goes to the Federation Council.

Federation Council

President

If the Federation Council passes the bill, it goes to the president for his signature.

The Legislative Process: Three Readings   **FIGURE 12.3**

Nearly all Duma deputies either join party factions or form their own groups. Factions and groups enjoy desirable privileges in the Duma, including the right to committee chairmanships, office space, and recognition in floor debate. Faction leaders are represented on the governing body of the Duma, the Council of the Duma.

The December 2003 elections gave the forces aligned with President Putin an overwhelming majority in the Duma, which they have used to centralize power. The pro-Putin party, **United Russia,** holds two-thirds of the seats in the Duma. About 80 percent of all single-member district deputies joined the United Russia faction—a good indication of its drawing power. United Russia took nearly all committee chairmanships, and eight out of the eleven seats of the Council of the Duma, which is the steering body for the chamber. Since United Russia votes with a high degree of discipline, the Duma consistently delivers the president legislative majorities. Other factions have very little opportunity to influence the agenda, let alone the outcomes of legislative deliberations. United Russia's control over the agenda and voting has turned the Duma into a rubber stamp for Putin.

Each deputy is a member of one of twenty-nine standing committees with specific policy jurisdictions. As bills are submitted to the Duma, they are assigned to particular committees, which collect and review proposed amendments before reporting out the bills for votes by the full chamber with the committee's recommendations.

The Federation Council is designed as an instrument of federalism in that (as in the U.S. Senate) every constituent unit of the federation is represented by two representatives. Thus the populations of small ethnic-national territories are greatly overrepresented compared with more populous regions. The Federation Council has important powers. Besides acting on bills passed by the lower house, it also approves presidential nominees for high courts, such as the Supreme Court and the Constitutional Court. It must approve presidential decrees declaring martial law or a state of emergency, or any acts altering the boundaries of territorial units. It must consider any legislation dealing with taxes, budget, financial policy, treaties, customs, and declarations of war.

Until a major reform pushed through by President Putin in the spring of 2000, the Council's members were the heads of the executive and legislative branches of each constituent territory of the federation. Now, however, each governor and each regional legislature names a representative to the Federation Council to serve on a full-time basis. The governors appoint their representatives, who are then confirmed by the legislatures. The regional legislatures elect their representatives. They can recall their representatives at any time.

There is a great deal of dissatisfaction over the current role of the Federation Council. Many believe that the composition of the chamber should be replaced with one providing that the members are popularly elected. This must be reconciled, however, with the constitutional requirement that the two members of the chamber from each of Russia's eighty-nine territorial subjects must represent the executive and legislative branches.

Executive-Legislative Relations

Relations between president and parliament during the Yeltsin period were often stormy. The first two Dumas, elected in 1993 and in 1995, were dominated by the communist and other leftist factions hostile to President Yeltsin and the policies of his government. This was particularly true in areas of economic policy and privatization. On other issues, such as matters concerning federal relations, the Duma and president often reached agreement—sometimes against the resistance of the Federation Council, whose members fought to protect regional prerogatives.

The 1999 election produced a Duma with a pro-government majority. President Putin and his government built a reliable base of support in the Duma for their legislative initiatives comprising a coalition of four centrist political factions. The 2003 election produced a still wider margin of support for the president in the Duma and an overwhelming majority for the United Russia party—which means that the president does not need to expend much effort in bargaining with the Duma to win its support for his policies. Generally speaking, the pro-presidential deputies in the Duma need the Kremlin much more than the Kremlin needs them. As a result, the balance of power in the political system under Putin has shifted steadily away from the parliament and toward the president. A major shift in the alignment of political forces in the society, however, could lead to a different relationship between executive and legislative power.

The Constitutional Court

The 1993 constitution provides for judicial review by the **Constitutional Court.** Its nineteen members are nominated by the president but are subject to confirmation by the Council of the Federation. The court is empowered to consider the constitutionality of actions of the president, the parliament, and lower level governments. The court has carefully avoided issuing any decisions restricting presidential powers in any significant way. However, it has decided a number of thorny constitutional issues, including the relations between the two chambers of parliament and the delineation of powers between central and regional governments. It has also consistently defended the rights of individual defendants in the criminal justice system. The court has also tended to uphold the sovereignty of federal law over the rights of the constituent territories of the federation.

Under Putin, the court has taken care to avoid crossing the president. Nevertheless, even the possibility that it might exert a measure of independent political influence has led Putin to propose moving the seat of the court to St. Petersburg. This is an ingenious way of distancing the court from the tight web of governing bodies located in Moscow and thus of marginalizing it politically.

Central Government and the Regions

Following the breakup of the Soviet Union, many Russians feared that Russia would also break up into a patchwork of independent fiefdoms. Certainly Russia's territorial integrity was subjected to serious strains. Under President Yeltsin, the central government granted wide autonomy to regional governments in return for political support. Yeltsin went so far as to sign a series of bilateral treaties with over forty regions to codify the respective rights and responsibilities of the federal government and the individual regional government. Under Putin, however, the pendulum of federal policy has swung back sharply toward centralization.

The demographic factor is one reason that Russia did not break up. Eighty percent of Russia's population is ethnically Russian. None of its ethnic minorities accounts for more than 4 percent of the total (the Tatars form the largest of the ethnic minorities, constituting about 5.5 million of the 142 million total population). Rebuilding national community in post–Soviet Russia has been helped by Russia's thousand-year history of statehood. Yet until 1991, Russia was never constituted as a nation-state: under the tsars it was a multinational empire, and under Soviet rule it was nominally a federal union of socialist republics. State policy toward nationality has also varied over the centuries. In some periods, Russia recognized a variety of distinct ethnic-national communities and tolerated cultural differences among them. In other periods, the state pressured non-Russian groups to assimilate to Russian culture.

Russia was formally established as a federal republic under the Soviet regime. In contrast to the Soviet Union, of which it was the largest component, only some of Russia's constituent members were ethnic-national territories.[6] The rest were pure administrative subdivisions, populated mainly by Russians. The non-Russian ethnic-national territories were classified by size and status into autonomous republics, autonomous provinces, and national districts. In many of them, the indigenous ethnic group comprised a minority of the population. As of 2007, Russia comprises 85 constituent territorial units, officially termed the "subjects of the federation." They represent 6 different types of units. Republics, autonomous districts (all but one of them located within other units), and the one autonomous *oblast* give formal political representation to ethnic minorities; *oblasts* (provinces), *krais* (territories), and two cities of federal status (Moscow and St. Petersburg) are treated as ordinary administrative subdivisions with no special constitutional status.

One of the centralizing measures President Putin has pursued is the absorption of smaller ethnic districts into larger neighboring units. Two such mergers have been approved and are being implemented. Several more such mergers are now being prepared. Most observers believe that the Putin administration seeks to eliminate most or all of the smaller ethnic units by merging them into their surrounding regions, thus reducing the patronage rights and political voice that come with their status as constituent members of the federation.[7]

The ethnic republics jealously guard their special status. From 1990 to 1992, all the republics adopted declarations of sovereignty, and two made attempts to declare full or partial independence from Russia. Only one, however, the Chechen Republic (**Chechnia**), resorted to arms to back up its claim. Chechnia is one of a belt of predominantly Muslim ethnic republics in the mountainous region of the North Caucasus, between the Black and Caspian Seas. Chechnia's president declared independence of Russia in 1991, an act Russia refused to recognize but did not initially overturn by force. When negotiations failed, however, in December 1994 Russian forces attacked the republic directly, subjecting its capital city, Groznyi, to devastating bombardment. This forced tens of thousands of Chechen and Russian residents to flee and led to a protracted, destructive war. Fighting ceased in summer 1996 but resumed in 1999. Federal forces had established control over most parts of Chechnia by early 2000, but Chechen guerrillas continue to carry out ambushes and suicide attacks against federal units.

Over time, the influence of radical fundamentalist Islam has increased among the Chechen rebels and they have resorted to terrorist attacks against civilian targets both in the North Caucasus region and in Moscow. One of the most shocking of these incidents was the seizure of a school in the town of Beslan, near Chechnia, in September 2004 (see Box 12.3). The brutal methods used by federal forces to suppress the uprising have fueled continuing hatred on the part of many Chechens against the federal government, which in turn facilitates recruitment by the terrorists. Observers hoped, however, that the death of the most notorious Chechen terrorist leader, Shamil Basaev, in July 2006, would weaken the guerrilla movement.

Chechnia, fortunately, is an exceptional case. In the other twenty ethnic republics, Moscow reached an accommodation granting the republics a certain amount of autonomy in return for acceptance of Russia's sovereign power. All twenty-one ethnic republics have the constitutional right to determine

Beslan

BOX 12.3

September 1 is the first day of school each year throughout Russia. Children, accompanied by their parents, often come to school bringing flowers to their teachers. A group organized by the Chechen warlord Shamil Basaev chose September 1, 2004, to carry out one of the most horrific incidents in the history of the Chechen wars. A group of heavily armed militants stormed a school in the town of Beslan, located in the republic of North Osetia, next door to Chechnia. Over 1,000 schoolchildren, parents, and teachers were taken hostage. The terrorists crowded the captives into the school gymnasium, which they filled with explosives to prevent any rescue attempt. The terrorists refused to allow water and food to be brought into the school to relieve the hostages' suffering. Negotiations over the release of the hostages failed.

On the third day of the seige, something triggered the detonation of one of the bombs inside the school. In the chaos that followed, many of the children and adults rushed to escape. The terrorists fired at them. Federal forces stormed the school, trying to rescue the escaping hostages and to kill the terrorists. Many of the bombs planted by the terrorists exploded. Ultimately, about 350 of the hostages died, along with all but one of the terrorists, and an unknown number of security troops.

The media covered the events extensively. The Beslan tragedy had an impact on Russian national consciousness comparable to that of September 11 in the United States. While there had been a number of previous attacks tied to Chechen terrorists, none had cost so many innocent lives. Although many Russians blamed corruption and poor organization among the police for allowing the terrorists to take over the school initially and for failing to prevent the destruction at the end, they also recognized that the terrorists had made it risky for the security forces to attempt a rescue for fear of provoking a massacre of the children.

Putin and other senior government officials claimed that the terrorists were part of an international terrorist movement aimed ultimately at the dismemberment of Russia itself. Putin studiously avoided linking the incident to Russian policy in Chechnia. In response to the crisis, Putin called for measures to reinforce national security. He also demanded increased centralization of executive power, including an end to the direct election of governors. Most observers assumed that Putin had wanted to make these changes anyway, and that the Beslan tragedy simply gave him a political opening to enact them. Beslan was a tragic indication that the insurgency that began in Chechnia may be spreading throughout the North Caucasus region.

their own form of state power so long as their decisions do not contradict federal law. All twenty-one have established presidencies. In many cases, the republic presidents have constructed personal power bases around appeals to ethnic solidarity and the cultural autonomy of the indigenous nationality. Often, they have used this power to establish personalistic dictatorships in their regions.

President Putin made clear his intention to reassert the federal government's authority over the regions. The reform of the Federation Council in 2000 was one step in this direction. Another was Putin's decree of May 13, 2000, that created seven new "federal districts." He appointed a special presidential representative to each district who monitors the actions of the regional governments within that district. This reform sought to strengthen central control over the activity

of federal bodies in the regions. Often, in the past, local branches of federal agencies had fallen under the influence of powerful governors.

Still another, very important, measure was the abolition of direct popular election of governors, including the presidents of the ethnic republics. Before 2005, regional chief executives were chosen by direct popular election. Since 2005, however, the president nominates a candidate to the regional legislature, which then approves the nomination (no legislature has dared to oppose one of Putin's appointments). Many citizens supported this change, believing that the institution of local elections had been discredited by corruption and fraud and that elections were more often determined by the influence of wealthy insiders than by public opinion. Critics of the reform accused Putin of creating a hypercentralized, authoritarian system of rule. Putin clearly hopes that appointed governors will be more accountable and effective, but past experience suggests that centralizing power by itself is unlikely to improve governance in the regions in the absence of other mechanisms for monitoring government performance and for enforcing the law.

Below the tier of regional government are units that are supposed to enjoy the right of self-government—municipalities and other local government units. Under new legislation, the right of local self-government has been expanded to a much larger set of units—such as urban and rural districts and small settlements—which has raised the total number of locally self-governing units to 24,000. In principle, local self-government is supposed to permit substantial policy-making autonomy in the spheres of housing, utilities, and social services (and to reduce the federal government's burden in providing such services). However, the new legislation—which is being phased in gradually—provides no fixed independent sources of revenue for these local entities. They thus depend for the great majority of their budgets on the regional governments. For their part, regional governments resist allowing local governments to exercise any significant powers of their own. In many cases, the mayors of the capital cities of regions are political rivals of the governors of the regions. Moscow and St. Petersburg are exceptional cases because they have the status of federal territorial subjects like republics and regions. Other cities lack the power and autonomy of Moscow and St. Petersburg, and they must bargain with their superior regional governments for shares of power.

Russia's postcommunist constitutional arrangements are still evolving. The political system allows considerable room for the arbitrary exercise of power and even, as under President Putin, the evisceration of democracy. Both Yeltsin and Putin have interpreted their presidential mandates broadly. Yeltsin used his decree power to carry out a massive privatization program. He also launched a brutal military campaign against the independence movement in the Chechen Republic without seeking parliamentary approval. In one eighteen-month period between 1998 and 1999, he named and dismissed his prime minister four times.

Putin has also used his presidential powers expansively. In 2000 he issued a decree creating seven federal superdistricts to facilitate central supervision of regional governments, and he appointed representatives to oversee them. By decree he also created a new consultative structure of regional governors called the State Council. This was an effort to mollify the governors, whom he had deprived of seats in the Federation Council. Both institutional changes were not envisioned by the constitution, but also were not specifically prohibited by it. The constitutional arrangements established under President Yeltsin had the potential to evolve toward democracy. A successful democratic transition, however, depends on more than a democratic constitution. The web of political institutions surrounding formal constitutional rules strongly shapes the way officeholders wield power and determines how effectively institutions hold leaders accountable for their actions. Informal rules can be far more important than formal rules. If rulers can circumvent formal limits on their power, constitutional structures may become irrelevant to the actual exercise of power.

Putin's style of rule resembles the pattern that political scientist Guillermo O'Donnell has called "delegative democracy."[8] In such a system, common in Latin America, a president may win an election and then proceed to govern as if he were the sole source of authority in the country. The president exercises so much power over other political structures, thanks to his control of the police and military and his access to patronage, that he can negate the nominal separation of powers written into the constitution. In such a system, parliamentarians may use their positions not to represent constituents or craft legislation but to trade favors and enrich their friends and family. Judges may deem it safer to tailor their decisions to the wishes of powerful state officials. The editors of major newspapers bury stories unfavorable to the authorities. Interest groups curry favor with officials rather than mobilizing their supporters around particular policy positions. The leaders of opposition parties learn to accept their role on the sidelines.

Under Putin this pattern of "hollowed-out democracy" has become evident. Without explicitly violating any constitutional limits on his power, and without abolishing elections or other democratic institutions, Putin has effectively negated the constitutional limits on his power built into the constitution. Using the president's extensive powers over the executive branch, he has neutralized and marginalized nearly all independent sources of political authority, while observing formal constitutional procedures. For

Boris Berezovsky was one of the most prominent oligarchs of the Yeltsin era. Today he lives in exile in Great Britain and faces criminal charges if he returns to Russia.

East News/Getty Images

example, he usually enacts his policy program by passing legislation through parliament rather than by relying on his decree power. But having used his control over electoral processes to secure overwhelming majority support in both chambers, parliamentary approval of his agenda is assured. As observers have pointed out, Putin appears to dislike the open give and take of democratic politics, preferring more familiar methods of behind-the-scenes bureaucratic maneuvering. Putin's use of presidential power presents a sharp contrast to the Yeltsin period. Yeltsin used his presidential powers erratically and impulsively. But Yeltsin respected certain limits on his power: he did not suppress media criticism, and he tolerated political opposition. Faced with an opposition-led parliament, Yeltsin was willing to compromise with his opponents to enact legislation. However, Yeltsin grew dependent on a small group of favored oligarchs for support and allowed them to accumulate massive fortunes and corrupt influence. Likewise, Yeltsin allowed regional bosses to flout federal authority with impunity because he found it less costly to accommodate them than to fight them.

The loss of state capacity under Yeltsin illustrates one danger of an overcentralized political system. When the president does not effectively command the powers of the office, power drifts to other centers of power. Putin's presidency illustrates the opposite danger. When Putin took over, he was faced with the task of reversing the breakdown of political control and responsibility that had accelerated under Yeltsin. Although he has repeatedly called for a system based on respect for the rule of law, he has also steadily restored authoritarian rule. He captured the contradictory quality of this vision in his 2004 message to parliament, when he said that creating "a free society of free people is the very most important of our tasks," but at the same time he warned that any attempts to effect a significant change in policy "could lead to irreversible consequences. And they must be absolutely excluded."[9]

RUSSIAN POLITICAL CULTURE IN THE POST-SOVIET PERIOD

Russian political culture is the product of centuries of autocratic rule, rapid but uneven improvement of educational and living standards in the twentieth century, and rising exposure to Western standards of political life. The result is a contradictory bundle of values in contemporary political culture: a sturdy core of belief in democratic values is accompanied by a firm belief in the importance of a strong state and sharp disillusionment with the way democratization and market reform worked out in Russia. In a 2005 survey, 66 percent of Russians agreed that "Russia needs democracy," but 45 percent said that the kind of democracy Russia needs is "a completely special kind corresponding to Russian specifics."[10] Fifty percent of the public regard Stalin as a positive figure in Russian history; only 36 percent assess him negatively.[11] Russians rate the Soviet regime before perestroika positively as a time of relative security and prosperity, but reject the notion of bringing back communism. Nearly half of the population (48 percent) agrees with the statement that it would have been better if perestroika had never been attempted, but 40 percent disagree.[12] Over 70 percent of Russians regret the breakup of the Soviet Union, but 72 percent say that restoring it is neither possible nor necessary.[13]

James Gibson sums up the findings of a number of studies by drawing three conclusions: one, there is rather extensive support in Russia for democratic institutions and processes so long as people see these as rights for themselves; two, there is much less support for extending rights to unpopular minorities; and three, the segments of the population who are the most exposed to the influences of modern civilization (younger people, more educated people, and residents of big cities) are also those most likely to support democratic values. These observations suggest that as Russia becomes more open to the outside world, support for democratic values will grow.[14]

Contemporary values and beliefs have been shaped by both long-term factors (such as the rise in educational levels over the decades of Soviet rule) and by short-term factors (such as the powerful impact of glasnost in raising popular aspirations for a standard of living close to that of the developed West). Public values were also shaped by the wrenching loss of familiar bearings as the old regime collapsed and with it, the very Soviet Union.

In his struggles with the communist opposition, Yeltsin encouraged people to imagine that his leadership would usher in a new era of prosperity and freedom. Instead, poverty, unemployment, and inequality rose sharply, and privation led to the enrichment of a small class of ultra-rich tycoons who flaunted their quickly amassed fortunes. Organized crime flourished. The modest but universal social safety net of the communist regime disintegrated. Little wonder that many Russians came to regard "democracy" as a bitter

joke and the market economy as a mechanism for exploitation—just as communist propaganda had taught. Democratization and economic liberalization became associated in Russians' minds with the breakdown of social and economic order since the late 1980s. Although Russians generally value the idea of democratic rights and freedoms, most people tend to consider them remote and unattainable in Russia.

Both nostalgia for the old order and aspirations for a better future set standards by which people judge the current regime harshly. Most Russians are highly critical of the performance of the current regime—apart from Putin. Russians think that the country's leaders are mainly concerned with their own power and wealth rather than with the country's well-being.

Surveys show that citizens have little faith in the current political system, although, as Table 12.1 shows, there is a good deal more confidence in Putin than in any other individual leader or institution.

Trust in Institutions, 2004   TABLE 12.1

	Percent Responding "fully merits confidence"
President of Russia	56
Church, religious organizations	43
Army	30
Press, radio, TV	26
Security organs	21
Regional (krai, oblast, republican) organs of power	19
Local (city, district) organs of power	19
Government of Russia	17
Courts	14
Procuracy	12
Federation Council	12
State Duma	11
Trade Unions	11
Police	10
Political Parties	5

Note: Question—"To what degree, in your view, does each of the following merit confidence?" Survey conducted September 2004. N = 2107. Margin of error 3%.

Source: Levada Center, Analiticheskii tsentr Yuriia Levady. http://www. levada.ru/press/2004092702.html (accessed 30 September 2004).

Moreover, as Figure 12.4 shows, the public distinguishes sharply between Putin and the government. Russians give Putin credit above all for reversing the deterioration of living standards: 24 percent of the population cite this as his main achievement. These figures show how successful Putin has been at taking credit for positive developments in the country and allowing the government to take the blame for continuing problems. Not surprisingly, Putin's popularity leads Russians to want to give him sweeping power over the political system. After the March 2004 presidential election, a nationwide survey found that 68 percent agreed with the statement that concentrating nearly all state power in Putin's hands "would be beneficial to Russia."[15] In 2005, 51 percent agreed with the proposition that the kind of president Russia needs is one "able to direct the work of the government, parliament, judiciary and regional organs of power with a firm hand"; 44 percent preferred one "who strictly observes the Constitution and is able to cooperate with other state bodies on the basis of the law."[16]

Russians' impatience with a separation of powers system (and their faith in Putin) does not mean that they do not also want democratic rights and freedoms for themselves. Indeed, paradoxically, many associate Putin with democracy. Over half of the population (55 percent) thought that following Putin's reelection as president in 2004 the country would develop as a democracy; the comparable figure in 2000 was only 35 percent. Russians prize their right to criticize the authorities: 76 percent of respondents think it is permissible to criticize Putin, and 86 percent think criticism of the government is permissible.[17] And a clear majority of Russians believe that Russia needs a political opposition (see Table 12.2).

The political culture thus combines contradictory elements. Russians do value democratic rights, but experience has taught them that under the banner of

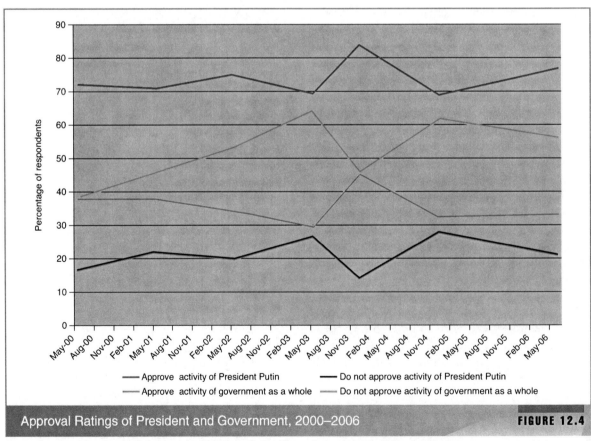

Approval Ratings of President and Government, 2000–2006

FIGURE 12.4

Source: Surveys of Russian population conducted by Levada Center (Moscow), reported on website: www.levada.ru.

Support for Principle of Democratic Opposition (in %)				TABLE 12.2
	Dec. 2002	Oct. 2004	Dec. 2005	June 2006
Definitely needed/ more needed than not	56	66	61	56
Definitely not needed/more not	24	21	25	20
Hard to say	20	13	14	24

Note: Question—"Is a political opposition to the authorities needed now in Russia?" Survey conducted 19–22 June 2006. N = 1600, 18 years old and older, in 128 towns and 46 regions.

Source: Levada Center, http://www.levada.ru/press/2006062901.html (accessed 13 July 2006).

democracy, politicians can abuse their power to the detriment of the integrity of the state and the well-being of society. They also feel powerless to affect state policy. Little wonder that a leader such as Putin can command such widespread support despite the general mistrust Russians have for the post-Soviet political institutions. Russians see him as restoring order following a protracted period of social and political breakdown. As Richard Rose and his colleagues argue, the reason Russians generally approve the current regime is not because they consider it to be ideal, but because it has improved economic well-being and they see little prospect for changing it.[18]

Surveys also reveal considerable continuity with the past in support for the idea that the state should ensure society's prosperity and the citizens' material security. More than in Western Europe or the United States, Russians believe that the state is responsible for providing a just moral and social order, with justice being understood as social equality more than as equality before the law. This pattern reflects the lasting influence of traditional conceptions of state and society on Russian political culture. Still, few would support the reestablishment of Soviet rule or a reversion to a military dictatorship. Most people think that the tremendous upheavals they have experienced since the late 1980s will result in an improved life—not soon, but "eventually."[19]

Political culture is also shaped by slower acting but more lasting influences, including the succession of generations, rising educational levels, and urbanization.[20]

The shift in values and beliefs has accelerated as new generations of young people are exposed to fundamentally different influences than those to which their parents were exposed. To a large extent, these differences are mutually reinforcing: the older generations tend to have lower levels of education and less exposure to the more cosmopolitan way of life of cities.

Political Socialization

The Soviet regime devoted enormous effort to political indoctrination and propaganda. The regime controlled the content of school curricula, mass media, popular culture, political education, and nearly every other channel by which values and attitudes were formed. The heart of Soviet doctrine was the Marxist belief that the way in which a society organizes its production—feudalism, capitalism, socialism, and so forth—determines the structure of values and beliefs prevalent in the society. The idea was that the ruling class in each society determines the basic ideology of the society. Therefore, Soviet propaganda and indoctrination emphasized that Soviet citizens were part of a worldwide working-class movement to overthrow capitalism and replace it with socialism, in which there would be no private property. Needing to knit together a highly diverse multinational state, the Soviet regime downplayed national feeling and replaced it with a sense of patriotic loyalty to the Soviet state and to the working class's interests in the worldwide class struggle.

Today the ideological content of Russian education has changed significantly, and there is much less overt political control over the formation of attitudes and values. In place of the idea of the class struggle and the international solidarity of the working class, textbooks stress love for the Russian national heritage. Historical figures who in the communist era were honored as heroes of the struggle of ordinary people against feudal or capitalist masters are now held up as great representatives of Russia's national culture.[21] Schoolbooks and mass media place heavy emphasis on loyalty to Russia as a state, tying it to Russian national and patriotic pride rather than to international working-class solidarity. This theme underlies Russia's effort to create a new sense of national community within the country's post-Soviet state boundaries.

State leaders also play on the strong undercurrent of desire for some sort of restored union among at least some of the former Soviet republics. Russian television broadcasts pay considerable attention to activities in the "near abroad," as Russians term the other former Soviet republics. Russians continue to feel tied to the other republics by decades of shared social, economic, cultural, and political experience. Putin and other politicians actively play on this sentiment, calling for the reinforcement of ties between Russia and its neighbors in the Commonwealth of Independent States (CIS). Sergei Shoigu, the relatively popular minister for Emergency Situation, noted during the parliament election campaign in November 2003 that he hoped "to live to see the day when we have one big country within the borders of the [former] Soviet Union." A former KGB chairman went so far as to say that "if we do not reassemble the Soviet Union, we have no future at all."[22] The neoimperial currents running through Russian political culture undercut the effort to create a new post-Soviet national community based on democratic values.

The authorities have also turned to the Orthodox Church as an aid in political socialization. They regard the Church as a valuable ally in building patriotic loyalty, national pride, and a framework of ethical behavior. The Church in turn seeks to protect its traditional status as Russia's state church, enabling it to block other Christian denominations from proselytizing in Russia. As of the fall of 2006, a required course on the fundamentals of Orthodox culture had been introduced into the school curriculum in nearly twenty regions, and about 20,000 Orthodox priests were serving as chaplains in the armed forces.[23]

Although the Putin regime has gone far to impose political controls over the mass media, it has not constructed the kind of comprehensive political socialization system that the Soviet state employed to indoctrinate citizens with the desired attitudes, values, and beliefs. Nevertheless, the authorities under Putin have promoted a particular political message intended to build support for their foreign and domestic policies. Print and broadcast media consistently emphasize the principles of sovereignty and a strong state along with those of democracy, market economics, and the rule of law. Putin's team works to create the impression that they are finding a moderate middle ground between the extremes of the past—totalitarian communism on the one hand, and unbridled oligarchic capitalism, on the other—and to restore continuity with the best traditions of Russia's political history.

Political socialization in Russia is much less subject to direct state control than it was in the Soviet era, and even then, awareness of the political and economic standards of the outside world filtered into the consciousness of the Soviet population. Today, the authorities seek to build loyalty to the state, confidence in the future, and acceptance of a highly centralized regime, while at the same time spurring Russians to modernize the economy. As time passes, Russians' support for Putin's model of "sovereign democracy" will depend on the regime's performance in meeting its own goals.

POLITICAL PARTICIPATION

In a democracy, citizens take part in public life both through direct forms of political participation (such as voting, engaging in party work, organizing for a cause, demonstrating, and lobbying) and indirect forms of participation (such as membership in civic groups and in voluntary associations). Both kinds of participation influence the quality of government. By means of collective action citizens signal to policymakers what they want government to do. Through these channels of participation activists rise to positions of leadership. But, despite the legal equality of citizens in democracies, levels of participation in the population vary with differences across groups in resources, opportunities, and motivations. The better-off and better-educated are disproportionately involved in political life everywhere, but in some societies the disproportion is much greater than in others. And where deep inequalities in the distribution of wealth and income reinforce differentials in political voice between rich and poor, democracy itself is at risk.[24]

The Importance of Social Capital

A healthy fabric of voluntary associations has been recognized since de Tocqueville's time as an important component of democracy. As Robert Putnam has shown, participation in civic life builds social capital—reciprocal bonds of trust and obligation among citizens that facilitate collective action. Where social capital is significant, people treat one another as equals rather than as members of social hierarchies. They are more willing to cooperate in ways that benefit the society and improve the quality of government by sharing the burden of making government accountable and effective.[25] For example, where people feel less distance from and mistrust toward government, governments are better able to float bonds to provide improvements to community infrastructure. People are more willing to pay their taxes, so that government has more revenue to spend on public goods—and less ability and less incentive to divert it into politicians' pockets. Both capitalism and democratic government rest on people's ability to cooperate for mutual benefit.

In Russia, however, social capital has historically been scarce compared with West European societies, and participation in civic activity has been extremely limited. Moreover, state and society have generally been separated by mutual mistrust and suspicion. State authorities have usually stood outside and above society, extracting what resources they needed from society but not cultivating ties of obligation to it. The communist regime further depleted the stock of social capital by coopting associations useful for the state and repressing those that threatened its interests. For this reason, social capital not only in Russia, but throughout the former communist bloc, is significantly lower than in other parts of the world.[26]

The weakness of intermediate associations linking political elites to ordinary citizens widens the mutual distance between state and society. Thus, although Russians turn out to vote in elections in relatively high numbers, participation in organized forms of political activity is low. Opinion polls show that most people believe that their involvement in political activity is futile, and they have little confidence that they can influence government policy through their participation.

Since the late 1980s, political participation, apart from voting, has seen a brief, intense surge followed by a protracted ebb. Membership in voluntary associations in contemporary Russia is extremely low. According to survey data, 91 percent of the population do not belong to any sports or recreational club, literary or other cultural group, political party, local housing association, or charitable organization. Four percent belong to sports or recreation groups, and 2 percent each say that they belong to a housing bloc, neighborhood association, or cultural group. Only half a percent report being a member of a political party. About 9 percent report attending church at least once a month, and about 20 percent say that they are members of trade unions. Attending religious services and trade union membership are very passive forms of participation in public life. Yet even when these and other types of participation are taken into account, almost 60 percent of the population still are outside any voluntary public associations.[27]

This is not to say that Russian citizens are *psychologically* disengaged from public life or that they are socially isolated. Half of the Russian adult population reports reading national newspapers "regularly" or "sometimes" and almost everyone watches national television "regularly" (81 percent). Sixty-nine percent read local newspapers regularly or sometimes. Sixty-six percent discuss the problems of the country with friends regularly or sometimes, and 48 percent say that people ask them their opinions about what is happening in the country. A similar percentage of people discuss the problems of their city with friends.[28] Russians do vote in high proportions in national elections—higher, in fact, than their American counterparts.[29]

Moreover, Russians prize their right *not* to participate in politics. Today's low levels of political participation are a reflection of the low level of confidence in political institutions and the widespread view that ordinary individuals have little influence over government. In one 2000 survey, 85 percent of the respondents expressed the opinion that they have no influence to affect the decisions of the authorities.[30] In the 2003 Duma elections, 4.7 percent of the voters expressed their dissatisfaction with the array of choices offered by checking the box marked "against all" on the party list ballot.[31]

The withdrawal from active political participation today results from the shattering of the expectations for change that rose to unrealistic levels in the late 1980s and early 1990s. Gorbachev's policy of relaxing controls on political expression and political participation stimulated a short-lived surge of involvement in many forms of public activity, including mass protests, such as strikes and demonstrations, as well as the creation of thousands of new informal organizations. But this wave subsided in the early 1990s. The disengagement and skepticism reflected in public life today reflects disillusionment with how conditions have turned out.

Elite Recruitment

Elite recruitment refers to the institutional processes in a society by which people gain access to positions of influence and responsibility. Elite recruitment is closely tied to political participation, because it is through participation in community activity that people take on leadership roles, learn civic skills (such as organization and persuasion), develop networks of friends and supporters, and become interested in pursuing political careers.

In the Soviet regime, the link between participation and elite recruitment was highly formalized. The Communist Party recruited the population into a variety of officially sponsored organizations—such as the Communist Party, youth leagues, trade unions, and women's associations. Through such organizations, the regime identified potential leaders and gave them experience in organizing group activity. The party reserved the right to approve appointments to any position that carried high administrative responsibility or that was likely to affect the formation of public attitudes. The system for recruiting, training, and appointing individuals for positions of leadership and responsibility in the regime was called the **nomenklatura** system. Those individuals who were approved for the positions on nomenklatura lists were informally called "the nomenklatura." Many citizens regarded them as the ruling class in Soviet society.

The democratizing reforms of the late 1980s and early 1990s made two important changes to the process of elite recruitment. First, the old nomenklatura system crumbled along with other Communist Party controls over society. Second, although most members of the old ruling elites adapted themselves to the new circumstances and stayed on in various official capacities, the wave of new informal organizations and popular elections brought many new people into elite positions. Today, the contemporary Russian political elite consists of a mixture of career types: some people have worked their way up through the state bureaucracy while others have entered politics through other channels, such as elective politics or business.

As in other areas of political life, old Soviet institutional mechanisms for recruitment are being restored under Putin. In the communist regime, the party maintained schools for training political leaders, where rising officials were given a combination of management education and political indoctrination. Today, most of those schools serve a similar function as academies for training civil servants and are overseen by Putin's presidential administration. Moreover, elements of the old nomenklatura system are being restored with a view to ensuring that competent and politically reliable cadres are available for recruitment not only to state bureaucratic positions but even for management positions in major firms.[32]

There are two major differences between elite recruitment in the communist regime and the present. The nomenklatura system of the Soviet regime ensured that in every walk of life, those who held positions of

President Vladimir Putin offers a reassuring word to Russian citizens.

AFP/Corbis

power and responsibility were approved by the party. They thus formed different sections of a single political elite and owed their positions to their political loyalty and usefulness. Today, however, there are multiple elites (political, business, scientific, cultural, etc.), reflecting the greater degree of pluralism in post-Soviet society.

Second, there are multiple channels for recruitment to today's *political* elite. Many of its members come from positions in the federal and regional executive agencies. Putin in particular has recruited officials for his administration heavily from among the police (the regular police and the security services) and from the military.[33] Other prominent political figures climbed the ladder by winning local or national elections, or after making successful business careers.

The formation of a business elite, in fact, is one of the most remarkable phenomena since the end of the Soviet regime. Many of today's successful businesspeople came out of the old Soviet nomenklatura, as old guard bureaucrats discovered ways to cash in on their political contacts and get rich quickly. Money from the Communist Party found its way into the establishment of many new business ventures, including several of the first commercial banks. As early as 1987 and 1988, officials of the Communist Youth League (**Komsomol**) saw the possibilities of using the organizations' assets to set up lucrative business ventures, such as video salons, banks, discos, tour agencies, and publishing houses.[34] They took advantage of their insider contacts, obtaining business licenses, office space, and exclusive contracts with little difficulty. Some bought (at bargain basement prices) controlling interests in state firms that were undergoing privatization, and a few years later found themselves millionaires or billionaires.

Other members of the new business elite rose through channels outside the state. Many, in fact, entered business in the late 1980s, as new opportunities for legal and quasi-legal commercial activity opened up. A strikingly high proportion of the first generation of the new business elite comprised young scientists and mathematicians working in research institutes and universities. The new commercial sector sprang up very quickly. By the end of 1992, there were nearly 1 million private businesses registered, with some 16 million people working in them.[35]

The new business elite are closely tied to the state, sometimes in order to capture benefits, and sometimes because state officials keep business on a short leash.

Financial-industrial conglomerates often cultivate strategic alliances with well-placed officials in the government. Both under Yeltsin and Putin, bureaucratic factions form around particular enterprises and industries. Businesses need licenses, permits, contracts, exemptions, and other benefits from government. Political officials, in turn, need financial contributions to their campaigns, political support, favorable media coverage, and other benefits that business can provide. In the 1990s, the close and collusive relations between many businesses and government officials nurtured widespread corruption and the meteoric rise of a small group of business tycoons, popularly known as oligarchs. The oligarchs took advantage of their links to President Yeltsin's administration to acquire control of some of Russia's most valuable companies. The prominence of the newly rich fed a strong public backlash that made it politically viable for President Putin to suppress some of them and destroy their business empires by police methods. The notion that businesspeople can make money honestly and benefit society by doing so strikes many people as a hopelessly naive proposition. Many therefore welcome a heavy-handed state to protect them from the power of the wealthy. But often when the state cracks down on a particular business firm, it is a maneuver by one bureaucratic faction to acquire control of a lucrative business asset from another, not a step toward the rule of law.

INTEREST ARTICULATION: BETWEEN STATISM AND PLURALISM

The political and economic changes of the last decade in Russia have had a powerful impact on the way social interests are organized. A far more diverse spectrum of interest associations has developed than existed under the communist regime. There are tens of thousands of nongovernmental organizations (NGOs)—a phenomenon that could not exist in the communist society, when the Communist Party oversaw all organizations. The pattern of interest articulation, however, still reflects the powerful impact of state control over society, as well as the sharp disparities in wealth and power that formed during the transition period. A few organizations have considerable influence in policymaking, while other groups have little. Patron-client networks between state officials and their patrons and their clients remain a persistent feature of political life.

The old regime did not tolerate the open pursuit of any interests except those authorized by the state. Interest organizations—such as trade unions, youth groups, professional societies, and the like—were closely supervised by the Communist Party. This statist model of interest articulation was upset by glasnost. Glasnost stimulated an explosion of political expression, which in turn prompted groups to form and to make political demands and participate in elections. It is hard today to imagine how profound was the impact of glasnost on Soviet society. Suddenly it opened the floodgates to a growing stream of startling facts, ideas, disclosures, reappraisals, scandals, and sensations. Gorbachev was clearly surprised by the range and intensity of the new demands that erupted. In loosening the party's controls over communication sufficiently to encourage people to speak and write freely and openly, Gorbachev also relinquished the controls that would have enabled him to limit political expression when it went too far.

As people voiced their deep-felt demands and grievances, others recognized that they shared the same beliefs and values, and made common cause with them, sometimes forming new, unofficial organizations. Therefore, one result of glasnost was a wave of participation in "informal"—that is, unlicensed and uncontrolled—public associations. Daring publications in the media allowed people with common interests to identify one another and encouraged them to come together to form independent associations. When the authorities tried to limit or prohibit such groups, they generated still more frustration and protest. Associations of all sorts formed: groups dedicated to remembering the victims of Stalin's terror; ultra-nationalists who wanted to restore tsarism; nationalist movements in many republics. The devastating explosion of the nuclear reactor at Chernobyl in 1986 had a tremendous impact in stimulating the formation of environmental protest, linked closely to nationalist sentiment in Belarus and Ukraine.[36]

The elimination of the state's monopoly on productive property resulted in the formation of new interests, among them those with a stake in the market economy. No longer does the state demand that organized groups serve a state-defined political agenda, as was the case under the old regime. Now groups can form freely to represent a diversity of interests, compete for access to influence and resources, and define their own agenda. The Justice Ministry estimates that there are

nearly half a million NGOs, although probably no more than a quarter of them are active at any given time.[37]

In some cases, NGOs are the successors of recognized associations of the old regime, such as official trade unions. Often these groups cling to their inherited organizational assets and continue to seek "insider" access to the state. Other groups sprang up during the glasnost period or later, but must work closely with legislative and executive authorities in order to gain access to meeting places and media attention.

There are elements of corporatism in the state's relations with interest groups under Putin because of the regime's preference for dealing directly with controllable umbrella organizations representing particular segments of society. Overall, however, the pattern of interest group activity is more pluralist than corporatist because in most cases, interest associations are too numerous, too weak internally, and too competitive for corporatism to succeed. But under Putin, interest articulation is becoming more statist as the regime has gradually increased political controls on nongovernment associations.

Although the pattern of comprehensive Communist Party control over nongovernmental associations that was characteristic of the Soviet regime is gone, the state still exercises substantial influence over NGOs. Under Putin, the rules governing their operation have tightened. A law enacted at the beginning of 2006 imposed new restrictions on NGOs, making it easier for the authorities to deny them registration and to shut them down. At the same time, the authorities warned that foreign intelligence services were sponsoring Russian NGOs for the purposes of intelligence-gathering and subversion. The political atmosphere for NGOs became considerably chillier.

Let us consider three examples of associational groups: the **Russian Union of Industrialists and Entrepreneurs (RUIE),** the **League of Committees of Soldiers' Mothers,** and the **Federation of Independent Trade Unions of Russia (FITUR).** They illustrate different strategies for organization and influence and different relationships to the state.

The Russian Union of Industrialists and Entrepreneurs

Most formerly state-owned industrial firms are now wholly or partly privately owned. More and more industrial managers respond to the incentives of a market economy rather than to those of a state social-ist economy. Under the old regime, managers were told to fulfill the plan regardless of cost or quality. Profit was not a relevant consideration.[38] Now, more managers seek to maximize profits and increase the value of their firms. Although many still demand subsidies and protection from the state, more and more would prefer an environment where laws and contracts are enforced by the state, regulation is reasonable and honest, taxes are fair (and low), and barriers to foreign trade are minimized. These gradual changes are visible in the changing political interests of the association that represents the interests of big business in Russia, the Russian Union of Industrialists and Entrepreneurs, or RUIE. The RUIE is the single most powerful organized interest group in Russia. Its members comprise both the old state indus-trial firms (now mostly private or quasi-private) and the newer financial-industrial conglomerates headed by the oligarchs.

In the early 1990s, the RUIE's lobbying efforts were aimed at winning continued state support of industrial firms and planning for a slow transition to a market economy. The RUIE also helped broker agree-ments between business and labor, and it was a source of policy advice for government and parliament. In 2000, the Putin administration let it be known that it wanted the oligarchs to join the RUIE and the RUIE to become the unified voice of big business. The Putin leadership also sponsored two other business associa-tions to articulate the interests of small and medium-size business.

Over time, the RUIE's role has changed according to the opportunities and limits set by the state author-ities. Under Putin, it has been a loyal, subordinate, and useful source of policy advice and political support for the government. It has expanded its in-house capacity for working with the government and the parliament in drafting legislation. On a wide range of issues—from land reform; tax law; pension policy; bankruptcy legislation; reform of the natural gas, energy, and rail-road monopolies; regulation of the securities market; and the terms of Russia's entry to the World Trade Organization—the RUIE has been active and influen-tial in shaping policy.

Yet the limits of RUIE's power as the collective voice of big business are clear. When the Putin regime began its campaign to destroy the Yukos oil firm start-ing in July 2003 (see Box 12.4), RUIE confined itself to

mild expressions of concern. Its members, evidently fearful of crossing Putin, chose not to defend Yukos' head, Mikhail Khodorkovsky, or to protest the use of police methods to destroy one of Russia's largest oil companies. Instead, they promised to meet their tax obligations and to do more to help the country fight poverty. Putin pointedly avoided meeting with RUIE and other business association leaders from November 2003 to July 2004—and then agreed to meet with them only on the condition that the subject of Yukos not be discussed. Perhaps if big business had taken a strong and united stand, they could have influenced state pol-icy. But the desire by each individual firm to maintain friendly relations with the government and fear of government reprisals undercut big business's capacity for collective action.

The League of Committees of Soldiers' Mothers

The Soviet regime sponsored several official women's organizations, but these mainly served propaganda purposes. During the glasnost period, a number of unofficial women's organizations sprang up. One such group was the Committee of Soldiers' Mothers. It formed in the spring of 1989 when some 300 women in Moscow rallied to protest the end of student defer-ments from military conscription. Their protest came hard on the heels of Gorbachev's withdrawal of Soviet forces from the decade-long war in Afghanistan, where over 13,000 Soviet troops were killed in bitter and demoralizing fighting. In response to the Soldiers' Mothers' actions, Gorbachev agreed to restore student deferments. Since then Soldiers' Mothers' movement has grown, with local branches forming in hundreds of cities, joining together in the League of Committees of Soldiers' Mothers. Their focus has expanded some-what but remains centered on the problems of military service. The league presses the military to eliminate the use of soldiers' labor in its construction battalions and to end the brutal hazing of recruits, which results in the deaths (in many cases by suicide) of hundreds of soldiers each year. The league also advises young men on how to avoid being conscripted.[39]

The onset of large-scale hostilities in Chechnia in 1994–1996 and 1999–2000 stimulated a new burst of activity by the league. It helped families locate soldiers who were missing in action or captured by the Chechen rebel forces. It sent missions to Chechnia to negotiate for the release of prisoners and to provide

Mikhail Khodorkovsky and the Yukos Affair

BOX 12.4

One of the most widely publicized episodes of the Putin era was the state takeover of the powerful private oil company, Yukos, and the criminal prosecution of its Chief Executive Officer, Mikhail Khodorkovsky. At the time of his arrest in October 2003, Khodorkovsky had been the wealthiest of Russia's new postcommunist magnates. His career began in the late 1980s when he was a young Komsomol activist working in the Moscow city government, and used his Komsomol resources and connections to start a bank and later to acquire— at a bargain basement price—80 percent of the shares of the Yukos oil company when the government privatized it. At first, like some of the other newly wealthy business tycoons, Khodorkovsky sought to squeeze maximum profit from the firm by stripping its assets. Soon, however, his business strategy changed, and he began to invest in the productive capacity of the firm. He made Yukos the most dynamic of Russia's oil companies. Khodorkovsky discovered that by emulating Western business practices, the company could increase its net worth and productive capacity. He reformed corporate governance practices and sought to have Yukos's shares listed on foreign stock exchanges. By improving the efficiency and transparency of the firm, Khodorkovsky found that share prices rose, and with them Khodorkovsky's own net worth. At its peak in 2002, the company's assets were estimated to be worth about $20 billion, of which Khodorkovsky owned nearly $8 billion. He was Russia's wealthiest citizen.

Meantime, seeking to improve his public image, Khodorkovsky created a foundation and launched several charitable initiatives. He recruited some distinguished international figures to his foundation's board. He became active in Russian politics, helping to fund the parties Yabloko and the Union of Rightist Forces, and sponsoring the election campaigns of several deputies to the State Duma. Critics accused him of wanting to control parliament and even of wanting to change the constitution to turn it into a parliamentary system. There was talk that he intended to seek the presidency.

Khodorkovsky himself refused to kowtow to the authorities. Without consulting with the Kremlin he began talks with foreign oil companies on selling a significant share of Yukos stock and signed an agreement with China under which Yukos would build a major oil pipeline from Siberia to China that would supply a quarter of China's oil imports.

By spring 2003, the Putin administration decided that Khodorkovsky and Yukos had grown too independent. In a series of actions beginning in July 2003, several top figures in Yukos and companies associated with it were arrested and charged with fraud, embezzlement, tax evasion and even murder. The police raided the offices of the company and of a number of its affiliates, and even one of the orphanages its foundation sponsored.

At the end of December 2003, the government began issuing claims against the company for billions of dollars in back taxes and froze the company's bank accounts as collateral against the claims. When Yukos failed to pay the full tax bill, the government seized Yukos' main production subsidiary, and auctioned it off to a cut-out firm, which three days later sold it to Russia's only state-owned oil company, Rosneft. Rosneft's board chairman, Igor Sechin, is deputy head of Putin's presidential administration and a long-time associate of Putin from St. Petersburg.

In October 2003, Khodorkovsky was arrested and charged with fraud and tax evasion. The courts refused to release him on bail. In May 2004, he was sentenced to nine years imprisonment and sent to a prison camp in Siberia. In 2006, the last remnants of the company were forced into bankruptcy.

Many reasons have been suggested for the government's campaign against Yukos and Khodorkovsky. Some have argued that Khodorkovsky, through his open involvement in party politics, violated Putin's rule that big business stay out of politics. Another explanation is that Yukos was a pawn in a struggle among intra-bureaucratic factions over the distribution of control over profitable business assets. Certainly Yukos's independence was at odds with Putin's policy of placing all major oil and gas companies under direct state control in order to use energy policy to advance the state's global interests.

Whatever the regime's motives, the Yukos affair shows that the authorities are willing to manipulate the legal system for political purposes when it suits them, that many of the most important political contests in Russia are fought out within the state bureaucracy rather than in the open arena of public politics, and that the fight to redistribute control of Russia's most lucrative natural resource assets continues to be a driving force in politics.

proper burial for the dead. It collected information about the actual scale of the war and of its casualties. It also continued to advise families on ways to avoid conscription and to lobby for decent treatment of recruits. Through the 1990s, it became one of the most sizable and respected civic groups in Russia. It can call on a network of thousands of active volunteers for its work. They visit wounded soldiers in hospitals and help military authorities identify casualties. One of the movement's greatest assets is its moral authority as mothers defending the interests of their children. This stance makes it hard for their opponents to paint them as unpatriotic or power-hungry.

The league plays both a public political role (for instance, it lobbied to liberalize the law on alternative civil service for conscientious objectors) and a role as service-provider. Much of its effort is spent on helping soldiers and their families deal with their problems. Recently the league formed a political party in order to build a broader base of public support for its policy goals in the area of military reform, conscription, health care, and human rights. Although it has continued its efforts to reform conditions within the military, its leaders clearly believe that reform requires open political pressure on policymakers. How successful it will prove in attracting votes remains to be seen.

Like many NGOs, the League of Committees of Soldiers' Mothers cultivates ties with counterpart organizations abroad, and it has won widespread international recognition for its work. For some groups, such ties are a source of dependence, as organizations compensate for the lack of mass membership with aid and know-how from counterpart organizations abroad. However, the league enjoys a stable base of public support in Russia. Its international ties have also probably helped protect the group in the face of the sometimes-hostile attitude of the authorities.[40]

The Federation of Independent Trade Unions of Russia

The Federation of Independent Trade Unions of Russia (FITUR) is the successor of the official trade union federation under the Soviet regime. Unlike RUIE, however, it has poorly adapted itself to the postcommunist environment even though it inherited substantial organizational resources from the old Soviet

trade union organization. In the Soviet era, virtually every employed person belonged to a trade union. All branch and regional trade union organizations were part of a single labor federation, called the All-Union Central Council of Trade Unions. With the breakdown of the old regime, some of the member unions became independent, while other unions sprang up as independent bodies representing the interests of particular groups of workers. Nonetheless, the nucleus of the old official trade union organization survived, and it is called the Federation of Independent Trade Unions of Russia. It remains by far the largest trade union federation in Russia. Around 95 percent of all organized workers belong to unions, which at least formally are members of FITUR. The independent unions are much smaller. By comparison with big business, however, the labor movement is fragmented, weak, and unable to mobilize workers effectively for collective action.

FITUR inherited valuable real estate assets from its Soviet-era predecessor organization, including thousands of office buildings, hotels, rest homes, hospitals, and children's camps. It also inherited the right to collect workers' contributions for the state social insurance fund. Control of this fund enabled the official trade unions to acquire enormous income-generating property over the years. These assets and income streams give leaders of the official unions considerable advantages in competing for members. But the FITUR no longer has centralized control over its regional and branch members. In the 1993 and 1995 parliamentary elections, for instance, member unions formed their own political alliances with parties. Thus internal disunity is another major reason for the relative weakness of FITUR as an organization. Much of its effort is expended on fighting other independent unions to win a monopoly on representing workers in collective bargaining with employers rather than in joining with other unions to defend the interests of workers generally.[41]

The ineffectiveness of the FITUR is also illustrated by the tepid response of organized labor to the severe deterioration in labor and social conditions in the 1990s, when there was much less labor protest than might have been expected. There were some strikes and protests, mainly over wage arrears. Surveys found that in any given year in the 1990s three-quarters of all workers received their wages late at least once.[42] Teachers were particularly hard hit by the problem of unpaid wages and organized numerous local strikes.

Waves of strikes by teachers shut down thousands of schools in the late 1990s. After 1999, protests subsided as the economy began to recover.[43]

Why was there not more labor protest? One reason is that workers depend on the enterprises where they work for a variety of social benefits that are administered through the enterprise, such as pension contributions, cheap housing, and access to medical clinics and day care facilities.[44] Another, however, is the close, clientelistic relationship between the leadership of the FITUR and government authorities. Like business, organized labor for the most part prefers to cultivate a clientelistic relationship with the political authorities rather than to stand independently of them. As a result, it is very difficult for labor to mount collective actions.

New Sectors of Interest In a time when people's interests are changing rapidly, interest groups search for new roles. Some old groups decline, while new organizations form. In Russia, many new associations have formed around the interests of new categories of actors. Bankers, political consultants, realtors, mayors of small cities, mayors of large cities, judges, attorneys, auditors, television broadcasters, political consultants, and numerous other professional and occupational groups have all formed associations to seek favorable policies or regulate professional standards. Environmental groups, women's organizations, human rights activists, and many other cause-oriented groups have organized. Most of these operate in a particular locality, but a few have national scope.

The rules of the game for interest articulation changed sharply after the communist regime fell, and are continuing to change more slowly as the new postcommunist regime defines a new framework for relations between state and society. In the Yeltsin period, lobbying frequently took corrupt forms, including bribery of parliamentary deputies and government officials. By the end of the 1990s, more collective action by business and other sectors of interest was evident, and there was more open bargaining over the details of policy. Under Putin, however, policymaking is more centralized again, and interest groups are more dependent on the goodwill of the president for access. Still, organized interests still press their demands through the mass media, the parliament, and the government, and public pressure does have some impact on policymaking.

PARTIES AND THE AGGREGATION OF INTERESTS

Interest aggregation refers to the process by which the demands of various groups of the population are combined into programmatic options for government. Although other political institutions also aggregate interests, parties in most countries are the quintessential structure performing this vital task. How well parties aggregate interests, define choices for voters, and hold politicians accountable is of critical importance to democracy.

In Russia, despite over a decade of postcommunist political development, the party system remains tenuous and fluid. There is considerable turnover in the parties that run in parliamentary elections from election to election. Politicians are constantly starting new parties, only to abandon them after the election. Voters have little sense of attachment to parties and more often associate them with particular politicians' personalities than with specific ideological stances. In the Duma, deputies do organize their political activity around party factions, but most of these parties have very weak roots in society. Party activity in Russia is organized more around *patronage*—the delivery of particularistic benefits to favored client groups—than around mobilizing support for the achievement of *programmatic* goals.[45]

Russia's party system has undergone a major transformation from the 1990s to the 2000s. In the first half of the 1990s, the struggle between democratic reformers and their communist opponents dominated party competition. Some parties allied themselves with the democratic movement, while others remain wedded to Marxist-Leninist ideology. There were also parties that sought to identify themselves with Russian nationalism. But although all three tendencies—democratic, communist, and nationalist—can still be found in the spectrum of Russia's political parties today, ideological differences have become much less central to party competition.

Instead, beginning in the mid-1990s and continuing into the 2000s, the authorities have made repeated efforts to create dominant parties built around patronage rather than programmatic appeals. Such a party is known as a **party of power.** To the voters, such a party presents an image of continuity and stability. For officeholders, a party of power is a vehicle for career advancement. In the 1990s there were several short-lived attempts to form parties of power, but under Putin the party United Russia has become *the* unquestioned party of power. United Russia presently casts such a long and commanding shadow over the political system that some observers believe that the Kremlin seeks to turn it into a replica of the ruling communist party of the Soviet era.

The party system in Russia is shaped by the rules of the electoral system as well as by the direct efforts of the Kremlin, big business, and regional officials to manipulate parties for their own purposes. The party list system used in parliamentary elections encourages ambitious politicians to join parties in order to run for office. But presidential elections have not stimulated party competition to the same degree. Because Russia's presidential system encourages the president to avoid making commitments to parties, presidential elections

have tended to concentrate attention on the candidates' personalities rather than on their policy programs, and therefore have undermined party development. Yet even in parliamentary elections, each new election presents voters with a substantially new set of party choices, making it hard for voters to develop any lasting attachments to parties or to make sensible judgments about parties' past or future performance.

Elections and Party Development

Table 12.3 indicates the results of the party-list voting in the 1993, 1995, 1999, and 2003 elections. The table groups parties into five categories: *democratic* (those espousing liberal democratic principles), *leftist* (those

Party-List Vote in Duma Elections, 1993, 1995, 1999, and 2003				TABLE 12.3
Party	**1993**	**1995**	**1999**	**2003**
Democratic Parties				
Russia's Choice	15.51	3.90	—	—
Union of Rightist Forces (SPS)	—	—	8.52	4.00
Yabloko	7.86	6.89	5.93	4.37
Party of Russian Unity and Concord (PRES)	6.76	—	—	—
Democratic Party of Russia (DPR)	5.52	—	—	.20
Centrist Parties				
Women of Russia	8.13	4.60	2.04	—
Civic Union[a]	1.93	1.60	—	—
Parties of Power				
Our Home Is Russia	—	10.10	1.20	—
Fatherland—All Russia (OVR)	—	—	13.33	—
Unity/United Russia[b]	—	—	23.32	38.20
Nationalist Parties				
Liberal Democratic Party of Russia (LDPR)[c]	22.92	11.20	5.98	11.60
Congress of Russian Communities (KRO)[d]	—	4.30	.62	—
Motherland (Rodina)	—	—	—	9.20
Leftist Parties				
Communist Party of the Russian Federation (CPRF)	12.40	22.30	24.29	12.80
Agrarian Party	7.99	3.80	—	3.69
Other parties failing to meet 5% threshold	10.98	26.81	12.55	11.10
Against all	4.36	2.80	3.34	4.80

[a]In 1995, the same alliance renamed itself the Bloc of Trade Unionists and Industrialists.
[b]In 2003, Unity ran under the name United Russia following a merger with the Fatherland party.
[c]In 1999, the LDPR party list was called the Zhirinovsky bloc.
[d]In 1999, this party was called "Congress of Russian Communities and Yuri Boldyrev Movement."

Source: Compiled by author from reports of Central Electoral Commission.

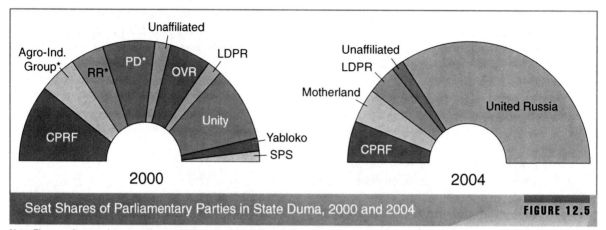

Seat Shares of Parliamentary Parties in State Duma, 2000 and 2004   FIGURE 12.5

Note: Figures taken as of January 2000 and May 2004. Percentages shift with time as members change factional affiliations. Note that United Russia was the result of a merger of the Fatherland party with Unity.

* These were groups made up of deputies elected in single-member districts who chose not to affiliate with any of the party-based factions, but were registered as official deputy groups on the basis of having at least 35 members. In the 2004 Duma, there were no such groups.

Source: Compiled by author from reports of State Duma.

advocating socialist and statist values), *centrist* (mixing leftist and liberal democratic appeals), *nationalist* (highlighting ethnic nationalism, patriotism and imperialism), and "*parties of power.*"

Figure 12.5 shows how the election results translated into the distribution of seats in the Duma to various party factions following the 1999 and 2003 elections. Under the mixed electoral system that was in force from 1993 through 2006, parliamentary factions varied in their composition. A few had substantial numbers of both list and single-member district (SMD) deputies, but most were composed predominantly of one type of member or the other. Some factions were "start-up" groups made up of independents elected in SMD races who did not wish to affiliate themselves with the party factions, while for others, the core of their membership were deputies elected on the party list. In the United Russia faction in the 2003–2006 Duma, about 60 percent of the members were from single-member districts—which means that 80 percent of SMD deputies elected in 2003 chose to join the United Russia faction. This is a good indication of the power of the United Russia bandwagon.

The 1989 and 1990 Elections The development of parties began with the elections under Gorbachev to the reformed Soviet Union and Russian Republic parliaments. Democratically oriented politicians coalesced to form legislative caucus in the Soviet Union's Congress of People's Deputies in 1989, and in turn helped a broad

coalition of democratic candidates run for the Russian Congress in 1990. In parliament, democratic factions competed for influence with communist, nationalist, agrarian, and other political groups. These parliamentary factions became the nuclei of political parties in the parliamentary election of December 1993.

The 1993 and 1995 Elections The 1993 election produced a shock—the proreform, pro-Yeltsin party, Russia's Choice, did unexpectedly poorly, while Vladimir Zhirinovsky's Liberal Democratic Party of Russia (LDPR) did unexpectedly well. Zhirinovsky's party is misleadingly named, because the flamboyant, extremist Zhirinovsky appeals to xenophobia, authoritarianism, and the nostalgia for empire rather than liberal or democratic values. The party's strong showing in the 1993 election was a signal of widespread popular discontent with the Yeltsin economic reforms.

The Communists (**Communist Party of the Russian Federation, or CPRF**) took about 10 percent of the seats. Altogether, the democratic factions received about 38 percent of the seats in the Duma, the left about 20 percent, and centrist factions about 20 percent. No political camp had a majority, but Zhirinovsky's oppositional stance meant the anti-Yeltsin forces had a narrow majority.

In the 1995 elections a wide array of political groups competed—far more than could possibly be accommodated given that the same 5 percent threshold rule was kept. Forty-three organizations registered and won a spot on the ballot. In the end, only four parties crossed the 5 percent threshold: the communists, Zhirinovsky's LDPR, the "Our Home Is Russia" bloc formed around Prime Minister Chernomyrdin, and the Yabloko party. Of these, the communists were the most successful, winding up with nearly a third of the seats in the Duma. Altogether, half of the votes were cast for parties that failed to win any seats on the party-list ballot.

The 1996 Presidential Election The 1995 parliamentary election was a test of strength for Russia's parties and leaders. The big unknown was how Yeltsin would perform in the 1996 presidential race. At the beginning of 1996 his approval was in the single digits.[46] During the campaign, Yeltsin succeeded in persuading voters that the election was about a choice between him and a return to communism.

This strategy worked. Yeltsin's displays of vigor during the campaign, his lavish promises to voters, and his domination of the media, all contributed to a surge in popularity and a victory over Gennadii Ziuganov, his communist rival (see Table 12.4).[47] The campaign took its toll on Yeltsin, however. Soon afterward he had major heart surgery and for much of his second term he was in poor health.

The 1999 Election The 1999 election was dominated by the question of who would succeed Yeltsin as president. Many federal and regional officeholders wanted to rally around a new "party of power" in order to protect their positions. A group of backroom Kremlin strategists formed a movement called Unity in late summer 1999. They wanted to create a political movement that state officials throughout the country could rally around in the parliamentary election. The party would serve as a political vehicle for Vladimir Putin, whom Yeltsin had just named prime minister and anointed as his successor. Conveniently for Putin, at the same time as Unity's formation and Putin's appointment, Chechen rebels launched raids into the neighboring region of Dagestan. Bombings of apartment buildings attributed to Chechen terrorists also occurred in Moscow and other cities. Putin's decisive handling of the military operations against the Chechen guerrillas gave him and the Unity movement a tremendous boost in popularity during the campaign. Unity, which had not even existed until late August, won 23 percent of the party-list vote.

Presidential Election Results, 1996 (in %)		**TABLE 12.4**
	First Round (June 16, 1996)	**Second Round (July 3, 1996)**
Boris Yeltsin	35.28	53.82
Gennadii Ziuganov	32.03	40.31
Alecksandr Lebed	14.52	—
Grigorii Yavlinskii	7.34	—
Vladimir Zhirinovsky	5.70	—
Svyatoslav Fedorov	0.92	—
Mikhail Gorbachev	0.51	—
Martin Shakkum	0.37	—
Yurii Vlasov	0.20	—
Vladimir Bryntsalov	0.16	—
Aman Tuleev	0.00	—
Against all candidates	1.54	4.83

Putin and the 2000 Presidential Race The presidential election of 2000 occurred ahead of schedule due to President Yeltsin's early resignation. Under the constitution, the prime minister automatically succeeds the president upon the premature departure of the president, but new elections for the presidency must be held within three months. Accordingly, the presidential election was scheduled for March 26, 2000. The early election gave the front-runner and incumbent, Putin, an advantage because he could capitalize on his popularity and the country's desire for continuity. Putin ran the Russian equivalent of a "rose garden" campaign, preferring to be seen handling the normal daily business of a president rather than going out on the hustings and asking for people's votes. He counted on the support of officeholders at all levels, a media campaign that presented a "presidential" image to the voters, and the voters' fear that change would only make life worse. His rivals, moreover, were weak. Several prominent politicians prudently chose not to run against him. As Table 12.5 shows, Putin's strategy worked brilliantly.

The 2003 and 2004 Elections Under Putin the ideological divide between communists and democrats that had marked the transition era disappeared. The political arena was dominated by the president and his supporters. The loyal pro-Putin party Unity was renamed United Russia after it absorbed a rival party, Fatherland

Gennadii Ziuganov rallies the Communist Party faithful under a portrait of Vladimir Lenin at a November 1998 anniversary celebration of the October Revolution.

Sergey Chirkov/AFP/Corbis

Presidential Election Results, March 26, 2000 (in %)	TABLE 12.5
Vladimir Putin	52.94
Gennadii Ziuganov	29.21
Grigorii Yavlinskii	5.80
Aman Tuleev	2.95
Vladimir Zhirinovsky	2.70
Konstantin Titov	1.47
Ella Pamfilova	1.01
Stanislav Govorukhin	0.44
Yuri Skuratov	0.43
Alexei Podberezkin	0.13
Umar Dzhabrailov	0.10
Against all candidates	1.88

(headed by Moscow mayor Yuri Luzhkov). United Russia held a near-monopoly in the party spectrum, squeezing other parties to the margins. The magnetic attraction of a successful party of power was demonstrated vividly in the 2003 parliamentary election, when United Russia won 38 percent of the party-list vote and wound up with two-thirds of the seats in the Duma. The communists suffered a severe blow, losing almost half their vote share, and the democrats did even worse. For the first time, none of the democratic parties won seats on the party-list vote. The result underscored Putin's drive to eliminate any meaningful political opposition. Such an impressive showing for United Russia assured Putin's reelection as president. The March 2004 race was a landslide. Putin won easily with 71.31 percent of the vote (see Table 12.6). European observers commented that the elections were "well administered" but hardly constituted "a genuine democratic contest" in view of the president's overwhelming control of media coverage of the race and the absence of genuine competition.[48]

As Russia enters the 2007–2008 electoral cycle, two closely related questions hang over the political system. First, as President Putin's second presidential term comes to an end, will he commit the power and prestige of his presidency to United Russia in order to make it a vehicle for his political legacy? Second, will United Russia become a long-lasting dominant party along the lines of Mexico's Partido Revolucionario Institucional (PRI)? For United Russia to survive as a party of power in the post-Putin era, it will need to control the channels of access to power for political officials at all levels, as well as win commanding majorities in federal and regional elections. This will require that the Kremlin—the large body of officials based in the presidential administration—commit its resources to United Russia to make it a long-term ruling party, something that it may not be willing to do.

Russian Presidential Election Results, 2004 (as % of valid vote)	TABLE 12.6
Vladimir Putin	71.31
Nikolai Kharitonov	13.74
Sergei Glaz'ev	4.10
Irina Khakamada	3.84
Oleg Malyshkin	2.02
Sergei Mironov	.75
Against all	3.45
Turnout	64.40

Source: Central Electoral Commission.

Party Strategies and the Social Bases of Party Support

Survey researchers have found some systematic differences in the bases of social support for parties. Such factors as household income, age, urban or rural residence, and education levels are related to differences in party preferences. These factors reflect the different types of images and appeals that parties present to voters.

Table 12.7 indicates how the parties differed in the social composition of their support in the 2003 Duma elections. Note that the table should be read downward. For example, it tells us that 64.5 percent of the

Social Bases of Support for Parties, Duma Parliamentary Election, December 2003 (in %)   TABLE 12.7

Party Support by Age Group	Motherland	LDPR	United Russia	CPRF	Other Party	Against All	Did Not Vote	Total
18–24	3.8	19.2	13.9	1.8	9.6	10.3	17.3	13.7
25–39	14.1	31.3	22.8	9.1	23.9	33.8	36.1	28.5
40–54	37.2	38.4	29.3	24.5	31.4	33.8	25.5	28.7
55+	44.9	11.1	34.0	64.5	35.1	22.1	21.2	29.1
Total	100	100	100	100	100	100	100	100
By Sex								
Male	43.6	60.6	38.0	49.5	44.1	43.3	46.6	45.3
Female	56.4	39.4	62.0	50.5	55.9	56.7	53.4	54.7
Total	100	100	100	100	100	100	100	100
By Education								
Incomplete secondary	35.9	20.2	29.9	43.1	25.1	16.7	26.8	28.0
Secondary, specialist	47.4	65.7	55.6	45.9	49.2	65.2	58.4	56.0
Incomplete higher, higher	16.7	14.1	14.5	11.0	25.7	18.2	14.9	16.0
Total	100	100	100	100	100	100	100	100
By Household Economic Situation								
Barely make ends meet	12.7	14.1	12.1	24.8	12.9	9.0	17.2	15.4
Enough for food	38.0	38.4	36.5	45.0	36.0	28.4	36.8	37.0
Enough for clothes	38.0	37.4	40.6	24.8	37.1	47.8	35.5	36.8
Enough for durables	11.4	10.1	10.8	5.5	14.0	14.9	10.4	10.8
Total	100	100	100	100	100	100	100	100

Key: LDPR: Liberal Democratic Party of Russia (Zhirinovsky's party) CPRF: Communist Party of the Russian Federation

Note: In each table, figures read downward. Each cell entry is the share of a given party's supporters represented by a given social category. Thus, of the supporters of the party Motherland, 3.8% were in the 18–24 age group; 29.1% of all voters were in the 55 years or older age group, but of Communist voters, 64.5% were in this age category.

Source: New Russia Barometer XII, 12–22 December 2003. www.russiavotes.org (accessed 19 July 2004). N = 1601.

communist voters were 55 and over. The table shows that age, gender, education, and economic situation all influence party choice. For example, the communists depended much more on older voters than do other parties, and on voters with lower levels of education and lower income levels. In contrast, United Russia drew its support from across the political spectrum. United Russia voters are distinctive because women predominate: 62 percent of their supporters were female. This fact is consistent with the observation that female voters in Russia tend to support parties promising stability and continuity in policy. In other respects, however, United Russia's base of social support is strikingly broad, suggesting that the party is successful in positioning itself as a nonideological catch-all party. It has benefited especially from its association with President Putin. As vague as its policy stances are, it has emphasized the message that it supports Putin unreservedly. Table 12.8 shows how much more popular United Russia is than any of its rivals.

For other parties, the 2003–2004 elections shattered their assumptions about their sources of support and forced them to rethink their strategies in an era when the Kremlin dominated the political stage so fully. For example, the communists traditionally relied on their inherited organizational networks, their habits of party discipline, a clear-cut ideological profile, and their association with the socialist legacy of the old regime to attract voters. Some party strategists, however, believe that they must change their message and their leadership in view of their dismal showing in 2003. Likewise, the democratic parties, such as the Union of Rightist Forces and Yabloko, both of which have fallen below the 5 percent threshold in national support, have joined forces in several regional elections. The nationalists found it difficult to identify any winning issues in the face of Putin's skillful manipulation of the idea of a strong state and continuity with Russia's past. Moreover, the Kremlin's ability to conjure up new parties overnight to peel off support from the existing nationalist and leftist parties made most politicians unwilling to commit themselves to any but the dominant party of power—United Russia.

Evolution of the Party System

Development of a viable competitive party system in Russia has been hampered by institutional factors, such as the powerful presidency, as well as by the authorities' practice of manipulating the political

	Of All Respondents	Of Those Intending to Vote and Holding a Preference
Party Support, 2006 (in %) — **TABLE 12.8**		
United Russia	26	47
CPRF	10	19
LDPR	5	10
Rodina (Babakov faction)	1	3
SPS	1	2
Yabloko	2	4
"For worthy life" (Glaz'ev)	1	2
Agrarian Party of Russia	1	1
Party of Pensioners	—	1
Against All	6	5
Don't intend to vote	17	—
Don't know whether will vote	8	—
Don't know whom to vote for	19	—

Note: Question—"If elections to Duma were to be held on Sunday, for which party would you vote?" Survey conducted 19–22 June 2006. N = 1600, 18 years old and older, in 128 towns and 46 regions.

Source: Levada Center, http://www.levada.ru/press/2006062901.html (accessed 13 July 2006).

arena. Strong presidentialism undermines the ability of parties to promise that electoral success will translate into policy influence, since the president can choose a government largely of his own liking. Moreover, both Yeltsin and Putin have avoided party affiliations, preferring to remain above the partisan fray. Under these circumstances, politicians have little incentive to invest their efforts in building up party organizations.

In addition, the authorities have directly undermined party competition by a number of manipulative tactics. These include sponsoring shadow leftist or nationalist parties to divide the opposition, denying their opponents access to the media, applying intense administrative pressure in state institutions to ensure that government employees vote as instructed, and, in some cases, resorting to outright fraud in tallying votes.[49] Ultimately the authorities seek to persuade voters that casting a vote for any but the party of power is futile. Putin's administration has been explicit about its goal of creating a party system in which United Russia enjoys a dominant but not exclusive position. Other parties on the right and left are allowed to exist as outlets for opposition sentiment, but are denied the ability to win elections or influence policy. Party competition is more nominal than real as a result. It does not serve to aggregate the interests of citizens or give voters meaningful choices over policy alternatives.

Some believe that Putin is restoring a political system similar to that of the old Soviet regime, where the ruling party suppressed all other political forces and ideologies. The model that Putin is constructing, however, allows limited rights for opposition parties and accepts that elections are a useful mechanism for conferring democratic legitimacy on rulers so long as United Russia wins. But the dependence of United Russia on Putin's popularity and administrative support means that its dominance of the political system beyond Putin's presidency is not assured. A future president may find it expedient to base his support on a different party, or no party at all. And over time, opposition parties may gradually gain political strength.

THE POLITICS OF ECONOMIC REFORM

The Dual Transition

Russia's transition was so wrenching because the country had to remake both its *political* and *economic* institutions following the end of communism. The move to a market economy created opportunities for some, and hardships for many more. Democratization opened the political system to the influence of groups that could organize to press for exclusive economic benefits for themselves. Many people who had modest but secure livelihoods under the communist regime were ruined by inflation and unemployment when the planned economy broke down. A smaller number took advantage of opportunities for entrepreneurship or exploited their connections with government to amass sizable fortunes. The Russian case illustrates the danger that a transition to democracy and a market economy can get stuck partway, as power is captured by powerful entrenched interests that take advantage of the initial steps toward reform, only to block any further steps toward competition and an open economy.

Stabilization Russia pursued two major sets of economic reforms in the early 1990s, macroeconomic stabilization and privatization. Stabilization, sometimes called **shock therapy,** is a program intended to staunch a country's financial breakdown. The government seeks to restore a macroeconomic balance between what society consumes and what it produces. It requires a painful dose of fiscal and monetary discipline by radically cutting government spending and tightening the money supply. Stabilization gives the national currency real value, which requires eliminating chronic sources of inflation by cutting state spending, raising taxes, lifting price controls, and ending protectionism. Structural reform of this kind always lowers the standard of living for some groups of the population, at least in the short run.

Initially it was believed stabilization would be opposed by those whose living standards suffered as a result of the higher prices and lower incomes, such as workers in state enterprises, government employees, and pensioners. In practice, however, those who benefited from the early steps to open the economy and privatize state assets then opposed any subsequent measures to carry economic reform through to its conclusion. This includes officials who acquired ownership rights to monopoly enterprises and then worked to shut out potential competitors from their markets. It also includes state officials who benefited from collecting "fees" to issue licenses to importers and exporters or permits for doing business, and entrepreneurs whose firms monopolize the market in their industry.[50] A fully competitive market system, with a level playing field for all players, would threaten their ability to profiteer from their privileged positions.

From Communism to Capitalism Communist systems differed from other authoritarian regimes in ways that made their economic transitions more difficult. This was particularly true for the Soviet Union and its successor states. For one, the economic growth model followed by Stalin and his successors concentrated much production in large enterprises. This meant that many local governments were entirely dependent on the economic health of a single employer. The heavy commitment of resources to military production in the Soviet Union further complicated the task of reform in Russia, as does the country's vast size. Rebuilding the decaying infrastructure of a country as large as Russia is staggeringly expensive.

The economic stabilization program began on January 2, 1992, when the government abolished most controls on prices, raised taxes, and cut government spending sharply. Almost immediately, opposition to the new program began to form. Economists and politicians took sides. The "shock therapy" program was an easy target for criticism, even though there was no consensus among critics about what the alternative should be. It became commonplace to say that the program was all shock and no therapy.

By cutting government spending, letting prices rise, and raising taxes, the stabilization program sought to create incentives for producers to increase output and to look for new niches in the marketplace. In theory, increases in production should have driven down prices. But Russian producers did not respond by raising productivity. As a result, society suffered from a sharp, sudden loss in purchasing power. People went hungry, bank savings vanished, and the economy fell into a protracted slump. Firms that were politically connected were able to survive by winning cheap credits and production orders from government, which dampened any incentive for improving productivity. Desperate to raise operating revenues, the government borrowed heavily from the International Monetary Fund (IMF) and issued treasury bonds at ruinously high interest rates. IMF loans came with strings attached—the government pledged to cut spending further and step up tax collections as a condition of accepting IMF assistance, which fueled the depression further. Communists and nationalists got a rise out of audiences by depicting the government as the puppets of a malevolent, imperialist West.

Privatization Stabilization was followed shortly afterward by the mass **privatization** of state firms. In contrast to the shock therapy program, privatization enjoyed considerable public support, at least at first. Privatization transfers the legal title of state firms to private owners. Economic theory holds that under the right conditions, private ownership of productive assets is more efficient for society as a whole than is state ownership because in a competitive environment owners are motivated by an incentive to maximize their property's ability to produce a return. Under the privatization program, every Russian citizen received a voucher with a face value of 10,000 rubles (around $30 at the time). People were free to buy and sell vouchers, but they could be used only to acquire shares of stock in privatized enterprises or shares of mutual funds investing in privatized enterprises. The program sought to ensure that everyone became a property owner instantly. Politically, the program aimed to build support for the economic reforms by giving citizens a stake in the outcome of the market transition. Economically, the government hoped that privatization would eventually spur increases in productivity by creating meaningful property rights. Beginning in October 1992, the program distributed 148 million privatization vouchers to citizens. By June 30, 1994, when the program ended, 140 million vouchers had been exchanged for stock out of 148 million originally distributed. Some 40 million citizens were, in theory, share owners. But these shares were often of no value, because they paid no dividends and shareholders could not exercise any voting rights in the companies.

The next phase of privatization auctioned off most remaining shares of state enterprises for cash. This phase was marked by a series of scandalous sweetheart deals in which banks owned by a small number of Russia's wealthiest tycoons—the so-called oligarchs—wound up with title to some of Russia's most lucrative oil, gas, and metallurgy firms for bargain basement prices. The most notorious of these arrangements became known as the **"loans for shares"** scheme. It was devised by a small group of magnates in 1995. They persuaded the government to auction off management rights to controlling packages of shares in several major state-owned companies in return for loans to the government. If the government failed to repay the loans in a year's time, the shares would revert to the banks that made the loans. The government, not surprisingly, defaulted on the loans, letting a small number of oligarchs acquire ownership of some of Russia's largest and most valuable companies.[51]

Consequences of Privatization On paper, privatization was a huge success. By 1996, privatized firms produced about 90 percent of industrial output, and about two-thirds of all large and medium-sized enterprises had been privatized.[52] In fact, however, the actual transfer of ownership rights was far less impressive than it appeared. For one thing, the dominant pattern was for managers to acquire large shareholdings of the firms they ran. As a result, management of many firms did not change. Moreover, many nominally private firms continued to be closely tied to state life-support systems, such as cheap state-subsidized loans and credits.[53]

The program allowed a great many unscrupulous wheeler-dealers to prey on the public through a variety of financial schemes. Some investment funds promised truly incredible rates of return. Most investors in Western companies would have regarded these claims as outrageous and fraudulent. Many people lost their savings by investing in funds that went bankrupt or turned out to be simple pyramid schemes. The Russian government lacked the capacity to protect the investors. Many people were disenchanted with the entire program as a result. Privatization was carried out before the institutional framework of a market economy was in place. Markets for stocks, bonds, and commodities were, and still are, small in scale and weakly regulated. The legal foundation for a market economy has gradually emerged, but only after much of the economy was already privatized. Banks do a very poor job of mobilizing private savings into investment in Russian companies. For much of the 1990s, the lack of liquidity in the economy meant that enterprises failed to pay their wages and taxes on time, and they traded with one another using barter. By 1998, over half of enterprise output was being "sold" through barter trade.

The government fell into an unsustainable debt trap. Unable to meet its obligations, it grew increasingly dependent on loans. As lenders became increasingly certain that the government could not make good on its obligations, they demanded ever higher interest rates, deepening the trap. Ultimately the bubble burst. In August 1998, the government declared a moratorium on its debts and let the ruble's value collapse against the dollar. Overnight, the ruble lost two-thirds of its value and credit dried up.[54] The government bonds held by investors were almost worthless. The effects of the crash rippled through the economy. The sharp devaluation of the ruble made exports more competitive and gave an impetus to domestic producers, but also significantly lowered people's living standards.

As Table 12.9 shows, economic output in Russia fell for a decade before beginning to recover in 1999. The recovery is not due to a structural reform of the economy. There has not been a substantial overhaul of the banking system or the way industry is managed. The economy is still vulnerable to a downturn in the international economic situation, because Russia remains highly dependent on exports of natural resources: exports of oil and gas make up over half of Russian exports and a fifth of Russian gross domestic product (GDP).[55] Still, a number of industries are showing real vigor. The oil industry has increased investment and output sharply and several oil companies have expanded their international distribution and marketing efforts. They have even invested in the agriculture and food processing sectors, which are also recovering. Following the 1998 crash, several domestic industries got a boost from the drop in the ruble's exchange value as their prices became competitive and imported products became sharply more expensive. In an economy that was as deeply depressed as Russia's, even a small infusion of cash has a multiplier effect, as enterprises are able to pay off arrears in back wages and taxes. In turn, these taxes allowed government to pay off its backlog of wages and pensions, in turn allowing consumer demand for industry's products to rise, and so on. These trends have raised living standards noticeably. Unemployment has fallen since the August 1998 crisis and the number of people living in poverty has declined by about one-third. President Putin has expressed satisfaction with the favorable trends in the economy, but has warned that they are not sufficient to achieve sustained and balanced development. He has called for doubling GDP in ten years, which would require average annual economic growth of 7 percent per year for the next decade.[56] However, some of Putin's actions—such as the moves to drive the oil firm Yukos into bankruptcy and imprisonment of its founder, Khodorkovsky—are having a chilling effect on business investment and make it that much harder for Russia to achieve high sustainable economic growth.

Social Conditions Living standards fell deeply during the 1990s. A small minority became wealthy, and some households improved their lot modestly. Most people, however, suffered a net decline in living standards as a result of unemployment, lagging income, and nonpayment of wages and pensions.

A much larger share of the populace lives in poverty than during the Soviet era. As of 2005, about 30 million people, or about 20 percent of the population, lived in poverty. High poverty rates are the result of unemployment and the lag of incomes behind prices. Unemployment, at about 7 percent, is much lower than its crisis level of 13 percent, but still is high for a country that was accustomed to nearly full employment in the Soviet period, and where the state-funded social safety net is weak.

	1991	1992	1993	1994	1995	1996	1997	1998	1999	2000	2001	2002	2003	2004	2005
Russian Annual GDP Growth and Price Inflation Rates, 1991–2005 (in %) — **TABLE 12.9**															
GDP	−5.0	−14.5	−8.7	−12.6	−4.3	−6.0	0.4	−11.6	3.2	7.6	5.0	4.0	7.3	7.1	6.4
Inflation	138.0	2323.0	844.0	202.0	131.0	21.8	11.0	84.4	36.5	20.2	18.6	15.1	12.0	11.7	10.9

Note: GDP is measured in constant market prices. Inflation is measured as the percentage change in the consumer price index from December of one year to December of the next.

Source: Press reports of Russian State Statistical Service (www.gks.ru).

As elsewhere in the former communist countries, unemployment has affected women more severely than men. Also vulnerable to the economic shock of the 1990s are groups whose incomes are paid directly out of the state budget, such as those living on pensions and disability payments, as well as teachers, scientists, and health care workers. Although they receive periodic increases in pay, these raises usually are insufficient to keep up with increases in prices.

Inequality has grown sharply since the end of the Soviet era. One commonly used measure of inequality is the Gini index, which is an aggregate measure of the total deviation from perfect equality in the distribution of wealth or income. In Russia, the Gini index nearly doubled during the early 1990s, rising from 26 in 1987–1990 to 48 in 1993–1994. Inequality in Russia was higher than any other postcommunist country except for Kyrgyzstan.[57] As the economy began to recover and poverty has declined, the gap between rich and poor has closed somewhat. Today, Russia's Gini index is just under 40, slightly lower than the level of the United States. The richest fifth of the population receive eight times as much income as do the poorest fifth in Russia, and the ratio is similar in the United States. But although Russia's total level of inequality is similar to that of the United States, the rapid growth of the gap between rich and poor since the end of the communist regime is a severe shock to a society brought up on the socialist doctrine of class equality.

An especially disturbing dimension of the social effects of transition has been the erosion of public health. Although public health had deteriorated in the late communist period, the decline worsened after the regime changed. Mortality rates have risen sharply, especially among males. Life expectancy for males in Russia is at a level comparable to poor and developing countries. At present, life expectancy at birth for males is just under fifty-nine years and for females seventy-two years. The disparity between male and female mortality—enormous by world standards—is generally attributed to the higher rates of abuse of alcohol and tobacco among men. Demographers have warned that at the present rate of mortality, 40 percent of Russia's 16-year-old boys will not reach their sixtieth birthday.[58]

Other demographic indicators are equally grim. Prime Minister Fradkov told a cabinet meeting in July 2006 that only 30 percent of newborn children "can be described as healthy," and that "there are more than 500,000 disabled children in need of various forms of treatment, and also some 730,000 orphans or abandoned children."[59] Rates of incidence of HIV and other infectious diseases, murders, suicides, drug addiction, and alcoholism are rising. Russia's leaders consider the demographic crisis to pose a grave threat to the country's national security both because of the growing shortage of labor in some regions and the army's inability to recruit enough healthy young men.[60] Every year Russia's population declines by about three-quarters of a million people due to the excess of deaths over births. Demographers estimate that Russia's population could fall by over one third by 2050. In his 2006 message to parliament, President Putin called for a series of measures to raise birthrates, reduce mortality, and stimulate immigration.

Setting the country on a path of self-sustaining economic growth, where workers and investors are confident in their legal rights, requires a complete overhaul of the relationship of the state to the economy. The Soviet state used central planning to direct enterprises on what to produce and how to use resources. Much of the economy was geared to heavy industry and defense production, and government ministries directly administered each branch of the economy. The postcommunist state must have an entirely different relationship to the economy in order to stimulate growth. It must set clear rules for economic activity, regulate markets, enforce the law, supply public goods and services, and promote competition. Shifting the structure of the state bureaucracy and the attitudes of state officials has been a Herculean task.

We can get some idea of the legacy of the communist system in the way the state was intertwined with the economy by looking at the structure of the state budget. Figure 12.6 shows the breakdown graphically for the 2006 federal budget. Total spending was set at 28.4 trillion rubles, or about $100 billion U.S. dollars. The share spent on national defense (at 23.5 percent) is higher than in the United States (19.8 percent of federal spending in 2006). The high shares of spending on general administration (22.5 percent) and law enforcement (19.1 percent) make it difficult for Russia to maintain an adequate social safety net or to rebuild its education and health care systems. The budget sur-

pluses of the last several years have made it possible for the government to meet its obligations, but spending was pared back so severely in the 1990s that many critical needs continue to go unmet.

Putin's government has recognized that the oil-and gas-fueled budget surpluses pose a serious danger of creating inflationary pressures in the economy. For this reason, like some other oil-rich states, Russia has created a "stabilization fund" that removes some of the revenues generated by high world energy prices from circulation and uses them to pay off external debt. By the beginning of 2006, the stabilization fund had accumulated some $44 billion, and political pressure was rising to spend it on social needs. President Putin also announced an ambitious program of spending on four high-priority projects to improve conditions in education, health care, housing, and agriculture. In addition to meeting some of the needs of these long-starved sectors, the spending should benefit Putin's allies in United Russia in the 2007 parliamentary elections.

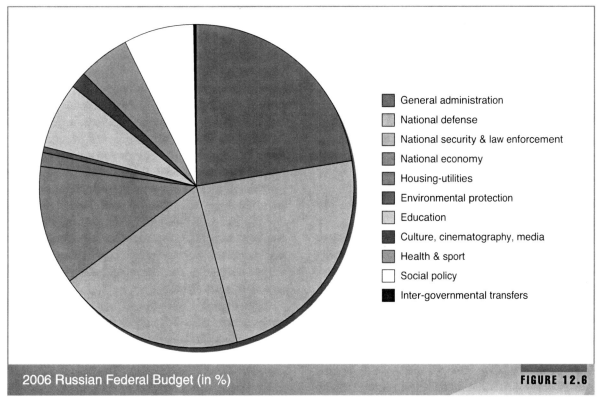

2006 Russian Federal Budget (in %)   **FIGURE 12.6**

- General administration
- National defense
- National security & law enforcement
- National economy
- Housing-utilities
- Environmental protection
- Education
- Culture, cinematography, media
- Health & sport
- Social policy
- Inter-governmental transfers

Source: Russian press reports.

RULE ADJUDICATION: TOWARD THE RULE OF LAW

The Law-Governed State

One of the most important goals of Gorbachev's reforms was to make the Soviet Union a **law-governed state (pravovoe gosudarstvo)** rather than one in which state bodies and the Communist Party exercised power arbitrarily. Since 1991, the Russian leaders have asserted that the state must respect the primacy of law over politics—even when they took actions grossly violating the constitution. The difficulty in placing law above politics testifies to the lingering legacy of the old regime's abuse of the legal system. President Putin too has emphasized the rule of law (in a strange but memorable phrase, he once called for the "dictatorship of law") even while his actions have sometimes flagrantly infringed on the independence of the judiciary.

The struggle for the rule of law began well before Gorbachev. After Stalin died, his successors ended mass terror and took significant steps to reduce the use of law for political repression. Still, throughout the late Soviet era, the Communist Party and the KGB often used legal procedures to give the mantle of legal legitimacy to acts of political repression. Although the prosecution of political dissidents has ended, the use of the legal system for political purposes by state authorities continues. Changes since 1991 represented some movement toward establishing an independent judicial branch, but under Putin political control over the legal system has started to grow again.

The major institutional actors in the legal system are the **procuracy,** the *judiciary*, and the **bar.** Each has undergone substantial change in the postcommunist period.

The Procuracy Russia's legal system traditionally vested a great deal of power in the procuracy; the procuracy was considered to be the most prestigious branch of the legal system. The procuracy is comparable to the system of federal and state prosecuting attorneys in the United States, but has more wide-ranging responsibilities and is organized as a centralized hierarchy headed by the procurator-general. The procuracy is charged with fighting crime, corruption, and abuses of power in the bureaucracy. It investigates crimes and official malfeasance and seeks to ensure that all state officials and public organizations observe the law. Moreover, the procuracy oversees the entire

system of justice. The procuracy has traditionally been the principal check on abuses of power by state officials. But it is inadequately equipped to meet the sweeping responsibilities that the law assigns to it, because of the difficulty of effectively supervising the vast state bureaucracy and overcoming the entrenched political machines of party and state officials.

The Judiciary In contrast to the influence that the procuracy has traditionally wielded in Russia, the bench has been relatively weak. Trial judges are usually the least experienced and lowest paid of the members of the legal profession, and the most vulnerable to external political and administrative pressure. Successful judicial reform requires greater independence and discretion on the part of courts. Judges are being asked to raise their standards of professionalism at a time of rapid change in law, legal procedure, and social conditions. In a few instances, judges have been murdered when they attempted to take on organized crime. Many judges have left their positions to take higher paying jobs in other branches of the legal profession, but caseloads have risen substantially.

State officials pay lip service to the principle of judicial independence but often violate it in practice by pressuring judges to render particular judgments in politically sensitive matters. At the same time, many reforms since the end of communism are intended to make the administration of justice more effective, and some increase the rights of defendants in criminal cases. For example, in the 1990s, trial by jury in major criminal cases was introduced in several regions on an experimental basis. Putin has backed its use nationwide. It is opposed by the procuracy because the prosecution has to work much harder to present a convincing case. It is also expensive, because court facilities must be expanded and jurors must be selected and paid. The goal of the jury system, however, is to make the judicial system more adversarial, so that the prosecution and the defense have equal status in the courtroom, and the judge becomes a neutral arbiter between them.[61]

The Russian judiciary is a unitary hierarchy. All courts of general jurisdiction are federal courts. There are also other specialized types of courts in addition to federal courts of general jurisdiction, among them the supreme courts of ethnic republics, local municipal courts (equivalent to justices of the peace), and military courts. Most criminal trials are held in district and city courts of general jurisdiction, which have original jurisdiction in most criminal proceedings. Higher-level courts, including regional and republic-level courts, hear appeals from lower courts and have original jurisdiction in certain cases. At the pinnacle of the hierarchy of courts of general jurisdiction is the Russian Supreme Court, which hears cases referred from lower courts and also issues instructions to lower courts on judicial matters. The Supreme Court does not have the power to challenge the constitutionality of laws and other official actions of legislative and executive bodies. The constitution assigns that power to the Constitutional Court. Under the constitution, the judges of the Supreme Court are nominated by the president and confirmed by the Federation Council.

There is a similar hierarchy of courts hearing cases arising from civil disputes between firms or between firms and the government called **commercial courts (arbitrazhnye sudy)**. Like the Supreme Court, the Supreme Commercial Court is both the highest appellate court for its system of courts as well as the source of instruction and direction to lower commercial courts. As with the Supreme Court, the judges of the Supreme Commercial Court are nominated by the president and confirmed by the Federation Council. In recent years, the Supreme Commercial Court has handed down a number of major decisions that clarify the rules of the economic marketplace.

The Ministry of Justice oversees the court system and provides for its material and administrative needs. Its influence over the judiciary is limited, however, because it lacks any direct authority over the procuracy.

The Bar Change of another sort has been occurring among those members of the legal profession who represent individual citizens and organizations in both criminal and civil matters: "advocates" (*advokaty*). They are comparable to defense attorneys in the United States. Their role has expanded considerably with the spread of the market economy. They have long enjoyed some autonomy through their self-governing associations, through which they elect officers and govern admission of new practitioners. In the past, their ability to effectively use their rights was limited, but in recent years their opportunities have risen markedly. Private law firms are proliferating. The profession is attractive for the opportunities it provides to earn high incomes. A number of lawyers have become celebrities by taking on high-profile cases.

Constitutional Adjudication One of the most important reforms in postcommunist Russia's legal system is the establishment of a court for constitutional review of the official acts of government. The Constitutional Court has authority to interpret the constitution in a variety of areas. It has ruled on several ambiguous questions relating to parliamentary procedure. It has overturned some laws passed by national republics within Russia, and struck down several provisions of the Russian Criminal Code that limited individual rights. Generally, in disputes between individuals and state authorities, the court finds in favor of individuals, thus reaffirming the sphere of individual legal rights. It has consistently upheld the sovereignty of the federal constitution over regional governments.

The most important challenge for the court, however, is the huge domain of presidential authority. The court has been reluctant to challenge the president. One of its first and most important decisions concerned a challenge brought by a group of communist parliamentarians to President Yeltsin's decrees launching the war in Chechnia. The court ruled that the president had the authority to wage the war through the use of his constitutional power to issue decrees with the force of law. In other, less highly charged issues, the court established legal limits to the president's authority. For instance, the court ruled that Yeltsin could not refuse to sign a law after parliament had overridden his veto. However, in the more authoritarian climate under Putin, the court has not issued any rulings restricting the president's powers. Generally the court is sensitive to the political climate surrounding it and takes care not to issue a ruling that would be ignored or opposed by the president.

Obstacles to the Rule of Law

Movement toward the rule of law continues to be hampered by the abuse of legal institutions by the political authorities and endemic corruption in state and society.

In the post-Soviet state the security police continue to operate autonomously. In the Soviet period, the agency with principal responsibility for maintaining domestic security was called the KGB (State Security Committee). The KGB exercised very wide powers, including responsibility for both domestic and foreign intelligence. Since 1991 its functions have been split up among several agencies. The main domestic security agency is called the Federal Security

A family in Chechnia surveys the damage to their home from the war.

Malcolm Lintron/Getty Images

Service (FSB). Although the structure and mission of the security agencies have changed, they have never undergone a thorough purge of personnel. No member or collaborator of the Soviet-era security services has been prosecuted for violating citizens' rights.

The security police are regarded as one of the more professionally competent and uncorrupted state agencies. However, despite being assigned new tasks, such as fighting international narcotics trafficking and terrorism, they still demonstrate a Soviet-style preoccupation with controlling the flow of information about the country. For example, in 2001 the security police sent a directive to the Academy of Sciences demanding that scholars report all contacts with foreigners. Many similar Soviet-era police practices have been revived under Putin.

Also under Putin, the legal system has been used as an instrument for suppressing potential political opposition. An example is the series of legal maneuvers taken against the owners of independent media. These included police harassment and criminal prosecution, as well as civil actions such as bankruptcy proceedings. For example, the owners of two television companies were forced to divest themselves of their media holdings and transfer ownership to companies loyal to the administration. As a result, Russia's two relatively autonomous national television companies lost their political independence; one respected liberal newspaper was shut down; and the entire media establishment was sent a strong signal that it would be wise to avoid crossing the current administration. Under Putin, only a small number of print media have retained a measure of political independence.

The heavy-handed use of procuracy, the police, and courts against the Yukos firm in a coordinated campaign to arrest the company's top leaders and dismantle the company represents another, particularly visible, instance of using the legal system for political ends.

Corruption Another serious obstacle to the rule of law is endemic corruption. Corruption increased substantially after the Soviet period. It is widespread both in everyday life and in dealings with the state. A large-scale survey by a Moscow research firm gives some indication of the nature and scale of corruption. At least half the population of Russia is involved in corruption in daily life. For instance, the probability that an individual will pay a bribe to get an automobile inspection permit is about 60 percent. The likelihood of paying a bribe to get one's child into a good school or college, or to get good grades, is about 50 percent. There is a 26 percent chance of paying a bribe to get a favorable ruling in a court case. The areas where the largest sums are spent are health care, education, courts, and automobile inspections; these alone account for over 60 percent of the money paid in bribes.[62]

Bribery in the dealings between business and the state is of a far larger magnitude. The survey's authors estimate that 82 percent of business firms engage in giving bribes to government officials, particularly those involved in licensing, taxation, and regulation. They calculated that the total annual cost of such corruption is $33.5 billion, a sum equivalent to about half of the federal budget.[63]

Corruption is hardly unique to Russia or to the former communist world. However, it is especially widespread in Russia and the other former Soviet states. Corruption on this scale imposes a severe drag on economic development, both because it diverts resources away from public needs, and because it undermines people's willingness to invest in productive activity.[64] Moreover, much corruption is tied to organized crime, which bribes government officials for protection and drives out legal businesses. For example, in a number of cases, criminal organizations have forced owners of legitimate businesses to sell out. The payment of protection money by businesses to organized crime groups is very widespread. The corruption of the police and courts ensures that such crimes go unpunished and forces legal businesses to compete in the corruption market with illegal ones.

Corruption in Russia has deep roots, and many Russians assume that it is ineradicable. Comparative studies of corruption demonstrate, however, that a culture of corruption can be changed by changing the expectations of the public and the government.[65] The key is for the political leadership to make a serious effort to combat corruption and to back up their commitment with institutional reform and sustained attention to the problem. In Russia, corruption is so pervasive that it is a significant drag on the economy and the political system.

Reforms of the legal system have made some progress toward realizing the goal of the rule of law. Since the early 1990s there have been a number of reforms that have the potential to strengthen the judiciary's independence from both political pressure and corruption. However, the authorities' habitual use of the procuracy and the courts for political purposes and the powerful corrosive effect of corruption continue to subvert the integrity of the legal system. In the long run, movement toward the rule of law will require that power be sufficiently dispersed among groups and organizations in the state and society so that neither private nor state interests be powerful enough to subordinate the law to their own purposes.

RUSSIA AND THE INTERNATIONAL COMMUNITY

Russia's thousand-year history of expansion, war, and state domination of society has left behind a legacy of autocratic rule and a preoccupation with defending national borders. The collapse of the Soviet regime required Russia to rebuild its political institutions, economic system, national identity, and relations with the outside world. During the Soviet period, state propaganda used the image of an international struggle between capitalism and socialism to justify its repressive control over society and its enormous military establishment. Now the country's leaders recognize that only through international integration can Russia hope to prosper. Under Putin the authorities aim to capture the benefits of economic integration with the developed capitalist world while at the same time building an authoritarian political order at home featuring direct state control of the strategically important sectors of the economy.

Gorbachev, Yeltsin, and Putin all believed that integration of Russia into the community of developed democracies was strategically important for Russia. Gorbachev was willing to allow communist regimes to fall throughout Eastern Europe for the sake of improved relations with the West. Yeltsin accepted the admission of East European states into the North Atlantic Treaty Organization (NATO) as a necessary condition for close relations with the United States and Europe. Putin has repeatedly emphasized that he regarded Russia's admission to the World Trade Organization (WTO) as critical for Russia's long-term economic success. Following the September 11, 2001, terrorist attacks on the United States, Putin immediately telephoned U.S. President George W. Bush to offer his support. Putin clearly saw an advantage for Russia in aligning itself with the United States against Islamic terrorism, which it identified as an immediate threat to its own security. Putin cited Russia's own war in Chechnia as part of the global struggle against Islamic terrorists.

Many elements of the political establishment criticized Gorbachev, Yeltsin, and Putin for making concessions to the United States and the West without receiving any benefits in return. Neither trade nor investment has blossomed as Russia had hoped, and Russia still depends on its raw materials exports to maintain a positive trade balance.

Russia has not fully embraced integration into the international community. It has expanded its military presence in several former Soviet republics, pressuring them to become satellites of Russia. In its brutal military campaigns in Chechnia, from 1994 to 1996, and then again from 1999 to the present, it has insisted that the war is a matter of domestic sovereignty and has refused to allow international human rights organizations to monitor Russian practices. The regime has forced the mass media to report a sanitized picture of the situation. Corruption and inefficiency in government, both at the central level and in many regions, deter foreign investors from making a serious commitment of resources. Russian leaders constantly urge foreign business to invest in Russia. But, as many foreign investors point out, why should they take a greater risk than Russia's own business community, which has sent some $300 billion to off-shore havens?

Russia thus has some distance to go before it is fully integrated politically or economically into the international community. Yet it is far more open than it was under Soviet rule, and its leaders recognize that they cannot retreat into isolation and autarky. Putin has made it clear, however, that Russia will accept international standards of democracy, human rights, and the rule of law only to the extent that they serve the state's strategic interests.

Russia's postcommunist transition has been difficult and incomplete. A framework of democratic institutions has been created, but increasingly, the informal rules governing the exercise of power are authoritarian. At the same time, the end of communism prompted the formation of tens of thousands of new social groups to organize for the protection of their interests. The spread of political and property rights has resulted in the emergence of a more pluralistic environment. Moreover, international factors—such as the dense network of international communications linking societies, the rapid expansion of cross-border trade and investment, and the global spread of norms and expectations centered on democracy, human rights, and the rule of law, together with the effects of domestic social changes such as rising educational levels—are likely to raise popular demands for democratic participation.

Russia's vast territory, weak government capacity, and tradition of state domination over society make it likely that the primary objective of its leaders for the foreseeable future will be to strengthen the state, both in its internal and international dimensions. The end of the communist regime and the dissolution of the Soviet Union damaged the state's capacity to enforce the laws, protect its citizens, and provide basic social services. Under Putin, the state has sought to rebuild its power by eliminating potentially independent sources of power in civil society and recentralizing executive power. At the same time, Putin seeks to knit Russia into the fabric of international trade and investment in order to promote economic development. In the long run, however, self-sustaining economic development will require the rule of law and effective institutions for articulating and aggregating social interests. The viability of Russia's postcommunist state will ultimately depend on how responsive and adaptive its institutions are to the demands of Russia's citizens in a globalized and interdependent world.

REVIEW QUESTIONS

- How did Yeltsin's "shock therapy" program contribute to the constitutional crisis of 1993?

- What effects did the constitutional struggles of 1992–1993 have on the features of the 1993 constitution?

- How has President Putin gone about strengthening the power of the central government at the expense of regional governments? What are his reasons for shifting the balance of power in this way?

- What are the main similarities and differences between the channels of elite recruitment under the Soviet system and today?

- Most Russians evaluate the pre-Gorbachev Soviet system favorably, yet would prefer not to bring it back. How would you explain this apparent contradiction?

- Why has United Russia been so successful as a "party of power?"

- What are the main obstacles to the rule of law in Russia? What changes in the political system would be required to overcome them?

KEY TERMS

bar

Chechnia

commercial courts
(*arbitrazhnye sudy*)

Communist Party of the
Russian Federation
(CPRF)

Constitutional Court

Federation Council

Federation of
Independent Trade

Unions of Russia
(FITUR)

glasnost

Gorbachev, Mikhail

governors

Komsomol (Communist
Youth League)

law-governed state
(*pravovoe gosudarstro*)

League of Committees of
Soldiers' Mothers

Lenin, Vladimir
Ilyich

loans for shares

nomenklatura

oligarchs

party of power

presidential decrees

privatization

procuracy

Public Chamber

Russian Union of
Industrialists and
Entrepreneurs (RUIE)

Security Council

shock therapy

Stalin, Joseph

State Council

State Duma

United Russia

Yukos

SUGGESTED READINGS

Aslund, Anders. *Building Capitalism: The Transformation of the Former Soviet Bloc.* Cambridge: Cambridge University Press, 2002.

Bahry, Donna. "Comrades Into Citizens? Russian Political Culture and Public Support for the Transition." *Slavic Review* 58, no. 4 (1999): 841–53.

Baker, Peter, and Susan Glasser. *Kremlin Rising: Vladimir Putin's Russia and the End of Revolution.* New York: Scribner, 2005.

Breslauer, George W. *Gorbachev and Yeltsin as Leaders.* Cambridge: Cambridge University Press, 2002.

Colton, Timothy J. and Stephen Holmes, eds. *The State After Communism: Governance in the New Russia.* Lanham, MD: Rowman & Littlefield, 2006.

Fish, M. Stephen. *Democracy Derailed in Russia: The Failure of Open Politics.* Cambridge: Cambridge University Press, 2005.

Hale, Henry. *Why Not Parties in Russia? Democracy, Federalism, and the State.* Cambridge: Cambridge University Press, 2006.

Hellman, Joel S. "Winners Take All: The Politics of Partial Reform in Postcommunist Transitions." *World Politics* 50, no. 1 (1998): 203–34.

Hill, Fiona, and Clifford Gaddy. *The Siberian Curse: How Communist Planners Left Russia Out in the Cold.* Washington, DC: Brookings Institution, 2003.

Huskey, Eugene. *Presidential Power in Russia.* Armonk, NY: M. E. Sharpe, 1999.

McFaul, Michael. *Russia's Unfinished Revolution: Political Change from Gorbachev to Putin.* Ithaca, NY: Cornell University Press, 2001.

Rose, Richard, and Neil Munro. *Elections Without Order: Russia's Challenge to Vladimir Putin.* Cambridge: Cambridge University Press, 2002.

Sakwa, Richard. *Putin: Russia's Choice.* London: Routledge, 2004.

Shleifer, Andrei, and Daniel Treisman. *Without a Map: Political Tactics and Economic Reform in Russia.* Cambridge: MIT Press, 2000.

White, Stephen, Richard Rose, and Ian McAllister. *How Russia Votes.* Chatham, NJ: Chatham House, 1997.

INTERNET RESOURCES

An invaluable source for daily news about Russia and neighboring countries is the Radio Free Europe-Radio Liberty Newsline: **www.rferl.org/newsline**

A useful daily e-mail newsletter containing news stories and commentary is Johnson's Russia list: **www.cdi.org/russia/johnson/**

A portal to a wide range of political resources on the Web is **www.politicalresources.net/russia.htm**

The University of Pittsburgh links to Web-based resources on Russia at: **www.ucis.pitt.edu/reesweb**

This is the home of "Friends and Partners," a joint Internet project by a team of Russians and Americans: **www.friends-partners.org**

The *Moscow Times* is an English-language daily newspaper published in Moscow, primarily for the expatriate community: **www.themoscowtimes.com**

The portal for the main institutions of the federal government—the president, the parliament, the government, and others—is **www.gov.ru/index.html.** Most of the content accessible through this site is in Russia, but some resources are in English.

The University of Strathclyde's Center for the Study of Public Policy provides a wealth of public opinion and electoral information from Russia: **www.RussiaVotes.org**

ENDNOTES

1. Richard Pipes, *Russia Under the Old Regime,* 2nd ed. (New York: Penguin Books, 1995).

2. Archie Brown, *The Gorbachev Factor* (New York: Oxford University Press, 1996).

3. For a comparison of the leadership styles of Gorbachev and Yeltsin, see George W. Breslauer, *Gorbachev and Yeltsin as Leaders* (Cambridge: Cambridge University Press, 2002); see also Archie Brown and Lilia Shevtsova, eds., *Gorbachev, Yeltsin, and Putin: Political Leadership in Russia's Transition* (Washington, DC: Carnegie Endowment for International Peace, 2001); Lilia Shevtsova, *Putin's Russia* (Washington, DC: Carnegie Endowment for International Peace, 2003); and Richard Sakwa, *Putin: Russia's Choice* (London: Routledge, 2004).

4. Konstantin Smirnov, "Vse pravitel'stvo: ekonomicheskii blok," *Vlast,* 28 June 2004, pp. 63–78; and World Bank, Russian Economic Report, June 2004. No. 8 (from website: www.worldbank.org.ru).

5. Many observers agreed that the point of the reform was to weaken the influence of local interests on Duma deputies, further centralizing power in the executive.

6. On nationality policy in the Soviet Union, see Terry Martin, *The Affirmative Action Empire: Nations and Nationalism in the Soviet Union, 1923–1939* (Ithaca, NY: Cornell University Press, 2001).

7. J. Paul Goode, "The Push for Regional Enlargement in Putin's Russia," *Post-Soviet Affairs* 20, no. 3 (July–September 2004): 219–57.

8. Guillermo O'Donnell, "Delegative Democracy," *Journal of Democracy* 5, no. 1 (1994): 55–69.

9. Quoted from text published on website Polit.ru, 26 May 2004.

10. From a survey conducted by the Levada Center in June 2005 and posted to its website: <http://www.levada.ru/press/2005070410.html>. The Levada Center is a widely respected independent public opinion survey firm.

11. From a survey in 2005 by the All-Russia Center for the Study of Public Opinion (VTsIOM) and reported by RFE/RL Newsline, 7 March 2005.

12. From a survey conducted by the Levada Center in January 2005 and posted to its website: <http://www.levada.ru/press/2005031100.html>.

13. Nationwide survey results conducted by the Public Opinion Foundation, reported by RFE/RL Newsline, 10 December 2001.

14. James L. Gibson, "The Resilience of Support for Democratic Institutions and Processes in the Nascent Russian and Ukrainian Democracies," in Vladimir Tismaneanu, ed., *Political Culture and Civil Society in Russia and the New States of Eurasia* (Armonk, NY: M. E. Sharpe, 1995), 57.

15. Yuri Levada, "Svoboda ot vybora? Postelektoral'nye razmyshleniia," published on website Polit.ru, 18 May 2004.

16. Levada Center, survey conducted October 2005; posted to website: <http://www.levada.ru/press/2005110901.html>.

17. L. Sedov, "Obshchestvenno-politicheskaia situatsiia v Rossii v iune 2004," from website of Levada Center <http://www.levada.ru/press/2004071402.print.html>.

18. Richard Rose, Neil Munro, and William Mishler, "Resigned Acceptance of an Incomplete Democracy: Russia's Political Equilibrium," *Post-Soviet Affairs* 20, no. 3 (2004): 195–218.

19. Richard Rose and Neil Munro, *Elections Without Order: Russia's Challenge to Vladimir Putin* (Cambridge: Cambridge University Press, 2002), 237.

20. Donna Bahry, "Society Transformed? Rethinking the Social Roots of Perestroika," *Slavic Review* 52, no. 3 (1993): 512–54.

21. Elena Lisovskaya and Vyacheslav Karpov, "New Ideologies in Postcommunist Russian Textbooks." *Comparative Education Review* 43, no. 4 (1999): 522–32.

22. RFE/RL Newsline, 1 December, 2003.

23. RFE/RL Newsline, 15 February 2006; 31 August 2006.

24. Daron Acemoglu and James A. Robinson, *Economic Origins of Dictatorship and Democracy* (Cambridge: Cambridge University Press, 2006); for studies of the effects of inequality on democracy in the United States, see Theda Skocpol and Lawrence R. Jacobs, *Inequality and American Democracy: What We Know and What We Need to Learn* (New York: Russell Sage, 2005).

25. Robert D. Putnam, *Making Democracy Work: Civic Traditions in Modern Italy* (Princeton, NJ: Princeton University Press, 1993).

26. Marc Morje Howard, *The Weakness of Civil Society in Post-Communist Europe* (Cambridge: Cambridge University Press, 2003).

27. Richard Rose and Neil Munro, *Elections Without Order: Russia's Challenge to Vladimir Putin* (Cambridge: Cambridge University Press, 2002), 224–25; Richard Rose, *Getting Things Done With Social Capital: New Russia Barometer VII* (Glasgow: Center for the Study of Public Policy, University of Strathclyde, 1998), 32–33.

28. Rose, *Getting Things Done.*

29. Turnout in the December 2003 parliamentary elections was reported to be 55.45 percent and for the presidential election in March 2004, 64.4 percent. In the United States, turnout of the voting-age population for the closely contested presidential election in 2000 was 51.3 percent.

30. VTsIOM survey findings, as reported on Polit.ru website, 10 January 2001.

31. A reform sponsored by President Putin and the United Russia party has moved to eliminate the "against all" option from future elections. Although the goal is to force voters to support one of the given parties, many observers—including the chairman of the Central Election Commission—warn that this change will reduce electoral turnout.

32. Eugene Huskey, "Nomenklatura Lite? The Cadres Reserve (*Kadrovyi reserv*) in Russian Public Administration" (NCEEER Working Paper, 24 October, 2003) (Washington, DC, National Council for Eurasian and East European Research).

33. Olga Kryshtanovskaya and Stephen White, "Putin's Militocracy," *Post-Soviet Affairs* 19, no. 4 (2003): 289–306.

34. Steven L. Solnick, *Stealing the State: Control and Collapse in Soviet Institutions* (Cambridge: Harvard University Press, 1998), 112–24.

35. Igor M. Bunin, ed., *Biznesmeny Rossii: 40 istorii uspekha* (Moscow: OKO, 1994), 366.

36. Jane I. Dawson, *Eco-Nationalism: Anti-Nuclear Activism and National Identity in Russia, Lithuania, and Ukraine* (Durham, NC: Duke University Press, 1996).

37. RFE/RL Newsline, 18 April 2006.

38. In a system where all prices were set by the state, there was no meaningful measure of profit in any case. Indeed, relative prices were profoundly distorted by the cumulative effect of decades of central planning. The absence of accurate measures of economic costs is one of the major reasons that Russia's economy continues to be so slow to restructure.

39. Article 59 of the constitution provides that young men of conscription age who are conscientious objectors to war may do alternative service rather than being called up to army service. Legislation specifying how this right may be exercised finally passed in 2002.

40. Several authors have examined the effect of Western aid on NGOs in Russia and other post-Communist countries. See Sarah L. Henderson, *Building Democracy in Contemporary Russia: Western Support for Grassroots Organizations* (Ithaca, NY: Cornell University Press, 2003); Thomas Carothers and Marina Ottaway, eds., *Funding Virtue: Civil Society Aid and Democracy* (Washington, DC: Carnegie Endowment for International Peace, 2000); and Sarah E. Mendelson and John K. Glenn, eds., *The Power and Limits of NGOs: A Critical Look at Building Democracy in Eastern Europe and Eurasia* (New York: Columbia University Press, 2002).

41. The FITUR reached a Faustian bargain with the government over the terms of a new labor relations code, which was adopted in 2001. Under the new legislation, employers no longer have to obtain the consent of the unions to lay off workers. But collective bargaining will be between the largest union at each enterprise and the management unless the workers have agreed on which union will represent them. Thus the new labor code favors the FITUR at the expense of the smaller independent unions.

42. Richard Rose, *New Russia Barometer VI: After the Presidential Election* (Glasgow: Center for the Study of Public Policy, University of Strathclyde, Studies in Public Policy no. 272, 1996), 6; and Rose, *Getting Things Done,* 15. In 1996, the question was: At any point during the past 12 months, have you received your wages or pension late? In 1996, 78 percent responded yes, 21 percent no. In 1998, the question was: At any point during the past 12 months, have you received your wages late? 75 percent responded yes, 25 percent no.

43. RFE/RL Newsline, 13 January 1997; 17 January 1997; 18 February 1997; 25 November 1998; 14 January 1999; 27 January 1999; 15 September 1999; 26 June 2000.

44. Linda J. Cook, *Labor and Liberalization: Trade Unions in the New Russia* (New York: Twentieth Century Fund Press, 1997), 76–77.

45. Two recent books detailing the obstacles to the formation of a stable competitive party system are Henry Hale, *Why Not Parties in Russia?* (Cambridge: Cambridge University Press, 2006); and Regina Smyth, *Candidate Strategies and Electoral Competition in the Russian Federation: Democracy Without Foundation* (Cambridge: Cambridge University Press, 2006).

46. Stephen White, Richard Rose, and Ian McAllister, *How Russia Votes* (Chatham, NJ: Chatham House, 1997), 254.

47. White, Rose, and McAllister, *How Russia Votes,* p. 241–70.

48. Quoted from a press release of the election observer mission of the Organization for Security and Cooperation in Europe, posted to its website immediately following the election, as reported by RFE/RL Newsline, 15 March 2004.

49. For an extensive overview of the tactics used by the authorities in Russia, Ukraine, and other post-Soviet countries to manipulate elections, see Andrew Wilson, *Virtual Politics: Faking Democracy in the Post-Soviet World* (New Haven, CT: Yale University Press, 2005).

50. Joel S. Hellman, "Winners Take All: The Politics of Partial Reform in Postcommunist Transitions," *World Politics* 50, no. 1 (1998): 203–34.

51. An excellent account of the "loans for shares" program, based on interviews with many of the participants, is Chrystia Freeland, *Sale of the Century: Russia's Wild Ride From Communism to Capitalism* (New York: Crown, 2000), 169–89.

52. Joseph R. Blasi, Maya Kroumova, and Douglas Kruse, *Kremlin Capitalism: Privatizing the Russian Economy* (Ithaca, NY: Cornell University Press, 1997), 50.

53. Blasi, Kroumova, and Kruse, *Kremlin Capitalism;* and Michael McFaul, "State Power, Institutional Change, and the Politics of Privatization in Russia," *World Politics* 47 (1995): 210–43.

54. Thane Gustafson, *Capitalism Russian-Style* (Cambridge: Cambridge University Press, 1999), 2–3, 94–95.

55. "OECD Economic Survey of the Russian Federation, 2004: The Challenge of Sustaining Growth" (Paris: OECD, 2004). (from website: http://www.oecd.org/document/62/0,2340, en_2649_201185_32474302_1_1_1_1,00.html.

56. President's annual message to parliament, from Polit.ru, 26 May 2004.

57. The World Bank, *Transition: The First Ten Years—Analysis and Lessons for Eastern Europe and the Former Soviet Union* (Washington, DC: World Bank, 2002), 9.

58. REF/RL Newsline, 8 March 1999.

59. RFE/RL Newsline, 20 July 2006.

60. Russian military commanders reported that one third of the men they had called up in the fall of 2004 were unfit to serve as a result of health problems. Polit.ru, 9 December 2004.

61. A vivid portrait of a recent jury trial in Moscow is presented by Peter Baker and Susan Glasser, *Kremlin Rising: Vladimir Putin's Russia and the End of Revolution* (New York: Scribner, 2005), 231–250.

62. G. A. Satarov, *Diagnostika rossiiskoi korruptsii: Sotsiologicheskii analiz* (Moscow: Fond INDEM, 2002), 16–17.

63. Ibid., 21.

64. Joel S. Hellman, Geraint Jones, and Daniel Kaufmann, "'Seize the State, Seize the Day': State Capture, Corruption, and Influence in Transition" (Policy Research Working Paper, no. 2444) (Washington, DC: World Bank Institute, September 2000).

65. Susan Rose-Ackerman, *Corruption and Government: Causes, Consequences and Reform* (Cambridge: Cambridge University Press, 1999), 159–74.

Section 4
Chinese Politics

POLITICS IN CHINA

Melanie Manion

Country Bio

CHINA

Population
1,307.56 million

Territory
3,705,386 square miles

Year of PRC Inauguration
1949

Year of Current Constitution
1982

Head of Party and State
Hu Jintao

Head of Government
Wen Jiabao

Languages
Standard Chinese or Mandarin (Putonghua, based on the Beijing dialect), Yue (Cantonese), Wu (Shanghaiese), Minbei (Fuzhou), Minnan (Hokkien-Taiwanese), Xiang, Gan, Hakka dialects, minority languages

Religions
Daoism (Taoism), Buddhism, Muslim 2–3%, Christian 1% (est.). Note: officially atheist.

On October 1, 1949, Mao Zedong, the peasant revolutionary who had led the Chinese communists in war against the Japanese and in civil war, pronounced a basic communist victory, proclaimed a new regime, and promised a new era for China. From the centuries-old Gate of Heavenly Peace in Beijing, Mao formally inaugurated the People's Republic of China (PRC). For nearly three decades after, until his death in 1976, Mao was the chief architect and agitator for a comprehensive project of revolutionary transformation designed to lead a largely backward agrarian people to modernization, prosperity, and (ultimately) communist utopia. A few years after Mao's death, his successors officially and publicly rejected most of the premises, strategies, and outcomes of this revolutionary project, essentially declaring it a failure. They launched a new era of reform, ongoing today. Economic reform in post-Mao China is nearly as radical and dramatic as the revolutions that toppled most of the world's communist regimes in 1989 and 1990. The resulting transformation is awesome.

Without publicly abandoning the ultimate goal of communism, Mao's successors have defined their current quest mainly in pragmatic economic terms, rather than utopian ideological terms. They have identified economic growth as the nation's highest priority and the Communist Party's main assignment. To achieve this objective, the communist party-state has largely retreated from thirty years of direct administration of the economy. Openly acknowledging the superiority of the capitalist experience, Chinese reformers are promoting a **"socialist market economy,"** with a place for foreign investors, private entrepreneurs, and stock markets. More than anything else, Chinese leaders have staked their legitimacy on the performance of this new economy.

While embracing economic markets, Chinese leaders have repeatedly rejected political pluralism. The communist party-state was in clear evidence in Beijing on June 4, 1989, when the People's Liberation Army employed its tanks and machine guns to clear the streets and main public square of thousands of protesters. The regime tolerates no open challenge to the Communist Party's monopoly on political power.

For most of the 1.3 billion ordinary Chinese, political reform is mainly reflected in a new official acceptance of a private sphere and a new official toler-ance of political apathy. Compared with the Maoist years, when a taste for the music of Beethoven signi-fied dangerous "bourgeois decadence," much less in daily life today is considered political. Moreover, under the new regime, ordinary citizens need not necessarily demonstrate active support for official policies and the political system—so long as they do not engage in active opposition. Chinese leaders have not charted a road toward liberal democracy, at least not purpose-fully. Instead, the political system has become merely authoritarian in its limited reach, rather than perva-sively totalitarian.

Yet, post-Mao reform is more than the retreat of the state from the economy and the imposition of fewer demands on citizens politically. A project of institutionalization is underway in China, to cre-ate an infrastructure promoting more transparency, stability, and responsiveness. In large part, this is to encourage investment and innovation, to support the goal of economic growth. At the same time, Mao's successors are also committed to political institution-alization for political reasons: to safeguard against the arbitrary dictatorship and disruptive politics of the Maoist past. The effort has included better-crafted laws and a new legality, more assertive repre-sentative assemblies, and popularly elected grassroots leaders.

Much of China's transformation in the past quarter-century is only partly a direct result of the various policies that constitute reform. It is at least as much a by-product of these policies. Reform has set in motion processes of economic, political, and social change that appear now largely beyond the control of leaders at the political center. Consider a few examples. Eased restrictions on population movement have created a "floating population" of more than 100 million inter-nal migrants, most of them from the countryside and seeking work in towns and cities, many of them unreg-istered squatters, all of them reflecting a new relation-ship between state authority, social welfare, and market opportunity. Local governments, empowered by a new fiscal federalism, pursue local economic growth with less and less heed to central guidelines. Growth in individual wealth and a telecommunications revolu-tion have produced an astonishing 110 million Internet users in China, linking Chinese to one another and to the outside world in ways that are nearly impossible to control.

CURRENT POLICY CHALLENGES

Meeting with the president of the United States in late 2005, China's President Hu Jintao frankly acknowledged that problems of political corruption, rural unrest, a growing wealth gap, and severe pollu-tion consume nearly all his time.[1] Some of these problems represent new policy challenges for Chinese leaders; others are not new, but their magni-tude and impact have only recently been under-stood. The new and ongoing policy challenges arise very significantly from China's economic successes in the past quarter-century.

Since 1978, Chinese leaders have agreed to be judged mainly by their ability to foster economic growth and deliver a better material life for Chinese citizens. China's development has in fact been very impressive. Its economy has grown at a rate of nearly 10 percent per year since 1980, a record of sustained growth comparable only to Japan and Korea in the lat-ter half of the twentieth century. In terms of purchas-ing power parity, China is now the world's second largest economy (after the United States) and third largest recipient of foreign direct investment (largest among developing countries). In 2006, it overtook Japan as the world's biggest holder of foreign exchange reserves.

Economic success has not been costless. It has provided more opportunities to pursue private gain, legally and also illegally through the abuse of public office. Despite decades of anticorruption efforts, year after year, ordinary citizens tell pollsters that corrup-tion is one of China's most serious problems. In the cities, Chinese poke fun at the perceived insincerity of the anticorruption reforms: "not daring *not* to fight corruption, not daring to fight corruption seriously." In the countryside, villagers rise up to protest abuses of power by "local emperors" imposing illegal fees and excessive taxes.

In recent years, the requisition, rezoning, and sale of agricultural land by local governments has pro-voked rural riots, usually suppressed with great vio-lence. Land is not privately owned, but contracted for agricultural use by Chinese farmers. Local govern-ments have seized on more lucrative opportunities for land use provided by real estate and industrial devel-opment. Farmers tend to be poorly compensated in these instances of eminent domain for local economic development (and local government profit). Top

Chinese leaders have condemned these actions, not least of all because arable land is already scarce.

The growing wealth gap fuels the perceptions of official abuse. Chinese policymakers have promoted a policy that "some get rich first." One result is rapidly rising inequality. Rural incomes are about 30 percent of urban incomes, and coastal regions have been advantaged over the interior. Urban Chinese in modern Shanghai enjoy annual incomes exceeding $2,000, while rural Chinese in backward Guizhou province make do with $200. Poorer Chinese deeply resent the newly conspicuous economic inequalities of the socialist market economy. While some struggle for a basic livelihood, there are also Chinese entrepreneurs and venal officials who travel in luxury sedans, do business on cellular phones, and feast ostentatiously at expensive restaurants. In 2006, Chinese authorities admitted to a Gini coefficient of 0.46, mostly reflecting a gap between urban and rural residents.[2] As the wealth gap has exploded within a single generation, it has great potential to impact social stability.

According to the Ministry of Public Security, in 2005, China experienced 87,000 "public disturbances," both urban and rural—up 7 percent from the previous year. Land takings, economic distress, and political corruption certainly provoked much of this unrest. A nontrivial number of rural "disturbances" are directed against pollution, which has displaced tens of millions of farmers.

Although the Chinese have developed a significant legal and organizational infrastructure of environmental protection in the past decade, environmental pollution and degradation have increased at a rate that far outpaces the capacity of the state to protect the environment. This reflects developmental priorities: indeed, as late as the mid-1990s, Chinese leaders routinely articulated the principle of "first development, then environment." The World Bank estimates that annually 300,000 Chinese die prematurely from air pollution. Children breath in the equivalent of smoking two packs of cigarettes per day. Sixteen of the world's twenty most polluted cities are Chinese cities—including Beijing, the site of the 2008 Olympic Games. The expanding ownership of private automobiles by the new middle class exacerbates the problem: Chinese domestically designed and manufactured automobiles emit ten to twenty times more pollutants than American or Japanese models.

As Chinese leaders confront their domestic challenges, they do so in a global context that they now actively engage. The U.S. government now uses the term "stakeholder" to describe the new role of China in the world. This has much to do with China's accession to the World Trade Organization (WTO) in 2001, which has further opened the economy, subjecting it to a new discipline of global competition and pushing development of the economic legal infrastructure. WTO accession agreements require China to fully open its banking sector to foreign investors in 2007—and this will accelerate an already rapid process of economic reform. China is not only an economic player, however. It has also shown its willingness to play a role in helping to resolve international crises, such as the production and testing of nuclear weapons by North Korea. As the only country with political influence over North Korea, China organized the six-party talks, bringing the United States to the negotiating table in a multilateral situation.

China has thoroughly abandoned the strictures of communist ideology, has experienced an awesome economic revolution, and is taking its place as an important world power. Yet, unlike most other communist regimes, which toppled in the face of popular uprisings, China has experienced no second political revolution. Today, it is still a communist party-state. Chinese policymakers have promoted limited liberalization, sometimes as an antidote to corruption at the grassroots. While they have opened up political processes to more diversified inputs, they have also firmly suppressed organized challenges to the Communist Party. A handful of leaders at the very top still monopolize the authority to choose what sorts of inputs from what sorts of groups are acceptable, and the decision rules are not always transparent.

Strikingly little remains of Mao's grand revolutionary schemes. Viewed from the perspective of the 1970s, the magnitude and pace of change in China in the past quarter-century are practically unimaginable. Chinese politics today is "post-Mao" politics in the sense that there is a new regime, not simply a change of leaders—and, given its dynamics, there appears to be no turning back. Of course, without a grasp of China's rich political history, it is not only impossible to appreciate what has (and has not) changed, but also impossible to understand the crucial context of post-Mao reform: what has been rejected.

HISTORICAL SETTING

When ordinary Chinese today are asked about what it is they, as Chinese, are most proud, many respond: "our long history." Chinese civilization emerged more than six thousand years ago. As a polity, imperial China was the longest-lived major system of governance in world history, enduring as a centralized state ruled with little change in political philosophy or bureaucratic organization for more than two millennia until the fall of the Qing, the last dynasty, in 1911.[3]

Traditional China was governed by an emperor and a unique bureaucracy of scholar-officials at the capital and in the localities, who gained their positions meritocratically through examinations that tested knowledge of the Confucian classics. Anyone was eligible to participate in the examinations, but successful performance required a classical education, usually through a private tutor, not available to most ordinary Chinese. **Confucianism** was basically a conservative philosophy. It conceived of society and the polity in terms of an ordered hierarchy of harmonious relationships. At the top of the hierarchy was the emperor, who maintained social order through his conduct as a moral exemplar. Confucianism blurred the distinction between state and society: it saw harmony (not conflict) as the natural social order; this harmony resulted because the virtuous emperor provided an example of correct conduct. Loyalty to the emperor was the highest principle in the hierarchy of relationships entailing mutual obligations throughout society.

Imperial Order to the Founding of the PRC

This remarkable imperial order began to crumble in the mid-nineteenth century, when Qing rulers proved unable to uphold their political authority and maintain territorial integrity in the presence of large-scale domestic rebellion and foreign economic and military encroachment. The republic founded in 1912 did not restore order or sovereignty to China, but effectively collapsed within a few years, as dozens of Chinese regional warlords ruling with personal armies competed for control of territory.[4] Nearly four decades of political upheaval and continuous warfare ensued, as the Chinese sought solutions to the problems of governance that had brought down the Qing.

The dominant problems were the struggle for national sovereignty and the struggle for peasant livelihood. The former involved two sorts of claims:

cession of Chinese territory in treaties imposed forcibly by Western powers beginning in the nineteenth century, and outright military invasion and occupation by the Japanese in the 1930s. As to the Chinese peasantry, poverty in the countryside due to socioeconomic conditions of exorbitant taxes, high rents, and usurious credit was aggravated by frequent floods and droughts, which usually brought ruin. An observer compared the condition of the Chinese peasant to a man standing up to his neck in water: one ripple would drown him.[5]

These two struggles were played out in the context of a competition to unify the country. By the 1920s, the **Nationalist Party** and army had emerged as the most prominent political and military force in the country. The Nationalists had their strongest social base in the urban areas; in the countryside, they were mainly dependent on the support of the landlord class. This largely explains Nationalist reluctance to implement land and social reforms to resolve the problems of Chinese peasants. Peasant poverty was exacerbated by absentee landlordism and the replacement of ties of mutual obligation with economic ties enforced by managing agents. Land distribution was not part of the Nationalist agenda; nor were tax controls or provision of cheap credit effectively implemented.

Between 1924 and 1927, the Nationalists allied with the communists in a battle to eliminate regional warlords and to unify China. By the late 1920s, the Nationalists had practically realized this aim. In 1927, they broke their alliance with the communists in a violent massacre that reduced the Communist Party from nearly 58,000 to 10,000 members. The break inaugurated a new civil war. In the end, the Nationalists were forced to retreat to the island of Taiwan in 1949.

By contrast with the Nationalists, the intellectual revolutionaries who founded the **Chinese Communist Party** in 1921 were unlikely contenders for power. The rise and eventual victory of the communists owe much to historic opportunities in the 1930s and 1940s. These opportunities were available for other forces to exploit too, but the communists exploited them best.[6] **Mao Zedong** emerged as leader of the communists in the mid-1930s, consolidating his leadership in the early 1940s.[7]

After the Nationalist attack in 1927, many communists retreated to the countryside. Mao had already reported on the spontaneous impulse for radical social change among the peasantry and had proposed a revolutionary strategy different from that suggested by communist theory or Russian experience. Mao rejected the idea that the Chinese communists could win power through a revolution of the small urban working class in China. Instead, he argued, a communist victory could be achieved only by providing leadership for a nascent rural revolution and building a guerrilla Red Army to surround the cities with the countryside. From a base in southeastern China, Mao and other communists implemented a program of political education and social change, including land redistribution. In 1934, a major Nationalist offensive forced them on a strategic retreat, the historic Long March, that ended at the caves of Yanan in China's northwest, where Mao and his communist forces, their numbers literally decimated, established their headquarters. From Yanan, they built on the strategy of rural revolution to further develop support in the countryside.

The second indispensable component in communist victory was the 1937 Japanese invasion of central China, beyond territory in the northeast that the Japanese had occupied since 1931.[8] Mao seized the strategic initiative to call for a truce in the civil war so that Chinese could unite to resist Japanese aggression. Nationalist leaders were initially wary. This combination of Nationalist reluctance and strong anti-Japanese sentiment in the cities and countryside earned the communists enormous popularity as the true nationalist resistance to foreign aggression. From 1937 to 1945, the communists grew in force from 40,000 to more than a million. Japanese defeat in World War II ended the alliance between Nationalists and communists. A new civil war began.[9] In four years, the communists won victory, as peasant revolutionaries and Chinese nationalists. Once in power, they turned their energies to the construction of socialism.

History of the PRC

The history of the People's Republic of China (PRC) can be divided into three major periods. In the first, between 1949 and 1957, the Chinese adopted a "lean to one side" strategy, emulating the experience of the first and most powerful communist state, the Soviet Union. The second period began in 1958, when the Chinese introduced their own model of revolutionary development. Except for a few years at the beginning of the 1960s, this Maoist model prevailed until Mao's

death in 1976. A short transitional period ensued, during which immediate problems of policy orientation and leadership succession were resolved with the arrest and trial of key radical leaders. In December 1978, the third period, a new era of reform, ongoing today, was inaugurated with a Central Committee declaration favoring learning from practical experience and rejecting the ideological constraints of Maoism—or any theory.[10] **Deng Xiaoping,** China's new "paramount leader," charted and presided over the reforms. In the same sense that Chinese politics in the two decades ending in 1976 are appropriately characterized as the Maoist years, the last two decades of the twentieth century belong most to Deng—despite important differences in the power of these two leaders and how they wielded it.

"Lean to One Side" The Chinese communists had won power largely by ignoring Soviet advice. Once in power, however, they looked to the Soviet Union for a plan to build socialism. They concluded a treaty of friendship and alliance in 1950. Soviet financial aid to China in the 1950s was not large. Mainly, aid was given in a massive technology transfer: over 12,000 Soviet engineers and technicians were sent to work in China; over 6,000 Chinese studied in Soviet universities, tens of thousands more in Soviet factories on short-term training courses. With this Soviet assistance, the Chinese developed heavy industry, establishing a centralized bureaucracy of planning agencies and industrial ministries to manage the economy according to five-year plans. They nationalized private industry. In the early 1950s, they sent communists down to the grassroots to instigate and organize land reform, a violent "class struggle." Each peasant household was classified according to land holdings, and land seized from landlords was redistributed to poor peasants, the majority of the peasantry.[11] Agricultural collectivization followed. This process was also essentially coercive, especially in its later stages, but not as violent as land reform.

The "lean to one side" period did feature some Maoist strategies, especially in political participation and socialization. The Chinese implemented many policies by mobilizing the masses in intensive campaigns, with essentially compulsory participation. For the Chinese communists, potential regime opponents—such as intellectuals and capitalists—were capable of being politically transformed through practices such as "thought reform." Communist leaders were sufficiently confident about the results of political education and regime accomplishments to invite nonparty intellectuals to voice criticism in the Hundred Flowers Campaign in 1957. When criticism was harsh, revealing weak support for the communist system, the leaders quickly reversed themselves. They launched an Anti-Rightist Campaign, which discovered more "poisonous weeds" than "blooming flowers." About a half million people, many of them intellectuals, were persecuted as "rightists" in a campaign that effectively silenced political opposition for twenty years.[12] Mass campaigns, political education, and political labeling were all coercive measures that resulted in the persecution of millions. To some extent, this coercion had a characteristic Maoist (and Confucian) element: fundamentally, it rejected the Stalinist version of political purge as physical liquidation, because it viewed the individual as malleable and ultimately educable. Yet, "enemies of the people" were not spared: one million to three million landlords and "counterrevolutionaries" were persecuted to death in the early 1950s alone.

In 1956, frictions in relations with the Soviet Union began to develop. Tensions increased throughout the 1950s, resulting in the withdrawal of aid and advisers and a Sino-Soviet split that shocked the world in 1960. Major irritants included Soviet reluctance to support efforts to "liberate" Taiwan, Soviet unwillingness to aid China's nuclear development, and a relaxation of Soviet hostility toward the United States. At about the same time, Mao was reconsidering his view of the Soviet model of development and developing his own radical model of building communism.

Great Leap Forward The first five-year plan had invested in heavy industry, not agriculture. Following the Soviet model, central planners had not diverted resources from industry to promote agricultural growth. In 1958, Mao proposed a strategy of simultaneous development of industry and agriculture to be achieved in two ways: (1) the labor-intensive mass mobilization of peasants to increase agricultural output by building irrigation facilities, and (2) the organization of primitive production processes to give inputs to agriculture (such as small chemical fertilizer plants and primitive steel furnaces to make tools) without taking resources from industry. A crucial element of Mao's solution was an increase in size of the collective

farms. In order to build irrigation facilities, local communist officials needed to control a labor force of large numbers of peasants, larger than the current collectives that grouped together a few hundred households. By combining several collectives into one gigantic farm, Mao hoped to realize economies of scale. In 1958, with prodding from above, the people's communes were born, grouping together thousands of households in one unit of economic and political organization managed by Communist Party officials.

The Maoist model was not simply an economic development strategy. It was fundamentally a political campaign, a point exemplified in the main slogan of the **Great Leap Forward:** "politics in command."[13] The Great Leap Forward abandoned most material rewards for moral incentives. By 1958, in Mao's view, Chinese peasants had demonstrated tremendous enthusiasm and were ready to leap into communism, if properly mobilized by local leaders. In the politically charged climate, economic expertise was denigrated and caution criticized as lack of faith in the masses. Leaders in Beijing set output targets high, demanding that local leaders believe in the ability of the Chinese people to accomplish miracles. By implication, failure to achieve high targets could be due only to poor leadership. A dangerous vicious cycle was set in motion: local leaders competed to demonstrate their political correctness; when communes failed to meet targets set in Beijing, local leaders calculated output imaginatively to report targets had been met or exceeded; production results were increasingly exaggerated as reports went to higher and higher levels; the response from Beijing to the falsely reported leap in output was a further leap in targets.

In 1958, dislocation associated with forming the communes and peasant mobilization to help meet high steel output targets by making steel in primitive furnaces was so great that the autumn harvest was not all gathered. That year too, a false belief in excess production led to reduction in areas sown in grain. Even with reduced acreage, peasant contributions to agricultural labor were decreasing due to physical exhaustion, weak material rewards, and the abolition of private plots (and, in some cases, private property for complete communization). In 1959, when top Chinese leaders met to consider these problems, the Minister of National Defense criticized radicalism in policy implementation. In response, Mao accused the minister of factionalism, turned the meeting into a referendum on his leadership, and challenged others to dare to attack the Leap's radical principles.

The meeting was a terrible turning point. With political correctness reasserted, radicalism returned. Moreover, just as the 1957 antirightist campaign had silenced opposition outside the party, Mao's 1959 accusations and threats effectively silenced opposition in the top echelons of party leadership.[14] That same year, large parts of China suffered from severe drought, others from severe flooding, in one of the worst natural disasters experienced in decades.

Retreat From the Leap Over the next three years, the famine cost an estimated 27 million lives.[15] China retreated from Maoist radicalism. Mao retreated from day-to-day management of public affairs, but continued in his position as Communist Party chairman. In the early 1960s, the communes ceased to be relevant to agricultural production. Instead, peasant households contracted with the state for production, selling the surplus in newly established free markets. In industry, there was a renewed reliance on material incentives, technical expertise, and profitability as the standard to judge performance. The education system emphasized the creation of a knowledgeable and highly skilled corps of managers and leaders. Policy processes took into account advice by experts, rather than reliance on mass miracles.

Cultural Revolution By the mid-1960s, Mao had further developed his radical critique of the Soviet model and extended it to the Chinese experience. In China, Mao saw a "new class" of economic managers and political officials, privileged by elitist policies that increased social antagonisms. In 1966, Mao argued that many communist leaders (notably, China's head of state, Liu Shaoqi, but also others, including Deng Xiaoping) were corrupt "capitalist roaders" who opposed socialism and must be thrown out of power. He launched the Great Proletarian Cultural Revolution, yet another exercise in radical excess. The **Cultural Revolution** was simultaneously a power struggle, an ideological battle, and a mass campaign to transform culture. Compared with the Great Leap Forward, its impact on the Chinese economy was minor; its impact on society was devastating.

For Mao, the enemy of socialism was within the Communist Party. Unable to rely on the party to correct

Defense Minister Lin Biao sits beside Chairman Mao Zedong and Premier Zhou Enlai during the Cultural Revolution. PLA soldiers wave the Little Red Book of quotations from Chairman Mao, a reflection of the cult of Mao that Lin helped to build.

SV Bilderdienst/The Image Works

its mistakes, Mao instructed secondary school and university students to overturn "bourgeois culture" and "bombard the headquarters." The Communist Party became effectively powerless as an organization. For the first time since 1949, Chinese were free to organize politically. Unconstrained by the party, Chinese engaged in political action legitimated by their own interpretations of Mao Zedong Thought. Students formed radical Red Guard groups to criticize and persecute victims, often chosen quite arbitrarily or for reasons more personal than political. In schools, factories, and government agencies, those in power were criticized and persecuted. Persecution was frequently physical. It was not uncommon for victims to be held in makeshift prisons, forced to do harsh manual labor, and subjected to violent public "struggle sessions" to force them to confess their crimes. Many were "struggled" to death, and many others committed suicide. Factional fighting was inevitable, as rival Red Guard groups fought for power, each faction claiming true representation of Mao Zedong Thought.[16]

In 1967, the country was near anarchy. The schools had been shut down; most party and government offices no longer functioned; transportation and communications were severely disrupted; factional struggles were increasingly violent contests, some of them armed confrontations. Having unleashed social conflict, Mao had been able to manipulate it—but not to control it. Mao called on the army to restore order, a process that began in 1969.

The 1970s were years of more moderate conflict, mostly played out as a struggle at the apex of power rather than in society generally. Radical leaders (including Mao's wife) who had risen to power in the Cultural Revolution supported a continuation of radical policies. Other leaders, reinstated by Mao to balance the power of the radicals, supported policies of economic modernization. The conflict was ongoing at the time of Mao's death in 1976. Within two years, the economic modernizers had won. China embarked on a new course of reform, different from anything in the experience of any communist system.

SOCIAL CONDITIONS

Chinese society has changed in various ways since the communists came to power. These changes include social structural transformations engineered by the regime, especially in the early decades. This section focuses on basic features that make up the social environment for Chinese politics that have not undergone fundamental transformation but have changed only in degree, if at all.

First among these is China's huge population. When the communists came to power in 1949, China's population was 540 million. Today China remains the world's most populous country, with a population of 1.3 billion. As in the 1950s, most Chinese live in the countryside, although the proportion has been changing more rapidly in recent years. In the 1950s, about 85 percent of Chinese lived in the countryside; by 1980 that proportion had decreased only slightly, to 82 percent. More than two decades of economic reform produced significant transformation. De facto relaxation of rural to urban migration restrictions liberated the underemployed farming population to seek work in cities. Rural industrialization and the growth of towns also changed the situation. By 2005, only 57 percent of Chinese lived in the countryside. An increasing proportion of this rural population work at least part-time in industry. Before economic reforms in the 1980s, state-owned enterprises dominated industry in China. Today, rural collective industry, in the form of township and village enterprises under the direction of local governments, is the most dynamic industrial sector.

The second basic feature involves geography. Although China is the world's second largest country in area, the population is concentrated in the eastern third of the land. This is largely because only about a quarter of China's land is arable. Population growth and reduction in cultivated area have greatly exacerbated the land shortage. Despite efforts to preserve arable land for farming, China's leaders have been unable to reverse the reduction in cultivated area. In part, this is a result of agricultural decollectivization and a return to household farming: land is used for property borders, burial grounds, and bigger houses. In recent years, local government land requisitions for lucrative residential and industrial development have further reduced arable land and provoked much rural unrest. The basic problem of feeding China's large population can be expected to continue to loom large as more Chinese grow prosperous and change their diet: eating more, and eating more meat and less grain.

The third feature is that China is a multiethnic state. At least 92 percent of Chinese are ethnically Han, but there are fifty-five recognized **ethnic minorities,** ranging in number from a few thousand to more than 16 million. Although minorities make up only a fairly small proportion of China's population, areas in which minorities live comprise more than 60 percent of China's territory, and much of this is in strategically important border regions.[17] This includes Tibet (bordering India) and Xinjiang (bordering three new post-Soviet states), which have experienced fairly continuous minority unrest over the decades. The Chinese have maintained considerable armed forces in these areas to quell secessionist efforts.

Finally, Han Chinese share the same Chinese written language, a unifying force in China for more than two millennia, practically defining what it is to be Chinese. The same written language is spoken in many different dialects, however, often making communication difficult. Mandarin, based on the dialect of the Beijing locality, is the official language promoted by the communist regime through the education system and mass media.

STRUCTURE OF THE PARTY-STATE

From top to bottom, Chinese politics has changed noticeably since the Maoist period. Yet, the essential form of the Chinese political system retains an organizational design borrowed decades ago from the Soviet Union and developed nearly a century ago in Russia by Lenin—the design of the communist **party-state.**

Design Features

Lenin viewed political legitimacy in ways that justify a monopoly of power by a communist party elite that is not popularly elected. He believed that ordinary citizens do not understand their own real interests and that larger interests of society are not best advanced by aggregating interests that citizens articulate. According to Lenin, as ordinary citizens typically lack revolutionary consciousness and knowledge of communist theory, they are incapable of making the correct choices that will lead from capitalism to socialism and toward communism—a utopia characterized by a high level of economic prosperity, an absence of social conflict, and a minimal role for government. Lenin proposed a solution to this problem: a political party and political system built on the principles of guardianship and hierarchy.[18] To these two principles, Chinese leaders

added the idea of the mass line, formulated by Mao in the 1940s. Guardianship and hierarchy define the communist party-state. The mass line adds another dimension, which moderates guardianship.

Guardianship describes the main relationship between the Communist Party and society. The party bases its claim to legitimate rule not on representation of the expressed preferences of a majority but on representation of the "historical best interests" of all the people. In theory, as most ordinary citizens do not know their best interests, society is best led by an elite vanguard party with a superior understanding of the historical laws of development. The Communist Party is therefore an exclusive organization—in China, membership is about 5 percent of the population—not a mass political party with membership open to all. The notion of Communist Party leadership is explicitly set forth in each of the four Chinese constitutions promulgated since 1949, as is some version of the notion of dictatorship. Currently, the constitution describes the political system as a socialist state under the "people's democratic dictatorship." As the Communist Party is the only organization with the politically correct knowledge to lead society, it is the authoritative arbiter of the interests of the people. In effect, dictatorship in the name of the people is Communist Party dictatorship. Party leaders today are more informed of public opinion than in the past, but there is no place in the Chinese political system (or in Leninist theory) for organized opposition to Communist Party leadership.

Chinese Communist Party guardianship is, in theory, informed by the practice of the **mass line.** The party leads, but its leadership is not isolated from the opinions and preferences of the mass public. The degree to which mass preferences actually find expression in public policy depends on their fit with larger goals determined by party leaders. Party leaders at all levels (but especially at the grassroots) are supposed to maintain a close relationship with ordinary citizens so that the party organization can transform the "scattered and unsystematic ideas" of the masses into "correct ideas" and propagate them "until the masses embrace them as their own." In this way, policy is supposed to flow "from the masses to the masses."[19]

Party Organization The internal organization of the Communist Party is organized around a hierarchy of party congresses and committees extending from the top of the system down to the grassroots. Lower party organizations are subordinate to higher party organizations, and individual party members are subordinate to the party as an organization. Inner-party rules for decisionmaking are based on the Leninist principle of **democratic centralism.**

In democratic centralism, democracy refers mainly to consultation. It requires that party leaders provide opportunities for discussion, criticism, and proposals in party organizations (often including lower party organizations) as part of the normal process of deciding important issues or making policy.

Centralism requires unified discipline throughout the party: top-level official party decisions are binding on party organizations and members. Centralism is never sacrificed to democracy. Party members are allowed to hold personal views contrary to party decisions and to voice them through proper party channels, but they are not free to act in ways that promote these views. According to the Communist Party constitution, the formation of "factions" or any sort of "small group activity" within the party is a punishable violation of organizational discipline. Communist Party hierarchy and the requirement that party members observe party discipline are designed as organizational guarantees that the party, in exercising leadership over society, acts as a unified force, responsive to the leadership of the highest level of party organization.

Ideology is today both less prominent and less coherent in Chinese politics than it was in the past. The principles of guardianship, hierarchy, and the mass line are not inconsequential abstractions, however. They have concrete practical implications, evident throughout the Chinese political system. Change in the system is evident too, of course, both as a product and by-product of policies of reform in the past two decades. Yet, while the political reforms of recent decades are not trivial, they do not add up to fundamental systemic change. For now, as in the past, the design of the communist party-state is a fair model of the organization of political power in China.

Two Hierarchies, with Party Leadership The design of the communist party-state is perhaps most evident in the organization of power in two hierarchies of political structures, illustrated in Figure 13.1. The focus in this section is politics at the national level, what the Chinese refer to as the political center of the system, but government structures are more or less duplicated at each level of the political system by Communist Party structures. In principle, there is a division of labor between party and government structures. In practice, the two often perform similar functions, with party structures and party officials exercising leadership over parallel government structures and government officials. This section on political structures distinguishes the party from the government, while elaborating on the variety of mechanisms the party uses to exercise control over officials in party and government structures. The following sections on policymaking and policy implementation emphasize that, because of the interconnectedness of party and government, distinctions between party and government are of only limited use in understanding decisionmaking in China. Both party and government structures have changed since 1949. The description in the following section focuses on the system that emerged in the reform era.

Government Structures

At the political center in Beijing, the key government structures are the **National People's Congress (NPC),** which is China's legislature, and the **State Council,** which exercises executive functions. Under the State Council are government ministries and commissions, which have ranged in number from thirty-two to 100 since 1949. Below the political center, government structures extend downward in a five-tiered hierarchy consisting of 31 provinces, 333 large cities, 2,862 counties, 41,636 townships, and 629,000 villages. Local government structures (local people's congresses, local governments, and government departments) are found at the provincial, municipal, county, and township levels. The provincial level includes four megacities (Beijing, Shanghai, Tianjin, and Chongqing). As shown in Figure 13.1, Chinese voters elect delegates to township and county people's congresses only. Municipal, provincial, and national congress delegates are elected by congresses one level down. At all five levels, congress delegates elect their governments. Villages are popularly elected self-governing rural grassroots organizations, not part of the formal government hierarchy.

National People's Congress According to the constitution, the highest organization of state authority is the NPC.[20] The NPC and its permanent body, the NPC Standing Committee, exercise legislative functions.

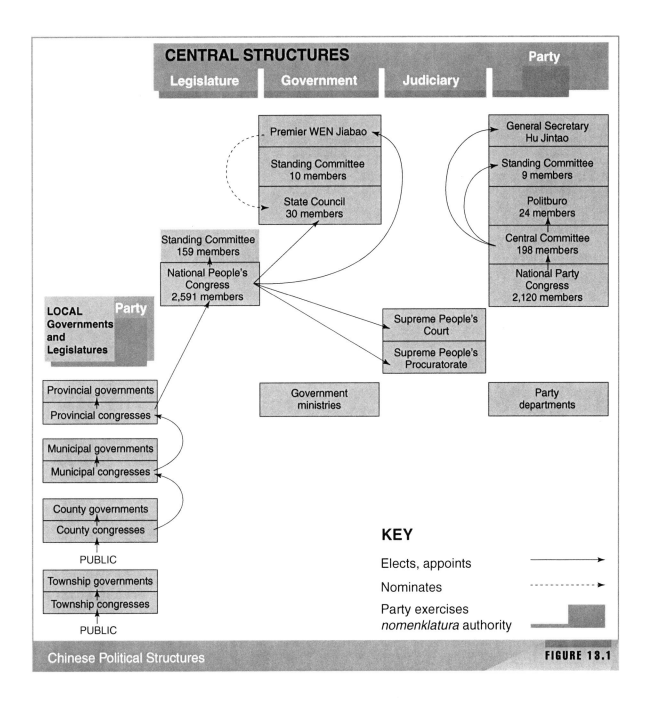

CENTRAL STRUCTURES — Chinese Political Structures — FIGURE 13.1

NPC delegates are elected for five-year terms by delegates in provincial-level congresses and the armed forces. Normally, NPC delegates assemble once annually for a plenary session of about two weeks (although they did not meet at all between 1965 and 1975). The number and composition of delegates are prescribed by law, but the NPC has always been huge. In 1986, the law set a ceiling of 3,000 delegates, which is about the

number elected to each congress since 1983. By law, urban Chinese are overrepresented: a 1995 law set the ratio of rural to urban Chinese per NPC delegate at 4:1—already less unequal than in previous years, due to legal change as well as urbanization.

Formally, the NPC has extensive powers, including amendment of the constitution, passage and amendment of legislation, approval of economic plans and government work reports, and appointment of top state and government leaders. For most of the year, when the NPC is not in session, its Standing Committee of about 150 members, who reside in Beijing and meet regularly throughout the year, serves as the working legislative assembly. The 1982 constitution considerably strengthened the role of the NPC Standing Committee. It now exercises all but the most formal powers of the NPC and prepares the agenda for the annual NPC plenary sessions, when the full NPC typically ratifies its interim legislative actions.

Is the NPC (and its Standing Committee) a "rubber stamp" assembly? For the Maoist years, the answer is clearly "yes." In recent decades, however, the NPC has become more assertive, and its Standing Committee has assumed a greater role in law making. This is part of political reform undertaken in response to the extreme institutional nihilism of the Cultural Revolution. NPC assertiveness is evident in an increase in delegate motions (by an order of magnitude) and, more significantly, in dissenting votes. The practice of unanimous approval, once automatic, has ended, sometimes with embarrassing results. In 1998, 45 percent of NPC delegates demonstrated their disapproval of the government's failure to control corruption by abstaining or voting against the work report of the chief procurator. While this high level of dissent remains unusual for votes on work reports, economic plans, and official appointments, dissenting votes of 20 to 30 percent on draft laws are not uncommon. Actual failure to pass legislation submitted to the NPC has occurred twice: a draft of the controversial Enterprise Bankruptcy Law was voted down in 1986, and a very restrictive draft of the Law on Public Demonstrations was voted down not long after the crushing of the 1989 mass protests. Both laws were sent back for substantial revision before securing the requisite majority approval in the NPC. A dramatic example of the new view of NPC authority occurred in 1989, when Hu Jiwei circulated a petition among fellow NPC Standing Committee members to call an emergency meeting of the NPC to exercise its constitutional power to repeal martial law.

The full NPC cannot be expected to function routinely as a credible legislature because it is too large and meets too infrequently and briefly. More important is the lawmaking role of the less cumbersome NPC Standing Committee. In the early 1980s, many party and government elders retired from important positions in central and provincial administration to the NPC Standing Committee. Instead of retreating from political life, these elders used the Standing Committee as a channel for political influence. Their enhanced role was institutionalized with the establishment of a Legislative Affairs Committee (with significant staff) and eight permanent specialized legislative committees to consider draft legislation. With these changes, the NPC (and its Standing Committee) can no longer be dismissed as a rubber stamp. The legislature remains institutionally weak, however, for two main reasons (discussed later in this chapter): the practice of executive-led government (which does not distinguish the Chinese system from parliamentary systems in other countries) and the practice of Communist Party leadership (which is more fundamental).

State Council In lawmaking, the State Council is the center of government activity, although this role too is newly enhanced.[21] The State Council is composed of the premier, who is head of government, and his cabinet of vice-premiers, state councillors, ministers, auditor general, and secretary general (currently thirty-six members, all formally nominated by the premier and appointed by the NPC). In 2003, Wen Jiabao became premier. The State Council has its own Standing Committee, which meets twice weekly, with members reporting on work in their assigned portfolios. As in parliamentary systems, the bulk of legislation is drafted by specialized ministries and commissions under the direction of the cabinet. Also, however, as most Chinese laws are drafted in general and imprecise language, they require detailed "implementing regulations" to have any effect. These regulations are typically drafted by State Council ministries (under the direction of the newly reestablished State Council Legislation Bureau) and promulgated by the ministries or State Council without consideration by the NPC or its Standing Committee.

Communist Party Leadership The Communist Party exercises direct leadership over government and legislative functions in a variety of ways. Before the NPC assembles, party leaders convene a meeting of all delegates who are members of the Communist Party (73 percent of NPC delegates in 2006). At these meetings, leaders discuss the NPC agenda and offer "hopes" of the party leaders for the forthcoming session, including suggestions about the tone (how open or restrained

NPC debate should be, for example). Also, NPC powers of appointment are effectively nullified by party control over candidate nomination and the usual practice of an equal number of candidates and positions. For example, although the NPC formally appoints the president, vice president, premier, and cabinet members, there has never been more than one nominee for these positions and candidate nomination is decided at the party meeting convened before the NPC assembles. The only positions for which NPC elections have ever featured choice are the 1988 and 1998 elections to the NPC Standing Committee. Those elections featured no choice for positions of leadership, however, and only limited choice for regular NPC Standing Committee membership (about 6 percent more candidates than positions).

As to lawmaking, Communist Party leaders have veto power over all legislation of consequence. The system of party review of legislation that emerged in the early 1990s rejects party micromanagement of the State Council or NPC Standing Committee work. Nonetheless, all important laws, constitutional amendments, and political laws submitted to the NPC or its Standing Committee must have prior approval by the party center. In short, the Chinese system is executive-led government, but with an important difference having to do with the role of the Communist Party.

The president of the PRC is head of state. This is a purely ceremonial office, held by **Hu Jintao.** Hu is also head of the Communist Party organization and of the Central Military Commission, in which leadership of military forces is formally vested. The commission was established as a government structure only in 1982, but its Communist Party counterpart functioned long before then and remains in existence, with the same membership in party and government structures.

Judiciary Judicial authority rests with the Supreme People's Court at the center and with local people's courts below. Formally, the Supreme People's Court is responsible to the NPC. Courts at lower levels are responsible to the people's congresses at their respective levels and also take direction from courts above them.

The Supreme People's Procuratorate, restored in 1978 after decades of neglect, is the central procuratorial agency. It sits at the top of a hierarchy of procuratorates extending down to the county level, each

formally responsible to a local people's congress and each also under the direction of the procuratorate above. The Supreme People's Procuratorate is responsible to the NPC.

Procuratorates act as a bridge between public security agencies and the courts. They supervise criminal investigations, approve arrests, and prosecute cases. Beginning in the mid-1980s, the most important role of the procuratorates has been investigation and prosecution of corruption. In each new congress session, the NPC appoints the chief justice of the Supreme People's Court and the chief procurator.

Party Structures

At the political center in Beijing, the key party structures are the National Party Congress and its Central Committee, the Politburo, and the Politburo Standing Committee. In addition, party departments are organized under a secretariat. Below the center, down to the township level, are local party congresses and local party committees.

National Party Congress As in the government hierarchy, while the formal power of Communist Party structures is directly proportional to size, actual impact on policy is inversely proportional to size. The Communist Party constitution vests supreme authority in the **National Party Congress,** but this structure is too big and meets too infrequently to play a significant role in political decisionmaking. The Central Committee determines the number of congress delegates and the procedures for their election. Since 1949, National Party Congresses have ranged in size from one to two thousand delegates, with recent congresses at about two thousand delegates. In the past, the congresses met irregularly, but party constitutions since 1969 have stipulated that congresses are normally convened at five-year intervals. This has been more or less the practice since 1969 and has been strictly observed in the post-Mao years, as shown in Table 13.1. The seventeenth party congress meets in October 2007.

National Party Congress sessions are short, about a week or two at most. A main function is to ratify important changes in broad policy orientation already decided by more important smaller party structures. Although party congresses yield no surprises, these changes receive their highest formal endorsement at

Chinese Communist Party Congresses and Growth of Party Membership, 1921–2005		**TABLE 13.1**
Congress	**Year**	**Party Members**
1st	1921	More than 50
2nd	1922	123
3rd	1923	432
4th	1925	950
5th	1927	57,900[a]
6th	1928	40,000
7th	1945	1.2 million
Founding of the PRC, 1949		
8th	1956	11 million
9th	1969	22 million
10th	1973	28 million
11th	1977	35 million
12th	1982	40 million
13th	1987	46 million
14th	1992	51 million
15th	1997	58 million
16th	2002	66 million
	2005	71 million

[a] Communist party membership dropped from 57,900 to 10,000 after April 1927, when the Nationalists broke the "united front" with the communists in a massacre that decimated communist forces and ignited civil war.

Source: *Beijing Review*, 41, no. 8 (1998): 22; *People's Daily*, 2 September 2002, and 19 June 2006.

the party congresses. Therefore, the sessions have the public appearance of major historic events. A second function of the National Party Congress is to elect the **Central Committee,** which exercises the powers of the congress between sessions. Official candidates for Central Committee membership are determined by the Politburo before the congress meets. According to the 1982 party constitution, elections to the Central Committee are by secret ballot, and wide deliberation and discussion of candidates precedes them. Of course, centralism prevails: elections rarely offer choice (or much choice) among candidates.

Central Committee The Central Committee is the Chinese political elite, broadly defined: it is a collection of the most powerful several hundred political leaders in the country. All Central Committee members hold some major substantive position of leadership, as

ministers in the central state bureaucracy or provincial party leaders, for example. Membership on the Central Committee reflects this political power—it does not confer it. In this sense, the Central Committee is less important intrinsically as a political structure than extrinsically, for the different sorts of interests and constituencies represented by its members.

Although the Central Committee does not initiate policy, changes in policy or leaders at the political center must be approved by it. This is done fairly routinely at plenary sessions now convened at least annually. Party leaders at the top rely on the bureaucratic and regional elites on the Central Committee to ensure that the "party line" is realized in practice. Central Committee membership brings these elites into the process as participants and, in effect, guarantors: in endorsing party policy, members also take on responsibility for its realization.

Politburo The Central Committee elects the **Politburo,** the Politburo Standing Committee, and the party general secretary—all of whom are also Central Committee members. These leaders are at the very apex of the political system. The composition of these structures is determined by party leaders before the party congress, and elections are mainly ceremonial, featuring no candidate choice. The Politburo is the top political elite, usually no more than two dozen leaders, most of whom have responsibility for overseeing policymaking in some issue area. Its inner circle is the Politburo Standing Committee, typically no more than a half-dozen leaders, who meet about once weekly, in meetings convened and chaired by the party general secretary. Members of the Politburo and its Standing Committee are the core political decision-makers in China, presiding over a process that concentrates great power at the top.

Top Leader and the Succession Problem Since the abolition of the position of party chairman in 1982, the top party leader is the general secretary, a position held by Hu Jintao since 2002 (see Box 13.1). The change in terminology reflects the effort to promote collective leadership, a reaction against norms of past years when Mao presided as nearly all-powerful chairman of the party until his death in 1976. Yet, if general secretaries in the 1980s and 1990s have been less powerful than Chairman Mao, this has mainly to do with the unusual elite politics of the post-Mao

BOX 13.1

Hu Jintao and the "Fourth Generation" of Leaders

In November 2002, Jiang Zemin relinquished to Hu Jintao the office of Communist Party general secretary. This event marked the first time in PRC history that the transfer of party leadership occurred as a regular matter at a party congress, rather than as a result of the death or political purge of the incumbent. Hu succeeded Jiang in his other offices in the years that followed: the presidency of the PRC in 2003, the chairmanship of the party Central Military Commission in 2004, and the chairmanship of the government Central Military Commission in 2005. Hu is a technocrat: he graduated in hydraulic engineering at the prestigious Qinghua University, which is known as China's MIT. He is typical of the "fourth generation" of Chinese leaders, the least dogmatic cohort to accede to top offices in Chinese politics. As president of the Central Party School in the 1990s, Hu supported bold studies of political reform, including reform of the party. However, as party leader, Hu has been less bold—promoting increased supervision of the mass media and strengthening control of Internet content, for example.

transition period and especially the role of Deng Xiaoping.[22]

In communist systems, the death of the top leader creates a succession crisis: there is no formal or generally acknowledged position of second-in-command and no regularized mechanism to choose a new top leader. Mao's death ushered in a power struggle at the top, won by Deng and his fellow modernizers. Deng, already in his seventies at the time of Mao's death, chose to eschew top formal leadership of party or government in the interest of resolving the problem of succession.

In the late 1970s, Communist Party elders who had formerly held important positions of power were reinstated after years of forced retirement during the Cultural Revolution. Within a few years, however, many of them retired (or semiretired) to the "second line," to serve as advisers and involve themselves only in major policy issues or broad strategy.

At the very top, a half-dozen elders, all senior communist revolutionaries in their eighties or nineties, continued to play key roles in decisionmaking and occupy formal positions of leadership, although not the top party or government positions. The best example, of course, was "paramount leader" Deng himself. Deng never held the top formal position of leadership in party or government, although he was on the Politburo Standing Committee until 1987 and chaired the Central Military Commission until 1989. Just below this very small group at the top, elders retired to advisory positions on a Central Advisory Commission, set up in 1982. Other elders "retired" to formal positions on the NPC. Younger leaders were promoted to the top positions on the "first line," to allow them to develop their own bases of support and authority, with the support of their elder patrons.

This arrangement did not provide a solution to the succession problem, however. In principle, elders on the second line used their prestige and informal power to support younger leaders in top executive positions. In practice, younger leaders on the first line, in the effort to establish their own authority, sometimes adopted positions at odds with the views of elder patrons. Friction with party elders resulted in two purges of top party executives in the 1980s: Hu Yaobang was dismissed as party general secretary in 1987 and his successor Zhao Ziyang was dismissed in 1989 (see Figure 13.2). The situation today is different: by the mid-1990s, most of the elders at the very top, including Deng, had "gone to see Marx," and the Central Advisory Commission had been dismantled, having served its purpose of easing leaders into retirement. After a dozen years as party secretary and beneficiary of Deng's support until Deng's death in 1997, Jiang Zemin stepped down in 2002, lending his support to Hu Jintao.

Party Bureaucracy The party has its own set of bureaucratic structures, managed by the Secretariat. The Secretariat provides staff support for the Politburo, transforming Politburo decisions into instructions for subordinate party departments. Compared with their government counterparts, party departments are fewer in number and have more broadly defined areas of competence.

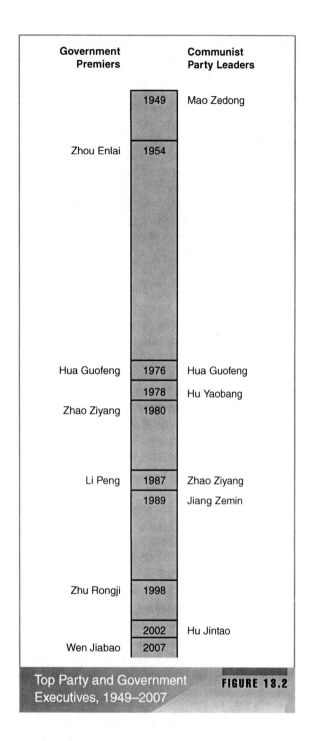

Government Premiers	Communist Party Leaders	
	1949	Mao Zedong
Zhou Enlai	1954	
Hua Guofeng	1976	Hua Guofeng
	1978	Hu Yaobang
Zhao Ziyang	1980	
Li Peng	1987	Zhao Ziyang
	1989	Jiang Zemin
Zhu Rongji	1998	
	2002	Hu Jintao
Wen Jiabao	2007	

Top Party and Government Executives, 1949–2007   **FIGURE 13.2**

People's Liberation Army

The **People's Liberation Army (PLA),** which includes the navy, air force, and army, has played a major role in Chinese politics. Party and army were practically inseparable until 1949. After 1949, the PLA participated in important nonmilitary functions, such as economic construction. In the Cultural Revolution, the PLA was brought more directly into politics to resolve violent factional struggles in society, at a time when party and government structures had been shattered. In 1989, the PLA was instrumental in crushing the mass protests.

The PLA does not dictate policy to party leaders, but it is the self-appointed guardian of Chinese sovereignty and nationalism, with a particular interest in preventing Taiwan's independence.[23] This issue has the greatest potential to spark military confrontation, and it is a matter the Chinese claim is completely domestic. Since the mid-1980s, the PLA has engaged in a program of military modernization and professionalization, increasing defense expenditures, procuring new weapons systems and technologies, and streamlining forces to realize a "smaller but stronger" force of 2.5 million. Despite these efforts, the military gap between China and the West is not narrowing, but widening, as western military technological advances continue at an increasingly rapid pace. The PLA is at least a decade behind in almost all weapons systems and remains predominantly a land force.

Party Dominance

Party and government structures from top to bottom are staffed by more than 40 million officials on state salaries. One important mechanism of party leadership, described earlier in this chapter, is the structural arrangement: the duplication of political structures and the dominance of party structures and leaders over government structures and leaders. The Chinese Communist Party exercises leadership in political structures in other ways too. Among the most important are overlapping directorships, "party core groups," party membership penetration, and the *nomenklatura* system. Mechanisms of party leadership specific to policymaking are discussed in later in this chapter.

Nomenklatura System The **nomenklatura system** is the most important mechanism by which the Communist Party exerts control over officials. In some sense, it is the linchpin of the political system. It refers to the management of all party and government officials in positions of even moderate importance by party committees. Party committees exercise authority over all major personnel decisions (such as appointment, promotion, transfer, and removal from office). Management authority is organized hierarchically and specified in lists of official positions. Any official at or above the rank of section chief is on such a list.[24] This amounted to about 8 million officials in the late 1980s, and the number must be considerably higher now.

Today, party committees, through their organization departments, directly manage all officials in positions one level down in the administrative hierarchy. At the top of the system, the Politburo exercises direct management authority over all officials at the provincial level in the territorial hierarchy and at the ministerial level in the bureaucratic hierarchy—about 7,000 officials in all (including the entire NPC Standing Committee, for example).

The extension of management authority downward in a hierarchy of dyadic relationships that are known to officials has important implications. Party leaders have a means of ensuring that the real constituency of every important official is the superior party committee—and ultimately the Central Committee and its Politburo. In looking ahead to career advancement, then, even officials who owe their positions formally to elections must look upward to "selectorates" of party committees rather than only (if at all) downward to electorates of congress deputies and ordinary citizens. Otherwise, they can be penalized. For example, for his effort in 1989 to assert NPC authority to repeal martial law, Hu Jiwei was expelled from the NPC Standing Committee.

Party Membership Another means by which the Communist Party exercises leadership over officials is in party membership penetration in political structures. The vast majority of officials in political structures (including government structures and positions filled by elections) are Communist Party members. At their places of work, officials are members of party committees, general branches, or branches located in a hierarchy of basic-level party organizations. They meet regularly to participate in party "organizational life," which is quite apart from their professional work. They are obliged to observe the inner-party discipline of democratic centralism. The routine activities of party branches in government offices are supervised by departments specially assigned to ensure that the Communist Party remains an active force in government structures. Because the party monopolizes

opportunities to get along and ahead in the Chinese political system, the organizational hierarchy and party discipline designed to guarantee unified party leadership over society also promote party leadership in political structures.

Party Core Groups Separate from the basic-level party organizations that bring party members in all workplaces under the Communist Party hierarchy are party core groups, formed in government structures only and composed of a handful of party members who hold the most senior positions.[25] The head of the party core group is normally also the head of the structure (for example, government ministers typically head party core groups of their respective ministries). Party core groups are appointed by the party committees one level up, and they answer to these party committees. While basic-level party organizations are mechanisms to promote unity and discipline under party leadership within political structures overall, party core groups are mechanisms to promote party leadership over leaders in their government host structures. Between 1987 and 1988, the system of party core groups was formally abolished (and many were actually dismantled) as part of a brief reform effort to separate party and government functions. Party core groups were quickly revived in 1989, however, after the purge of Zhao Ziyang, the leader most closely associated with the reform.

Overlapping Directorships Finally, the structural distinctions illustrated in Figure 13.1 mask some overlap of directorates in party and government structures. Hu Jintao is concurrently head of state, head of the party, and chairman of the Central Military Commission of both government and party. The practice of "wearing two hats" (party and government) has always been common. Premier Wen Jiabao is also at the apex of party power, as a member of the Politburo Standing Committee. Wu Bangguo, who chairs the NPC Standing Committee, is also a member of the Politburo Standing Committee. Overlapping directorships were much more extensive in the past than they are now. Membership of local party committees and their parallel governments used to be indistinguishable. In the 1980s, overlapping directorships were retained at the political center, but practically eliminated at lower levels. There is some evidence that they are returning.

Elite Recruitment Some key features of elite recruitment emerge from the discussion earlier in this chapter. First, membership in the Communist Party is a prerequisite for political elite status. Over the decades, the party has changed its focus of recruitment in society, reflecting larger changes in policy orientation. In the 1950s, for example, the party recruited most intensely among industrial workers, to build a more traditional Communist Party from a largely peasant base. In the Cultural Revolution of the 1960s and 1970s, radical leftist standards dominated—and recruitment was directed toward the less educated and less well-connected. In the 1980s and 1990s, the party focused its recruitment effort on intellectuals, professionals, and (more ambivalently) private entrepreneurs—all social groups identified as important for China's development as a prosperous nation (see Box 13.2).

Second, the party controls not only accessibility to this fundamental prerequisite for elite status, but also possesses a powerful organizational mechanism to recruit and promote elites: the *nomenklatura* system. Both appointed and elected leaders are vetted for office, level by level, such that a party committee at some level is the real constituent for leaders below. Beijing has not relinquished this key power, despite significant economic decentralization in recent decades.

What determines who gets along and ahead in the Chinese political system? That is, what criteria have leaders at higher levels viewed as most important for promotion? While much is made of the role of informal politics in China, a systematic study of provincial leaders from 1949 to 1998 shows that economic performance is the most important determinant of elite promotion in the post-Mao era of reform.[26] Leaders in provinces with higher economic growth or revenue contributions to the center during their tenure are less likely to be demoted or retired from office. In short, to win the support of their real constituents in Beijng, provincial leaders have to "deliver the goods." This is not surprising, considering that leaders in Beijing have staked their claim to legitimacy on precisely this outcome.

Rule by Law

The principle of "rule of law" is traditionally associated with liberal democratic ideals. It implies a particular relationship between individuals and the state, the essence of which is protection of individual rights by limitations on arbitrary state power. Such limitations are enshrined in the law and in legal institutions. This notion makes no sense in traditional communist ideology: law is a weapon of the state to use in exercising dictatorship. In 1978, however, Chinese leaders began to revive and develop important ideas and institutions of legality that had flourished for a brief period in the

---

"Red Capitalists"

BOX 13.2

In the mid-1980s, many party and government officials plunged into the private sector economy, shedding their offices but not their Communist Party membership. With little fanfare, the party also began to recruit private entrepreneurs as new members—a practice that reflected the party's commitment to economic growth, but met strong opposition from many as an abandonment of basic communist tenets. How could millionaire exploiters represent Chinese workers and peasants? When private entrepreneurs lent their support to protesters in 1989, leaders imposed a ban on their recruitment into the party. More than a decade later, in 2000, party leader Jiang Zemin introduced a convoluted new formula to justify welcoming them back: the "three represents," added in 2004 to China's constitution. In this formula, the party does not simply represent workers and peasants, but represents developmental needs of the advanced social productive forces, the promotion of advanced culture, and the fundamental interests of the greatest majority of the people. In 2001, on the party's eightieth anniversary, Jiang proposed lifting the ban on recruitment of private entrepreneurs into the party. His proposal was soon implemented. Today, one-third of private entrepreneurs are party members. Even though "red capitalists" still account for only a very small proportion of party members, their inclusion reflects a highly significant policy.

1950s. The new Chinese legality acknowledges **rule by law.**[27] Briefly, this means: there are laws, and all are equally subject to them. As the second principle is often violated, this may seem a trivial advance. It is not. The ongoing effort to establish rule by law in China has already changed the way Chinese act and think, in important ways.

Socialist Legality The initial Chinese experiment with "socialist legality" began with the promulgation of the first constitution in 1954 and ended in 1957 with the Anti-Rightist Movement. Legalistic perspectives were rejected as examples of "bourgeois rightist" thinking. Legal scholars and legal professionals were criticized and labeled as "rightists." Work on development of criminal law stopped. Legal training and legal scholarship practically ceased. Defense lawyers disappeared from the legal process. Party committees took direct control of legal proceedings. The abandonment of law reached a peak during the Cultural Revolution, when violent "class struggle" and "mass justice" substituted for any regularized procedures to resolve social conflicts. This degree of radical lawlessness was not characteristic of the entire Maoist period, but a general official hostility to law prevailed from the late 1950s.

Legal Reform Legal reform began in 1978. The legal system, barely functioning at the time, required urgent action for a number of reasons. First, there was an immediate need to establish legitimacy by righting past wrongs: investigating and reversing verdicts of dubious legality issued during the Cultural Revolution were a high priority. Second, Deng Xiaoping and other leaders wanted not only to restore public order and stability after years of chaos and uncertainty, but also to express their commitment to system building as a substitute for arbitrary political rule. Finally and not least of all, Chinese leaders hoped that the new legality would encourage economic investment and growth by promoting predictability—through transparent rules and impartial rule adjudication.

Rule by law requires laws. Nearly thirty years after the founding of the PRC, there was no criminal law. In 1978, Chinese leaders appointed committees of legal specialists to pick up work set aside for decades and to draft criminal codes for immediate promulgation. In 1979, the NPC passed the first criminal law and criminal procedure law. In the years that followed, as

government agencies issued interim regulations that amended and clarified the hastily drafted laws, the NPC Legislative Affairs Committee worked on legal revisions. In 1996 and 1997, the NPC passed substantially amended and more precise versions of the laws. The 1997 amended criminal law takes into account changes in the Chinese economy that have created opportunities for economic crimes almost unimaginable in 1979 (such as insider securities trading). It abolishes the vaguely defined crimes of "counterrevolution." The 1996 amended criminal procedure law grants the accused the right to seek counsel (a right rejected in the 1950s) at an early stage of legal proceedings.

Rule by law implies equality before the law. This idea stands in sharp contrast to both the politicized view of law in communist ideology and routine practices in the Maoist years. In 1978, the NPC restored the procuratorates, which had been abolished in the 1960s. A new important role of procuratorates in the 1980s and 1990s became the investigation and prosecution of official crimes, for which procuratorates have full independent responsibility, according to law. Chinese leaders have regularly and prominently voiced a commitment to equality before the law, stating that officials who abuse public office and violate laws must be punished. Equality before the law, labeled "bourgeois" in the 1950s, is featured in the 1982 constitution—which also, for the first time, subjects the Communist Party (not only party members) to the authority of the law. At the same time, as described later in this chapter, there has been an explosion of corruption in recent years. In practice, the Communist Party, through its political-legal committees and its system of discipline inspection committees, routinely protects officials from equality before the law in cases involving abuses of power.

At the end of the 1970s, most Chinese were ignorant of laws and mistrustful of legal channels, a reasonable position when politics routinely superceded law. In the 1980s, the authorities launched a number of campaigns to educate ordinary citizens about the content of important laws and about certain ideas, such as equality before the law. Developing legal norms when legality has been actively denounced (not merely neglected) for decades has been difficult. Yet, ordinary Chinese do use law to pursue their interests. One indicator of the effect of the legal education effort is the growth in lawsuits against government agencies and officials under the administrative litigation law. The

Cyber cafés are popular with urban Chinese youth. Even with some 50,000 cyber-police, it is impossible to fully monitor Internet activity.

AP Images

number of such lawsuits processed in the legal system has increased steadily since passage of the law in 1989. Even in cases not won outright in court, out-of-court settlements that favor plaintiffs have become sufficiently common to make lawsuits worthwhile.[28]

Criticism of Legal Practices Legal reform has provoked criticism of Chinese law and legal practices outside China.[29] Three examples illustrate. First, Chinese criminal law stipulates the death penalty in "serious circumstances" of smuggling, rape, theft, bribery, trafficking in women and children, and corruption. In periodic intensive efforts to "strike hard" at crime, the authorities have resorted widely to capital punishment. Critics argue that capital punishment is excessively harsh for these crimes. Second, by design, criminal proceedings are inquisitorial (not adversarial), focused on determination of punishment (not guilt). As cases are prosecuted only after sufficient evidence has been collected to demonstrate guilt, most prosecutions result in guilty verdicts. The right to seek counsel at an early stage of proceedings is recognized in the law, but the requirement is only that a public defender be assigned no later than ten days before trial. By that time, the case has been prepared for prosecution and usually a confession (for which the law promises leniency) has already been obtained. This practice of "verdict first,

trial second" has been questioned and debated inside China and criticized outside China. Finally, despite abolition of specifically political crimes of counter-revolution, the Chinese authorities acknowledge "several thousand" political prisoners. While human rights groups estimate the number to be much larger, all critics view the situation as essentially inconsistent with the new law.

Nonetheless, the new legality has produced significant change. Today more than ever before, the Chinese state is more constrained by laws, while Chinese citizens are freer from political arbitrariness because of laws. Abuse of authority is acted on differently from before. The law is a weapon, because the regime has invested heavily in it. To the extent that, in practice, a double standard for citizens and officials persists, the law is a political weapon, which ordinary citizens can take up against perceived injustice. The official effort to build rule by law, by making law salient, has produced a basis for "rightful resistance" to hold the regime accountable to its own proclaimed standards.

POLITICAL SOCIALIZATION

One result of the economic policy of opening up to the outside is that Chinese leaders today cannot control information as in the Maoist years.[30]

Mass Media Ordinary Chinese are now routinely exposed to news and opinions about public affairs in their country through access to Hong Kong (which maintains relatively free and critical mass media) and the outside world in newspapers, books, radio and television broadcasts, and the Internet. Moreover, Chinese connect with one another to transmit information as never before: in blogs, bulletin boards, e-mail, telephone, and text messages. China imported its first mobile phone facilities in 1987; by mid-2006, the country had more than 420 million mobile phone subscribers, the largest number in the world. One result of the telecommunications explosion and the opening to the outside world is the dilution in importance of the state-dominated mass media. In 1978, there were fewer than 900 periodicals and 200 newspapers with a provincial circulation in China; today, there are nearly 9,500 periodicals and nearly 2,000 newspapers.

To be sure, not all messages in the media are acceptable. Yet, most of the new media outlets do not touch on politics, offering instead the latest perspectives on sports, fashion, music, and movie stars. New academic journals carry lively scholarly discussions about the economy, law, and politics, however. Moreover, Chinese journalists expose government wrongdoings and thwart official efforts to suppress news of disasters.

At the same time, Chinese leaders reserve the right to shut down publications that in their view go too far. A government watchdog department monitors the media, focusing especially on coverage of Taiwan, party leaders, major political events, and the interpretation of party history—all explicitly defined in regulations as politically sensitive topics "of importance to state security and social stability." Media content has been scrutinized more carefully in recent years. At the same time, the most effective censorship the authorities can exercise in the new context is self-censorship—which generally operates fairly well. This is especially the case with Internet chat rooms and bulletin boards, which are otherwise nearly impossible to monitor, despite a force of some 50,000 cyber-police.

Education System The new content and style of political socialization are clearly evident in the education system. Mao's successors inherited an educational system designed to build communist values—and fundamentally at odds with the priority of economic growth. During the Cultural Revolution, high school graduates were sent to factories or farms to acquire work experience and learn from the masses. University entrance examinations were replaced with recommendations by grassroots leaders, focusing on revolutionary political credentials. With the persecution of scholars and denigration of expert knowledge in the

China is no longer a bicycle nation. Chinese-designed and manufactured automobiles emit ten to twenty times more pollution than American or Japanese Models.

Justin Guariglia/The Image Works

universities, the content of university education was redesigned to include more politics in every specialization. Graduates were more "red" than expert. An entire decade was lost. The generation that missed out on an education during this decade is known today as the "lost generation."

Today, with the return of the university entrance examinations and huge numbers of Chinese studying in foreign universities, the respect for expertise is thoroughly restored. Indeed, in fall 2006, on instructions from top party and government departments, colleges across the country reduced the seven compulsory courses on political ideology and party history to four, in the first major curricular change in twenty-five years.

POLITICAL CULTURE

Older and middle-aged Chinese have experienced not only the radicalism of the Maoist years, but also more than two decades of "reform and opening" to the outside world. Young Chinese have only the personal experience of the relatively open post-Mao years, including the decade of the 1990s that saw the "third wave" of democratization, with the triumph of democracy in nearly every communist country. When asked about the most memorable event in their lifetime, Chinese of all ages talk mainly about recent events, such as the post-Mao reforms.[31] Surely recent changes, both inside and outside China, have left their imprint on the way Chinese view their government and their relationship to political authorities.

Because Maoist-era leaders regarded social science with great suspicion, we have no good baseline of public opinion data by which to assess change over time in the beliefs of ordinary Chinese. We can say something about the Chinese political culture today, however, based on survey research in China, including surveys organized and conducted by political scientists based in the United States. What is the orientation toward politics of ordinary Chinese? In particular, to what extent do the beliefs of Chinese seem conducive to political change in the direction of further democratization?

Political Knowledge An important building block for democracy is a citizenry knowledgeable about politics and interested in public affairs, so as to be able to

monitor the performance of representatives and leaders. Most ordinary Chinese follow public affairs at least weekly, mainly through radio or television programs and somewhat less through newspapers, but politics is not something that is a regular topic of discussion in China. A majority say they *never* talk about politics with others, a stark reflection of lack of active interest.

Political knowledge and interest are not uniformly distributed in China, of course. A more active knowledge and interest are seen among men, the more highly educated, and Chinese with higher incomes, which is not so different from what we observe in other countries. Not surprisingly, Chinese in Beijing are much more interested in politics than Chinese overall; in fact, they discuss politics very frequently. Yet, even if we consider the situation of Chinese overall, which includes the relatively less knowledgeable and less interested rural population, political knowledge in China today is higher than in Italy in the early 1960s and political discourse higher than in Italy or Mexico in the early 1960s.[32]

Political Values How do the Chinese view their communist government? With the increased availability of information on other countries, including liberal democracies, do the Chinese see their relationship with political authorities differently? Moreover, does the Chinese political culture reflect traditional values—the influence of Confucianism, which conceived of legitimacy to rule in moral terms?

Perhaps the most interesting perspective on contemporary Chinese political culture is a comparative one that considers its fate across three different Chinese political systems. An extraordinary survey of a representative sample of Chinese in mainland China, Hong Kong, and Taiwan, conducted in 1993 and 1994, provides this perspective and helps to sort out different influences of traditional culture, political system, and socioeconomic development.[33] Figure 13.3 compares responses of ordinary Chinese in the PRC, Hong Kong, and Taiwan to questions about political relationships. Two questions tap orientations to popular accountability and political liberty. Another frames relationships in traditional Confucian terms of virtuous leadership. Altogether, these questions probe Chinese support for values commonly associated with liberal democracy. The responses reveal a fairly consistent, easily interpretable, and striking pattern.

First, there seems to be a strong impact of political system. A majority of Chinese in the PRC reject every democratic value, and support for democratic values is generally lowest in the PRC. This is not surprising. By the early 1990s, when this survey was conducted, Taiwan's process of democratization was well underway. Hong Kong, while still under British colonial rule, had enjoyed very significant civil liberties for decades and was taking initial steps to increase electoral competition.

Second, the influence of non-Chinese political socialization is evident. The traditional Confucian orientation to the moral state is least evident in Hong Kong: nearly three-fourths of Hong Kong Chinese reject the view that everything should be left up to virtuous leaders. By contrast, this view finds strong support in the PRC. Chinese in Taiwan are somewhere in the middle, perhaps reflecting rule by a Chinese government but a society long open to outside influences.

Third, and perhaps most interesting of all for speculation about support for democratization in the PRC, the responses show an impact of socioeconomic development. This is most evident in a comparison of responses in the PRC overall with those in urban China only. Urban Chinese are much more supportive of democratic values than are mainland Chinese generally.

In sum, traditional Chinese orientations to moral leadership appear to prevail in the PRC, and high proportions of the population have orientations unfavorable to democratization.[34] Barring the introduction of very major political change by the leaders themselves, popular disgruntlement about the performance of the government appears unlikely to transform itself into collective action for regime change. Overall, the responses suggest that mainland Chinese are "elitist

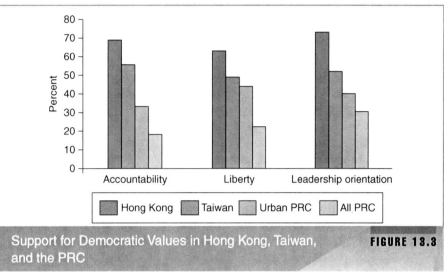

Support for Democratic Values in Hong Kong, Taiwan, and the PRC   **FIGURE 13.3**

Percent expressing *disagreement* with statements below.

Accountability: "Top government officials are like the heads of a big family. We should follow all their decisions on national issues."

Liberty: "The government should have the power to decide which opinions (perspectives) are to be circulated in a society and which are not."

Leadership orientation: "We can leave everything to morally upright leaders."

Source: Yun-han Chu and Yu-tzung Chang, "Culture Shift and Regime Legitimacy: Comparing Mainland China, Taiwan, and Hong Kong," in Shiping Hua, ed., *Chinese Political Culture, 1989–2000* (Armonk, NY: M. E. Sharpe, 2001), 332–33. Based on surveys conducted in 1993 and 1994.

and authority-oriented," and this contributes to the stability of the communist regime.[35]

POLITICAL PARTICIPATION

In the communist party-state, political participation, interest articulation, and interest aggregation differ from the processes normally found in liberal democratic systems. The source of difference is, of course, different conceptions of the relationship between leaders and citizens: the notion of guardianship is fundamentally incompatible with liberal democratic notions of representation. The Communist Party organization claims to represent the interests of all society. It rejects, as unnecessary and unacceptable, political parties other than itself. While there has been change in political processes in recent decades, the "officially acceptable" forms of political participation, interest articulation, and interest aggregation in the Chinese political system continue to reflect the relationship of guardianship between party and society. This section discusses political participation; the next section explores interest articulation and aggregation.

Changes in the Rules An important aspect of political reform undertaken after Mao's death in 1976 has been the redefinition of what constitutes "officially acceptable" political participation in the Chinese system. Guidelines for the new political participation are evident in three categories of rule changes that have routinized participation and reduced its burden for ordinary Chinese. The changes reflect an official reaction against the disruption that characterized mass participation in the Maoist years (especially during the Cultural Revolution), an official assumption that economic growth is predicated on order and stability, and an official recognition that changes in economic relationships require adjustments in political relationships.

The first category of rule changes involves political participation, which has become essentially optional for ordinary Chinese since the early 1980s. In the first thirty years of communist rule, for a broad range of political activities, failure to participate was considered tantamount to opposition to the communist regime. Today, politics intrudes far less in the lives of ordinary Chinese. The scope and demands of politics have shrunk. The single most important measure signifying this change is the official removal, in 1979, of all class and political labels. After thirty years, the Chinese are no longer formally identified by class background or past "political mistakes." Not only does politics no longer dominate daily life, but in the diminished sphere of political activities, political apathy is no longer risky for ordinary Chinese.

The second category has been the assiduous avoidance by the regime to rouse the mass public to realize policy objectives. In the Maoist years, by contrast, the quintessential form of political participation was the **mass mobilization campaign**—intensive, large-scale, disruptive group action, implemented by grassroots leaders. The Great Leap Forward launched in 1958 and the Cultural Revolution launched in 1966 were essentially mass campaigns, on a gargantuan scale. Typically in mass campaigns, grassroots party leaders, responding to signals from the political center, roused ordinary Chinese to achieve regime goals of various sorts, often aimed at identified categories of enemies—such as "counterrevolutionaries" in 1950–1951; the "landlord class" in 1950–1952; the "rightists" in 1957; and the "unclean cadres" in 1962–1963. Mass-campaign

methods were adopted for nonpolitical objectives too, such as the ill-conceived and ecologically harmful effort to eradicate "four pests" (sparrows, rats, flies, and mosquitoes) in 1956. Participation in campaigns was virtually compulsory. Only three years after Mao's death, Chinese leaders issued an official rejection of mass campaigns as a mode of political participation. Many leaders who emerged at the top echelons of power in the late 1970s had themselves been victims of persecution in the Cultural Revolution. The social disorder of campaigns was rejected as antithetical to the new priority of economic growth.

The third category is the rejection of mass mobilization as the dominant mode of political participation. Chinese leaders have instead encouraged ordinary citizens to express their opinions and participate in politics through a variety of regular official channels, some new, others newly revived: offices to receive complaints, centers and telephone hotlines to report abuses of power, and letters to newspaper editors, for example.[36] Not least of all, the authorities have introduced important reforms in elections. As a consequence, political participation in China is varied and extensive in scope. Table 13.2 shows findings from a survey conducted in Beijing in the 1980s and 1990s. The extent of citizen participation in a wide range of activities is quite remarkable, not at all the picture of Maoist mobilization.

Elections and an electoral connection between citizens and leaders are integral to liberal democratic conceptions of representation. For this reason, governments and nongovernmental organizations in liberal democracies have paid close attention to electoral reforms in China.

Local Congress Elections Elections to local people's congresses in the Maoist years were political rituals, featuring no candidate choice and no secret ballot. Voters directly elected deputies to township-level congresses only; at higher levels, deputies were elected by congresses at the level immediately below. Such elections served as vehicles of regime legitimation, popular education, and political socialization, but they did not really allow ordinary citizens to choose representatives.

In 1979, a new election law introduced direct election of deputies to county-level congresses, mandated secret ballots rather than public displays of support,

Political Participation in Beijing (percent reporting having participated in political act)		**TABLE 13.2**
Political Act	**1988**	**1996**
Voting for deputies in 1988 local congress elections	71.5	81.0
Contacting leaders of workplace	51.2	54.2
Complaining through bureaucratic hierarchy	43.0	47.5
Voting for leaders in workplace	34.8	16.1
Complaining through trade unions	18.9	24.4
Using connections (*guanxi*)	15.5	16.6
Complaining through political organizations	15.0	17.7
Slowing down on the job	12.6	9.3
Writing letters to government officials	12.5	15.3
Persuading others to attend campaign meetings for congress deputies	8.9	13.0
Complaining through congress deputies	8.6	14.1
Persuading others to attend campaign or briefing meetings at workplace	7.7	5.4
Organizing others to fight against leaders	7.6	3.0
Writing letters to newspaper editors	6.8	8.3
Persuading others to vote for certain leaders in workplace elections	5.7	3.5
Whipping up public opinion against workplace leaders	5.1	1.7
Persuading others to vote for certain deputies in congress elections	4.7	8.0
Giving gifts in exchange for help	4.6	8.0
Persuading others to boycott unfair workplace elections	4.6	2.9
Reporting to complaint bureaus	4.0	8.1
Persuading others to boycott unfair congress elections	3.7	6.8
Bringing cases to court	1.2	4.5
Participating in strikes	0.9	2.6
Participating in demonstrations	0.4	1.4

Source: Tianjian Shi, "Mass Political Behavior in Beijing," in Merle Goldman and Roderick MacFarquhar, eds., *The Paradox of China's Post-Mao Reforms* (Cambridge: Harvard University Press, 1999), 155.

and required the number of candidates to be one and a half times the number of deputies to be elected.

Although local Communist Party organizations continue to play a key leadership role in election committees, essentially vetting candidates, not all candidates can win under current rules. Some officially nominated candidates lose elections. Indeed, some candidates officially designated for government office lose elections. A growing number of candidates who are not Communist Party members have competed and won in elections. A smaller number of government executives nominated by deputies are not official candidates and win without official endorsement.[37] An electoral victory signifies some degree of popular support, while losing signifies a problematic relationship with the mass public. At a minimum, the new rules are a means for the Communist Party organization to gauge popular views about local officials, diversify the pool from which leaders are recruited, and monitor local leaders. To be sure, the new rules have not produced radical change. Nor can such an outcome be expected without further change in rules: no platform of opposition to the Communist Party is permissible.

Village Committees China also now has nearly two decades of experience with rural grassroots democratization, formally approved in November 1987 when the NPC, after over a year of debate, passed a provisional version of the Organic Law on Village Committees. A final revised version was passed in November 1998.

The law defines **village committees** as "autonomous mass organizations of self-government," popularly elected in elections featuring choice among candidates for three-year terms and accountable to a village council comprised of all adult villagers.

The introduction of popularly elected village committees in 1987 was designed to strengthen state capacity to govern in the aftermath of agricultural decollectivization. In the early 1980s, the people's communes had been dismantled and replaced with township governments. Land and other production inputs were divided among peasant households to manage on their own, free markets were opened, most obligatory sales to the state were abolished, and private entrepreneurship was promoted.[38] The results of these reforms were successful by most economic standards, but disastrous in their consequences for rural leadership. As villagers gained greater economic initiative and autonomy, the power of the Chinese party-state to exact compliance was enormously weakened. By the mid-1980s, village leadership had seriously atrophied. Leaders were enriching themselves at the expense of the community, and villagers were resisting their efforts to implement unpopular policies. Violent conflicts between villagers and village leaders had become common. The revitalization of village committees in 1987 was designed to make the countryside more governable by increasing accountability. Presumably, villagers would be more responsive to leaders elected from below rather than those imposed from above as before.

In 1998, when the NPC affirmed the experience of village elections, most villages had undergone at least three rounds of elections, with enormous local variation in implementation. In many villages, the village Communist Party branch controlled candidate nomination, there was no candidate choice for the key position of village committee director, and voting irregularities were common. Even in villages that made serious progress—with genuinely competitive elections, widespread popular participation in candidate nomination, and scrupulous attention to voting procedure—real managerial authority often resided not with the popularly elected village committee but with the village Communist Party branch. Even today, too little is known to generalize about overall progress in village elections, its determinants, or its consequences.[39] Certainly, to the degree that the practices of grassroots democracy acquire the force of routine and expectations accumulate, however slowly, among

nearly 750 million Chinese in more than 600,000 villages, political participation in the countryside will change profoundly.

"Unacceptable" Political Participation   More dramatic than the reforms that have redefined officially acceptable political participation has been the political action of ordinary Chinese in city streets and squares beginning in the late 1970s. With strikes, marches, posters, petitions, and occupation of public spaces, ordinary citizens have acted as if political reform comprehended or condoned mass political action and public disorder. The official record suggests the contrary, however.

In 1980, the right to post "big-character posters" (usually criticisms of leaders, written by individuals or groups and posted on walls), introduced during the Cultural Revolution, was removed from the Chinese constitution. In 1982, the constitutional right to strike was rescinded. As for mass protests, the official view was made clear in 1979 with the introduction of the "four fundamental principles" that political participation must uphold: (1) the socialist road, (2) Marxism-Leninism-Mao Zedong Thought, (3) the people's democratic dictatorship, and (4) the leadership of the Communist Party. Of these principles, only the last is necessary to restrict political participation effectively, as the content of the first three has become what party leaders make of it. Participants (especially organizers) face real risks of physical harm and criminal punishment. Why then did ordinary citizens engage in mass protests with increasing frequency in the 1970s and 1980s? Why did urban worker and peasant unrest increase in the 1980s and 1990s?

Different sorts of "officially unacceptable" political participation have different explanations, but none can be explained without reference to the post-Mao reforms. On the one hand, economic reforms have produced some socially unacceptable outcomes: more (and more visible) inflation, unemployment, crime, and corruption, for example. Rural unrest has typically been triggered by local corruption and exaction of excessive (often illegal) taxes and fees. Urban unrest—strikes, slowdowns, and demonstrations—has increased too, as state enterprises struggle to survive in the socialist market economy. A number of enterprises have been closed down; many have engaged in massive layoffs; others have been unable to pay bonuses and pensions. For the first time since

1949, many urban Chinese have been living on fixed incomes, no incomes, or unpredictable incomes as the cost of living increases.

Protesters and Reformers In 1989, a different sort of urban unrest captured the attention of the world news media and, consequently, of the world. The demonstration that brought a million people to Tiananmen Square was the third major political protest movement since Mao's death. The first was in 1978–1979, the second in 1986–1987. All three were officially unacceptable, all were linked in some important way to official reforms and reformers, and all ended in failure for mass protesters (and resulted in setbacks to official reforms too).[40]

Despite links between protesters and official reformers, the post-Mao movements were not mass mobilization campaigns. As they were not explicitly initiated by the regime, once underway they could not be easily stopped with an official pronouncement from the political center. Instead, the authorities turned to coercive force wielded by the police, the armed police, and ultimately the army to terminate the protests with violence.

Protests are officially unacceptable mainly because of their form of expression. The official consensus since December 1978 has been that the most important priority for China is economic growth, with social order and stability are prerequisites for growth. Mass protests are distinctly disorderly. Further, as a form of political participation, mass protests are a symptom of regime failure in two senses. By turning to the streets to articulate their demands, protesters demonstrate that official channels for expressing critical views are not working and that they do not believe the Communist Party's claim that it can correct its own mistakes. Further, protesters are clearly not alienated from politics: while they reject official channels of participation, they are not politically apathetic; indeed, they articulate explicitly political demands despite serious risks and the difficulty associated with organizing outside the system. In short, political protests signify that mass political participation can neither be contained within official channels nor deterred with a better material life.

For the most part, despite some radical elements, the protests have not been blatantly antisystem in their demands. This does not appear to be merely strategic. Rather, the protests are something of a rowdy mass counterpart to the official socialist reform movement, exerting more pressure for more reform, and (while officially unacceptable) often linked with elite reformers.

In the **Democracy Movement** of 1978–1979, Deng Xiaoping publicly approved many of the demands posted on Democracy Wall and published in unofficial journals, which called for a "reversal of verdicts" on individuals and political events. The demands were an integral part of the pressure for reform that surrounded the meetings of top leaders in

In 1989, ordinary Chinese participated in the largest spontaneous protest movement the communists had ever faced. A lone protester shows defiance of regime violence in his intransigent confrontation with a Chinese tank.

AP Images

Wei Jingsheng and the "Fifth Modernization"   BOX 13.3

In late 1978, in an atmosphere of great change that included official "reversals of verdicts" of the Cultural Revolution, many Chinese began to gather regularly at a large wall close to Beijing's Tiananmen Square to post, read, and discuss political posters. One of the boldest posters to appear on Democracy Wall was an essay by Wei Jingsheng. It argued that the ambitious new program to modernize agriculture, industry, national defense, and science and technology could not succeed without a "fifth modernization"—democracy. Wei wrote: "The hated old political system has not changed. Are not the people justified in seizing power from the overlords?" Wei published even more critical essays in his unofficial journal *Explorations,* one of more than fifty such journals circulating at the time. In March 1979, he posted an attack on Deng Xiaoping, asking: "Do we want democracy or new dictatorship?" Wei was tried and convicted of "counterrevolutionary crimes" and "leaking state secrets" to foreigners. Some fifteen years later, Wei was released from prison, only to be rearrested for dissident activities. In 1997, after years of pressure from human rights groups and governments outside China, China's most famous political dissident was released and exiled to the United States, where he continues to criticize the Chinese authorities.

---

late 1978, allowing elite reformers to argue for major changes in policy and political orientation. The poster campaign and unofficial journals were tolerated. To be sure, when a bold dissidenter named Wei Jingsheng demanded a "fifth modernization," by which he meant democracy of a sort never envisaged by the communists, the Chinese authorities promptly sentenced him to a fifteen-year prison term (ostensibly for revealing state secrets) and introduced the "four fundamental principles" to establish the parameters of acceptable debate[41] (see Box 13.3).

When the Communist Party congress convened in late 1987, party leader Zhao Ziyang acknowledged conflicts of interest in society at the current time. The years 1988 and 1989 were high points for political liberalization. The political criticism expressed in Tiananmen Square in 1989 largely echoed public views of elite reformers in the party and government. From the perspective of communist authorities, the real danger in 1989 was not the content of mass demands but the organizational challenge: students and workers organized their own unions, independent of the party, to represent their interests.

The challenge was exacerbated by an open break in elite ranks when Zhao Ziyang voiced his support for the protesters and declared his opposition to martial law. Other party and government leaders and retired elders, including Deng Xiaoping—many of whom had been victims of power seizures by youths in the Cultural Revolution—viewed the problem as a basic struggle for the survival of the system and their own positions. The movement was violently and decisively crushed with tanks and machine guns in the **Tiananmen massacre** of June 4, 1989.[42]

All three protests ended in defeat for the participants: prison for the main protest organizers in 1979, expulsion from the Communist Party for intellectual leaders in 1987, and prison or violent death for hundreds in 1989. The defeats extended beyond the mass protest movement to encompass setbacks to the official reform movement too. When demands for reform moved to the city streets, more conservative leaders attributed the social disorder to an excessively rapid pace of reform. The result was a slower pace or postponement of reforms. Twice, the highest party leader was dismissed from office as a result of the mass protests (Hu Yaobang in 1987 and Zhao Ziyang in 1989), and the official reform movement lost its strongest proponent.

INTEREST ARTICULATION AND AGGREGATION

Most ordinary citizens engage in interest articulation without interest aggregation. This takes the form of personal contacts to articulate individual concerns about the effects of policies on their lives. Much of this interest articulation takes place at the workplace. As shown earlier in Table 13.2, more than 50 percent of those surveyed in Beijing in the 1980s and 1990s had engaged in precisely this sort of low-level politics. And more than 15 percent of those surveyed had made use of personal connections. For the most part, the function of interest aggregation is monopolized by the Communist Party, although the party's role in interest aggregation is being diluted and the methods it employs have also evolved.

Organizations under Party Leadership Under the formal leadership of the Communist Party are eight "satellite parties," a legacy of the communist pre-1949 strategy of provisional cooperation with noncommunist democratic parties.[43] These parties have no real role in policymaking, but they are represented (with prominent nonparty individuals) in the Chinese People's Political Consultative Conference. In 1989 the Central Committee proposed greater cooperation with the noncommunist parties by regular consultation with their leaders on major policies—or at least a stronger effort to inform the parties of Communist Party policies. Of course, this proposal referred only to the eight officially tolerated parties. In 1998, the authorities arrested, tried, and imprisoned a veteran of the 1978–1979 Democracy Movement who attempted to register a fledgling China Democracy Party.

The other older formal organizations that aggregate like interests in the Chinese political system are the "mass organizations," extensions of the Communist Party into society, nationwide in scope and organized hierarchically. The All-China Federation of Trade Unions and the Women's Federation remain active and important mass organizations today. Mass organizations are led by Communist Party officials, who are specially assigned to these positions and who take direction from party committees. The main function of these organizations is not to aggregate and represent group interests for consideration in the policymaking process, but to facilitate propagation of party policy to the relevant groups. Essentially, mass organizations represent the interests of the Communist Party to the organized "interest groups" it dominates, not vice versa. The classic description of this relationship refers to mass organizations as "transmission belts" for the Communist Party.

NGOs and GONGOs A very different set of associations emerged in the late 1980s with official encouragement. These "social organizations," over 170,000 in

number, range widely in form and focus. In form, they include genuine nongovernmental organizations (NGOs) and government-organized nongovernmental organizations (**GONGOs**). Some GONGOs are essentially front organizations for government agencies, set up to take advantage of the interest of foreign governments and international NGOs to support the emergence of Chinese civil society. Other GONGOs have strong and mutually beneficial relationships with NGOs, acting as a bridge to government agencies. In focus, GONGOs and especially NGOs cover a wide range of interests and activities.

Among the most interesting GONGOs are the business associations set up to organize firms: the Self-Employed Laborers Association, the Private Enterprises Association, and the Federation of Industry and Commerce. The Federation of Industry and Commerce, which organizes the largest Chinese firms, has independent resources that have permitted it to create a separate organizational network (chambers of commerce), a national newspaper, and a financial institution to provide credit to members.

Among NGOs, the 250 organizations that focus on environmental issues are at the vanguard of NGO activity.[44] The largest, best funded, and best organized environmental NGOs focus primarily on species and nature conservation and environmental education. With strong support from the media, these NGOs often work with central authorities to expose and counter local government failure to implement environmental laws and policies. One environmental NGO trains lawyers to engage in enforcement of laws, educates judges about the issues, and litigates environmental cases.

Individual environmental activists have also organized to influence political decisions. A good example is the independent publication of *Yangtze! Yangtze!*, a collection of papers by scientists and environmentalists critical of the world's biggest and most controversial hydroelectric project, the Three Gorges Dam. The study was released in early 1989 with the aim of influencing the widely publicized NPC vote to approve dam construction. Although it failed to halt approval, nearly a third of NPC delegates voted against the project or abstained—prompting the government to postpone dam construction until the mid-1990s (see Box 13.4).

Considering the "Leninist organizational predisposition" to thwart organizational plurality, the

The Three Gorges Dam

BOX 13.4

The Three Gorges Dam, essentially completed in May 2006, is the biggest, most costly, and most controversial hydropower station ever built. It was conceived to regulate the flow of the Yangtze, the third most powerful river in the world. Three times in the past century, the river has flooded, killing hundreds of thousands of people. The new dam will supply an estimated 10 percent of China's electric power, for industrial production and "basic electrification" of the countryside. Building it displaced more than a million people. Environmentalist opponents of the dam are concerned about damage to the ecosystem and endangerment of some species of fish and birds. Other critics are concerned about flooding more than 100 significant archeological sites. Opposition to the dam also focuses on safety issues: problems of sedimentation may cause floods upstream and weaken foundations of cities built on silt downstream. Most opponents suggested building several smaller dams, rather than one mega-dam. Central to these concerns are doubts that the government sufficiently considered expert advice in designing the project—which was a dream of Chinese leaders since 1919 and took on meaning as a political accomplishment.

encouragement of NGO emergence and activity in the Chinese context seems puzzling.[45] It is explained by the closure of many state enterprises and the downsizing of government at all levels, in the 1980s and 1990s, creating a need for the growth of social organizations to take on some former government functions, especially social welfare functions. Essentially, this change shifts the burden from government to society. The 1998 plan to downsize the central government bureaucracy explicitly noted that many functions "appropriated by government" must be "given back" to society and managed by new social associations. This plan opened the political space for the emergence of NGOs. The authorities also recognize that NGOs can help the center monitor local government policy implementation; this is the role that environmental NGOs have played most prominently, for example.

For the most part, NGO activity is in fact well within the parameters of officially acceptable political participation. Most groups do not seek autonomy from the state, but rather seek "embeddedness" within the state. To be autonomous is to be outside the system and relatively powerless, unable to exercise influence. In sum, for the most part, the emerging Chinese civil society aggregates and articulates its interests without challenging the state.

To be sure, the authorities have taken measures to guarantee that NGOs work with (not against) them. An elaborate set of regulations requires social organizations to affiliate with a sponsor that is responsible for their activity, to register with the government, and to have sufficient funding and membership. The regulations also prohibit the coexistence of more than one organization with the same substantive focus at the national level or in any particular locality. This preserves the monopoly of the official mass organizations to represent the interests of women and workers, for example.

In practice, however, it is simply impossible really to control NGO activity: some NGOs register as businesses, others thrive as Internet-based virtual organizations, and government sponsors cannot monitor the organizations registered as their affiliates. For example, the All-China Women's Federation is responsible for more than 3,000 social organizations dealing with women's issues. In this context, Chinese NGOs can be expected to continue to grow.

It is important to note that one significant social group lacks a legitimate organizational channel (even a mass organization) that aggregates its interests: farmers. To the extent that Chinese farmers engage in collective action to articulate their interests, it is largely through petitions and protests.

POLICYMAKING AND IMPLEMENTATION

Today, it is inconceivable that a scheme such as the Great Leap Forward could be launched and implemented as it was in the 1950s. Controversial policies are no longer adopted at the whim of a single leader;

experts play a significant role in policy formulation; experimentation in selected localities precedes widespread implementation; and local authorities no longer slavishly sacrifice local development goals to meet unrealistic campaign targets dictated by the center.

The single most important difference distinguishing policy processes of the 1950s from those of the 1990s and after, however, is the recent greater reliance on consultation and consensus building among a wider range of bureaucratic, local, and economic players. This change is partly due to economic reforms that provide increased opportunities and incentives for players to devote resources to projects outside the state plan rather than to state-mandated projects. In discussing policy processes, the Chinese often refer to the following expression: "The top has its policy measures; the bottom has its countermeasures." Having renounced campaigns and purges, policymakers at the top have instead worked to forge agreements with a variety of players at the political center and in the localities so that policies adopted are implemented, not ignored or radically reshaped in the course of implementation. At the apex of the system, consultation has become even more important, because no leader possesses either the experience or the personal prestige of a Mao Zedong or a Deng Xiaoping.

The political structures described at the beginning of this chapter are essential points of reference for the description of policymaking and policy implementation here. However, key features of policy processes are not well illustrated by consideration of these formal structures alone. As elaborated below, the formal distinction between party and government structures is less relevant than it appears; at least one key structure does not appear on formal organizational charts; and authority is more fragmented and less well-bounded than formal structure suggests.

Policymaking

Policymaking in China today is less concentrated and more institutionalized than ever before. It involves three sets of institutional players: the party, the government, and the legislature, shown in Figure 13.4. It is also useful to distinguish three tiers in the policymaking process. Different party, government, and legislative structures at different tiers interact at different stages of the process. Moreover, a number of

individual players overlap, appearing in more than one set of institutions. This section traces the process by which major policies emerge and are eventually formalized as laws. It is worth noting, however, that many important policy decisions do not go through the legislature at all. For example, the State Council has the power to issue administrative regulations, decisions, instructions, orders, and measures to local governments; central government ministries issue their own departmental regulations, clarifications, and responses to respective local government departments; the Communist Party Politburo and individual party departments have their own separate systems of regulations, decisions, instructions, orders, and measures issued to counterparts in the localities and lower levels of the party bureaucracy.

Three Tiers in Policymaking At the very top tier are the leaders at the apex of the party: in the Politburo and its Standing Committee. The party generalists at this tier are each typically responsible for at least one broad policy area. As a group, they make all major policy decisions. Formally, the Politburo has the ultimate authority to determine major policies, but it probably meets in plenary session only about once monthly for a morning to ratify policies already approved by the Politburo Standing Committee. It is useful to recall here that the leaders at the top of the party hierarchy include not only party leaders but also the prime minister and the NPC chairman. Overlapping directorships help coordinate major decisionmaking across the three sets of institutions.

The most thorough consideration of policy options and shaping of policy decisions occur at the second tier—within **leading small groups (LSGs),** which are defined by broad policy areas.[46] LSGs are headed by leaders at the top tier of the party, although deputy heads are likely to be outside the top tier. LSGs have sweeping mandates to preside over policy research, formulation of policy proposals, sponsorship of policy experiments in the localities, and drafting of policy documents. LSGs bring together all the senior officials with responsibility for different aspects of a policy area.[47] They exercise leadership as policies emerge onto an initial agenda, and they make specific recommendations to the Politburo Standing Committee once policies are ready to move onto the legislative agenda. They are a crucial coordinating mechanism in the policymaking process, linking top

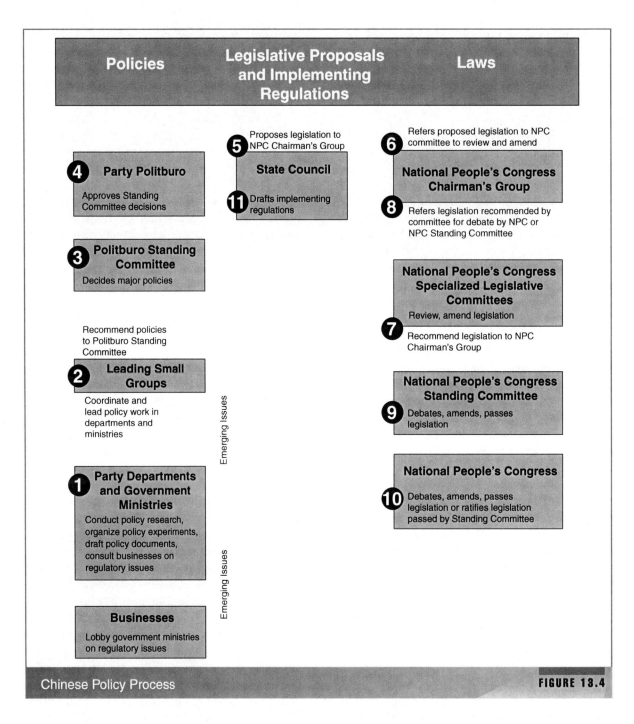

Chinese Policy Process   FIGURE 13.4

decisionmakers to bureaucracies and bridging institutional systems.

Coordinating mechanisms are particularly important to policymaking in the Chinese system because authority is formally structured so as to require the cooperation of many bureaucratic units, nested in separate chains of authority. The fragmentation of formal authority and its resolution by formal and informal coordinating mechanisms at the top of the system have led some scholars to characterize the Chinese system as one of **fragmented authoritarianism.**[48]

In what ways is formal authority fragmented? The best example is the system of dual subordination. On the one hand, authority is organized in systems of vertical bureaucracies in hierarchies that extend from ministries at the center to lower-level departments in the localities. Each ministry under the State Council is at the top of a hierarchy of subordinate departments that exist at the provincial, county, and township levels of government. On the other hand, the central ministry and subordinate departments are all government departments and, as such, are subordinate to their respective governments too. The Chinese refer to the two structural arrangements as "lines" and "pieces." Authoritative communications are channeled from top to bottom (vertically, in lines) and also from governments to their departments (horizontally, in pieces). The two sorts of authority come together only at the center, at the level of the State Council. Simply put, then, all local government departments have two bosses in their formal authority relationships—not to mention their relationships with party departments in the same issue area and party committees with *nomenklatura* authority over them. In Chinese terminology, there are "too many mothers-in-law." This structure of formal authority routinely creates blockages in policy processes. Many policy issues cannot be resolved at lower levels but must be pushed up to a sufficiently high level, such as an LSG, that spans many authority structures and can overcome bureaucratic impasses below.

Below leading small groups, at the third tier, are the relevant party departments and government ministries. As LSGs have little staff of their own, the research centers and staff in departments and ministries at the third tier do the actual work of gathering information and drafting policy documents. Increasingly, with a high proportion of policy related to economic matters, government ministries play a key role—but at this tier it is the specific policy area that determines which bureaucratic players are most involved.

From Agenda Setting to Implementing Regulations There are five main stages in policymaking and lawmaking: agenda setting; inter-agency review; Politburo approval; NPC review, debate, and passage; and the drafting of implementing regulations.[49] The two stages that have the most impact on substance are interagency review and drafting of implementing regulations. The State Council dominates both these stages.

LSGs provide leadership and coordination among party departments and government ministries, from which draft proposals emerge. Leaders of departments and ministries are continuously considering relevant policy issues and waiting for (or creating) opportunities to push proposals onto the agenda. A draft proposal is on the agenda when it is assigned to interagency review.

Interagency review is usually a very prolonged process, still at the third tier, initially involving only the most relevant ministries but gradually incorporating a wider group of departments, localities, and other players. At some point, either the State Council Legislation Bureau or the Legislative Affairs Work Committee approves a drafting group for the law. The last phase of interagency review is opinion solicitation. By then, most of the law's content has already been decided. This does not imply that relevant nonbureaucratic players are shut out of the policy process, however—at least in economic policymaking.

New case studies of the government–business relationship in China show that marketization has prompted Chinese firms to take an active interest in the many industrial policies and regulations that impact their competitiveness.[50] Businesses interact regularly with government departments on midrange policies, such as industry standards, tax rates, prices, and international competition—mostly regulatory issues that do not go through the legislative process. Interacting takes two forms: consultation and lobbying. On the one hand, government departments now routinely take the initiative to consult with relevant businesses before drafting industrial policies and regulations, calling meetings of key players or inviting them to formal hearings, for example. Similarly, business executives, including foreign business executives, now routinely lobby government officials to influence policy in favor of the firm or industry. Larger firms have the most direct and regular access to government officials, although large state-owned enterprises (SOEs) appear to have more access than large foreign firms, perhaps a legacy of interaction under central planning or the enormous importance of these players to social stability. Businesses lobby all departments relevant to policies that impact them, with one unsurprising exception: despite the influence of environmental regulations on industry competitiveness, businesses typically ignore the State Environment Protection Agency (SEPA)—reflecting an assumption that environmental protection is at odds with economic profits.

For policies that will involve passage of legislation, after interagency review, a draft proposal is included on the Legislation Bureau's or Legislative Affairs Work Committee's annual legislative plan. Politburo approval precedes NPC passage of any major piece of political, economic, or administrative legislation, although this practice is not formally required in any legal document.

Officially, legislation may be proposed by the State Council, its ministries, or groups of NPC delegates. Not surprisingly in this quasi-parliamentary system, the overwhelming majority of legislation is proposed by the State Council and its ministries at the third tier. Although it is unusual for laws to pass through NPC review without amendment, a bill approved in principle by the Politburo is not normally opposed in the NPC.

The NPC review stage begins with referral (by the NPC Chairmen's Group) of the draft legislation to a specialized legislative NPC standing committee for review and amendment. The structure that links party and legislative institutions at this stage is the NPC Standing Committee party group. After draft legislation is recommended by an NPC legislative committee, the party group (acting officially through the NPC Chairmen's Group) decides whether the draft will be debated in the NPC Standing Committee or the full NPC. It is common for the NPC Standing Committee to debate and revise draft legislation many times before voting on passage. When draft legislation encounters significant opposition in the NPC, a vote is usually postponed to avoid a public show of opposition.

After a law is passed, implementing regulations are drawn up, usually by the State Council Legislation Bureau. Implementing regulations transform laws into language that can be applied by local governments and subordinate departments throughout the country. Through implementing regulations, the State Council regains design control over policy before releasing it for implementation.

Policy Implementation

Although the state has partially retreated from direct control over many aspects of the economy, politics, and society in recent decades, the proportion of decisions affecting all three spheres that is made at the

political center in China remains higher than that in liberal democracies. Considering this scope, the fragmented structure of authority, and the size and regional diversity of the country, policymakers are seriously constrained in their efforts to elicit effective policy implementation, despite the recent trend toward greater consultation and consensus building to bring relevant departments and localities into the policy process at an earlier stage.

This section discusses problems of policy implementation in China. It is worth pointing out here, however, that despite problems and their consequences for unsuccessful policy implementation, the Chinese authorities have achieved impressive policy success in two areas designated as vitally important for the country's development: promoting economic growth and controlling population growth. They have been less successful in another policy area: environmental protection. These examples of policy performance are discussed at length later in this chapter. Here, the focus is on general issues in policy implementation.

Monitoring The major issue of policy implementation is the monitoring problem, especially serious in China because of the constraints noted earlier.[51] How do China's policymakers ensure that central-level decisions are translated into actions at lower levels? Central authorities have a very limited capacity to monitor the many aspects of the economy, politics, and society affected by their policies. To cope, they adopt fairly simplistic performance indicators. Not only are these problematic as accurate measures of compliance, but also they can produce unanticipated results. Additionally, policymakers rely mainly on departments and localities, which have their own particular interests to pursue, for much of the information on which to base evaluations of performance. Leaders at the political center have attempted in recent years to develop channels of information independent of ministries and local governments. The National Bureau of Statistics has been given more resources and responsibilities to gather and compile information relevant to policymaking and assessment of policy performance. Research institutes and public opinion polls have also played a greater role in channeling different sorts of information to leaders at the political center. The State Auditing Administration and the Ministry of Supervision, both newly established in recent years, are designed to improve central capacity to measure and monitor implementation. Nonetheless, central authorities are unable to verify most reports independently. As a result, information is routinely distorted to make policy implementers appear compliant. Policymakers appear to take this bias into consideration when assessing implementation.

Policy Priorities As policymakers routinely communicate multiple (and conflicting) policy objectives downward through several channels, local authorities must arrive at a reasonable ordering of policy priorities. In deciding priorities, local objectives as well as the apparent priorities of the political center are considered. Local governments and parallel party committees are multitask agencies. Policy priorities communicated in documents channeled down from Beijing in the functionally specialized line hierarchies of government may not be treated as policy priorities by local governments. Policies appear more likely to be implemented in conformity with central directives when signals from the center indicate that top leaders have reached a consensus among themselves and are paying attention. This sort of signal is generally communicated through documents issued by executive organizations (not simply central ministries) of the Communist Party (not simply the government). Party executives may also signal their attention to the implementation of policy issues by speaking at work conferences convened to assess progress in particular areas or establishing an ad hoc leading small group to manage a particular policy problem.

Adapting Policy to Local Conditions Chinese politics presents no electoral incentives for top leaders to line up public policy with the expressed preferences of special interest groups or ordinary voters. To be sure, policymakers consult the players they view as relevant to policy outcomes. Yet, with restrictions on investigation or criticism by the mass media and the prohibition on organized opposition groups, policymakers face relatively little routine outside pressure in formulating policies. Despite increased consultation of players below the top tiers, the policymaking process is relatively closed compared with liberal democracies. In a structural context that limits widespread input and provides no electoral connection to policymakers at the top, reshaping policy in the course of policy implementation is often the most effective way for officials

to influence policy outcomes. Leaders at the political center accept a certain amount of "adaptation of central policy to local conditions"—indeed, this is a stock phrase of Chinese politics.

Corruption

Economic reform has produced unprecedented growth and prosperity, but also the conditions for new forms of **corruption**. Since the early 1980s, the economy, no longer centrally planned but not fully marketized, has provided opportunities for officials to gain privately from abuse of their control over resources, contracts, and permissions. On the one hand, the new opportunities for corruption may have eased resistance by officials with the most to lose from economic reform. On the other, abuse of public office to pursue private gain has grown in scope, scale, volume, and severity to become one of the gravest challenges facing the regime, even threatening the Chinese armed forces.[52] In public opinion polls conducted over the years, Chinese citizens consistently view corruption as a serious social problem, often the most serious problem. The huge 1989 mass protests, as much about corruption as about democracy, reflected and aired this view.

Chinese leaders are alarmed about corruption, recognizing the threat to regime legitimacy and political stability. Since 1982, they have waged a nearly continuous corruption control effort. While corrupt officials have been prosecuted and punished, the battle against corruption suffers from a basic contradiction between Communist Party leadership and rule by law in China. In principle, as described earlier, equality before the law is a core component of the new legality. In practice, the Chinese legal system has not been used to full effect to control corruption. An important obstacle is a structural one, reflecting a more basic political obstacle. In 1978, party leaders reinstated discipline inspection committees, specialized departments subordinate to party committees at each level of the party hierarchy. Discipline inspection committees investigate misconduct and enforce ethical and political standards for party members. As the preponderance of officials are party members, discipline inspection committees investigate corruption. Regulations require the transfer of criminal cases to procuratorates, but party investigations and party punishments generally precede criminal investigations. Procuratorates routinely encounter obstacles in their efforts to prosecute such cases, not only because officials call up networks of cronies for support but also because successful prosecution is botched when officials have sufficient time to destroy evidence. In principle, the system holds Communist Party members to a higher standard of conduct than ordinary citizens. In practice, exemption from prosecution and substitution of disciplinary action for criminal punishment are very common for officials (but not for ordinary citizens). Public cynicism about corruption control is understandable. In the instances that high-ranking officials are removed from office and sentenced through the legal system, many interpret it as the outcome of a political power struggle.

The problem of corruption and corruption control reflects a basic contradiction between the principles of Communist Party leadership and rule by law. If law is supreme, then the party is subordinate to law and under supervision by procuratorates and courts, not vice versa. So long as party leaders cannot commit to supervision by an impartial legal system, the building of a legal infrastructure will not amount to rule by law. Yet, to commit to such supervision calls into question party leadership and the foundations of the communist party-state.

POLICY PERFORMANCE

In late 1978, China's leaders defined economic growth as the most important policy priority for decades to come. Despite disagreement about the appropriate pace and scope of economic reform, there has been consensus on a broad strategy of retreat from direct state intervention. The Chinese state has been achieving more by directly controlling less. This strategy has applied not only to economic goals but also to most other policy goals in the reform era. This includes environmental protection, which is less well suited to such a strategy. The important exception has been population control, which Chinese leaders identified as a major policy priority in the late 1970s. The one-child family policy introduced in 1978 features the Chinese state in a more directly interventionist role in population control than ever before.

This section examines the performance of policies of economic reform, environmental protection, and compulsory family planning, focusing on the role of the state in achieving policy goals.

Economic Growth

Although the Chinese have moved only slowly on political reforms, they have been bold in economic reforms. Since 1978, Chinese leaders have staked their political legitimacy on economic growth, more than anything else. For the most part, the gamble has succeeded. Chinese economic growth, illustrated in Table 13.3, has averaged just under 10 percent per year since 1980.[53] Real per capita income has grown rapidly, to more than $1,700 in 2005 or nearly $6,000 in purchasing power parity (PPP). Although China is still very much a developing country, it is the world's second largest economy in PPP terms. Economic reform has been a remarkable success story. It has been achieved through three major strategies: opening up the economy to the world outside; marketizing the economy; and devolving authority downward to create incentives for local governments, enterprises, households, and individuals to pursue their own economic advancement.

In the late 1970s, Chinese leaders rejected the economic autarky of Maoist "self-reliance," instead opening up the country to foreign trade and investment. As shown in Table 13.4, China had become a major trading economy, moving toward a trade surplus in 1990. The favorable trade balance has allowed China to amass one of the world's largest foreign exchange reserves. It has also created frictions with the United States and some other trading partners. Foreign-invested firms are responsible for much of China's

Economic Performance, 1980–2005 (in constant yuan)	**TABLE 13.3**	
	GDP (billion yuan)	**GDP per Capita (yuan)**
1980	452	460
1985	898.9	853
1990	1,859.8	1,634
1995	5,749.5	4,854
2000	8,825.4	7,086
2005	18,232.1	14,025
	U.S. $2,279 billion	U.S. $1,753 ($6,800 PPP)

Sources: State Council Information Office, China Internet Information Center at http://www.china.org.cn; National Bureau of Statistics of China, Statistical Communique, 28 February 2006 at http://www.stats.gov.cn; 2005 PPP figure is from Central Intelligence Agency, *World Factbook* at http://www.cia.gov/cia/publications/factbook/.

Foreign Trade, 1978–2005 (in U.S. billion constant dollars)		TABLE 18.4	
Year	Trade Volume	Imports	Exports
1978	20.64	10.89	9.75
1979	29.33	15.67	13.66
1980	38.14	20.02	18.12
1981	44.03	22.02	22.01
1982	41.61	19.29	22.32
1983	43.62	21.39	22.23
1984	53.55	27.41	26.14
1985	69.60	42.25	27.35
1986	73.85	42.91	30.94
1987	82.65	43.21	39.44
1988	102.79	55.27	47.52
1989	111.68	59.14	52.54
1990	115.44	53.35	62.09
1991	135.70	63.79	71.91
1992	165.53	80.59	84.94
1993	195.70	103.96	91.74
1994	236.62	115.61	121.01
1995	280.86	132.08	148.78
1996	289.88	138.83	151.05
1997	325.16	142.37	182.79
1998	323.95	140.24	183.71
1999	360.63	165.70	194.93
2000	474.29	225.09	249.20
2001	509.65	243.55	266.10
2002	620.77	295.17	325.60
2003	850.99	412.76	438.23
2004	1,154.55	561.23	593.32
2005	1,421.90	659.95	761.95

Source: National Bureau of Statistics of China, *2006 China Statistical Abstract* (Beijing: China Statistics Press, 2006), 169.

exports, reflecting the country's appeal—through preferential policies, cheap labor, and a potentially huge market—as a destination for foreign direct investment (FDI). China attracts more FDI than any other developing nation; overall, it is the world's third largest recipient of FDI. The role of FDI in promoting economic growth through exports has compensated for the weakness of Chinese private capital as the country emerged from its socialist economic past.

Post-Mao leaders inherited a centrally planned economy, organized according to a Stalinist model borrowed from the Soviet Union in the 1950s. They did not initially set out with a stated goal or program to create a socialist market economy. Indeed, the goal to create a market system was not officially affirmed until 1993. Rather, economic reform proceeded incrementally, in a process often described as "crossing the river by groping for stones." Initially, some top party leaders envisaged only a small secondary role for the market economy, as a "bird in a cage" of the planned economy. By the mid-1990s, however, the Chinese economy had basically "grown out" of the plan.[54] In 1998, the Chinese approved a "shareholding system" that is essentially privatization, thinly disguised to maintain ideological orthodoxy.

The emergence of scarcity prices, reflecting market supply and demand, to replace prices determined bureaucratically by central authorities is a good example of this incrementalism. Initially, the government pursued a "two-track" pricing system: it maintained bureaucratic prices for some key industrial inputs, but allowed scarcity to determine prices of other commodities. Some scarcity prices were determined fully by market forces; others were allowed to rise and fall within a range. Over time, the number of commodities with bureaucratic prices was steadily decreased. By the mid-1990s, two-track prices were a thing of the past.

Finally, a key economic reform strategy has been decentralization. Leaders in Beijing have devolved authority to empower local governments, enterprises, households, and individuals. Agricultural decollectivization in the early 1980s was the first such reform, replacing collective farming with household farming. Individual entrepreneurs emerged at about the same time, engaging in small-scale production or providing services (such as transportation of commodities to markets) long ignored under central planning. Existing rural enterprises were allowed to expand into practically any product line, rather than being restricted to "serving agriculture," as before. Most of these industries were organized as "collective enterprises," with formal ownership by the township or village community and with strong direct involvement of local government in management. These small-scale township and village enterprises (TVEs) proved themselves adaptable to the demands of the new market environment. They drove much of China's rapid growth in the 1980s and into the 1990s. Fiscal arrangements negotiated in the mid-1980s also favored local governments, at the expense of the center; in a renegotiation in the mid-1990s, the central government gained back some revenues, but without removing incentives for local economic initiative.

The reform of the state-owned enterprise (SOE) system began in the mid-1980s. Initial reforms created incentives to boost production by replacing government appropriation of all SOE profits with a system of taxing profits—allowing SOEs to retain a portion of profits. Of course, until prices reflected scarcity, the incentives remained weak. More important, SOEs employed (and employ) a very high proportion of urban workers. This effectively put SOEs on a "soft budget constraint": as local governments feared worker unrest, unprofitable SOEs did not fear bankruptcy; they could count on state banks to bail them out. In 1993, the Chinese authorities announced that one-third of SOEs were loss-making and one-third barely breaking even. In 1994, the Company Law was passed to provide a legal framework for corporatization. A strategy of "targeting the large, releasing the small" emerged: Beijing continued to nurture about 1,000 large SOEs, encouraging them to form giant conglomerates, assisting them with loans but imposing greater financial discipline; the smaller SOEs were left to confront market forces and reorganize themselves through mergers, takeovers, conversion into shareholding companies, or outright closure. This dual process of corporatization and reorganization continues today, with increasing privatization through conversion to shareholding and greater political toleration of SOE closures and sales, including sales to foreign partners.

Environmental Degradation

China's rapid economic growth has resulted in serious environmental damage. Environmental pollution and degradation have increased at a rate that outpaces the capacity of the Chinese state to protect the environment.[55] Township and village enterprises contribute more than half of pollutants of all kinds, dumping their untreated waste directly into rivers and streams and relying heavily on coal for energy. Use of coal, a major source of air pollution but a vital contributor to energy supply (see Box 13.5), has doubled since the economic reforms. Water scarcity poses a major challenge: prices do not reflect scarcity because most water is directed toward agriculture for irrigation, and local governments fear rural unrest will erupt with meaningful water price increases. Integration into the global economy

has made China a global market for resource-intensive goods, such as paper and furniture—producing a massive drop in forest coverage with increases in logging by Chinese and multinational businesses. China has also become a destination of choice for some of the world's most environmentally damaging industries.

Environmental economists at the World Bank and other organizations estimate the cost to the Chinese economy of environmental degradation and resource scarcity at 8 to 12 percent of GDP annually. This includes health and productivity losses associated with air pollution and water scarcity costs in lost industrial output. Even so, through the mid-1990s, leaders and the Chinese media continued to articulate the principle of "first development, then environment." The ideal of sustainable development, prominent in official

The policy of "first development, then environment" has taken a heavy toll. Pollution far outpaces the government's capacity for environmental protection.

Topham/The Image Works

Shutting Down 5,000 Coal Mines

China depends on coal for more than 65 percent of its growing energy needs, but in 2005 the central government ordered more than 5,000 coal mines shut down. China's mines are the most dangerous in the world: in that year alone, nearly 6,000 Chinese coal miners died in mining accidents, almost 80 percent of the world's total mining fatalities. The mines ordered closed were both unsafe and illegal. Many were lucrative small-scale mines, managed as township or village enterprises. Others were privately owned, often with local officials holding private (strictly illegal) shares. Mine managers routinely flout safety standards, taking local government acquiescence for granted. The miners generally resign themselves to the high risks, because mining pays better than alternative employment in agriculture. In such conditions, despite laws, orders, and rhetoric on industrial safety, dangerous mines will continue to operate. Undoubtedly, they include many mines shut down in 2005.

rhetoric today, was incorporated into the economic planning process only in 1992.

Over the past decade, China has erected a legal and bureaucratic infrastructure of environmental protection. In 1984, the State Council established a central government department responsible for environmental matters; in 1989, the NPC adopted an environmental protection law; and in 1993, a specialized legislative environmental protection and natural resources committee was established in the NPC.

Nonetheless, in the policymaking process, the environmental bureaucracy is weak in negotiations with the many ministries with developmental priorities. The problem is even more serious at the local level. The laws that emerge tend to be too diluted and general to provide useful guidelines for enforcement.

The Chinese tally a great number of enforcement successes over the past decade: the resolution of more than 75,000 environmental law violation cases, the closure of more than 16,000 enterprises for illegal discharge of pollutants, and the issuance of more than 10,000 warnings to environment polluters.[56] Yet, the devolution of authority to local governments, a strategy that unlocked economic growth, constitutes a fundamental obstacle to enforcement.

Although local environmental protection bureaus (EPBs) are nominally accountable to both the State Environmental Protection Agency (SEPA) in Beijing and their local governments, they depend on local governments for their growth and survival—budgets, career advancement, staff size, and allocation of resources, such as vehicles and office buildings. Local government developmental priorities practically always dominate efforts to enforce environmental standards, especially when enterprises are collective enterprises or firms with a large number of workers. Pollution discharge fees are routinely not collected (or not fully collected), and legal requirements to improve pollution control capacity are routinely waived. The 2006 policy decision to consider environmental protection performance, including energy use, in evaluating local governments may have some impact, but its importance is unlikely to trump economic growth in the near future.

Environmental protection is also underfunded. The five-year plan adopted in March 2006 budgeted 1.6 percent of GDP for environmental protection—an increase over past years but nonetheless an amount that Chinese scientists believe is well below what is needed to produce notable improvements. At the same time, the Chinese set an ambitious policy goal: 10 percent of its energy needs to be supplied by environmentally friendly renewable sources by 2010.

Population Control

While reducing state intervention to promote economic growth, policymakers have increased their intervention involving a new policy priority: population control. For most of the Maoist years, population planning was not actively promoted. In 1978, with the population close to a billion and amid rising concern about meeting economic goals and ensuring basic livelihood, employment opportunities, and social security support at the current rate of population growth, China's leaders declared population control a major policy priority. State-sponsored family planning was added to the constitution, and an ideal family size of one child was endorsed as national policy. According to this policy, most couples are required to stop childbearing after one or two births. Married couples in urban areas, with few exceptions, are restricted to one child. In rural areas, married couples are subject to rules that differ across provinces. In some provinces, two children are normally permitted; in others, only one child is permitted; in most provinces, a second child is permitted only if the first is a girl.

One-Child Family Policy The **one-child family policy** is inherently difficult to implement in China, particularly in the countryside, where nearly 60 percent of Chinese live.[57] There, the population is relatively poorly educated and has poor access to public health facilities—circumstances that do not facilitate an effective family planning program. Traditional views about the family prevail: as in most agrarian societies, big families and many sons are viewed as ideal. Moreover, in China, a married daughter joins the household of her husband, while a married son

remains in the household to support aging parents. Decollectivization and the return to household farming in the early 1980s enhanced the value of sons compared to daughters, for their labor power. The dismantling of the commune system has also left the state less able to monitor compliance, just as the new economic independence of peasants has left the state less able to enforce compliance. Finally, population control involves the state as the dominant decisionmaker in choices that are traditionally viewed, in China as elsewhere, as private family matters.

Despite the inherent difficulties, the Chinese have succeeded in curbing population growth dramatically, as is illustrated in Figure 13.5. A population structure normally resembles a pyramid: with relatively unchanged rates of births and deaths, the proportion of population from top to bottom is progressively bigger. The population pyramid in Figure 13.5 deviates from this form in a few places. The first, located at about the middle of the pyramid, reflects fewer births as well as differentially more deaths among the young in the disaster following the Great Leap Forward, in the cohort aged 45–49 in 2005. The second, evident beginning with the cohort aged 25–29 in 2005, reflects the impact of

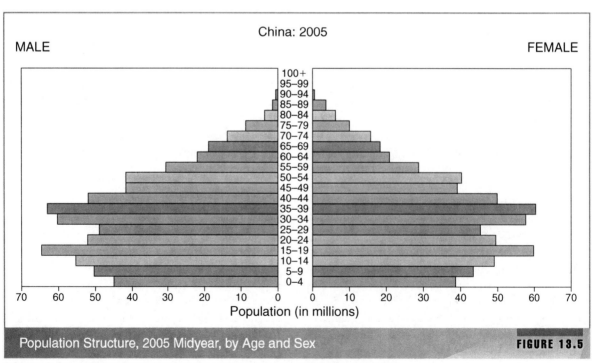

Population Structure, 2005 Midyear, by Age and Sex   **FIGURE 13.5**

Source: U.S. Census Bureau, International Data Base at http://www.census.gov/ipc/www/idbpyr.html.

family planning policies introduced in the 1970s. Variation in policy emphasis by leaders at the political center is reflected in variation in number of births, beginning in the mid-1970s. Implementation of the one-child family policy began in 1979. In 1983, responding to concerns at the political center, implementation became more coercive. From 1984 through the late 1980s, the policy was relaxed and implementation in the countryside faltered due to difficulties associated with decollectivization. Births rose immediately. From 1989 to the present, policy implementation has been stringent. Urban-rural outcomes differ significantly, however. In the cities, the one-child family appears to be the accepted norm. In the countryside, however, any relaxation of policy has been reflected in immediate big increases in births.[58]

Policy Implementation Policy implementation has taken a number of forms: a legal requirement of late marriage, a requirement of insertion of an intrauterine device after a first birth, and a requirement of sterilization of one partner after a second birth. There are incentives to sign a one-child family certificate after the first birth, including priority in entrance to schools and funding for health fees for the child. Fines are imposed on the family for policy violations. Birth planning workers at the grassroots are given birth quotas from higher levels, which they allocate on the basis of family circumstances. From the perspective of leaders at the political center, abortion is a sign of failure, not success, in policy implementation. At the grassroots, from the perspective of birth planning workers, however, the obvious fact is that abortions do not add above-plan births. Undeniably, birth planning workers have incentives to encourage abortions and face few disincentives for doing so.

Perverse Outcomes In recent years, policymakers have expressed concern about a perverse result of compulsory family planning: the shortage of young girls, compared with boys. Recent figures show atypical birth disparities: a national average of 118 newborn boys to 100 newborn girls in 2005. These figures compare with an international average of about 106 boys to 100 girls.

The shortage of girls reflects the traditional Chinese preference for male children in the context of compulsory family planning. Traditional practices of female infanticide as well as abandonment and severe neglect of girls beyond infancy have led to excess female infant mortality. Not least of all, missing girls are increasingly the result of sex-selective abortion, made possible with the widespread use of ultrasound technology in the early 1980s. These practices prompted top legislators to consider criminalizing such abortions, although ultimately they decided against it.

China's success in reducing population growth has strong supporters and detractors outside the country. The official Chinese response to criticism from human rights advocates has focused on "economic rights" that the government argues would be denied to all Chinese in the decades to come if population growth is not brought under control.

HONG KONG

In 1842 and 1860, the island of **Hong Kong** and adjacent territory on the Chinese mainland were ceded by treaty to Britain in perpetuity. In 1898, more adjacent territory was ceded in a ninety-nine-year lease. These cessions were largely the outcome of British victory in wars fought to impose trade on China. For nearly a century, Hong Kong (including the adjacent territories) was a British colony, ruled by a governor appointed in London. Hong Kong flourished economically, with a disciplined labor force of Chinese immigrants, a free-market economy, and a government commitment to rule of law and civil liberties but not elected government.

In 1984, the Chinese communist authorities elaborated the principle of **"one country, two systems,"** applicable to Hong Kong after 1997. China and Britain signed a joint declaration: Hong Kong would revert to Chinese sovereignty in 1997, but would continue to enjoy "a high degree of autonomy." The Chinese agreed that Hong Kong would enjoy economic, financial, and monetary autonomy, maintaining its capitalist system, legal system, and way of life for fifty years. At midnight on June 30, 1997, Hong Kong became a special administrative region of communist-ruled China.

The British had made little effort to democratize politics in Hong Kong through the 1980s. The governor had consulted business elites and other key constituencies on policy affairs, but there had been no elected legislature or government. Nor had political parties really developed in such an environment. All this changed in 1989.

The Tiananmen massacre galvanized Hong Kong Chinese and British expatriates into efforts to accelerate the pace of political democratization before 1997. In 1991, in the first direct elections to the Legislative Council, only a third of the legislative deputies were directly elected. In 1995, a controversial electoral reform bill introduced by Governor Christopher Patten guided elections: for the first time, ordinary Hong Kong citizens elected all deputies in the Legislative Council. Hong Kong's most liberal democratic parties won overwhelmingly in geographic voting districts. Openly pro-Beijing forces did poorly.

Communist authorities rejected the elections and the legislature as violations of the Basic Law, Hong Kong's miniconstitution passed in China's National People's Congress in 1990. They supervised selection of a chief executive and provisional legislature in 1996. At the moment of the historic handover, this chief executive and provisional legislature officially replaced the governor and the legislature elected in 1995.

Since the handover, Beijing authorities have been less heavy-handed than feared. Hong Kong today enjoys most of the same civil liberties as under British rule. Human rights organizations and pro-democracy organizations that monitor and support progress in the PRC have bases in Hong Kong. Hong Kong newspapers provide information about politics in the PRC and are critical in ways not permitted on the mainland. Chinese communist authorities hope that success in implementing "one country, two systems" in Hong Kong will woo Taiwan back to the PRC too.

TAIWAN

Taiwan, governed by the Nationalists as the **Republic of China** since 1945, lies a mere 100 miles off the east coast of the Chinese mainland. Communist "liberation" of Taiwan became moot when the United States sent its Seventh Fleet to the Taiwan Strait, declaring an American interest in the security of Taiwan after the outbreak of the Korean War in the 1950s. For the next three decades, the Chinese routinely bombarded

offshore islands of Taiwan and continued to threaten liberation by military force. For the most part, however, it was a cold war—and until the 1970s, Taiwan was the clear winner, enjoying international recognition as the sole legitimate representative of China.

In the 1970s, two major events affected Taiwan's status. In 1971, Taiwan lost its membership in the United Nations and its seat on the Security Council to China. In 1979, the United States recognized China diplomatically, downgrading the relationship with Taiwan to one of unofficial liaison. Today, fewer than thirty countries recognize Taiwan. These events have put China in a position of relative strength.

The two sides have engaged in negotiations on and off over the years. Since democratization in the late 1980s, Taiwan's leaders are more constrained than ever to represent majority public opinion, which does not support unification with the mainland. The election of a pro-independence party candidate to the presidency in 2000 exacerbated friction across the Taiwan Strait.

CHINA'S POLITICAL FUTURE

Two main themes have run through this study of Chinese politics today. First, despite very significant economic liberalization and a nascent political institutionalization, Chinese politics takes place within the boundaries of what is still essentially a communist party-state. Second, the dramatic changes sweeping the Chinese economy, polity, and society, many of which now seem beyond the control of political leaders, are as much a by-product of reform as a direct product of reform policies. The first theme cautions against liberal democratic optimism when considering China's political future. The second reminds us that the script of the political future will not be written by Chinese communist leaders alone.

In this new century, China must confront a number of key issues that will significantly determine its development. Can structures and processes that bolster and foster economic growth safeguard against the threat of more significant political liberalization and eventual democratization—which remain unacceptable to the Chinese authorities?

Around the world, political change in recent decades has created an age of democratization—the result, in many countries, of revolutions that toppled communist regimes older than the Chinese regime. Will the "third wave" of world democratization reach China early in the twenty-first century?

Certainly, liberal democratic ideals and practices are quite alien to Chinese culture. Chinese history provides no examples of democratic rule, and the Chinese cultural tradition expresses no concerns to protect individuals by checking state power. Past experience and cultural tradition, then, offer little encouragement to those looking for the seeds of democratization in China.

Yet, authoritarianism has not survived intact with economic modernization in many East Asian countries that have a similar lack of historical and cultural foundations for democracy. To be sure, even with continued economic growth, China will differ from these countries for many years to come. It will be bifurcated in its development: middle-class prosperity is emerging in the big cities and coastal regions, but Chinese in the countryside will remain relatively poor for some time.

With reform, for most ordinary Chinese, the party has demanded less and delivered more in recent decades. Unlike communist parties that gained (and held) power with the aid of Soviet troops and tanks, the Chinese Communist Party has indigenous and nationalist roots. Barring a major economic crisis, it is less likely to collapse in the face of the sort of mass discontent that toppled communist regimes in Eastern Europe. More likely, in the medium term at least, the party will continue to transform China in the years to come and to transform itself in order to continue to rule.

KEY TERMS

Central Committee
Chinese Communist Party
Confucianism
corruption
Cultural Revolution
Democracy Movement
democratic centralism
Deng Xiaoping
ethnic minorities
fragmented
    authoritarianism

GONGOs
Great Leap Forward
guardianship
Hong Kong
Hu Jintao
leading small groups
    (LSGs)
Mao Zedong
mass line
mass mobilization
    campaign

Nationalist Party
National Party Congress
National People's
    Congress (NPC)
nomenklatura system
one-child family policy
one country, two systems
party-state
People's Liberation Army
    (PLA)
Politburo

Republic of China
rule by law
socialist market economy
State Council
Taiwan (Republic of
    China)
Tiananmen massacre
village committees

SUGGESTED READINGS

Bianco, Lucien. *Origins of the Chinese Revolution, 1915–1949.* Stanford, CA: Stanford University Press, 1971.

Chang, Jung. *Wild Swans: Three Daughters of China.* New York: Anchor, 1991.

Economy, Elizabeth C. *The River Runs Black: The Environmental Challenge to China's Future.* Ithaca, NY: Cornell University Press, 2004.

Goldman, Merle, and Roderick MacFarquhar, eds. *The Paradox of China's Post-Mao Reforms.* Cambridge: Harvard University Press, 1999.

Gries, Peter Hays, and Stanley Rosen, eds. *State and Society in 21st-century China: Crisis, Contention, and Legitimation.* New York: RoutledgeCurzon, 2004.

Lieberthal, Kenneth. *Governing China: From Revolution Through Reform.* 2d ed. New York: Norton, 2004.

Nathan, Andrew J. *Chinese Democracy.* Berkeley: University of California Press, 1986.

Spence, Jonathan D. *The Search for Modern China.* New York: Norton, 1990.

Weston, Timothy B., and Lionel Jensen, eds. *China Beyond the Headlines.* Lanham, MD: Rowman & Littlefield, 2000.

Wong, Jan. *Red China Blues.* Sydney, Australia: Doubleday, 1996.

INTERNET RESOURCES

www.china.org.cn/english. China Internet Information Center, State Council Information Office. Authorized website of Chinese government, link to National People's Congress. Access to government White Papers, news, statistical data.

www.stats.gov.cn/english/. National Bureau of Statistics. Official monthly and yearly statistics, including downloadable Excel files.

www.chinadaily.com.cn. *China Daily.* News from China directed toward external readership.

http://english.peopledaily.com.cn/. *People's Daily.* Official newspaper of Communist Party of China.

www.scmp.com. *South China Morning Post.* News about Hong Kong and mainland China, from Hong Kong.

www.wws.princeton.edu/~lynn/chinabib.pdf. Contemporary China bibliography, Professor Lynn White, Princeton University.

www.uschina.org/. United States–China Business Council. Analysis and advocacy of policy issues of interest to U.S. corporations engaged in business relations with China.

ENDNOTES

1. *New York Times*, 17 April 2006.

2. Lou Jiwei, Deputy Minister of Finance, *People's Daily* online, 22 June 2006. Bai Jinfu, a former deputy director of a research center under the State Council, estimates the Gini coefficient to be 0.50. See *South China Morning Post* online, 11 July 2006.

3. For a good, very readable discussion of Chinese history beginning with the late Ming (seventeenth century) and extending into the 1980s, see Jonathan D. Spence, *The Search for Modern China* (New York: Norton, 1990). Other good historical overviews include Charles O. Hucker, *China's Imperial Past: An Introduction to Chinese History and Culture* (Stanford, CA: Stanford University Press, 1975); and Immanuel C. Y. Hsu, *The Rise of Modern China*, 5th ed. (New York: Oxford University Press, 1995).

4. See Hsi-sheng Chi, *Warlord Politics in China, 1916–1928* (Stanford, CA: Stanford University Press, 1976); and Edward A. McCord, *The Power of the Gun: The Emergence of Modern Chinese Warlordism* (Berkeley: University of California Press, 1993).

5. R. H. Tawney, *Land and Labour in China* (London: Allen & Unwin, 1932).

6. See especially Lucien Bianco, *Origins of the Chinese Revolution, 1915–1949* (Stanford, CA: Stanford University Press, 1971). See also Benjamin Schwartz, *Chinese Communism and the Rise of Mao* (Cambridge: Harvard University Press, 1951).

7. The classic political biography of Mao is Edgar Snow, *Red Star Over China* (New York: Grove Press, 1968). Of the many excellent studies by Stuart R. Schram, see especially *The Political Thought of Mao Tse-tung*, rev. ed. (New York: Praeger, 1969); *The Thought of Mao Tse-tung* (Cambridge: Cambridge University Press, 1989), and his biography of Mao, *Mao Tse-tung*, rev. ed. (Harmondsworth: Penguin, 1967). After Mao's death, scholars appraised Mao and his legacy from a variety of perspectives in Dick Wilson, ed., *Mao Tse-tung in the Scales of History: A Preliminary Assessment* (Cambridge: Cambridge University Press, 1977).

8. See Chalmers A. Johnson, *Peasant Nationalism and Communist Power: The Emergence of Revolutionary China* (Stanford, CA: Stanford University Press, 1962).

9. See Suzanne Pepper, *Civil War in China: The Political Struggle, 1945–1949* (Berkeley: University of California Press, 1978).

10. For a good selection of essays offering a comprehensive overview of PRC history, see Roderick MacFarquhar, ed., *The Politics of China: The Eras of Mao and Deng*, 2nd ed. (Cambridge: Cambridge University Press, 1997). Other good discussions of post-Mao history are found in Richard Baum, *Burying Mao: Chinese Politics in the Age of Deng Xiaoping* (Princeton, NJ: Princeton University Press, 1994); and Harry Harding, *China's Second Revolution: Reform After Mao* (Washington, DC: Brookings Institution, 1987). Good discussions of particular topics of reform are found in Merle Goldman and Roderick MacFarquhar, eds., *The Paradox of China's Post-Mao Reforms* (Cambridge: Harvard University Press, 1999).

11. The classic account is by William Hinton, who observed land reform before 1949 in *Fanshen: A Documentary of Revolution in a Chinese Village* (New York: Viking, 1966).

12. Roderick MacFarquhar, ed., *The Hundred Flowers Campaign and the Chinese Intellectuals* (New York: Praeger, 1960); and Fu-sheng Mu, *The Wilting of the Hundred Flowers Movement: Free Thought in China Today* (London: Heinemann, 1962).

13. See Dali L. Yang, *Calamity and Reform in China: State, Rural Society, and Institutional Change Since the Great Leap Famine* (Stanford, CA: Stanford University Press, 1996).

14. See Frederick C. Teiwes, *Politics and Purges in China: Rectification and the Decline of Party Norms, 1950–1965* (Armonk, NY: M. E. Sharpe, 1979); and Frederick C. Teiwes, *Leadership, Legitimacy, and Conflict in China: From a Charismatic Mao to the Politics of Succession* (Armonk, NY: M. E. Sharpe, 1984).

15. See Jasper Becker, *Hungry Ghosts: Mao's Secret Famine* (New York: Free Press, 1996).

16. Some of the best accounts of the Cultural Revolution are biographical or autobiographical. See, for example, Gordon A. Bennett and Ronald N. Montaperto, *Red Guard: The Political Biography of Dai Hsiao-ai* (Garden City, NY: Doubleday, 1971); Jung Chang, *Wild Swans: Three Daughters of China* (New York: Anchor, 1991); Yuan Gao, *Born Red: Chronicle of the Cultural Revolution* (Stanford, CA: Stanford University Press, 1987); Liang Heng and Judith Shapiro, *Son of the Revolution* (New York: Knopf, 1983); Anne F. Thurston, *Enemies of the People: The Ordeal of the Intellectuals in China's Great Cultural Revolution* (Cambridge: Harvard University

Press, 1988); Daiyun Yue and Carolyn Wakeman, *To the Storm: The Odyssey of a Revolutionary Chinese Woman* (Berkeley: University of California Press, 1985); and Nien Cheng, *Life and Death in Shanghai* (New York: Grove Press, 1986).

17. See Dru C. Gladney, *Muslim Chinese: Ethnic Nationalism in the People's Republic* (Cambridge: Council on East Asian Studies, Harvard University, 1991); and Stevan Harrell, ed., *Cultural Encounters on China's Ethnic Frontiers* (Seattle: University of Washington Press, 1995).

18. An excellent discussion of guardianship is found in Robert A. Dahl, *Democracy and Its Critics* (New Haven, CT: Yale University Press, 1989), ch. 4. On Leninism in general, see especially Alfred G. Meyer, *Leninism* (Cambridge: Harvard University Press, 1957).

19. Mao Zedong, "Some Questions Concerning Methods of Leadership," in *Selected Works of Mao Tse-tung*, vol. 3 (Peking: Foreign Languages Press, 1965), 117–22.

20. On the changing role of the NPC, see Murray Scot Tanner, *The Politics of Lawmaking in Post-Mao China: Institutions, Processes, and Democratic Prospects* (New York: Oxford University Press, 1999); and "Breaking the Vicious Cycles: The Emergence of China's National People's Congress," *Problems of Post-Communism* 45, no. 3 (1998): 29–47. For an historical perspective, see Kevin J. O'Brien, *Reform Without Liberalization: China's National People's Congress and the Politics of Institutional Change* (Cambridge: Cambridge University Press, 1990).

21. See Murray Scot Tanner, "How a Bill Becomes a Law in China: Stages and Processes of Lawmaking," *China Quarterly*, no. 141 (1995): 39–64.

22. See the selection of essays in David Shambaugh, ed., *Deng Xiaoping: Portrait of a Chinese Statesman* (New York: Oxford University Press, 1995).

23. Tai Ming Cheung, "The Influence of the Gun: China's Central Military Commission and Its Relationship With the Military, Party, and State Decision-Making Systems," in David M. Lampton, ed., *The Making of Chinese Foreign and Security Policy in the Era of Reform* (Stanford, CA: Stanford University Press, 2001), 61–90; and Michael D. Swaine, "Chinese Decision-Making Regarding Taiwan, 1979–2000," in *The Making of Chinese Foreign and Security Policy in the Era of Reform*, 289–336. On military modernization, see David Shambaugh and Richard H. Yang, eds., *China's Military in Transition* (Oxford: Clarendon Press, 1997); and David Shambaugh, "The People's Liberation Army and the People's Republic at 50: Reform at Last," *China Quarterly*, 159 (1999): 660–72.

24. See Melanie Manion, "The Cadre Management System, Post-Mao: The Appointment, Promotion, Transfer, and Removal of Party and State Leaders," *China Quarterly*, 102 (1985): 203–33; John P. Burns, *The Chinese Communist Party's Nomenklatura System* (Armonk, NY: M. E. Sharpe, 1989); and "Strengthening Central CCP Control of Leadership Selection: The 1990 *Nomenklatura*," *China Quarterly*, 138 (1994): 458–91.

25. See Hsiao Pen, "Separating the Party From the Government," in Carol Lee Hamrin and Suisheng Zhao, eds., *Decision-Making in Deng's China: Perspectives From Insiders* (Armonk, NY: M. E. Sharpe, 1995), 153–68.

26. See Zhiyue Bo, *Chinese Provincial Leaders: Economic Performance and Political Mobility Since 1949* (Armonk, NY: M. E. Sharpe, 2002). For an earlier discussion of elite recruitment and mobility, based on case studies, see David M. Lampton, *Paths to Power: Elite Mobility in Contemporary China* (Ann Arbor: Center for Chinese Studies, University of Michigan, 1986).

27. For an overview of the change, see Richard Baum, "Modernization and Legal Reform in Post-Mao China: The Rebirth of Socialist Legality," *Studies in Comparative Communism* 19, no. 2 (1986): 69–103. For notions underlying the change, see Carlos W. H. Lo, "Deng Xiaoping's Ideas on Law: China on the Threshold of a Legal Order," *Asian Survey* 32, no. 7 (1992): 649–65. For a description of the law in practice in post-Mao China, see James V. Feinerman, "Economic and Legal Reform in China, 1978–91," *Problems of Communism* 40, no. 5 (1991): 62–75; Pitman B. Potter, ed., *Domestic Law Reforms in Post-Mao China* (Armonk, NY: M. E. Sharpe, 1994); "The Chinese Legal System: Continuing Commitment to the Primacy of State Power," *China Quarterly*, no. 159 (1999): 673–83; and Stanley B. Lubman, *Bird in a Cage: Legal Reform in China After Mao* (Stanford, CA: Stanford University Press, 1999).

28. See Minxin Pei, "Citizens v. Mandarins: Administrative Litigation in China," *China Quarterly*, 152 (December 1997): 832–62.

29. See, for example, Donald C. Clarke and James V. Feinerman, "Antagonistic Contradictions: Criminal Law and Human Rights in China," *China Quarterly*, 141 (1995): 135–54.

30. See the account of "thought work" in Daniel Lynch, *After the Propaganda State: Media, Politics, and "Thought Work" in Reformed China* (Stanford, CA: Stanford University Press, 1999).

31. M. Kent Jennings and Ning Zhang, "Collective Memories in the Chinese Countryside" (paper presented at the Annual Meeting of the International Society of Political Psychology, July 2002, Berlin). Chinese who were adolescents during the Cultural Revolution also recall that event as memorable, more so than do Chinese in other age groups.

32. See Tianjian Shi, "Cultural Values and Democracy in the People's Republic of China," *China Quarterly*, 162 (2000): 540–59; and Yang Zhong, Jie Chen, and John Scheb, "Mass Political Culture in Beijing: Findings From Two Public Opinion Surveys," *Asian Survey* 38, no. 8 (1998): 763–83. For a comparative perspective, see Gabriel A. Almond and Sidney Verba, *Civic Culture: Political Attitudes and Democracy in Five Nations* (Princeton, NJ: Princeton University Press, 1963).

33. Yun-han Chu and Yu-tzung Chang, "Culture Shift and Regime Legitimacy: Comparing Mainland China, Taiwan, and Hong Kong," in Shiping Hua, ed., *Chinese Political Culture, 1989–2000* (Armonk, NY: M. E. Sharpe, 2001), 320–47. See also Tianjian Shi, "Cultural Values and Political Trust: A Comparison of the People's Republic of China and Taiwan," *Comparative Politics* 33, no. 4 (2001): 401–19.

34. This is the conclusion of Tianjian Shi, based on analysis of the same survey data. See "Cultural Values and Democracy in the People's Republic of China." See also Andrew J. Nathan and Tianjian Shi, "Cultural Requisites for Democracy in China: Findings From a Survey," *Daedalus* 122, no. 2 (1993): 95–123.

35. Two independent sets of surveys, including surveys of the more politically knowledgeable and interested Beijing population, conclude this in almost exactly the same words. See Shi, "Cultural Values and Democracy in the People's Republic of China"; and Zhong, Chen, and Scheb, "Mass Political Culture in Beijing."

36. See the excellent discussion of forms of political participation in Tianjian Shi, *Political Participation in Beijing* (Cambridge: Harvard University Press, 1997), ch. 2.

37. On the Maoist period, see James R. Townsend, *Political Participation in Communist China* (Berkeley: University of California Press, 1967). On post-Mao elections, see Andrew Nathan, *Chinese Democracy* (Berkeley: University of California Press, 1985); Robert E. Bedeski, "China's 1979 Election Law and Its Implementation," *Electoral Studies* 5, no. 2 (1986): 153–65; Barrett L. McCormick, *Political Reform in Post-Mao China* (Berkeley: University of California Press, 1990); J. Bruce Jacobs, "Elections in China," *Australian Journal of Chinese Affairs*, 25 (1991): 171–200; and Melanie Manion, "Chinese Democratization in Perspective: Electorates and Selectorates at the Township Level. Report from the Field," *China Quarterly*, 163 (2000): 133–51.

38. On rural decollectivization, see especially Daniel Kelliher, *Peasant Power in China: The Era of Rural Reform, 1979–1989* (New Haven, CT: Yale University Press, 1992); and Kate Xiao Zhou, *How the Farmers Changed China: Power of the People* (Boulder, CO: Westview Press, 1996).

39. See Melanie Manion, "The Electoral Connection in the Chinese Countryside," *American Political Science Review* 90, no. 4 (1996): 736–48; Tianjian Shi, "Economic Development and Village Elections in Rural China," *Journal of Contemporary China* 8, no. 22 (1999): 433–35; Anne F. Thurston, *Muddling Toward Democracy: Political Change in Grassroots China* (Washington, DC: United States Institute of Peace, 1999); and Lianjiang Li, "Elections and Popular Resistance in Rural China," *China Information* 16, no. 1 (2002): 89–107.

40. On protest movements in the 1970s and 1980s, see especially Andrew J. Nathan, *Chinese Democracy* (Berkeley: University of California Press, 1985); Jeffrey N. Wasserstrom and Elizabeth J. Perry, eds., *Popular Protest and Political Culture in Modern China: Learning From 1989* (Boulder, CO: Westview, 1992); and Gregor Benton and Alan Hunter, *Wild Lily, Prairie Fire: China's Road to Democracy, 1942–1989* (Princeton, NJ: Princeton University Press, 1995).

41. James D. Seymour, ed., *The Fifth Modernization* (Stanfordville, NY: Human Rights Publishing Group, 1980).

42. On the 1989 protests, see Michel Oksenberg, Lawrence R. Sullivan, and Marc Lambert, eds., *Beijing Spring, 1989: Confrontation and Conflict, The Basic Documents*, (Armonk, NY: M. E. Sharpe, 1990); Han Minzhu and Hua Sheng, eds., *Cries for Democracy: Writings and Speeches From the 1989 Chinese Democracy Movement* (Princeton, NJ: Princeton University Press, 1990); Tony Saich, ed., *The Chinese People's Movement: Perspectives on Spring 1989* (Armonk, NY: M. E. Sharpe, 1990); Jonathan Unger, ed., *The Pro-Democracy Protest in China: Reports From the Provinces* (Sydney: Allen & Unwin, 1991); and Craig Calhoun, *Neither Gods Nor Emperors: Students and the Struggle for Democracy in China* (Berkeley: University of California Press, 1995).

43. See James D. Seymour, *China's Satellite Parties* (Armonk, NY: M. E. Sharpe, 1987).

44. See Fengshi Wu, *New Partners or Old Brothers? GONGOs in Transnational Environmental Advocacy in China*, China Environmental Series, no. 5 (Washington, DC: Woodrow Wilson Center Press, 2002); and Elizabeth C. Economy, *The River Runs Black: The Environmental Challenge to China's Future* (Ithaca, NY: Cornell University Press, 2004), 129–76.

45. For good discussions of NGOs and their relationship to the state, see especially Tony Saich, "Negotiating the State: The Development of Social Organizations in China," *China Quarterly*, 161 (2000): 124–41; and Bruce Dickson, *Red Capitalists in China: The Party, Private Entrepreneurs, and Prospects for Political Change* (Cambridge: Cambridge University Press, 2003), 1–28.

46. The most thorough description and thoughtful analysis of leading small groups is by Carol Lee Hamrin, "The Party Leadership System," in Kenneth G. Lieberthal and David M. Lampton, eds., *Bureaucracy, Politics, and Decision Making in Post-Mao China* (Berkeley: University of California Press, 1992), 95–124. See also David M. Lampton, ed., *The Making of Chinese Foreign and Security Policy in the Era of Reform* (Stanford, CA: Stanford University Press, 2001), especially the contribution by Lu Ning, "The Central Leadership, Supraministry Coordinating Bodies, State Council Ministries, and Party Departments," 39–60.

47. These areas are defined in very comprehensive terms, such as party affairs, national security and military issues, foreign affairs, legal issues, personnel, finance and the economy.

48. See Kenneth Lieberthal and Michel Oksenberg, *Policy Making in China: Leaders, Structures, and Processes* (Princeton, NJ: Princeton University Press, 1988).

49. See Murray Scot Tanner, "How a Bill Becomes a Law in China: Stages and Processes in Lawmaking," *China Quarterly*, 141 (1995): 39–64; and *The Politics of Lawmaking in China: Institutions, Processes, and Democratic Prospects* (Oxford: Oxford University Press, 1999).

50. Scott Kennedy, *The Business of Lobbying in China* (Cambridge: Harvard University Press, 2005).

51. See David M. Lampton, ed., *Policy Implementation in Post-Mao China* (Berkeley: University of California Press, 1987); and Yasheng Huang, "Administrative Monitoring in China," *China Quarterly*, 143 (1995): 828–43.

52. See especially Ting Gong, "Forms and Characteristics of China's Corruption in the 1990s: Change With Continuity," *Communist and Post-Communist Studies* 30, no. 3 (1997): 277–88; Xiaobo Lu, "Booty Socialism, Bureau-preneurs, and the State in Transition," *Comparative Politics* 32, no. 3 (2000): 273–94; Yan Sun, "Reform, State, and Corruption: Is Corruption Less Destructive in China Than in Russia?" *Comparative Politics* 32, no. 1 (1999): 1–20; and James Mulvenon, *Soldiers of Fortune: The Rise and Fall of the Chinese Military-Business Complex, 1978–1998* (Armonk, NY: M. E. Sharpe, 2001).

53. This (economic growth rate) is based on official Chinese statistics, which probably overstate real growth rates. One estimate suggests average annual rate of gross domestic product (GDP) growth in the 1980s and 1990s may have been as low as 7.9 percent rather than the official figure of 9.9 percent. Of course, this estimate would still have made China one of the five most rapidly growing economies in the world. See Nicholas R. Lardy, *China's Unfinished Economic Revolution* (Washington, DC: Brookings Institution, 1998). More recently, Thomas G. Rawski has ignited controversy with his significantly lower estimates of growth for 1998–2001 (i.e., annual growth rates ranging from 2.5 to 4.0 percent), based on low energy consumption. See "How Fast Is China's Economy Really Growing?" *China Business Review* 29, no. 2 (2002): 40–43.

54. See Barry Naughton, *Growing Out of the Plan: Chinese Economic Reform, 1978–1993* (Cambridge: Cambridge University Press, 1996).

55. Two excellent recent sources on the environment are Elizabeth C. Economy, *The River Runs Black: The Environmental Challenge to China's Future* (Ithaca, NY: Cornell University Press, 2004); and Kristen A. Day, ed., *China's Environment and the Challenge of Sustainable Development* (Armonk, NY: M. E. Sharpe, 2005).

56. State Council Information Office, 2006 White Paper on the Environment, "Environmental Protection in China (1996–2005)".

57. See Susan Greenhalgh, Zhu Chuzhu, and Li Nan, "Restraining Population Growth in Three Chinese Villages, 1988–93," *Population and Development Review* 20, no. 2 (1994): 365–95.

58. See the excellent study by Judith Banister, "China: Population Dynamics and Economic Implications," in Joint Economic Committee, U.S. Congress, *China's Economic Future: Challenges to U.S. Policy* (Armonk, NY: M. E. Sharpe, 1997), 339–60. On coercion in implementation, see John Aird, *Slaughter of the Innocents: Coercive Birth Control in China* (Washington, DC: AEI Press, 1990).

INDEX

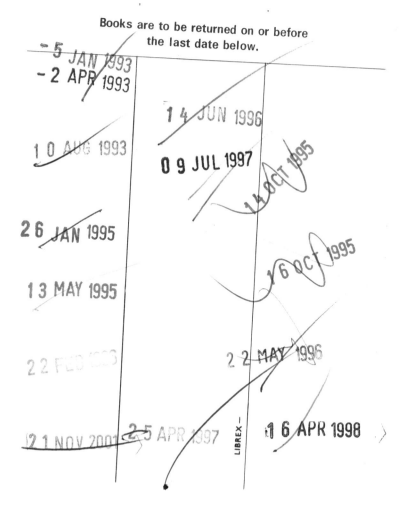